War and Change in the Balkans

Nationalism, Conflict and Cooperation

edited by

Brad K. Blitz

D0551912

CAMBRIDGE UNIVERSITY PRESS
Cambridge, New York, Melbourne, Madrid, Cape Town, Singapore, São Paulo

Cambridge University Press
The Edinburgh Building, Cambridge CB2 2RU, UK

Published in the United States of America by Cambridge University Press,
New York

www.cambridge.org
Information on this title: www.cambridge.org/9780521677738

© Cambridge University Press 2006

First published 2006

Printed in the United Kingdom at the University Press, Cambridge

A catalogue record for this publication is available from the British Library

ISBN-13 978-0-521-86042-0 hardback
ISBN-10 0-521-86042-3 hardback

ISBN-13 978-0-521-67773-8 paperback
ISBN-10 0-521-67773-4 paperback

Contents

Contributors

IVO BANAC, is the author of *With Stalin Against Tito* and *The National Question in Yugoslavia*. A former director of the Institute of South-Eastern Europe at the Central European University, he is Bradford Durfee Professor of History at Yale University (On-leave). He served as minister for the environment in Croatia and was elected to the Croatian Parliament in the 2003 elections.

MARK BARTOLINI, was a spokesperson and press officer for the International Rescue Committee in the former Yugoslavia from 1995–96. He has served in Bosnia, Croatia and Kosovo and as humanitarian expert. He is currently Vice-President for Government Relations at the International Rescue Committee.

BRAD K. BLITZ, received his Ph.D. from Stanford University and has held several academic positions in the USA and United Kingdom, including a visiting fellowship at the Refugee Studies Centre, Oxford University. He is currently Reader in Political Geography at Oxford Brookes University.

FRASER CAMERON, is Director of Studies at the European Policy Centre, Brussels. A former British diplomat, he served in New York, Bonn and East Berlin before joining the European Commission. Until 2001, he was Head of the Political and Academic Affairs Section in the Delegation of the European Commission in Washington DC. He is the author of a number of books and articles on European affairs, including *The Enlargement of the European Union* and *The Foreign and Security Policy of the European Union: Past, Present and Future*.

DANIELE CONVERSI, is Senior Lecturer in Politics at the University of Lincoln. He has taught at the Government and History Departments. at Cornell and Syracuse Universities, as well as at the Central European University, Budapest. He is the author of *The Basques, the Catalans, and Spain, German-Bashing and the Break-up of Yugoslavia* and editor of *Ethnonationalism in the Contemporary World*.

PETER GALBRAITH, is the former US Ambassador to Croatia. He is the principal designer of the Erdut Agreement that brought an end to the Serb–Croatia fighting in Eastern Slavonia, Croatia.

CAROLE HODGE, is Research Fellow at the University of Glasgow and is the author of *Britain and the Balkans 1991 until the present.*

BRYAN HOPKINSON, is former British Ambassador to Bosnia and analyst with the International Crisis Group in Bosnia. He is currently director of Political Affairs in the UN Mission in Kosovo.

ALI KARAOSMANOGLU, is Professor of International Relations at Bilkent University in Ankara. He is a specialist in Turkish foreign policy and is a member of the Foreign Policy Institute in Ankara, and of the Political and Social Studies Foundation of Istanbul.

KEMAL KURSPAHIC, is former Editor-in-Chief of Oslobodjene, the daily Sarajevo newspaper and is currently the Caribbean Regional Representative of the United Nations *Office on Drugs and Crime* in Barbados. He is the author of *As Long as Sarajevo Exists* and *Prime Time Crime: Balkan Media in War and Peace.*

BRANKA MAGAS, is author of *The Destruction of Yugoslavia* and co-editor of *The War in Croatia and Bosnia-Herzegovina 1991–95.* A former member of the editorial board of *New Left Review*, she is currently finishing a manuscript on the history of Croatia.

NOEL MALCOLM, is Senior Research Fellow at All Souls College, University of Oxford. A former columnist for *The Telegraph* and Political Editor of *The Spectator*, he is the author of several studies on the Balkans, including *Bosnia: A Short History* and *Kosovo: A Short History.* In 2001 he was appointed Fellow of the British Academy.

SRDJA POPOVIC, was a leading human rights lawyer in Belgrade and also former editor of VREME. After spending a decade in New York he returned to Belgrade where he currently lives.

DAVID ROHDE, has covered the conflicts in the former Yugoslavia for *The Christian Science Monitor* and *The New York Times* and was awarded the 1996 Pulitzer Prize for foreign reporting. He is the author of *Endgame: The Betrayal and Fall of Srebrenica.*

ANDREW ROSSES, is Professor of History at the University of Toronto. He is preparing a volume, *Macedonia and the Macedonians: A History*, for the Studies of Nationalities Series, published by the Hoover Institution Press, Stanford University.

GEORGE SCHÖPFLIN, is former Jean Monnet Professor of Political Science and Director of the Centre for the Study of Nationalism at the School of Slavonic and East European Studies, University of London. He is the author of *Politics in Eastern Europe 1945–1992* and *Nations, Identity, Power* as well as of many other works, including numerous articles on ethnicity and nationhood. In June 2004, he was elected to the European Parliament and is one of Hungary's first MEPs.

PHILIP SHASKO, is Professor of History at the University of Wisconsin Milwaukee. His research interests and teaching are in Russian/Soviet and Southeast European social and intellectual history since the eighteenth century. He is currently working on a study of glasnost and the quest for civil society in Russia from Peter the Great to the revolutions of 1917.

WILLIAM A. STUEBNER, is Affiliate Professor in the Peace Operations Policy Program at George Mason University and former Executive Director of the Alliance for International Conflict Prevention and Resolution. In 1994 he served as special adviser to the prosecutor of the International Criminal Tribunal for the Former Yugoslavia and Chief of Staff and Senior Deputy for Human Rights of the OSCE Mission to Bosnia and Herzegovina.

THANOS VEREMIS, is Professor of Modern History at the University of Athens, Department of European and International Studies, and Vice President of the Hellenic Foundation for European and Foreign Policy (ELIAMEP) and President of the National Council for Education. His publications include: *Action without foresight: Western Involvement in Yugoslavia; The Greek Army in Politics: From Independence to Democracy; Greece's Balkan Entanglement.*

Acknowledgements

This volume is the product of many people. Professor Ivo Banac provided the initial idea for this study and gathered together an outstanding collection of scholars and journalists when he convened a conference on the Balkans organised by the South European Studies Programme at the Central European University and Students Against Genocide at Stanford University in the Summer of 1997. Since then this volume has taken many forms and I am indebted to the contributors for their patience and dedication to this project. It has been a privilege working with each of them and I am most grateful for the relationships that have been forged as a result of our collaboration.

Valerie Millholland and Miriam Angress at Duke University provided much enthusiasm for a critical publication on the conflicts in the former Yugoslavia and offered an initial contract. Valerie and Miriam responded quickly to my proposal and then waited as an early draft of the manuscript was revised to take into account the conflicts in Kosovo and Macedonia and the radical shift in international policy that occurred in 1999. Although we have opted to publish this book with Cambridge University Press, the interest shown by Duke University Press sustained this project over several years.

The move to Cambridge University Press could not have gone more smoothly. I am especially grateful to John Haslam and Karen Matthews for their support and for attracting such professional reviewers. Jackie Warren, Jo Breeze and Sheila Kane superbly managed the production and copyediting processes, respectively. From the very beginning, it has been a pleasure to work with Cambridge University Press. I would also like to record my appreciation to Michelle Bridges at Macmillan for permission to reproduce Noel Malcolm's chapter from his acclaimed study, *Kosovo: A Short History* and to George Schöpflin for permission to reproduce his essay in this volume.

Over the years, I have been encouraged by friends and colleagues. Tin Gazivoda and John Tillinghast deserve a special mention for their constant enthusiasm. Academic colleagues Martin Baldwin-Edwards,

Daniele Conversi, Tom Gallagher, Carole Hodge, Sabrina Ramet and Andrew Rossos directed me to additional sources and provided much needed feedback on earlier drafts. In addition, a team of superb post-graduate students provided invaluable assistance in the preparation of the final manuscript. Blake Hinderyckx, Robert Guzman, Stephanie Stuart, Kristin Tamblin proofread each chapter; Wendy Cuesto, Angie Ratliff, Allison Torbet provided much needed research assistance as I checked facts and dates; and Serena Rodriguez and Tenecia Sicard assisted with the formatting and assembly of the final document. A special note of thanks goes to my polyglot assistant Eleftheria Georgiadi who dealt with the tedious task of revising a bibliography in multiple languages.

I am also grateful for the institutional support I received while I prepared this manuscript and would like to acknowledge the US Institute of Peace, the Institute of Social Science Research at Middlesex University, the Research Sub-Committee at Roehampton University and the Refugee Studies Centre, University of Oxford.

Last but not least, a very special note of appreciation to my family for their understanding and unlimited patience as I have retreated at various times to finish off this project. I could not have done so without Hayley's welcome support and without Romilly's equally welcome distractions.

1 War and Change

Brad K. Blitz

For over a decade events in the former Yugoslavia dominated Western attention. The issues of secession, conflict and the horrific abuses that took place in Croatia, Bosnia and Kosovo gave rise to a series of diplomatic conferences and plans which put the former Yugoslavia and surrounding states on the map as an international trouble spot. Thousands of journalists were drawn to the region and witnessed crimes first hand alongside the victims of aggression.[1] Their reports from the battlefield also ensured that the abuses committed against the peoples of Croatia, Bosnia and later Kosovo would enter permanent record. Previous experience of war reporting in Vietnam and even in the first Gulf War just a couple of years earlier could not compare to the live reports, combined with satellite imagery, which brought home the horrors of war and produced a chronicle of conflict in 'real time'. Neither Western politicians nor the Western public could escape the reality of the siege of Sarajevo where the media lived among the local population and provided a detailed account of daily suffering under occupation. As sociologists Mestrovic and Cushman write in their discussion of genocide in Bosnia, what distinguishes the conflicts in the former Yugoslavia from previous wars is that this time we knew about the events as they were happening.[2] For this reason, the events in the Balkans and the responses they generated in Western capitals form a particularly important chapter of contemporary history and also set the scene for subsequent reporting, not least of all in Iraq.

There are many explanations for the break-up of Yugoslavia including domestic-interest-based arguments which centre on competing claims made by rival ethno-national groups[3] and economic-based theories in which structural conditions and unrealistic austerity programmes imposed by the International Monetary Fund (IMF) are blamed for destroying the existing socialist state and the constitutional order.[4] At first glance these arguments appear quite attractive.

In the first argument, the claim that rival ethno-national groups unsettled the political design of the former Socialist Federal Republic of

Yugoslavia (SFRY) is often attributed to selective scholastic writings on nationalism and the role that ethnic attachments play in nation-state formation. From the 1960s to mid-1980s theoretical studies of nationalism flourished and in the absence of empirical research stressed the importance of political and ethno-national congruity for stability. Ernest Gellner, for example, claimed that the expression of nationalist sentiment was the result of the violation of this principle of congruity. Elsewhere, others such as Ellie Kedourie maintained that nationalism pretended to supply the criterion for the exercise of state power and was derived from the natural occurrence of national blocs. In this setting, nationalism was the inevitable product of state formation and political transition.

If the first argument is based on theoretical claims, the second argument can find greater evidentiary support in national and macro-economic studies of the later 1980s. Yugoslavia's economic position had undeniably worsened throughout the 1980s and after Tito's death Yugoslavia's debt stood at $20 billion, representing a quarter of the national income at the time. By the late 1908s, the former socialist showcase was subject to mass redundancies, and economic conditions deteriorated just as nationalist ideologies were given greater voice both at home and next door in Central Europe. Further, the role of international financial institutions in the destabilisation of much of Latin America during the 1980s lent weight to the claim that Yugoslavia was yet another victim of harsh structural adjustment policies which included currency devaluations, wage freezes, price controls and debt repayment programmes set by Western institutions.

There are several counter arguments to the above claims, some of which are explored in this book. The central question that must be posed is why it was that Yugoslavia, unlike other multinational and socialist states, descended into war as it did? Also, while the above accounts focus on ideological positions and structural conditions, they simultaneously ignore the role of political leaders in Yugoslavia's new direction in the 1980s – an essential theme of this study. A useful starting point in our analysis is a review of Yugoslavia's history as a multinational state and the ideologies that sustained its political leadership both during and after the communist period.

The relationship between communism and nationalism in Yugoslavia played a central role in Yugoslavia's demise. As George Schöpflin argues in his now classic article, 'Nationhood, communism and state legitimation',[5] at a point when its neighbours were looking to the West, democratic option in Yugoslavia was defeated by a strong ethno-national consciousness among the Serbian population that felt itself to have been suppressed under communism and this feeling was actively manipulated by political leaders, above all Slobodan Milošević. It is important to recall that in the Socialist Federal Republic of Yugoslavia ethnic tension was institutionalised and played out within the state apparatus both during and after the communist period. Contrary to popular opinion, the creation of a socialist state did not placate nationalist agitators but simply incorporated them in a different political system. Most obvious was the way in which the old nationality disputes continued within the Yugoslav communist movement which became increasingly 'nationalised' after the mid-1960s. Attempts to rebalance the Socialist Federal Republic of Yugoslavia were notable in the early Titoist plans to deprive Serbia of its hegemony over the state by devolving power to the republics by means of a new constitution in 1974. However, this constitution included a number of contradictory provisions: on the one hand, it devolved power to the six republics and two autonomous regions (including Kosovo); on the other, it was also predicated on the rule of the central Communist Party.

After Tito's death in 1980, Serbian communists challenged the constitution and sought to re-establish Serbia's hegemony over the federal state, most dramatically by cancelling Kosovo's autonomy in 1987. As Branka Magas writes, in a chapter in this volume, the next phase of Yugoslavia's troubles was sparked by the attempts of the Serbian political elite and Milošević's own agents to devise a policy of unionism as a means of preserving their hegemony. This policy, which set the scene for a Greater Serbia project exploited the nationalist ideals of Serbian intellectuals and married them to a programme that could only be carried out by means of population transfers. In the name of protecting Serbs from the fall-out of Slovenia's and Croatia's secession from the Socialist Federal Republic of Yugoslavia, Milošević was able to legitimise his unionist aims and used his most powerful weapon, the Yugoslav National Army.

The processes by which political elites contrived to undermine the possibility of a smooth transition from communism by fostering tensions between Yugoslavia's ethnic communities have been described in considerable detail elsewhere[6] but it is useful to recall that Yugoslavia remains an anomaly among post-communist states precisely because the drive to separatism and eventual secession was activated not by disgruntled minorities in the periphery but as Daniele Conversi argues from the political elites at the very centre.[7] In other contexts, the circulation of former communist elites in the late 1980s was associated with recentralisation and the development of new markets as seen in Russia and elsewhere in the former Soviet Union.[8] However, what distinguished

Milošević's Yugoslavia was the way in which the Belgrade political establishment was prepared to regroup around the politics of ethnic antagonism and xenophobia even over material interests.[9] The rationale for this regrouping was to preserve the establishment figures' legitimacy in the hope of maintaining Serbia's hegemony over the fragile federation. As an era of single-party rule was coming to an end, the people and institutions that characterised communism in Yugoslavia thus helped to legitimise the nationalist path. The formal dissolution of the League of Communists (SKJ) in January 1990 ensured that there was no central arena in which the issue of Yugoslavia's potential transition from communism to democracy could be addressed.[10]

Other factors furthered weakened the prospect of a democratic transition. Structuralist critics are correct to point out that the deterioration of the Yugoslav economy in the 1980s with inflation reaching 1,950 per cent by 1989, also hampered Yugoslavia's political evolution. Further, it is important to stress that in the absence of a defined post-communist polity, the growing unrest between the republics which contrasted with peaceful elections and transition from single-party rule elsewhere in Eastern Europe, was ripe for manipulation by the national media.[11] Above all, the emergence of a determined leader in Slobodan Milošević, who was able to exploit the Communist Party's extensive organised networks, was an essential factor in Yugoslavia's demise. While scholars debate the merits of leadership as an explanatory variable in international relations, Milošević filled a political void at a critical time and thus his role (and his wife's influence over his leadership) was of paramount significance for the future of Yugoslavia.[12] Similarly, the rise of Franjo Tudjman in Croatia cannot be underestimated. As Yossi Shain and Juan Linz note in their important study of interim governments and democratic transitions, since interim periods are characteristically marked by 'uncertainty, anxiety and high expectations concerning the future distribution of power and loyalties … the nature and action of the interim government are of enormous political moment' and in this context the role of political leaders is also of paramount importance.[13]

The wars that followed in Croatia, Bosnia and Kosovo raised additional questions regarding the involvement of external actors. One central question that remains in dispute is how did foreign actors, above all the United States and the governments of Western Europe, react to events in the Balkans and influence the conduct and eventual conclusion of these conflicts? Several scholars charge that, in addition to the economic policies of international financial institutions, the West encouraged the break-up of Yugoslavia, and they blame Germany in particular for destabilising the region by recognising Slovenia and Croatia in advance of the European Union and United States. Yet, as Ivo Banac and George Schöpflin write in this volume, such causal arguments are overly simplistic and do not help to explain the initial rationale for war which they believes lies in Yugoslavia's history as a multinational state. Elsewhere, Daniele Conversi contends that the attempt by some to displace blame and focus on external actors reflects a post-Cold War anxiety over a recently unified Germany rather than a detailed consideration of other explanations including personal culpability.[14]

The debate over Germany's recognition of the former Yugoslav republics does, nonetheless, raise some important questions over the West's conduct during the conflicts in the former Yugoslavia. After the first Gulf War, why did the West refuse to intervene and put a stop to the conflicts in Croatia and Bosnia? While scholars disagree over the motives for inaction – the range of explanations include the claim that Yugoslavia fell outside the interests of the United States, a gross over-estimation of Serbian military strength and the mistaken belief that the war in Bosnia would end quickly, and fear of igniting a wider war between Greece and Turkey – the West's refusal to intervene cannot be divorced from the legacy of Cold War policies and preferences that had guided the West for the previous fifty years. In spite of the brief incursion in the Gulf in 1991, the crisis in the former Yugoslavia presented the first major test for the Atlantic powers in the dawn of the post-Cold War era and there was little evidence from the West that it had established a new robust framework which it could apply to the changing times. The Soviet Union had disintegrated with remarkably little violence, leaving Washington and its European partners at a loss for foreign policy guidance. As a result of this unspectacular break-up, the West was not compelled to review the assumptions which had dominated its diplomatic tenets over the previous fifty years. Unfortunately for the peoples of the former Yugoslavia, above all the citizens of Croatia and Bosnia, one constant of Cold War foreign policy had been the United States' preference for dealing with large multilateral states as opposed to smaller independent actors.

In the early 1990s, the American preference for conducting diplomacy through large configurations was given added weight by the short-lived appearance of regional trading blocs in Asia and North America, and particularly the accelerated move towards closer political and economic integration in the European Union. In addition, with the previous rationale of containing Communism now a distant memory, the evolving US foreign policy doctrine shifted from ideology-based policy-making to consensus politics which necessarily gave the European states greater influence over international matters in which the two Atlantic partners had common concerns. During the initial conflicts, the international consensus favoured keeping Yugoslavia together as a loose federation even though facts on the ground suggested that under the new leadership of Slobodan Milošević a powerful Serbian elite was centralising control and destroying the remnants of the socialist federal state. The most egregious attack on the constitutional order was evidenced by the revocation of autonomy in three of Yugoslavia's federal units, Kosovo, Vojvodina and Montenegro, and by denying their people freedoms guaranteed under the 1974 constitution. This was the start of the West's reluctant relationship with the former Yugoslavia.

From 1991 until 1999, the West's response to Milošević and the violence he created in the former Yugoslav republics was reactive and self-deceptive at best. Warren Zimmerman recounts in his *Origins of a Catastrophe*, the former US ambassador to Yugoslavia was entrusted with implementing the Bush administration's policy of 'unity and democracy' even though the constitutional order had been destroyed prior to his arrival. As Human Rights expert Srdja Popovic writes in this volume, American policy at this time was characterised by 'confusion, wishful thinking, procrastination, evasions, a lack of focus and determination'. At its worst, the West's response to the conflict in the Balkans was characterised by a tendency to moral equivalence in which Western states refused to reign in aggressors and simultaneously punished victim states such as Bosnia. Indeed, the most compelling evidence of such Western bias was seen in the imposition of an arms embargo against Bosnia which left the small state exposed to Milošević's powerful army as it began its programme of 'ethnic cleansing' and unleashed a genocidal campaign against the non-Serbian population in 1992. It was not until the Kosovo crisis in 1999 that the Cold War preferences described above were laid to rest and a new Western doctrine of selective intervention was heralded.

By 1999, the West had experimented with a number of tactics that failed to produce a halt in Milošević's brutal campaigns, this time in Kosovo. After failing to bring security to the region by means of high-level diplomatic conferences, the deployment of peacekeepers, intermittent air strikes and formal peace agreements, the situation facing the West was all too familiar. As Milošević stationed troops on the border of Kosovo, Western governments were finally forced to review their foreign policies and consider increasingly vocal protests for intervention. After years of prevarication during which thousands of innocents were killed, US President Bill Clinton and British Prime Minister Tony Blair publicly reversed their policies of non-intervention when they issued the attack on Milošević and authorised NATO to bomb targets within Serbia. In the hope of forestalling Milošević's murderous assault on Kosovo's Albanian population, Clinton and Blair made the case for defending a people against the probable threat of genocide, crimes against humanity and other gross abuses of human rights. Writing in *Newsweek*, Tony Blair acknowledged that the West had learned by 'bitter experience not to appease dictators' and that 'Milošević's policy of ethnic cleansing must be defeated and reversed' as part of a new internationalism.

We need to enter a new millennium where dictators know they cannot get away with ethnic cleansing or repress their peoples with impunity. In this conflict we are fighting not for territory but for values. For a new internationalism where the brutal repression of whole ethnic groups will no longer be tolerated.[15]

Most importantly, Blair recognised that inaction in Bosnia had led to hundreds of thousands of deaths and that the previous policy was, in his own words, a mistake.

This policy shift, which finally put an end to Milošević's expansionist ventures, ultimately paved the way for a change of leadership in Serbia and gave rise to claims that Western foreign policies could be grounded on liberal humanitarian principles. Two years after his incursions into Kosovo, Slobodan Milošević was removed from Serbia and taken to the International Criminal Tribunal in the Hague where he died in custody as he was on trial for crimes against humanity. Many questions still remain to be answered. The peoples of the former Yugoslavia are now faced with the challenge of consolidating new democratic regimes and engaging in the arduous task of reconciliation with their neighbours. While Montenegro and Kosovo test out new independent structures, their neighbours will prepare for the equally daunting prospect of securing membership to the European Union.

This book is about war and change in the Balkans during the Milošević years and up to the present day. The contributors to this volume provide a range of assessments of the wars in the former Yugoslavia and explanations for the ways in which these conflicts have been settled. Several of these are based on historical analysis but there are also personal accounts from journalists, diplomats and civil servants who draw upon their own experiences of war and political change in the former Yugoslavia. In addition, the scholars included in this study assess the impact the conflicts have had on foreign actors and the neighbouring countries which are now preparing to enter the European Union following the example of the former Yugoslav Republic of Slovenia, and thus the current study seeks to provide a contemporary historical account of political developments across Southeastern Europe.

For analytical purposes, one can discern four key transformations that enable us to explore the effects of war and change in the Balkans. These are: (1) the transformation of formal state structures, the demise of Yugoslavia and the creation of new states; (2) the importance of nationalist ideologies in the preparation for war and their subsequent decline in the post-conflict era; (3) the role of international actors as policy-makers, implementing agencies and arbiters; and, finally (4) the process of democratisation and integration into European structures. The authors in this volume address the above themes over the course of this volume, which is divided into two parts to provide balance and reflect the often conflicting agendas of local actors in the former Yugoslavia and the international community both during and after the conflict.

The first part of this book develops the analytical framework by focusing on the key political structures, ideologies and institutions that are central to any study of transition. The demise of Yugoslavia and the rise of nationalist sentiment are explored in chapters by George Schöpflin on state construction and state failure and Ivo Banac on the politics of national homogeneity. While Schöpflin's article focuses on the way in which communism sustained nationalism and provided a source of conflict in the former Socialist Federal Republic of Yugoslavia, Banac considers the role nationalist ideologies played in the mobilisation of ethnic groups and the conduct of war aims in the 1990s. Noting the failure of previous partitions and population transfers, Banac laments the way in which a settlement was imposed on Bosnia. The future for a truly multiethnic and European identity is held out as the best possible conclusion to the disastrous effects of partition and displacement in the Balkans. These chapters are complemented by an important study of Milošević and the personality of leadership by Srdja Popović. While the notion of leadership as a variable in international relations is subject to considerable debate, few would contest Milošević's preeminence as the architect of conflict in the former Yugoslavia.

The role of international actors is then considered by Daniele Conversi who examines the way in which Germany's recognition of Slovenia and Croatia was used as a means of dividing support for a concerted European policy, to the benefit of Slobodan Milošević. The effects of European policies on the conduct of the war, the genocide in Bosnia and its eventual reorganisation are discussed in an important essay by former editor of the Sarajevo daily *Oslobodjene*, Kemal Kurspahic. In his chapter, 'From Bosnia to Kosovo and Beyond: Mistakes and Lessons',

Kurspahic writes that the mission of ending the war in Bosnia was not compatible with the task of building foundations for a lasting peace and, as a result, half of Bosnia's population was left homeless, in exile and unable to return. In the years since the Dayton Agreement was first signed, efforts have been made to ensure freedom of movement between Bosnia's two entities, but as Kurspahic notes the state remains divided along cantonal and ethnic lines where there is great disparity among the regions and populations. As we move further away from Dayton, it is clear that the original Belgian-style model for Bosnia was fraught with difficulties in terms of design and has led to the exponential involvement of the international community to ensure its implementation.[16]

This section concludes with two analyses of international involvement from the vantage point of supranational institutions that are central to the reconciliation process, the International Criminal Tribunal for the Former Yugoslavia (ICTY) and the European Union. William Stuebner chronicles the development of the ICTY and the role that the United States played in its early years and describes how the problems of intelligence ultimately slowed down the work of the chief prosecutor. In a personal account of the development of the ICTY, Stuebner chronicles how dedicated civil servants advanced the cause of justice during their terms in office but were nonetheless constrained by budgets and other essential resources. Fraser Cameron then reviews the European Union's involvement in the region and the difficulties it encountered during the inception of its common foreign and security policy. He notes how the former Yugoslavia provided an important testing ground for the European Union and how more than ten years later, the EU's involvement in the Balkans pushed it to develop a greater range of external policy instruments which are in use today.

The second part of the book focuses on the experiences of the former Yugoslav republics and their neighbours and the subsequent attempt at regional stabilisation and European integration. It begins with the Macedonian crisis of 1991 which is set apart from the chronicles of war and destruction in Croatia, Bosnia and Kosovo that follow. Andrew Rossos argues that the Macedonian crisis in 1991 was not instigated by the break-up of Yugoslavia but had been a constant since the Congress of Berlin in 1878. In Rossos' account, the Macedonian crisis was caused by the determined opposition by some of its Balkan neighbours. Macedonia's declaration of independence was, in his view, the only way to resolve the Macedonian question. Rossos credits the Glikorov government which skillfully avoided war and ultimately enabled the newly independent state to survive the Greek embargo.

Croatia was less fortunate than Macedonia and its fate is explored in two chapters which examine the origins and conduct of the first war of 1990–91 and the difficulties of enforcing a peace. In the first of two chapters, Branka Magas argues that the intention behind the attacks by the Yugoslav National Army was to drive out local populations and, as the war continued, to destroy any cultural or civic monuments which were associated with secessionist states and alien cultures. In the second study, former US ambassador to Croatia, Peter Galbraith, provides a personal account in which he describes American attempts to bring peace to Croatia. Galbraith recalls the high-level discussions that led to the relatively unknown Erdut peace agreement that ended the conflict in Croatia's Danube region and paved the way for the Dayton Peace Agreement.

The campaigns of terror and vandalism in Croatia were to spill over into Bosnia, as Serbian paramilitary units imported the politics of ethnic purity to Croatia's neighbour. The cumulative effects of these campaigns is recorded in a remarkable piece of investigative journalism by Pulitzer Prize winning author David Rohde who documents the most horrific outcome of the battle for ethnic purity – the fall of Srebrenica and the massacre of thousands of Bosnian Muslims by Serbian forces which has since been recognized as an act of genocide by the International War Crimes Tribunal.

The focus then shifts from Bosnia to Kosovo. In the first of three studies, Noel Malcolm discusses the diplomatic efforts in 1999 which aimed to avert war over Kosovo, and provides a useful introduction to the KLA. Malcolm's attempt to demystify the sources of conflict in Kosovo is followed first by Mark Bartolini's account of NATO's air campaign, from the perspective of humanitarian organisations on the ground, then an assessment of the international community's attempts to administer the province, following NATO's intervention, by Bryan Hopkinson, chief political officer to the United Nations in Kosovo. Hopkinson reviews the work of the UN mission in Kosovo and considers the factors which made it so difficult to govern and which are central to Kosovo's final status talks.

Relations between NATO members Greece and Turkey, as well as NATO hopefuls Bulgaria and Albania, and their relationship with Russia are analysed in chapters by regional experts Thanos Veremis, Ali Karaosmanoglu and Philip Shashko. Veremis and Karaosmanoglu record how public opinion in Greece and Turkey was divided by NATO's actions against Belgrade and provide explanations for such divisions. Veremis's account sheds light on the 'anti-Americanism' exhibited in Greece and dispels any notion that the Greek population was in sympathy with coreligionists, as others have suggested. Karaosmanoglu then considers the range of interests behind Turkey's policies. The transition and transformation of Bulgaria, a country that teetered on the brink of ethnic cleansing but seized the opportunity to embrace a new Euro-Atlantic identity, is addressed by Philip Shasko. In his detailed history of contemporary Bulgaria, Shasko comments on the importance of US and European engagement for Bulgaria and the region. His chapter contrasts with Carole Hodge's study of Albania and its relations with its neighbours, Greece and Italy. In spite of massive financial support from the European Union, Hodge argues in this penultimate chapter that Albania is economically dominated by its neighbours who have historically sought to undermine its independence and failed to develop its resources.

Finally, this volume concludes with a review of some current problems regarding the transition from war to peace. Brad K. Blitz considers the challenges of reintegrating returning refugees and reconstructing states that have experienced brain drain and have lost much of their multiethnic flavour as a result of forced migrations and the destruction of local economies.

Notes

1 Several Pulitzer Prizes were awarded for reporting and writing on the conflicts in the Balkans and the impact of the genocide in Bosnia in particular. For their accounts, see Roy Gutman. *A Witness to Genocide: The 1993 Pulitzer Prize-Winning Dispatches on the 'Ethnic Cleansing' in Bosnia*, New York: Macmillan, 1993; David Rohde, *Endgame: The Betrayal and Fall of Srebrenica, Europe's Worst Massacre since World War II*, Boulder, CO: Westview, 1998; and, Samantha Power, *A Problem from Hell: America and the Age of Genocide*, New York: Basic Books, 2002.

2 Thomas Cushman and Stjepan Mestrovic (eds.), *This Time We Knew: Western Responses to Genocide in Bosnia*, New York: New York University Press, 1996.

3 See Misha Glenny, *The Fall of Yugoslavia: The Third Balkan War*, New York: Penguin Books, 1994.

4 See also Susan L. Woodward, *Balkan Tragedy: Chaos and Dissolution after the Cold War*, Washington, DC: Brookings Institute Press, 1995.

5 George Schöpflin, 'Nationhood, communism and state legitimation', *Nations and Nationalism* 1, 1 (1995), 81–91.

6 Branka Magas, *The Destruction of Yugoslavia: Tracing the Break-up 1980–92*, New York: Verso, 1993; Laura Silber and Allan Little, *The Destruction of Yugoslavia: Death of a Nation*, London: BBC/Penguin Books, 1997.

7 See Daniele Conversi, 'Central secession: towards a new analytical concept? The case of former Yugoslavia', *Journal of Ethnic and Migration Studies*, 26, 2 (April 2000), 333–56.

8 See Yossi Shain and Juan Linz (eds.), *Between States: Interim Governments in Democratic Transitions*, New Haven, CT: Yale University Press, 1995; and Olga Krishtanovskaia and Stephen White 'From nomenklatura to new elite' in V. Shlapentokh, C. Vanderpool and B. Doktorov (eds.), *The New Elite in Post-Communist Europe*, College Station, TX Texas AandM University Press, 1999.

9 Norman Cigar, *Genocide in Bosnia: The Policy of Ethnic Cleansing*, College Station, TX: Texas A and M University Press, 1995.

10 Paula Lytle, 'Electoral transitions in Yugoslavia', in Shain and Linz, *Between States*, pp. 237–54.

11 For a detailed account of the way in which after serving Yugoslavia's communist party for decades many journalists shifted their loyalties to support nationalist ideologues in their warmongering, see Kemal Kurpahsic. *Prime Time Crime*, Washington, DC: United States Institute of Peace Press, 2003.

12 For a good account of Milošević's rise see Adam Lebor, *Milošević: A Biography*, London: Bloomsbury, 2004; and Louis Sell, *Slobodan Milošević and the Destruction of Yugoslavia*. Durham, NC: Duke University Press, 2004.

13 Shain and Linz, *Between States*, p. 7.

14 Daniele Conversi, *German-Bashing and the Breakup of Yugoslavia*, Seattle: University of Washington/ Henry M. Jackson School of International Studies (The Donald W. Treadgold Papers in Russian, East European and Central Asian Studies, no. 16, March 1998).

15 Tony Blair, 'A new generation draws the fine', *Newsweek*, 19 April 1999.

16 See Gerald Knaus and Felix Martin, 'Lessons from Bosnia and Herzegovina: travails of the European Raj', *Journal of Democracy*, 14, 3 (2003), 60–74.

2 Yugoslavia: state construction and state failure

George Schöpflin

The particular dilemma and tragedy of Yugoslavia might be described with only a little cynicism as the product of a major historical error. In a very real sense, the state was founded on a weak basis because of a set of serious misunderstandings; some of them were deeply structural, others contingent and derived from a cognitive screening out of long-term factors by short-term ones. Indeed, there is a case to be made for the proposition that the concentration on short-term problems can produce really major headaches in the long term.

The above argument needs to be grounded in both the interpretation of the nature of state foundation and the actual historical data. How states come into being or how they fail tends to be an underinvestigated area, yet the success or otherwise of the modern state does to a very considerable extent depend on the actual contingent circumstances of its birth. There is an argument to be made that such contingent factors continue to influence its operations, not least through its foundation myth which generally encodes something of the purposiveness of the state in question. When the purposiveness of a state remains caught in the contingent factors of its birth and if it cannot readily transcend these, the chances of its success are diminished.

All this raises a further question or set of questions to do with what states are actually for and whether the purpose of states has changed over time. Here the key moment is the rise of the modern state. Whereas the pre-modern state was static and could operate with a fairly high degree of coercion, the modern state, because it is dynamic, presupposes a much higher level of consent. After all, the modern state has quite extraordinary expectations of its subjects: that they entrust it with a high level of power to organise, to regulate, to rationalise, to tax and to coerce and that generally they trust those who exercise power over them. This is extraordinary because it assumes that rulers and ruled concur in the broad aims of power, which the ruled believe that power will not be exercised to their detriment, but to their advantage. Democracy is the most developed form of this dispensation, but other modes of establishing consent are also possible, though as economic and technological change advances, the intensity of two-way exchanges must increase too and democracy is the most effective way of achieving this.

Hence the function of states in the modern world is to act as a framework for the exercise of power in a fast changing world, to provide stability and make provision for change. The way in which a state establishes its rules, both implicit and explicit, will shape the patterns of power and simultaneously the aims which the exercise of power is intended to serve. What is critical in this context, however, is that the state cannot shape the aspirations of society *in toto*. Society has its own agendas, its own expectations and moral imperatives; states must heed these or else come up against the problem of consent and the withdrawal of consent. State failure can be seen as the loss of consent to be ruled by that particular state.

So how, then, is consent to be attained and maintained? The classical answer is that consent between rulers and ruled is achieved through the civic contract which is encoded in the doctrine of state sovereignty. The population of a particular state is said to have consented to that state, the rulers of which regard themselves a ruling only by virtue of that contract and thus consensually. A moment's thought will show that this does not deal very effectively with the problem of dissent. While dissent from policy issues can be readily integrated into the concept of the civic contract, the withdrawal of consent from the state as such cannot. Indeed, and this is the particularly significant lesson of Yugoslavia, although states in Europe look well established, immanent and unquestionable, their existence in their present form is under challenge in several places and should not be taken for granted.

Those in power have a vested interest in preempting the very question of the existence of the state and seek to do so by making the existing dispensation unquestionable, by making the status quo 'normal and natural' and thus cognitively beyond challenge. But that is not the same as an explicit, overt civic contract. That is an altogether different process, one used widely in the world; that of making certain questions unaskable by sacralising them. Sacralisation can take various forms. It can be attained by creating and maintaining a state over a very long period of time, so that its origins are vague and the population accepts it as the only possible form of living. France generally falls into this category.

However, there is generally more to sacralisation than a straightforward cognitive closure. The really effective way of constructing consent is to base it on culture. And it is at this moment that this analysis arrives as its most controversial point, the linking of consent to ethnicity.

In essence, the core of the argument here is that one of the features of a shared culture is that it encodes the bonds of solidarity that tells the embers of a collectivity what their tacit obligations are to one another, what they share and what they do not. Crucially, solidarity does not presuppose consensus.[1] Indeed, solidarity makes a range of disagreement possible by establishing the outer boundaries of disagreement. But when it comes to the establishment and maintenance of states, the function of solidarity is to exclude the questioning sketched above. The name given to this cultural solidarity is ethnicity.

Ethnicity has its own purposiveness. Once in being, an ethnic community will do virtually everything it can to ensure that it survives and it employs a very wide range of instruments to ensure its cultural reproduction.[2] The ultimate aim is to gain universal recognition for itself as a community of moral worth, as a bearer of collective values on the same terms as all the others.[3] At the end of the day, moral worth is about imposing a pattern on the world that gives meaning to the myriad conflicting impressions and experiences that individuals encounter in their lives. Ethnicity is a central means of creating coherence and order in what would otherwise be chaos.[4] Through this coherence, individuals recognise mutual bonds and obligations. They acquire moral worth in their own eyes by being members of a community of shared solidarity.

Thus the solidarity that underlies ethnicity is the central element in ensuring that consent to the state remains in being. People who share an ethnicity also share an understanding of what their community is and what the metaphorical and physical boundaries of that state are or should be. By and large, members of the same ethnic group do not seek secession, indeed they will not have the group consciousness which could give rise to the questioning that might produce secession.

So what, may I ask, are the bases of ethnicity? There is a range of answers to this question, and again the answers given today are more complex and more sophisticated than they were a century ago. One can debate the nature of ethno-genesis, but as far as Europe is concerned, an ethnic group has to have an awareness of itself as a collectivity, a sense of its own past and future and a set of markets by which it differentiates itself from other groups. All other factors are contingent. Some ethnic collectives will make use of various materials, like say, language and religion, while for others these are less important. What is significant is the actual quantity of usable materials. Where these are plentiful, especially where the shared past is dense and complex, the identity fashioned out of it will reflect this.

The palette of choice is significant too. The greater the range of raw materials, the more easily a community will be able to adapt to different challenges. It is important to recognise in this context that self-definitions are not fixed, but will shift according to circumstances, that these identities are fluid and seemingly opportunistic. This is one of the aspects of collective identities and of their being intellectually impoverished.[5] In fact, invention will only operate where there is resonance; the past that is used must be recognisable by the collectivity in question as theirs. As long as a particular strand in the self-definition remains capable of energising the population, as long as it prompts a moment of self-recognition, it will be effective.

A further problem, of particular significance with respect to Yugoslavia, is that of overlaps. It can happen that more than one group will lay claim to a particular piece of history or language or religion as a badge of identity. In such situations, there will certainly be a contest and maybe conflict. Given that any conflict of this kind will be about the deepest levels of identity, it will inevitably be bitter and seen as highly threatening by those involved.

It would, however, be misleading to regard ethnicity as the sole determinant and creator of group political identities. Much of the debate about nations and nationalism omits a key aspect of the nature of nationhood: the state and civil society are also vital in the construction of identity, indeed, given the nature of the modern state, it is very hard to see how the activity of the state could fail to transform identities in various ways. The modern state has an enormous capacity to reshape the way in which a society regards itself, through legislation and through moral suasion, not least through its control of the education system.[6] It is, in fact, at this point that the coincidence of interest of the state and ethnic group is clearest. The ethnic group has an overriding concern for its own survival, in its cultural reproduction. The state has an equivalent concern in ensuring the reproduction of consent. The two meet through the medium of education, where much of this reproduction takes place.

The outcome of this state of affairs is that individuals of different ethnicities can acquire the same state (étatic) identities. They have been socialised into dealing with the states in a particular way even when their consent to the state may not be wholehearted. Their expectations of how a state functions, what it can and cannot do, have been shaped by that state experience. This adds up to an identity which can divide groups of the same ethnicity, and can create differences that will persist over very long periods of time. An example is Romania, where political patterns, notably voting behaviour, in Transylvania (a part of Hungary until 1918) are markedly different from those in the Regat.

What emerges from a study of states, their success and failure, is that success requires that they have a legitimising ideology that is capable of mobilising and remobilising consent, in other words that the population feel that the state continues to articulate their deepest aspirations. The coincidence between the legitimate ideology and the aspirations does not have to be perfect, but the gap cannot be too great, otherwise the existence of the state is endangered.

By and large, state failure is not much studied. Yet any closer look at the history of Europe in the twentieth century will show that it is more widespread than it appears. If the criteria of state failure are taken to be complete disappearance, the loss or acquisition of territory (gaining territory is a problem because it creates major tasks of integration and transformation of state purposiveness), foreign conquest or loss of empire, then Switzerland is the only state in Europe to have not undergone this trauma. The implication is that states are far more fluid than they seem, that changes are a part of the political repertoire, but because that state failure really is traumatic, everything is done to screen out this reality.

This proposition also says something about how the European political tradition deals with the problem of non-consent. Although coercion is not unknown (e.g., the Spanish Civil War was fought at least in part about the relationship between Castile and the Basque country and Catalonia), the general European approach is reluctant to accede to secession and new state formation. The period between 1945 and 1991 (the end of the Soviet Union) was unusual in that this fluidity was temporarily frozen because of the Cold War; that era is definitively over and Yugoslavia is one of the casualties.

The third element of the modern nation is the civic dimension, the nature of civil society, citizenship and the complex web of interactions between different groups and between individuals, groups and the state. Society acts on the state and vice versa; conflicts of interest are settled by the criteria that a particular community has evolved. These conflicts are settled much more easily when all the members of the community in question share a set of cultural norms, i.e., they share the same ethnicity. Because ethnicity encodes some of the deepest moral assumptions and aims of a collectivity, there is a general tendency for intra-collective communication to be more effective than communication with non-members. This does not mean that such communication is impossible, just that it is more complex and more likely to result in misunderstanding.

What is significant about the impact of civil society on nationhood is that where society is well established and self-confident, it finds it easier to take its own existence and identity for granted and does not have to concern itself with its own survival and self-reproduction. This makes it much easier for a nation with a strong civil society to live with the codes of other ethnic groups. Correspondingly, where civil society is weak, that self-confidence will be weaker too and the nation in question will be much more inclined to see issues in ethnic terms.

When the lessons of these theoretical considerations are applied to Yugoslavia, the flaws in that state – flaws that were built into the state from the outset – became clearer. This argument is not aimed at suggesting that the experiment in setting up a South Slav state was doomed from the outset, rather, that its founders seriously underestimated the extreme difficulty in running a multiethnic state in the modern world. Again, it is not argued here that this was the outcome of malign intentions. The flaw derived from a misunderstanding of the nature of nationhood, crucially because of the reductionist definition that was employed.

The argument in favour of the South Slav state was that the South Slavs share an ethnicity and, therefore, they should all be in the same state. The word 'ethnicity' was not, of course, used at the time. The term then current was 'race', a word not without the extraordinarily negative connections that it bears today. But the content of 'race' was only partly biological. Its essence was language. The universal assumption in the analysis of nationhood was that the people speaking the same language were members of the same nation and should in consequence be living in the same state, hence the South Slavs (generously including the Slovenes and Macedonians in the same language group) were all members of one nation.[7]

This initial assumption was the single most important flaw in the creation of Yugoslavia because it ignored all other factors in the make-up of nationhood. Serbs and Croats spoke the same language, hence they were all members of the same nation and should, therefore, be living in the same state. As a syllogism this may work, but as sociology it was poor stuff. And, as cannot be emphasised too often, any ideology based on inadequate sociology will be faced with the choice of either abandoning its project or constructing the conditions that would then justify the ideology. In the South Slav context, this meant homogenising the various different ethnicities until they really were one.

To be fair, this was not quite as outrageous at the time as it appears today. Such projects of social engineering were common enough in the nineteenth century, as dominant ethnic groups sought to assimilate weaker ones through their control of the state and the educational system. France is the classic example, but neighbouring Hungary had made a similar attempt; the Hungarian failure should have served as a warning to the South Slavs, but it was ignored, largely because they were misled by the question of language.

Exclusive emphasis on the language meant that other key elements of identity were ignored and, when they interfered with the project, were suppressed. Of vital significance in this connection was that the Croats – the most important dissonant actor – really did have very different experiences from the Serbs and that their identity, the way in which they defined themselves as a community of moral worth, could not be reconciled with the vision of Yugoslavia held by the Serbs. The outcome was stress and friction. Despite the shared language – to which I shall return – there were many other markers and aspirations that separated the two communities.

In the first place, while the Croats did indeed launch the entire concept of Illyrianism, the basis of the South Slav idea, Illyrianism was not the only Croatian project. The nineteenth century saw the formulation of Croatian rights as an alternative vision of the Croatian project, in which Croats were clearly and unmistakably different from the Serbs,[8] but the contingent circumstances of 1918 made this position inaudible.

Second, the Croatian identity was heavily marked by the experience with Budapest. While the Croatian perspective on Hungary tends to be negative, the reality is that the bulk of the Croatian elite acquired its view of politics in the struggle with Hungary and, to some extent, with Vienna. A Croatian elite with certain political skills, especially those of bargaining would produce results, even if those results were not necessarily what the Croats had set out to achieve. The Croatian étatic identity already existed.

Third, the Croats had a longer-term historical and literary tradition of their own, one marked by contact with Venice, Vienna and the German speaking world. A Croatian way of creating coherence was already in being. This too, marked them out as different from the Serbs.

Finally, and rather importantly, there was religion. The difference was not merely the obvious one, that of differences between Eastern and Western Christian dogma. Rather, religion gives rise to a mediated identity derived from religion and religious styles. The ways of making the world are heavily influenced by the dominant religious identity of the community in question. In essence, as a result of the Counter-Reformation in the seventeenth century, much of Central Europe was re-Catholicised on a Protestant basis, that is to say that Catholic and Protestant values were in conflict. The Catholicism that resulted gave saliency to certain features of style and content. These included an emphasis on hierarchy and obedience, on display, on form over content, complexity over simplicity, the attempt to include all phenomena even if they are left unexplained, and gloss over inconsistencies.

Counter-Reformation Roman Catholicism accepted the 'complexities of opposites', the *complexion oppositorum*, in which doctrinal opposites are brought into a kind of order so that unity may be enhanced.

The Serbian experience was wholly different. The Serbian experience had been one of resistance by force and the successful establishment of the Serbian state in the face of Ottoman hostility. The state experience and étatic identity of the Serbs was one of rather low levels of integration, given the limited capacity of the Serbian state (poor quality bureaucracy, high levels of illiteracy, corruption, the tendency to ignore regulations, personalisation of politics). At the same time, the Serbian project was regarded as unfulfilled, in as much as sizable numbers of undisputed Serbs continued to live under Austria-Hungary (Croatia, Vojvodina, Bosnia).

For the Serbian elite, this was a classic irredenta that had to be brought into the Serbian state by the equally classic methods of expansion through force and conquest. This last factor was highly significant in 1918, because the contingent events conspired to create precisely this symbolic experience. Threatened by Italian expansion, a section of the Croatian elite called on the Serbian government to send their armed forces into Croatia and Slovenia. What was experienced as liberation by the Croats was integrated in Serbian experience as yet another military expansion.

The question of language still misleads some observers. Their position is a simplistic philological one and does not differ from the nineteenth-century position. According to the argument, people who speak the same language as defined philologically all belong to the same nation. The problem is that language as a cultural, let alone political, phenomenon is quite different from philology. Although many people dismiss the role of politics in the definition of language, it is real enough.

After all, philologically the language of the United States and the United Kingdom is the same, the difference between them has arisen through politics and geography, but it is more than real enough. The same is true for France and Wallonia, where there is not even a sea boundary to separate one from the other. The cultural aspects of language show that, over time, the different experiences of two communities speaking the same language philologically differentiates their language as well, as words begin to acquire different meanings, carry different emotional charges and evoke different responses. From this perspective, Serbian and Croatian were culturally different languages and culture, as argued in the foregoing, has a central role in the definition of nationhood through ethnicity. This set of differences between the two dominant ethnicities that made up Yugoslavia constituted the first and greatest flaw in the new state.

Then, the next integrating factor in the new state was to be the monarchy. This proposition again shows that it came from a different era, but monarchy was widely believed to have stabilising qualities that republics lacked. Possibly the sacralised quality of kingship lay behind this, the belief that despite the secularisation undergone by Europe since the Enlightenment, some kind of divine sacrament endowed monarchs with a higher political sense than mere presidents could command.

Whatever the truth or otherwise of this argument, the difficulty in the case of the South Slav kingdom was that Serbs and Croats had different expectations of kingship in the light of their pre-1918 experience. For the Serbs the monarch was theirs; for the Croats he was emphatically not theirs, given that he had resided in Vienna and Budapest. Furthermore, when they approached the king, they expected him to be relatively detached with respect to the Croats and not to adopt a strongly centralising position which ignored their wishes. Not surprisingly, the monarchy rapidly lost whatever legitimacy it may have had in the eyes of the Croats.

To these deep structural flaws can be added the contingent errors of perception and practice made by both Croatian and Serbian actors. Many of them certainly were errors and not antagonistic machinations, but such was the mutual sensitivity that there was no space for error and each move was interpreted in the harshest light. To take one example, the Croatian elite concluded that the Constituent Assembly of 1921 was so determinedly anti-Croat that there was no point in attending. This was fairly clearly not the case.

Serbian attitudes were still comparatively fluid and there was still room for argument. In the absence of the Croats, however, the Vidovdan constitution really was highly centralising and did ignore Croatian susceptibilities. This was a self-fulfilling prophecy that came true. But, having said that, the decision to promulgate it on St Vitus Day, 28 June, a day heavily redolent of Serbian modes and perceptions (battle of Kosovo Polje in 1389, the anniversary of the assassination of Franz Ferdinand in 1914), was tactless, to say the least. It confirmed Croats in their belief that they had been right to stay away and legitimate their fears.

The remainder of interwar history simply moved along these predetermined lines of polarisation. Each step taken by one side or the other confirmed the actors in their conviction of the malign, intransigent, hostile nature of the other. Compromise was impossible with such people. The only answer, they believed, was force and yet more force. In effect, it was not until a significant part of the Serbian elite came together to recognise that centralisation would not work, that the Croats would not be homogenised into Serbian modes, that some kind of compromise could be sought. But the 1939 *sporazum* (the compromise between Serbian and Croatian elites) was too late, Croatian attitudes had hardened and there was virtually no support left for Yugoslavia.

The events of the war are vital in understanding several processes. Central to these is the state failure and refoundation, but to these should be added the scars of the war itself,[9] a conflict that became an inter-ethnic massacre that, in the immediate aftermath of the war, to some extent delegitimated violence as an acceptable instrument of politics and created an atmosphere in which interethnic cooperation was no longer anathema. The destruction of old elites contributed to this change. In reality, the events of the war should be seen as a deep gulf between old and new, which made possible various options previously unthinkable. The communists both seized the opportunity offered by this gulf and contributed to the new options.

When they talked of a new order, they meant it. The new order would give rise to a new state radically different from the old, in which the ills of the old order would be swiftly remedied. The communists also enjoyed the immense advantages of having been untainted by the state failure, and of their association with what appeared at the time to be the most successful and the most dynamic ideology of the new world. This strength was also their greatest weakness. Any ideology and movement attempting to build a new world face a key problem which is generally ignored – the past.

Because the revolutionaries are themselves suffused by their belief in the order that they are bringing into being, they assume that they are untainted by the old and that everyone else will readily accept the new world that they are creating. This establishes a Manichean mindset, in which the legacy of history – the real, living, authentic past – is dismissed as a hostile conspiracy, because of the vain attempt to eliminate history itself. In reality, bits of the past will always live on and successful political projects are those that manage to graft the new onto the old without serious discontinuities. The Yugoslav communists were not interested in these subtleties, they already had the answer in the founding of the state, with its completely different purposiveness and foundation myth. In this endeavour, they overlooked, as they were bound to, one fatal flaw. By tying the existence of the Yugoslav state to communism, they predicated that existence on the perpetual success of communism. In 1945 it was clearly impossible to envisage a time when communism would be so eroded that its weakness would threaten the future of the state; but by the mid-1980s, this was not quite such an extraordinary proposition.

To these structural weaknesses in the communist project, there should be added two others. In the first place, communism was a direct descendant of Enlightenment rationalism and communists believed that rational construction was not only viable, but expressly desirable. Implicit processes were denied or written off as legacies of the past. Obstacles that existed in the form of values and attitudes different from theirs were dismissed as irrational or alien or hostile. Second, the entire Marxist project had a very particular and peculiar relationship with ethnicity. At the level of theory, the two are incompatible, in as much as Marxism insists that the individual's primary and original identity, aspirations and world-view are derived from the material base. Ethnicity derived it from culture. Hence the persistence of ethnicity faced Marxism with two insurmountable problems: how to account for the survival of ethnic identities, and what to do with them.

The solution was to define them as relics of the past and to give them formal existence as something that would wither away. This intellectual trap left Yugoslavia's communist rulers incapable of dealing with the resurgence of ethnic identity politics except by suppression, which then revived the responses of the interwar period. The consequence was that they were incapable of rebuilding a system that would give genuine expression to the ethnic reality of Yugoslavia and of allowing these realities some space within communist hegemony. Of course, that would have meant a formal dilution of the community ideology, hence of their legitimacy to rule, so it was not a step that could be taken until the very end.

The alternatives were unfortunate. Ethnic identities were initially suppressed and a Yugoslav identity was superimposed on them. But as the effectiveness of communism as a system waned, an off-stage ethnicity became more and more an accepted point of reference. The official language of politics was marked by an ever-growing gap between the condemnations of ethnic nationalism and its reality. That gap too helped to undermine the legitimacy of the system and the state.

The central difficulty was that for Yugoslavia to be able to survive as a state, the communists would have had to collude in their own political demise and act as midwives to a democratic order; and they would have had to do it before the erosion was too far advanced, in other words before they saw any reason for it. This was evidently too much to expect.

To the foregoing, there are a number of contingent factors to be added as instrumental in the collapse of the state. The first of these is the role of Tito himself.[10] Tito was pivotal in the refoundation of the state and central to the maintenance of its cohesion. At the same time, unfortunately, he proved too limited in his vision to recognise that the

Yugoslav order that he had created would, after all, have to come to terms with ethnic identities and allow them some room in politics. The various ethnic communities in Yugoslavia then had not been superseded by the communist Yugoslav identity – an étatic, pseudo-civic identity – because that ethnicity was not provided. Tito was too inflexible, too much a captive of his authoritarianism, too caught up by his own towering authority to be able to recognise the true sociological process that his own very real success had launched.

Then Tito's enormous prestige, authority and power brought with it the major disadvantage that it was all but impossible for a reasonably open-minded and sophisticated successor generation to take its place. Tito, like the jealous despot that he was, saw to it that it was third and forth-grade politicians who succeeded him. The post-1971 purges saw the best successor generation taken off the political scene to be replaced by party hacks. This proved to be a tragedy, because the system that Tito constructed could only be made to function by him or someone like him. After his death in 1980, the system drifted, the centre failed to hold and the power of the republics waxed. Increasingly, the reality of power was out of alignment with the purposiveness of the state.

Further, neither Tito nor Kardelj, chief ideological tailor of the system, had a true understanding of conflict and of the ways of resolving it.[11] Crucially, because they both understood ethnicity as a malign relic of the past, they were incapable of seeing the need for building instruments of ethnic conflict management. Tito had two ways of dealing with ethnic conflict – suppression and personal intervention. Nor would he do anything to establish procedures that are routine and accepted by all in the field of inter-ethnicity. The outcome was that the ethnic distribution of offices, resources and prestige was random and unpredictable and became a source of conflict and unregulated contest rather than one of reassurance. The experience of other multiethnic systems is unequivocal on the need to routinise an ethnic key. Titoism refused to do so because he believed that ethnic identity was inherently negative.

The outcome of this was that elites, for whom an ethnic identity, along with a Yugoslav identity, was authentic, tended to give saliency to the former. This process was much enhanced by the grave weakening of the federal centre after the 1960s. Once the power of the secret police was broken with the fall of Alexander Ranković and attacks on 'Unitarianism', the code-word for Serbian power, gained ground, the republics emerged as serious centres of power. The 1974 constitution secured this new arrangement by accepting the republican veto.[12] Consequently, it was perfectly rational for elites to adopt a republican identity and these were to some extent inherently ethnic (other than Bosnia-Hercegovina).

As these elites increasingly identified with republican power, they adopted its symbolic and real characteristics. It was at this point that the absence of a legitimate expression of ethnic identities in the public sphere turned into a real threat. These identities were authentic, they informed politics, but they always had to be disguised by another language, by another political vocabulary. The only way out would have been to recognise these identities as real, to provide the mechanism for reconciling them and gradually to transform the system from a pseudo-consociational one to a real consociationalism. But that came up against the rock of the communist ideology, the one upon which the state itself was to be shipwrecked.

The only counterweight to these republican elites was the federal bureaucracy and the armed forces. Neither could be the core of an all-Yugoslav identity because they drew their legitimacy from the ruling ideology and, once that was gone, their position was fragile. The spectacle of JNA, the Yugoslav armed forces, looking for a political home in the summer of 1991, after Croatia and Slovenia had opted for independence, illustrated this process vividly and with a tragic outcome. The seceding republics had no further use for the JNA, which they saw as inherently pro-Serbian, and which saw them as destructive of Yugoslavia. The gap in perceptions was evident – for the Croats and the Slovenes, 'Yugoslavia' had become symbolic of Serbian power, while for the JNA the Yugoslav state was an essential entity to make its existence valid and legitimate.

The nature of non-elite ethnicity was just as relevant. In the immediate aftermath of the war, it is reasonably clear that war-weariness and disgust at the interethnic killing had led many people to conclude that their ethnic identities were less significant as a source of meaning than had been the case before the war. Until the 1960s these ethnic identities coexisted with a Yugoslav identity, even when people continued to identify themselves with their ethnic affiliation. The question then arises as to why this Yugoslav identity declined. Even at its peak, it was never able to attract even 10 per cent of the population (those who returned their identity as 'Yugoslav, nationally undetermined' in the censuses).

The explanation has to be sought in a number of factors. First, there was the process of republicanisation already mentioned. Just as republics attracted elites, so they also attracted non-elites.[13] This did not mean, at that stage, that the ethnic identity excluded the Yugoslav one, but the former gradually gained in its power to resonate. Some of this had to do with the failures of the system, both the failure to construct meaningful interethnic mechanisms and in the general sense, that as ethnicity was slightly illicit, its place in the official Yugoslav order was never clear, it could pose as a superior alternative without being called on to deliver.

Then, ethnic identities prospered through the failure of the Yugoslav one. Yugoslavism as a doctrine was too closely bound up with communism and, given the propensity of communists to centralise power, it was associated with Serbian power. This made it hard for non-Serbs to see a genuinely all-Yugoslav identity as attractive to them. The Yugoslav identity was an étatic identity that, by definition, had limited democratic content. As long as the Yugoslav state was non-democratic, the identity that it propagated was similarly non-democratic.

This applied even to the much vaunted slogan of *'bratsvo i jedinstvo'* (brotherhood and unity), the supposed cornerstone of 'nationalities policy'. The slogan was always imposed and not assumed voluntarily. There was always an element of threat and coercion behind it: 'if you are not nice to your fellow Yugoslavs, we have ways of making you nice'. Indeed, the first direct intervention by the JNA into Yugoslav politics was over the Croatian crisis of 1971. This element of coercion effectively removed any incentive for people to learn interethnic accommodation from below. A traditional, pre-communist mode of such accommodation coexisted, sometimes uneasily, with brotherhood and unity, but neither had full legitimacy.

To these factors there should be added the sociology of Yugoslav urbanisation. As everywhere else in the communist world, industrialisation was rapid and undertaken without much thought for its consequences.[14] Urban ghettos were built and rural migrants were decanted into them, with all the attendant ills that are so familiar from every other part of the world. Crucially, no attempt was made to construct an urban identity that would respond to the needs of these migrants, how they were to conduct themselves as urban workers and citizens, other than a vague proletarian identity (this was less clear-cut than in the Soviet world).

The outcome was the ruralisation of the city. Rural modes, rural thought-worlds, rural values and attitudes persisted. Central in this connection was the persistence of ethnic allegiance as the key source of meanings. Contact with members of other ethnicities reinforced it rather that diluted it. It was only in cities where there already existed a tradition of interethnic accommodation from before the communist period that ethnic relations could be regulated.[15] Time helped to some extent. Where members of two communities had lived in the same tower block for a couple of decades, this might make matters easier, but even then, when the decisive test came after 1991, it turned out that suspicion and hostility prevailed over tolerance.

Once again, the absence of a clear-cut Yugoslav identity that was relevant to inter-ethnic relations and was felt to be authentic, proved to be a far-reaching flaw in the system. It meant that once the system came to be tested, there was only a minority prepared to stand up for it. The majority was either actively hostile or passive or open to mobilisation along ethnic lines and, at that moment, all the myths of the ethnic order could be brought into play; these proceeded to be stronger, as they generally are, than the actual ground level experience of accommodation. Yugoslav counter-myths were too feeble to have much effect.[16]

Finally, a word about the international context of Yugoslavia. International support for states helps them to remain in being and to overcome the threat of state failure. States help one another almost instinctively, presumably on the tacit assumption that the failure of one state is a reflection on them all. Yugoslavia was undoubtedly the beneficiary of this approach. In the interwar period the Yugoslav state came to be seen as a stabilising factor in the Balkans, as the instrument for keeping the lid on otherwise troublesome and quarrelsome ethnic groups, and it resumed this role after 1948 as the non-Soviet communist state that kept the Soviet Union out of the Adriatic.[17]

Even when the doctrine of human rights began to make headway in Europe, Yugoslavia's poor record was simply overlooked on strategic grounds. The kind of criticism that was levelled at other communist states, like Czechoslovakia, was regarded as 'undesirable', not least because the Yugoslav authorities were successful in presenting their dissidents as ethnic troublemakers (e.g., those imprisoned in the post-1972 purge in Croatia and their counterparts in the other republics). The same went for Yugoslavia's tilt towards the Soviet Union, as in 1967 when it granted Warsaw Pact aircraft over flying rights to supply Egypt in the Six Day War; the West simply ignored this. The Yugoslav leadership, for its part, used its adherence to the doctrine of non-alignment to generate prestige and support in the Third World.

From the international perspective, therefore, Yugoslavia's problems began when its roles as intermediary and as buffer state between the West and the Soviet Union began to lose their value in the mid-1980s. The attempt to construct a European identity and legitimisation for Yugoslavia – the intermediary role was too great to sustain by that stage – could not gain much support because of the legacy of the past and the country's adherence to a communist legitimisation. Nevertheless, when the cracks in the edifice of the state grew visible the West ignored these and continued to back a state that was enjoying less and less domestic support.

It is open to question whether earlier Western attention to Yugoslavia in 1989–90 might have preempted the polarisation that led to the collapse. The level of intervention needed would have been very far-reaching and the will to intervene in this fashion was not there. Besides, by 1990 the West was suffering from bureaucratic overload as communism was collapsing generally and the question of German unification arrived on the agenda.

Furthermore, there was a real Western fear that allowing Yugoslavia to break up would serve as a precedent for the disintegration of the Soviet Union. There is a lesson to be drawn from all this. International pressure is seldom sufficient to maintain a state if it lacks domestic legitimacy and if the consent to sustain if is absent. This lesson, it would appear, has still to be absorbed by the West. The attempts to enforce the Dayton Agreement and keep Bosnia together are strangely reminiscent of the way in which Western attitudes are marked by a belief that whenever possible states must be sustained, whether their domestic bases justify this or not.

Notes

1 David I. Kertzer, *Ritual Politics and Power*, New Haven, CT: Yale University Press, 1998.
2 Pierre Bourdieu, *The Field of Cultural Production*, Cambridge: Polity, 1993.
3 Donald Horowitz, *Ethnic Groups in Conflict*, Berkeley, CA: University of California Press, 1985.
4 Mircea Eliade, *The Myth of Eternal Return: Cosmos and History*, London: Penguin Books, 1954.
5 Eric Hobsbawm and Terence Range (eds.), *The Invention of Tradition*, Cambridge: Cambridge University Press, 1983.
6 Ernest Gellner, *Nations and Nationalism*, Oxford: Blackwell, 1983.
7 Ivo Banac, *The National Question in Yugoslavia*, Ithaca, NY: Cornell University Press, 1984.
8 Djurdja Knežević, 'The enemy side of national ideologies: Croatia at the end of the 19th century and in the first half of the 20th century' in Lazlo Kontler (ed.), *Pride and Prejudice: National Stereotypes in 19th and 20th Century Europe: East and West*, Budapest: Central European University Press, 1995, pp. 105–18.
9 Milovan Djilas, *Wartime*, New York: Harcourt Brace, 1997.
10 Stevan Pavlowitch, *The Improbable Survivor: Yugoslavia and its Problems, 1918–1988*, London: Hurst, 1988; Milovan Djilas, *Tito: The Story from Inside*, New York: Harcourt, Brace, 1980.
11 Paul Shoup, *Communism in the Yugoslav National Question*, New York: Columbia University Press, 1968.

12 Leonard J. Cohen, *Broken Bonds: Yugoslavia's Disintegration and Balkan Politics in Transition*, Boulder, CO: Westview, 1995.

13 Laslo Sekelj, *Yugoslavia: The Process of Disintegration*, New York: Columbia University Press, 1993.

14 Andrei Simic, *The Peasant Urbanites: A Study of Rural–Urban Mobility in Serbia*, New York: Seminar Press, 1973.

15 Dževad Karahasan, *Il centro del mondo: Sarajevo, esilio di una cittá*, Milan: Il Saggiatore, 1995.

16 George Schöpflin, *The New Politics of Europe: Nations, Identity, Power*, London: Hurst, 2000.

17 Rebecca West, *Black Lamb and Grey Falcon*, London: Macmillan, 1942.

3   The politics of national homogeneity

Ivo Banac

There is an underlying pattern that continues across the conflicts in the former Yugoslavia, from the attack on Slovenia right the way through to the campaign in Kosovo and even its spill-over into Macedonia in 2001, namely that ethnic cleansing and the construction of nationally homogeneous states were not the consequence of but rather the aim of war. This proposition might not have been obvious to all parties in the encounter at the beginning of the war, but it became their common stock in the course of the conflict. The leaders of Serb, Croat, Bosniac, Kosovar Albanian and other national communities, with variations, evidently believed that national homogeneity, that is, statehood without minorities, constituted political stability and offered the only genuine chance for peace. In order to illustrate this it is necessary to investigate the behaviour of the national leaderships.

Serbian conduct: As in all other matters, Milošević led the way. Although taciturn in public statements, he was explicit in defence of national homogenisation as early as January 1989 in the following statement at the Twentieth Session of the League of Communists of Yugoslavia Central Committee:[1]

I ... ask the critics of homogenization, why are they disturbed by the homogenization of peoples and human beings in general if it is carried out on the basis of just, humane, and progressive ideas, in one's own interests, and is of no harm to others? Is this not the meaning, the aim, to which humanity has always aspired? Surely the sense of human community is not to be inhomogeneous, divided, even when its aspirations are progressive and humane?[2]

But had Milošević not been so forthcoming in reconciling the communist notions of unity with national homogenisation, his political behaviour would have told the story. It was Milošević who turned the propaganda machinery of Serbian party-state through his appointees (Zivorad Minović, editor-in-chief of the daily *Politika* and Dugan Mitević, general director of Belgrade TV) into vehicles of national ideologisation. The Serbian press and electronic media promoted national stereotypes, systematically dehumanised Kosovar Albanians, Croats and Bosnian Muslims, insinuated notions of Serb historical victimisation, and aggrandised the role of Serbia and its historical mission in the Balkans. The Serbian media created the preconditions for an ethnically pure Great Serbia that could be accomplished only by war.[3]

Another instrument of national homogenisation and war were the paramilitaries, permitted and encouraged by Milošević, and who were given logistical support by Serbia's security apparatus. Such notorious units as Arkan's Tigers, Seselj's Chetniks, and the White Eagles of the Serbian Renaissance Movement were responsible for carefully orchestrated massacres,[4] 'strategic rape' and the introduction of terrorist regimes in various Croatian and Bosnian localities that were meant to spread panic and intimidation and compel whole national communities to go into exile. The 'regular' armies of Serb parastates – Krajina and Republika Srpska, then followed their work.

But even where paramilitaries were not directly involved, where peace prevailed throughout the war, as in Banja Luka, the largest Bosnian city under Serb control, ethnic cleansing was practised from the beginning. The usual pattern was to create symbolic delegitimation of non-Serb communities (systematic destruction of mosques or occasional razing of Catholic churches), followed by the recruitment of the non-Serbs into units for forcible labour, followed by arrests and removal into concentration camps (Manjaca, Omarska) and ending with the expulsion of survivors.

The goal of Serbian policy, which was originally shared by Milošević's ex-communists and groups far to their right, was the establishment of an ethnically cleansed Great Serbia, which would include Serbia and most of Bosnia-Hercegovina, certainly its inner rim. When this goal became untenable, Milošević shifted to a more realistic policy of holding to the lands conceded to the Serbs by the international community. That meant the abandonment of dependencies in Croatia and a certain cooling to the most extreme pretensions of Karadžić. When the Croat offensive commenced in 1995, Serbia offered no military help to Milan Martić's Krajina parastate. Milošević 's generals only prepared an orderly retreat. In fact, the exodus of Serbs from Croatia also aided the cause of Serbia's homogenisation, by however backhanded means. The inflow of Serbs from Croatia and Bosnia was interpreted as the strengthening of Serbian national juices in a setting destabilised by Albanian, Muslim, Hungarian and other minorities. The loss of Kosovo in 1999, however unanticipated, and the possibility of Montenegro's independence, however resisted, nevertheless offered a possibility of

Serbia's greater homogenisation. Little Serbia may not be preferable to Great Serbia, but it would certainly be more homogeneous.

Milošević's backpedalling in Great Serbianism can be appreciated in terms of his paramount need to maintain himself in power. Because of general disillusionment and the crisis of Great Serbian ideology, Milošević's tactical inventiveness generated new ideological constructs. His 'leftist' visage, which was dominant after Dayton, was spurred by his conjugal ideologist, Mira Markovic-Milošević, whose party, the United Yugoslav Left (JUL), made some inroads among a segment of urban technical intelligentsia and the hapless minorities in Vojvodina and the Sandzak. The JUL masked the option of Milošević's technocrats, who professed to be 'Yugoslav' and 'progressive', but not anti-Milošević. Like them, Milošević, too, increasingly turned to the communist origins of Serbia's ruling party, celebrating its Partisan heritage and promoting a form of pseudo-Yugoslavism. His 'leftist' vestments did not prevent him from initiating war operations and the pursuit of ethnic cleansing in Kosovo, but created an illusion that he was not identical to Vojislav Seselj's Radicals, the chauvinist right-wing party with which he continued to share power in Serbia until the elections in 2000. As a result, Milošević was able to control the whole gamut of Serbian political options. He had the option of being 'leftist', 'rightist' or anything in between. He was 'Yugoslav' or narrowly Serbian, as he chose. More importantly, he could be a partner of the West or the greatest enemy of the 'new world order'. But, whatever the option, he had to dominate.

Croatian conduct: It must always be borne in mind that the political establishment of Serbia was not changed in the course of communism's systemic demise in Eastern Europe. The policy of national homogenisation and war permitted the change of ideological garb for Serbia's old communist establishment. Moreover, Milošević kept parts of Yugoslavia's old federal apparatus (JNA) under his control. The Croat leadership of Tudjman had a far more difficult task of pursuing a transitional course, establishing a new political elite (albeit aided by significant sections of the old communist apparatus), and fending off pressure from Milošević's. Hence, it is puzzling that Tudjman never strayed from a course of unbridled national discrimination and limited defence.

To put it another way, Croatia's best option was to counter Serbian expansionist nationalism with a policy of civic nationhood, enlisting the Serbs of Croatia into a common front against Milošević, which could have included the other republics (Bosnia-Hercegovina, Montenegro, Macedonia), Serbia's autonomous provinces (Kosovo, Vojvodina) and even the Serbian opposition. That would have meant discouraging of narrow Croat nationalism, with its limiting symbols and historical references, some of which were offensive to the Serbs. Admittedly, had such a policy been pursued it would not have stayed Milošević's hand. But it could have slowed it. Instead, Tudjman's behaviour was anything but restrained. He did nothing to prevent the mass expulsion of Serbs from important positions in public administration and the other areas of public trust. In fact, he encouraged a radical 'lustration' of Serbs.

As for defence, when the war started, Tudjman pursued a self-limiting war, which conceded much to Serbian ambitions. This is less evident in the Croatian phase of the war, although many questions can be raised about why the arms meant for the defence of Vukovar and Dubrovnik frequently ended in western Hercegovina, among Tudjman's hard-core supporters. But, it is perfectly obvious in the Bosnian war. The HVO and the Croatian army, without which the HVO would not have been possible, yielded key strategic areas to the Serbs. Without their cooperation the Serb corridor in Bosnian Posavina would have been cut off in 1992–93, leading to the encirclement of 'Western Serbia' (Krajina and northwestern Bosnia). Nor would the Bosnian Croats voluntarily have withdrawn from Jajce and many other towns adjacent to the Serb strongholds to the southwest of Banja Luka.[5]

The logic of Tudjman's behaviour, too, must be sought in the belief that national homogenisation and the establishment of 'ethnically pure' states constitute stability. Tudjman's book *Nacionalno pitanje a suvremenoj Europi*, contains many sections that support this proposition. In the book, Tudjman approvingly cites the population exchanges between Turkey and Greece after 1923, whereby 'Turkey gained the preconditions for its development as a national state.'[6] He promotes the idea of 'reasonable territorial division and joint coexistence' between the Cypriot Greeks and Turks, cautioning:

historical experiences, unfortunately, hardly provide examples in which reasonable considerations and solutions won over narrowly selfish interests – not just material interests, but even suicidal hegemonist impulses and revanchist incentives.[7]

As for Bosnia-Hercegovina, Tudjman's views on the 'federal status' of this republic within Yugoslavia were consistently negative. For him, federal Bosnia-Hercegovina 'was more often a source of new divisions between the Serb and Croat population than their bridge'.[8] For Tudjman, the Bosnian Muslims were really Croats. Their option for an alternative (Bosniak) identity could only benefit the Serbs and hence advance the hour of Bosnia's 'reasonable territorial division'. The agreement with Milošević at Karadjordjevo in March 1991 was the final step in that direction.

Tudjman's Bosnian strategy was division by construction of separate territorial-political units in the overwhelmingly Croat areas of western Bosnia. This 'Hercegovinian option' included the building of the parastate of Herceg-Bosna, the establishment of the HVO paramilitary force, and the stirring up of hostilities against the Muslims. The course of the latter endeavour closely paralleled the lessons learned from Milošević's nationalist mobilisation. The official Croatian press and state-controlled electronic media incited hatred against the Muslims. Their work was followed by ethnic cleansing in the Croat-controlled parts of Bosnia-Hercegovina, again on the Serb model.[9] The concentration camps at Dretelj, Gabela and the Rodoc Heliodrome, as well as the destruction of Muslim religious sites and antiquities, most dramatically in Stolac, were aspects of this policy.[10]

Another aspect was the voluntary withdrawal of Croats from central Bosnia and Sarajevo. Croat officials encouraged the exodus of Croats from these areas, often in conflict with the Catholic church, which opposed the moves that would have deprived it of its flock. The point was to strengthen the Croat areas of western Hercegovina and the depopulated parts of Croatia (Istria, Dalmatian islands). After the Serb exodus from Krajina and parts of western Bosnia in 1995, efforts were made to resettle Bosnian Croat refugees on the lands left vacant by the Serbs – a policy which accelerated in the years immediately after the conclusion of the war and continues to this day.[11] In short, the official Croat response to Serbian challenges, pressures and, ultimately, military aggression, was entirely 'ethnic'.

Bosniak conduct: Official Croatia adopted Milošević's concepts against its own long-term interests. Nevertheless, some have argued that Croatia enjoyed more stability after the war than it did in 1991. No such argument can obtain in Bosnia's case, certainly as far as the Bosniak community is concerned. The history of concessions to the logic of national homogeneity is, therefore, in part a story of growing desperation. It is also a story of nationalist mobilisation and of 'modern' nationalist subversion of Islam.

Alija Izetbegovic's Islamic Declaration (1970) was not a programme for the Islamisation of Bosnia, but it was a programme for the 'Islamisation of Muslims'. Tragically, the latter was accomplished by the war that Izetbegovic sought to avoid, but which also had the effect of destroying Bosnia-Hercegovina. Izetbegovic's Declaration[12] recognised that Islam was not only a religion, that the 'shortest definition of the Islamic order ... [is] the unity of religion and law, education and power, ideals and interests, spiritual community and state, voluntariness and compulsion'.[13] The treatise affirms the contradiction between Islam and non-Islamic systems. Moreover,

Islamic order can be realized only in countries in which the Muslims represent the majority of the population. Without this majority, Islamic order is reduced to state power alone (because the other element – Islamic society – is missing) and can turn itself into violence. Non-Islamic minorities within the confines of an Islamic state, provided they are loyal, enjoy religious liberties and all protection. Muslim minorities within the confines of non-Islamic [state] communities, provided their religious liberties, normal life, and development are guaranteed, are loyal to – and are obliged to carry out all obligations to – that community, except those that harm Islam and Muslims.[14]

Written under communism and in the Yugoslav state, where Muslims were a minority whose religious liberties were frequently violated, this was certainly a challenge to Tito's order. Applied to ex-Yugoslav Bosnia-Hercegovina, in which Muslims (as a religious category) were a minority, this programme had controversial connotations, which were readily seized on, in turn, by Milošević's and Tudjman's propagandists, but it does not imply the establishment of a nationally homogeneous Bosnian Muslim state, which in any case would have been impossible in 1992. Since 1992, however, Serb and Croat national homogenisations have reordered Bosnia-Hercegovina by armed force and ethnic cleansing. This was inevitable precisely because multinational and multi-confessional Bosnia in every respect was at odds with the logic of national homogenisers. The war for the establishment of nationally homogeneous states was turned into a war for the division of Bosnia.

Bosnian Muslim reaction to this horrific challenge was initially disbelief, then panic, and finally a turning inward. The aim of a united and integral multinational Bosnia-Hercegovina was never abandoned, but the content of that aim was increasingly compromised, frequently under pressure from the international community, which obstructed Bosnia's armament and self-defence.[15] Bosnian Muslims were aware of the negative implications of Muslim nomenclature in their national identity. After their failure in parrying international incredulity on the non-religious reading of their name, they opted for the term 'Bosniak', the archaic common name for all the inhabitants of Bosnia-Hercegovina. This opened them to charges that they were trying to assimilate Bosnian Serbs and Croats. As their mosques were being blown up, their women raped, and their people most inhumanely removed from many of their ancestral sites, their response was to seek shelter in Islam. This opened them to accusations that they were accepting 'fundamentalism'. Inured to all hostile charges, they started flaunting secularised Islam (not the Islam of faith, but the Islam of identity) in Bosnian state institutions, particularly in the army. Under pressure of their refugees who were flooding the cities of Sarajevo, Tuzla, Zenica and eastern Mostar, they looked the other way as anti-separatist Serbs and Croats were becoming the new victims of discrimination.

The familiar logic of national homogeneity made strong inroads among the Bosniaks after the war and the question remains whether the leadership of Izetbegovic's SDA, or for that matter of the other pre-dominantly Bosniak parties, wanted to revive multicultural Bosnia – whether they were convinced that the Serb and Croat efforts to build nationally homogeneous states from parts of Bosnia-Hercegovina (among other pieces of available territory) required the acceptance of a mini-Bosniak 'entity' as a substitute for increasingly unreal Bosnia-Hercegovina. The first option would have required a long-term strategy that simultaneously appealed to the Bosnian Serbs and Croats and would have risked the revival of warfare against the diehards who still exercise enormous influence over the districts of Bosnia-Hercegovina that are still controlled by Serbs and Croats and in which both Belgrade and Zagreb have a hand. While Bosnia is still divided, both options seem – at least for now – to have been defeated by the continuing presence of the high representative which has pushed through many important reforms. The second option implies the slow strangulation of the Bosniak community. Both options risk the revival of warfare.

Albanian conduct: There is no question that Yugoslavia's Albanians endured abysmal treatment at the hands of Serbian nationalists in both Yugoslav states. Insurgency of the sort championed by Azem Bejta in the 1920s and Shaban Polluzha in the 1940s was never far from the surface. The exception was the relatively liberal period from 1968 to 1981, when, in Kosovo at least, they enjoyed significant autonomy and developed their own social and cultural elite. Everything after 1981, and especially after the formal abolition of autonomy in 1989, was an unremitting brutalisation within an apartheid society. State and public institutions, schools, hospitals, associations, etc. were purged of Albanians and became staffed almost uniformly by Serbs, which was all the more reason to wonder at the infinitely patient and pacific response that the Albanians proffered to the Milošević regime through most of the 1990s. In fact, they had little choice. The strategist of passive resistance, Ibrahim Rugova, pointed out in 1992 that it is 'better to do nothing and stay alive than to be massacred'.

Necessity compelled Rugova's Democratic League of Kosovo (LDK) to make a virtue out of non-contact with the dominant Serbs, who did not mind that the Albanians behaved exactly as expected. At a time when Yugoslavia was crumbling even the twice-purged-over Albanian deputies of the Kosovo provincial assembly (114 in number) summoned the courage to proclaim Kosovo a federal republic (2 July 1990). Although Belgrade dissolved the assembly because of its impudence, the body (more exactly its Albanian part) continued its parallel existence and, on 7 September 1990, at a clandestine meeting, adopted a constitution for their phantom republic. On 22 September 1991, at the height of the war in Croatia, the deputies proclaimed the independence of Kosovo and then carried out an almost public referendum in favour of independence, in which the overwhelming majority of eligible Albanian voters supported their leadership. In May 1992, the LDK carried out parliamentary and presidential elections, which the party and Rugova won easily. The Milošević regime did not deign to interfere with these proceedings in any consistent manner. This was the time when it was busy destroying Bosnia and it could hardly afford the second front in Kosovo. Besides, Rugova was not confrontational. Although his parallel parliament left fourteen seats vacant for Serbs and Montenegrins, he pursued a policy of no contact.

With the support of large and self-organised Kosovar Albanian emigration 'President' Rugova created a parallel society. Apart from the Serbian institutions, Rugova's LDK built parallel Albanian schools, hospitals and associations. Albanians generally used every loophole offered by the regime, taking seriously (and to great pecuniary advantage) Milošević's minimalist privatisation sops. But they made no common front with the enemies of the regime. The Serbian opposition admittedly did nothing to win the support of Kosovar Albanians, promising them less than what they accomplished all by themselves. Still, various claimants to power in Serbia learned not to count on the Kosovars. Rugova and Milošević started to depend on each other.

This incongruous situation could be mutually advantageous as long as it did not acquire permanent features. After Dayton, where the Kosovo issue was studiously ignored, a new impatient generation of Albanians came to the fore. Some of the new militants had roots in the sectarian 'Marxist-Leninist' groups that supported the Enver Hoxha regime of Albania during the 1980s. Some were veterans of the Croatian army. The handiwork of their impatience was the Kosovo Liberation Army (UCK, founded already in 1993, but hardly important until 1996), which Rugova predictably proclaimed a Milošević agency. In 1997, as a result of chaos and the collapse of the state in Albania, arms became readily available to the would-be Kosovar insurgents. By the spring of 1998 they were on the march, using guerrilla tactics, and aided by the new examples of Milošević state terror. At the end of a series of massacres, pacifist tactics were entirely discredited. The Washington-exacted Albanian signature at Rambouillet was possible only because there was no expectation of Serbian acceptance.

Kosovar Albanians did not graduate to the politics of national homogenisation by the usual route. Their brutalisation at Serbian hands throughout the twentieth century was a typically Third World story. The continuity of the Serb presence in Kosovo ultimately made little difference in a situation that was Algerian in character. The flight and expulsion of Serbs from Kosovo is therefore in some ways reminiscent of the *pieds noirs*. And even Rugova, however episodic, was not really arguing for an integrated Kosovar society. Still, Albanian national homogenisation will probably not lead to a Great Albania. Kosovar Albanians in the meanwhile have learned a great deal about the 'mother country'. They now feel superior to their kinsmen from Albania, and in many ways they are. Moreover, the overriding Western presence in Kosovo will create dependent relationships that will be specific to this area of Albanian settlement. Ironically, too, it will foster the sort of modernisation that will end the restraints of traditional society, including those that governed the rules of ethnic and confessional coexistence inherited from imperial Ottoman times.

International aspects: The politics of national homogeneity were played out in a larger international context in which international entanglements played an increasingly more important role, frequently pursued by affinities that were not necessarily enthusiastic or even logical. Serbia's cause was frequently aided by Russia and Greece, and more distantly by some of the other Eastern Orthodox states, as well as by India and China, but also Libya and Iraq. At key points some of the West European powers (Britain, France, Italy and Spain) also found understanding for Serbia, or better, sought to prevent its collapse. Bosnia's cause was championed, however lukewarmly, by the West in general, but especially by the United States. Turkey, Iran and the other Islamic countries (including some distant ones, such as Pakistan and Malaysia) had their own reasons for the support of various processes in Bosnia (Turkey supported secularised Bosniak nationalism whereas Iran and Saudi Arabia promoted imported strains of nationalised Islam). Germany, Austria, Hungary and the Holy See initially aided Croatia, but this support evaporated with the growing evidence of Tudjman's abuses and Croatia's disastrous role in Bosnia-Hercegovina. From 1994 Croatia was a client of the United States; from 2004 onwards, its future seems clearly within the EU fold. During the war, and afterwards, Croatia also benefited from good relations with Turkey. The affinities of the NATO intervention in 1999 resemble the Bosnian pattern, with opposition to the intervention being voiced, at least on an unofficial level, especially in Macedonia, Bulgaria, Russia and Greece, but also in Italy. This does not quite make for a proxy war, but certain patterns cannot be overlooked.

The part played by the United States is especially important. During the Second World War, the United States played a secondary role in the Allied Balkan strategy. Only after the Soviets, in 1948, expelled Tito from the company of 'people's democracies' did the United States start lending a helping hand to a totally isolated and until then markedly anti-Western regime. This led to a special relationship that was mutually beneficial. To Tito, it meant a virtual guarantee for his regime, which enjoyed the tacit support of all American administrations. To Washington, Yugoslav non-alignment was a bait for the other East European leaderships, which were, in effect, told that they could hold on to their power and ideology without being dependent on Moscow. Nicolae Ceausescu of Romania took the hint. His was the last Comecon communist regime to collapse, a while before Yugoslavia's started to wobble.

American policy wedded Washington to the maintenance of everything that was counterproductive about Yugoslavia. When Slobodan Milošević appeared on the scene, Ambassador John Scanlan represented him as a reformer precisely because Milošević embarked on a seemingly ameliorative recentralisation project. And in June 1991, when it became self-evident that Yugoslavia could not survive as a federation, Secretary of State James A. Baker still tried to keep it going, thereby encouraging Milošević to think that his planned military campaigns against Slovenia and Croatia would meet with Washington's approval.

In a sense they did. The Bush administration was obsessed with the dangers of Soviet collapse and the nuclear threat supposedly implicit in the break-up of the Soviet federation. It is ironical that Yeltsin, whom Washington originally saw as a troublesome anti-Gorbachev meddler, managed to construct a coalition with the reformers in the republics and carry out the peaceful dissolution of the USSR against American wishes. In Belgrade, where Washington had invested enormous resources over decades, the dissolution occurred, too, without any American input, and moreover, violently, and on an anti-reform basis.

It is possible to assess the early stages of Yugoslavia's demise variously, but the fact remains that American non-intervention in the fall of 1991, when Serbian paramilitaries and the JNA tore into Croatia, encouraged Milošević's new adventures in Bosnia. Nor did the January 1992 American non-recognition of Slovenia and Croatia help. This was merely bureaucratic obstinacy by a compromised Bush team that included the majority of the State Department's Yugoslav experts (Eagleburger, Scowcroft).

Under Clinton matters were mended somewhat, but initially only symbolically. The recognition of Bosnia in April 1992 did not stop Milošević from unleashing his most horrendous war. Nor did the sanctions make an impression, even in their specifically Serbian parts. It is not a vast exaggeration to claim that Washington initially did not significantly help the legitimate government of Bosnia-Hercegovina, whatever its failings, but consistently obstructed its self-defence. The arms embargo did not hurt Milošević but rather the Bosnians. The consequences were the growth of extremism in Bosnia and the virtual destruction of the country.

In 1994 Washington decided on another tactic. By that time, it had become evident that Tudjman's Bosnian policy was an aspect of Milošević's own anti-Muslim war. Since Washington's diplomatic influence over Tudjman was far more compelling than in the case of Milošević, the Croatian regime was obliged to stop its military operations in Bosnia, to make peace with the Bosniaks, and to sanction a Croat–Bosniak federation in the areas of Bosnia not held by the Serbs. This shotgun marriage, otherwise known as the Washington agreement, had its dark side, but it forced a change in Tudjman's alliance with Milošević.

The Clinton administration was determined not to use US troops in Bosnia, but a convenient proxy against Bosnian Serbs was increasingly an attractive option. Neither the Croats nor the Bosniaks could be given a decisive advantage, nor was it judged appropriate to permit the complete rout of the Serbs. The war, according to the Clinton administration, could only end without any obvious winners or losers. The Bosniaks were forced into an alliance with the Croats and the latter started receiving US military advisers and materiel. After the massacre at Srebrenica the United States was increasingly determined to teach the Bosnian Serbs a lesson. Milošević, too, was able to see the wisdom of this policy. When the Croatian army went after the Krajina Serbs in August 1995, its campaign, logistically aided by the Pentagon, continued into Bosnia, but not to the point of routing the Banja Luka Serb enclave, which the US troubleshooter Richard Holbrooke actually prohibited.

The result was the negotiated Dayton Agreement, that is, an effectively partitioned Bosnia. There was much in the small print, but the UN troops (IFOR, SFOR, which included the Americans), who participated in patrolling the partition, were never in real peril. The problem was that the Dayton Agreement legitimated Milošević (and also Tudjman). Also, apart from a deal on Serbian withdrawal from the Croatian Danube borderlands, there were no attempts at Dayton to diffuse the other ticking bombs – notably Kosovo. Holbrooke's cuddling of Milošević was a betrayal of the Kosovar Albanian non-violent movement of Ibrahim Rugova. But precisely because the United States bought Milošević's cooperation in Bosnia by ignoring the issue of Kosovo, Kosovar Albanians learned that no changes in their position would take place until they themselves raised the price of benign neglect. Enter the UCK, which created a very difficult situation for Milošević, not so much in terms of actual military threat as in the revival of political interest in the Kosovo question. Milošević could not give up on Kosovo. That would have been impossible for a politician who rose to power as a champion of Serbian rule over Kosovo. But he could retreat before the power of NATO intervention, which he, moreover, did not expect. The absence of earlier interventions taught him that all American pressure could be ignored or extended. His American-sponsored role as a Dayton peacemaker made him oblivious to the growing resentment of his policies in the West. The intervention that came too late had to convince Milošević and the rest of the world (NATO, too) that the US-led alliance was no idle threat.

This was done in the worst possible way. Had the goal of the operation been to unseat Milošević, to denazify Serbia and to create a democratic polity in rump Yugoslavia, the Kosovo endgame to the Yugoslav wars would have been worth it. But that could be accomplished only by the use of ground troops, something that was politically unacceptable both to Washington and most of its European allies. As a result, the prolonged NATO bombing campaign only succeeded in restoring the ethnically cleansed Kosovar Albanians to their homeland. In every other way it was a political failure: (1) Milošević became stronger than he had been before the NATO intervention; as the final showdown demonstrated, with the arrest of Milošević, the opposition had no chance of unseating him by legal means. (2) Kosovo effectively is divided as a result of the NATO/UN inability to stem the tide of Albanian revanchism and Milošević's infiltration. (3) The military strategy applied against rump Yugoslavia proved useful to Russian efforts against Chechnya and elsewhere.

The debate over the role of the international community in the Yugoslav wars is generally uniform. On the one side, stand the principled opponents of all intervention, including of such placebo efforts as the Stability Pact (1999), which merely provides an appearance of action, on the other various paper hawks who divorce military intervention from credible political programmes and insist on narrowly defined Western interests, always with an eye on Moscow. The best help from the international community was always concrete and quite beyond the false dilemmas connected to interventionism. The United Nations' International Criminal Tribunal for the Former Yugoslavia (ICTY) at the Hague was probably the best deterrent to those who would follow the logic of ethnic cleansers and a good corrector to the unprincipled diplomacy that was entirely too common in international dealings with Milošević, Karadžić, Tudjman and the rest.

Regional prospects: The politics of national homogeneity, however 'typically European' in the interpretation of various partitionists, did not establish more legitimate patterns of statehood in the successor states of Yugoslavia and never were successfully countered by the international community. If anything, the discrepancy between statehood and ethnicity, which was the source of Yugoslavia's ills, was continued in every tiny part of the broken state, just as in Hans Andersen's tale of the broken mirror that distorted beauty and goodness, and exaggerated ugliness.

In the northwest, in Slovenia and Croatia some improvements in this picture are evidenced by the decisions to admit Slovenia in 2004 and Croatia some years later, as full members of the European Union. But the slow pace of the Račan and Mesić leadership in Croatia, and the election of moderate nationalist Ivo Sanader in 2004 remind us of the strength of the ethnicist hold over the national ideologies in all areas of former Yugoslavia. The degrees of illegitimacy in post-Yugoslav statehood and the inability of the new states to address the question of minorities in a successful way demonstrate the great potential for new conflicts in the former Yugoslavia. Ethnic cleansing can be read to mean a simpler ethnic map, but it does not promote non-ethnic (or civic) nationhood. Even after the exchange of population and the effective partition of Cyprus, Greece and Turkey have not yet found a path to constructive engagement. Likewise, the successor states of Yugoslavia are not likely to show an early success in this area. The battle, ultimately, will not be won in the Balkans, but in Western Europe. If it becomes possible to be French and simultaneously Muslim and black, then it might be possible to be Macedonian and simultaneously Muslim and Albanian-speaking. The demise of Yugoslavia perhaps came too late from the point of view of European national-state integration and too early in the shaping of a cross-national European identity.

Notes

1 For an account in Milošević's own words, see Slobodan Milošević, *Godine rasjzleta*, Belgrade, 1989. His actions have also been detailed in other valuable

biographies such as Louis Sell, *Slobodan Milošević and the Destruction of Yugoslavia*, Durham, NC: Duke University Press, 2003.

2 Milošević, *Godine raspleta*, p. 334.

3 For a comprehensive account of the role that state-run media played in the development of the wars, see Kemal Kurspahic, *Prime Time Crime: Balkan Media in War and Peace*, Washington, DC: US Institute of Peace Press, 2003.

4 In the initial indictment issued against Vojislav Seselj by the International Criminal Tribunal for the former Yugoslavia (Case number IT), the prosecutor acknowledged that among the criminal charges raised against him, Seselj made inflammatory speeches with the aim of instigating others to carry out crimes, including the expulsion of Croat civilians from parts of Vojvodina, and 'espoused and encouraged the creation of a homogeneous "Greater Serbia" ... by violence and thereby participated in war propaganda and incitement of hatred towards non-Serb people'. See *International Criminal Tribunal for the Former Yugoslavia, The Prosecutor of the Tribunal Against Vojislav Seselj, Indictment (Case No. IT), Initial Indictment 14 February 2003*: www.un.org/icty/indictment/english/ses-ii030115e.htm.

5 For an excellent account of the military course of the wars in Croatia and Bosnia see Branka Magas and Ivo Zanic, *The War in Croatia and Bosnia-Hercegovina 1991–95*, London: Frank Cass, 2001.

6 *The National Question in Contemporary Europe*. This book was published by an *émigré* press in 1982 and an English-language version was published by Columbia University Press in 1981.

7 Ibid., p. 118.

8 Ibid., p. 152.

9 The application of the Serbian model was particularly noted in the ICTY indictment of Jadranko Prlic and others. In this indictment, several others, including former Croatian President Franjo Tudjman, Minister of Defence Gojko Susak, Croatian Army General Janko Bobetko and president of the Croatian Community of 'Herceg Bosna' Mate Boban were accused of participating in a joint criminal enterprise which used forced labour, deportation and terror to advance its war aims (Case IT 04.74).

10 Among the charges raised against Jadranko Prlic, Bruno Stojic, Slobodan Praljak, Milvivoj Petkovic, Valentin Coric and Berislav Pusic are: instigation and fomentation of political, ethnic or religious strife, division and hatred; use of force, intimidation and terror; appropriation and destruction of property; detention and imprisonment; forcible transfer and deportation; forced labour.

11 For an account of the way ethnic Croats from Bosnia were settled in ethnic Serb homes, see Brad K. Blitz, 'Refugee returns in Croatia: contradiction and reform', *Politics*, 23, 3 (2003), 181–91.

12 See Alija Izetbegovic, *Islamska Deklaracija*, Sarajevo, 1990. Also published in English.

13 Ibid., p. 19.

14 Ibid., pp. 37, 38.

15 For an informative account of the Bosnian government's attempt as self-defence, see Marko Attila Hoare, *How Bosnia Armed*, London: SAQI Books/ Bosnia Institute, 2004.

4   Milošević's motiveless malignancy

Srdja Popovic

Throughout the eight years of conflict in the former Yugoslavia, Western, and particularly American policy in the region has been characterised by confusion, wishful thinking, procrastination, evasions and a lack of focus and determination.

The most likely reason for such behaviour on the part of the United States may simply have been that, in 1991, Yugoslavia was very low on the State Department's list of priorities.[1] This was a time of great turmoil in the world. The end of the Cold War, the fall of communism, and the unification of Germany were certainly all events of epochal and global significance that by far outweighed the petty ethnic bickering of Yugoslav leaders. Especially since, at this time, Yugoslavia was considered the most promising candidate, among former communist states, for a smooth transition into both the parliamentary system and an open market economy, as well as integration into European economic and political institutions. Focused on larger global events and confident in Yugoslavia's capacity for a smooth transition, Western diplomats underestimated the potential of these petty tensions to escalate into violence.

At the time, optimism was rampant; the United States swore by 'multilateralism' hoping to engage Russia in the Security Council and work out global problems by consensus. Little was understood, at the time, about the terrible consequences now encountered by people who had spent half a century or more under the rock of communist rule; little understood about the humiliation of the Soviet Union, yesterday's mighty empire, now pushed into bankruptcy and political disarray. And most tragically of all, the celebratory mood of the West prevented them from recognising that, despite the fact that the threat of the Soviet Union had disappeared, the United States could not simply disengage from Europe, just as NATO, far from being an obsolete organisation, still had a significant role to play. The dangers created by the dissolution of the bipolar world, by a disintegration of the entire balanced field of political forces, were completely ignored. The West also failed to recognise that with the disappearance of the old world order once imposed upon the world by two hegemonies from above, the possibility was created for the emergence of a new 'order'. This was created from below by small players, newly released from the rigid old structure and now free to settle their accounts with their neighbours.

For the West, and the United States especially, the fall of communism was a positive development – a victory. And so they failed to recognize that from an internal perspective the situation was fraught with instability and hidden dangers. It was for these reasons that the conflict in the former Yugoslavia found the United States, whose first reflex was to leave the problem to the Europeans, unprepared; after all, Yugoslavia was 'Europe's backyard'. The United States was busy cutting down on military spending, getting out of the recession, celebrating the end of the Cold War and going through presidential elections.

When Europeans, left without American leadership, turned out to be unable to formulate a common foreign policy towards Yugoslavia, the United States decided to dump the problem on the United Nations – to act only 'multilaterally'.[2] It seems that, by this time, it was already clear to American policymakers that the United Nations might not be up to the task, and that this move was meant merely to sweep the problem under the UN carpet.[3]

The UN quickly assumed a 'neutral' and 'evenhanded' position and the whole process came to a dead end while the US pretended not to notice. The US was satisfied with the situation, in which the 'neutral' UN peacekeepers acted as self-appointed hostages and prevented any military action. Yet such action was the only thing that could have stopped the blood bath organised by Milošević, first in Croatia and then in Bosnia.

Needless to say, 'multilateralism' did not work, as Russia was happy to reinstate itself as a global player and a factor in the international arena. The 'evenhanded' stance taken by the UN could not have been effective, as the whole Yugoslav drama was a one-man show run by Milošević. Both the UN and the United States grossly misjudged this man around whom the vortex of violence turned, and this was perhaps the biggest mistake made by the United States, the UN, and the entire international community from the beginning of the Yugoslav conflict. This misjudgement, along with the failure to understand what the nature of the conflict was in the first place, later caused a string of wrong decisions to be made.

The nature of the conflict was perceived from the very beginning, especially in the United States, in ideological terms: Milošević was 'a Communist', and Tudjman and Izetbegovic were 'democrats'.

However, at that point in time, what was playing out in Yugoslavia was not about ideology; it was a simple power struggle.

After the death of Tito, who ruled as an absolute dictator, an enormous power vacuum was felt throughout the country. The Presidency which replaced him, and which was supposed to reach its conclusions by consensus, was practically paralysed. The whole political system had been adapted to revolve around a single figure and a single will. Tito's authority was not rooted in his institutional post as the president, but in his role as the head of the Communist Party and, even more importantly, in his role as the commander in chief. It had been made obvious during the party purges, especially in the early seventies, that Tito's main strength had come from the Yugoslav Army.[4] No single member of the Presidency, or, for that matter, all of them put together, could have fulfilled such a role.

The first result of this power struggle was the splintering of the Communist Party into six disparate parties. Since Tito no longer delegated the power from the top, party leaders sought support from below, by casting themselves as representatives of the interests of their respective republics.

Faced with the fall of communism, these six parties started to form alliances mainly along the lines of reformers and hard-line conservatives. Milošević, threatened by aggressive and militant anti-communists and royalists in Serbia, opted for the hard-line conservative option; he soon found himself politically defeated and isolated.

It is important to understand that he did not choose this position as a result of deeply ingrained political belief. Rather, he chose it because he alone realised that this was the best way to secure the real power, which did not belong to the Communist Party but to the highly indoctrinated Yugoslav army.[5]

Thus, although apparently defeated and isolated within Yugoslavia, Milošević still held the trump card: the army. Nobody in Yugoslavia at the time realised that this power struggle would be resolved by force, except Milošević. He recognised that the political battle was lost, and he was well positioned and prepared for the military battles in which he would be overwhelmingly superior. He made this clear during his famous Gazimestan speech when he masked his pursuit of power with such nationalist rhetoric as 'us against them', promising to 'defend Serbian interests' and, if necessary, To do so 'with military means'.

The main effect of the speech was that it generated a great deal of fear, not only among non-Serbs in Yugoslavia, but also among Serbs who suddenly 'realised' the 'gravity' of the situation and the stakes involved.

Although at this point Milošević had the support of the army, a simple putsch was too risky to undertake as it might have provoked foreign intervention. Milošević lacked two things in order to effectively use the military force at his disposal: institutional control over the army and casus belli (a viable 'provocation').

According to the constitution, the commander in chief was the Presidency and, within the Presidency, Milošević controlled only four votes: those of the representatives of Serbia and its puppets, Montenegro, Kosovo and Vojvodina. In order to obtain even these votes, Milošević had to deprive Kosovo and Vojvodina of autonomy, and stage a putsch in Montenegro. But after all this, he still lacked one vote that would enable him to control the army.

Milošević then made a clever and bold move: he pushed Slovenia out of Yugoslavia (true to his double-talk, he accused them of separatism). This move solved both of his problems; without Slovenia he controlled the majority in the Presidency, but even more significantly, he created the casus belli. He knew that Croatia would run for the door the moment Slovenia left Yugoslavia, i.e., the moment Milošević got hold of the army. At this moment, Milošević knew he would be given an opportunity to use the army in order to prevent Croatia from taking the Serbian minority out of Yugoslavia.

Slovenia readily agreed to leave. Milošević's threats and aggressive rhetoric were already spreading fear throughout the country. The Slovenians were perfectly aware that by jumping out of the boat they would overturn it, but the stakes were too high, and they opted for independence.

Milošević met with Slovenian President Kucan in May 1991. After their meeting they issued a joint statement in which Milošević agreed for Slovenia to leave the Federation and in which Kucan expressed his 'understanding for the wish of all Serbians to live in a single state'.

The 'war' with Slovenia, which lasted ten days and had just a few casualties, was a show; Milošević never intended to hold them back. In a sense, it was just an overture playing the main theme, a foreshadowing of what would ensue if and when Croatia decided to follow the Slovenes. Croatia did follow and Milošević used the army 'to protect the Serbs' in Croatia. With the army in play, the potential power he had held in his hands hence became tragically real.

The popular perception in the West that the consequent armed conflict amounted to Milošević's 'fight against separatists' was also false. Borisav Jović, then president of the Presidency and Milošević's right-hand man testifies in his book Poslednji Dani SFRJ (Last Days of SFRY), about a conversation he had with Milošević in June of 1990: 'He agrees with the plan to force Slovenia ... out of Yugoslavia'.[6]

Milošević and Jović knew that once the Slovenes left, a threatened Croatia would try to follow. Jović also states in his book that Veljko Kadijević, the chief of staff, had the following plan for Slovenia: to 'respond forcefully ... then withdraw ... This will boost the Army morale, scare Croatia, and appease the Serbian people.'[7]

But pushing Slovenia out was not enough. Milošević and his apparatchiks had to be certain that Croatia would follow their script. On 26 January 1991, Jović writes in his dairy: 'The war should be started by Croatia.'[8] To this end, they devised a plan whereby Croatia would be forced to act, and apparently without provocation from Belgrade. On 25 February 1991 Jović reported on an idea from the chief of staff, Veljko Kadijević: 'Serbs in Krajina should be encouraged, not publicly but secretly, to secede from Croatia.'[9] In his own book, Kadijević also boasts of how the JNA 'fulfilled its tasks of preparing both politically and militarily the Serbs in Croatia' for war.[10] Quite contrary to perceptions at the time, Milošević did not go to war in order to prevent Croatian secession and the dissolution of Yugoslavia. According to Jović, on 21 January 1991 during a telephone conversation concerning the ongoing crisis, the Croatian representative in the Presidency, Stipe Mesić, informed Jović that Croatia might choose to leave Yugoslavia in response to the threats coming from Belgrade. Jović warns Mesić that he is 'choosing war', and promptly informs Milošević of the conversation. Jović describes Milošević's reaction in the following words: 'He was exuberant: excellent'.[11]

The West's tendency to blindly accept Milošević's claim that he was 'protecting Yugoslavia from separatists' is even more difficult to understand in view of the fact that Serbia designed the first separatist constitution as early as 28 September 1990. This was more than a year before 8 October 1991, when Croatia and Slovenia declared independence.

In article 72, Serbia is declared a 'sovereign and independent' country, with its own Army, Ministry of Foreign Affairs and National Bank etc. In article 135, Serbia declared that it was no longer bound by the laws of SFRY. In the spring of 1991, the Serbian parliament enacted a series of its own laws on monetary and fiscal policy, international relations, and customs (all previously regulated by the federal parliament). When reproached by Jović for the separatist content of the Croatian constitution during the 125th session of the Presidency, the Croatian representative Mesić justly replies: 'We have done exactly the same as Serbia, we just copied your constitution and we knew we would be attacked for doing so'. It is hard to understand how the Western powers, including the United States, could have been confused and blinded for so long by Milošević's absurd claims that he was just 'protecting the unity and territorial integrity of Yugoslavia', when there was so much evidence to the contrary.

Hundreds of books have been written by diplomats, journalists and self-proclaimed experts who have tried to explain all the intricacies, twists and turns, plots and subplots of the Yugoslav war,[12] but the basic script was rather straightforward and simple. The whole prolonged affair boils down to a simple, single event: the moment Milošević secured control of the army. From this moment on, all the republics (Slovenia, Croatia, Bosnia, Kosovo and, even today, Montenegro and Vojvodina) just wanted to escape Milošević's jurisdiction and establish a firm international border between themselves and his aggressive, dangerous and unpredictable regime.[13] Even the Serbs from Serbia fled his jurisdiction in hundreds of thousands by emigrating, especially the young and better educated segments of the population. All the events that followed were just a complication of this basic plot – a bunch of sideshows and distractions.

The United States failed to take a clear position from the start. During Secretary of State Baker's visit to Yugoslavia a few months before the war erupted, the United States took the position that they were in favour of preserving the territorial integrity of Yugoslavia in accordance with the principle of stable borders as expressed in the Helsinki Accords.[14] But, as the United States favoured the reunification of Germany, they were compelled to shift their position to the principle of self-determination.[15] The United States sent mixed signals: they allowed Milošević to hide behind his 'preserving the territorial integrity of Yugoslavia', but then encouraged Croatia's secession as an act of self-determination of the Croatian people.

The misinformed perception that the conflicts were motivated by ideological differences (communist *versus* democrats), and their ambivalent position in relation to the two different and contradicting principles described above (territorial integrity *versus* self-determination), made US policy in Yugoslavia both confused and confusing. The United States failed to recognise the simple picture of one man who had gained control of the army by unconstitutional means (the annexation of Kosovo and the putsch in Montenegro) in the power struggle that had erupted after Tito's death, and who was now determined to use it to defeat his political opponents. Milošević's control of the army and his readiness to use it set the stage for his one-man show.

Milošević not only wanted the war, but also needed it in order to be able to dictate the agenda. Once he threatened to use force, all of the other participants, including the international community and the United States, merely reacted to his moves. His discouraging success was the result of the obvious fact that the United States had no intention of intervening militarily, and that the Yugoslav Army had overwhelming superiority over the other players within Yugoslavia.

As Milošević was running the whole show, it would have made all the difference had he been properly understood from the very beginning. But, from the very beginning, Milošević's motives were misinterpreted. The attempts to appease him, to somehow engage him, to apply too much carrot and no stick, to negotiate with him, to 'help him save face', and to see the non-existent 'other side' of the issues were all steps in the wrong direction.

Not only did these steps do nothing to stop his aggression, but they also actually encouraged it. To be fair, Milošević's character and personality are both very unusual. In his case, analogies, the favourite tool of diplomats, did not work. This was so because men of Milošević's personality and character rarely rise to positions of power, except in extraordinary and highly turbulent, revolutionary circumstances.[16] His 'motiveless malignancy', to borrow Coleridge's words, is a rare trait among politicians in normal times, even within the Communist Party through which he rose to power.

It is a pity how rarely diplomats seem to read poets. This type of personality has been described in literature with great clarity and deep understanding:

The villain, on the other hand, is shown from the beginning as being a malcontent, a person with a general grudge against life and society. In most cases this is comprehensible because the villain has, in fact, been wronged by Nature or Society. [Both of Milošević's parents committed suicide].

[His] primary satisfaction is the infliction of suffering on others, or the exercise of power over others against their will. [He has] the pleasure of making a timid conventional man become aggressive and criminal ... [he] will not let him alone until he consents to murder.

[His actions are] a demonstration ... that man does not always require serious motive for deceiving another. [He is] a practical joker ... and all practical jokes are anti-social acts. The satisfaction of the practical joker is the look of astonishment on the faces of others when they learn that all the time they were convinced that they were thinking and acting on their own initiative, they were actually the puppets of another's will.

The success of a practical joker depends upon his accurate estimate of the weakness of others, their ignorance, their social reflexes, their unquestioned presuppositions, their obsessive desires, and even the most harmless practical joke is an expression of the joker's contempt for those he deceives.

The practical joker despises his victims, but at the same time he envies them because their desires, however childish and mistaken, are real to them, whereas he has no desire which he can call his own.

Yet the professional practical joker is certainly driven like a gambler, to his activity, but the drive is negative, a fear of lacking a concrete self, of being nobody.

[Since his] ultimate goal is nothingness, he must not only destroy others, but himself as well.

The 'villain' described is Iago and the quotations are taken from W. H. Auden's essay, 'The Joker in the Pack'.[17] This analysis of a fictional character, written fifty years ago in a literary essay on a Shakespeare tragedy, defines Milošević's actions, his personality and his motives more accurately than the hundreds of pages that have been written on him by journalists, diplomats and political analysts.

Milošević had recognised the weakness of the Serbian population that was created by the vacuum of national identity they found themselves in after the death of Tito, and he played a morbid practical joke on them. Imposing the kind of strong leadership they had grown used to, he led them to the worst kind of criminal and aggressive behaviour imaginable: genocide. The nationalist card was simply the easiest means to this end.

If we accept Auden's characterisation of Milošević, we can easily understand that Milošević was neither a communist nor a Serbian nationalist, and that it was impossible to appease him, to deal with him, to bribe him or to shame him. He was able to stay always a step ahead in this political game ruled by interests (including a personal self-interest) and trade-offs, since he had no such interests and no real stake because he was playing with counterfeit money.

Even the more recent conventional wisdom that he was 'only interested in preserving power' seems wrong; for Milošević, power was just a tool that enabled him to play his practical jokes. It was evident that he shunned the usual opportunities to enjoy power, such as interviews, public appearances, rallies and ovations, and his supporters, such as his wife, who spoke of him as a 'very modest man' and, tellingly, 'extraterrestrial' according to Mihalj Kertes, former minister of the interior.[18] His political statements were usually made by others, by the puppets whose movements he controlled like a ventriloquist behind the scenes: his wife, the Academy of Sciences, Šešelj and members of the 'government' (the composition of which was shuffled and reshuffled constantly).

Had Milošević been understood earlier, the number of his victims could have been reduced considerably, and less time would have been lost in futile attempts to 'deal' with him. The passivity of the US administration was compounded when, as a result of extensive coverage of the Yugoslav war, public criticism of US policy and demands for military action started to mount. Still unwilling to get militarily involved due to the high political cost of such action, the US administration developed an extensive public campaign to fend off critics, which resulted in an elaborate misrepresentation of the Yugoslav conflict.

The administration tried to persuade the American public that however terrible were the pictures that they watched every evening on CNN, there was 'nothing that could be done' because the conflict was a result of 'centuries of hatred', that it was driven by 'blind forces of history', that it was a 'problem from hell', that 'there are no good guys in that conflict' and that the only viable strategy was that which is used for forest fires – 'let it burn itself out'.

Such misguided persuasion was probably a bigger mistake than the one that it was supposed to cover up. Passivity was bad enough, but the explanations given for such passivity, for example, 'what can you do against the blind forces of history', were much worse since they played straight into the hands of Milošević, whose propaganda kept repeating the same mantra: the conflict had erupted spontaneously, he had nothing to do with it, Serbia is not at war.

Of course, there was nothing spontaneous about the conflict. Most of the victims were produced by the professionals of the Yugoslav Army, by the Serbian police and by paramilitary groups whom the Serbian police organised, armed and shipped to the frontlines.

It was only in its later stages that the conflict also assumed some traits of a civil war, because it was impossible for civilians to remain neutral. It was at this later stage, roughly after 1992, that members of various ethnic groups flocked together and armed themselves as an act of self-preservation. It was also at this stage that non-Serbs started to retaliate against their Serbian neighbours for the atrocities committed by Milošević's professionals. Milošević must have been delighted to learn that, according to the State Department, 'There were no good guys in the conflict'. Being the main culprit, instigator and executioner, he readily agreed on many occasions that 'all sides are committing atrocities', thus equating the victims with the aggressors, and appearing to hold an 'objective' position at the same time.

Milošević was well aware that the hatred between Serbs on one hand, and the Croats and Bosnians on the other, was not the cause of the conflict, but the result of the brutal and unprovoked crimes perpetrated against the others (especially in Bosnia) by the Serbian side (his Army and his police). He also knew that these crimes were so terrible that they would create enough hatred for the war to be able to perpetuate itself. Of course he was happy to hear that this hatred was 'centuries old'.

Both the American and Serbian media repeated these mantras from day to day in enormous circulation. Miloševic understood this weakness of the American position, and he exploited it to the best of his ability. A great deal of denial still present among Serbs today was caused by the fact that American foreign policy and media emphatically reinforced Miloševic's own propaganda.

At the time, this created among the Serbian population a feeling of omnipotence and triumph, for either the Americans were fooled by Miloševic, or else the Western powers were, through their inactivity, actually allowing Miloševic to get rid of the Muslims, an opinion frequently entertained in Serbia during the war. The State Department's attempts to justify US passivity by claiming that the conflict was a spontaneous eruption of centuries old hatred had a devastating effect on the course of the war. From an objective point of view, passivity turned into complicity.

This allowed Miloševic to retain the initiative right to the end. As Auden wrote of the tragedy of Othello: 'I cannot think of any other play in which only one character performs personal action – all the deeds are Iago's – and all the others without exception only exhibit behaviour'.[19] All the deeds were Miloševic's; everybody else just exhibited 'behaviour', including the United States.

Even the grand finale, when the United States led the coalition finally into military intervention to stop the genocide in Kosovo, cannot truly be considered anything else than Miloševic's 'deed'. Richard Holbrooke testifies that during their last encounter, he asked Miloševic: 'Do you realize fully what will come next?' to which Miloševic calmly responded, 'Yes, you will bomb us.'[20]

The State Department's 'behaviour' can hardly be viewed as taking action in Kosovo; rather, the State Department painted itself into a corner by harsh rhetoric at Rambouillet by threats it hoped would never have to be carried through.[21] Miloševic's resilience when faced with bombing, and his stubbornness during the bombing, again came as a complete surprise to the State Department.

Even at the end of the game, the State Department did not understand that Miloševic cared nothing for the suffering inflicted on 'his own people' or the destruction of 'his own country' and the isolation of Yugoslavia, and that he welcomed this new opportunity for 'making the timid and conventional man aggressive and criminal'. In one of Miloševic's courts in Valjevo, President Clinton was 'indicted [in absentia] for war crimes'. However farfetched it may seem, the use of a court to promote Milošević's political ends fits perfectly with his stubborn character.

Milošević initially profited from the anti-Western sentiment aroused by the bombing of Serbia, as well as from the desperation of his own population plunged into poverty by the bombing. As for the subsequent isolation, even though it was short lived, it allowed him to settle his accounts with the pro-Western 'fifth column' and the 'traitors' of the opposition without having to worry about the niceties of human rights and democratic standards. Milošević never cared about losing Kosovo.

So, what could have been done differently? First, the late Yugoslav prime minister, Ante Marković, should have been helped by every possible means to preserve the formal unity of Yugoslavia; even if that meant injecting some of the billions of dollars later spent on interventions, peacekeeping, reconstruction and conferences. Even the offer of blue helmets in the face of the Milošević/Yugoslav Army conspiracy – if it led only to the subsequent dissolution of Yugoslavia – would have prevented the carnage that ensued.

Second, once Croatia and Bosnia carved out their own independent states, and these states were then internationally recognized, they should have been defended by the international community as members of the United Nations exposed to foreign aggressions. Most certainly, it was the duty of all members of the United Nations (including the United States), under the Convention on the Prevention of Genocide, to intervene in Bosnia. The State Department took pains to avoid even whispering the word 'genocide' and instead used Milošević's carefully and cynically calibrated expression 'ethnic cleansing' in its place.

A man of Milošević's profile with a lethal weapon in his hand could have been and should have been stopped as early as possible. This could only be accomplished by superior force. The United States initially declined to act as a world policeman and then chose to do so at an inappropriate moment, which was at a great cost and done hesitantly and messily. It attacked a sovereign state and interfered with its internal affairs. Of course, it had to be done, but it was done much too late, improperly, and even then half-heartedly, on Milošević's own terms.

In the end, it required considerable international pressure, and a public divide between the late Prime Minister Zoran Djindjić and President Koštunica to force Milošević out of Serbia to the Hague where he died, while on trial accused of crimes against humanity in Kosovo, Bosnia and Croatia. Indignant, until the end, he prepared his own defence and challenged the legitimacy of the Tribunal. Although he died before justice could be served, the 'malcontent' did finally reach the dock.

Notes

1 See Walter Zimmermann, *Origins of a Catastrophe*, New York: New York Times Books, 1996. This book is especially valuable given his longstanding relationship with Milošević.
2 See Mark Thompson, *Paper House: The Ending of Yugoslavia*, New York: Pantheon Books, 1994.
3 For a scathing attack on the European Community's actions and the effects of the US handover to the United Nations, see also Mark Almond, *Europe's Backyard War: The War in the Balkans*, London: Heinemann, 1994.
4 See James Gow, *Legitimacy and the Military: The Yugoslav Crisis*, London: Pinter; New York: St. Martin's Press, 1992.
5 For an excellent analysis of the decay of the Titoist political system in the 1980s, focusing on the increasing concentration of legitimacy at the republican level, and on the counter-productive attempts of the Yugoslav Army to restore the legitimacy of the federal regime, see Gow, *Legitimacy and the Military*.
6 Borisav Jović, *Poslednji dani SFRJ*, Belgrade: Politika, 1995, p. 161.
7 Ibid., p. 349.
8 Ibid., p. 263.
9 Ibid., p. 277.
10 Veljko Kadijević, *Moje vidjenje raspada*, Belgrade: Politika, 1993, p. 128.
11 Jovic, *Poslednji*, pp. 256–7.
12 See, for example, Robert Thomas, *Serbia under Milošević: Politics in the 1990s – How Milošević Won and Exercised Power*, London: Hurst & Company, 1999.
13 See Branka Magas and Ivo Zanic (eds.), *The War in Croatia and Bosnia-Hercegovina 1991–1995*, London: The Bosnian Institute/Frank Cass, 2001.
14 Baker, 1995.
15 For an account of the end of the Cold War from the perspective of the then secretary of state, see James Addison Baker and Thomas M. DeFrank, *The Politics of Diplomacy: Revolution, War, and Peace, 1989–1992*, New York: Putnam, 1995.
16 Adam LeBor's *Milošević: A Biography* contains several interviews with the Milošević family and inner circle. It presents an image of cold, calculated determination on the part of both Milošević and his wife, Mirjana Marković, who was herself arrested in 2001 and charged with abuse of office before a Serbian court in 2003.
17 W. H. Auden, *The Dyer's Hand*, Random House: New York, 1967.
18 Mihalj Kertes, a former interior minister and head of the Yugoslav customs, was central to the logistics of the Serb wars in Croatia, Bosnia and Kosovo. He helped funnel the arms, equipment and money to the Serb militias and paramilitaries in Croatia and Bosnia in the run-up to the 1991–95 wars.

19 Auden, *Dyer's Hand*.
20 See Richard Holbrooke, *To End a War*, New York: Random House, 1998.
21 Peter J. Boyer, 'General Clark's battles', *The New Yorker*, 17 November 2003. This article documents the Clinton administration's reluctance to intervene until it was absolutely unavoidable, as well as their mistaken view of Milošević.

5   Germany and the recognition of Croatia and Slovenia

Daniele Conversi

Introduction

A central myth that accompanied the West's incapacity to tackle the crisis in the Balkans throughout the 1990s was the legend of Germany's attempt to 'gain a warm port' in the Mediterranean via the recognition of Croatia and Slovenia. Although some will recognise here the distortions of Belgrade's nationalist propaganda, many of these stereotypes were bought wholesale by leading Western political and academic circles. Even though the criticism against German foreign policy was mostly veiled and did not envision imaginary threats of a new *Lebensraum*, the mainstream interpretations remain to this day a kind of exculpation for the general Western failure by putting the entire blame on a single country whose decisions were nevertheless marginal to the development of the crisis.

As the European Union (EU) recognised Slovenia's and Croatia's independence on 16 December 1991, this act was submitted to a barrage of international criticism. Critics charged that the step was premature, precipitating the ensuing dramatic developments – even though recognition occurred well after the JNA (*Jugoslavenska Narodna Armija*) embarked on a ten-day conflict with Slovenia and subsequently engaged in a much longer war leading to the occupation and 'ethnic cleansing' of nearly one third of Croatia.

With the exception of Michael Libal's book, this theme has not been systematically addressed in the academic literature.[1] Other research remains at a more dispersed level, while recent work on the topic is relatively limited.[2] In most of the literature, the idea that Germany's policy of recognition was erroneous and misguided, and even that it was one of the causes of the war, remains implicitly or explicitly uncontested. This is the approach adopted, for instance, by the former Yugoslav ambassador to the European Community, Mihailo Crnobrnja;[3] by the former US ambassador in Belgrade (until 1992), Warren Zimmermann;[4] by Britain's 'peace mediator' and EU representative to the International

Conference on the former Yugoslavia, Lord Owen;[5] and, most notably, by Susan Woodward, senior adviser to the UN's special representative in former Yugoslavia, Yasuki Akashi.[6]

Most, though not all, of this literature is far from being scholarly or academic, so no one should be surprised at precipitate conclusions relying on shallow and cursory analyses. What is most meaningful is that all of the above personalities were directly involved in the crisis as international mediators, advisors or diplomats. Since they could be held accountable for at least part of the accompanying events, there is an understandable urge of self-disculpation with a view to whipping imaginary culprits.

However, the same trend has also appeared in academic works, for instance in a tightly argued article by Beverly Crawford published in the mainstream International Relations journal *World Politics*.[7] The article's guiding assumption is that there existed a sort of tacit international understanding on the issue of not recognising Slovenia and Croatia (and the other republics), and that, with its 'unilateral' move, German 'defection' constituted a form of breach, double-crossing and infringement of such unsaid accord.

In virtue of its political and economic weight, Germany's role in influencing the EU decision was certainly greater than that played by several other states which simultaneously pushed for recognition – this pressure began as early as 27 June 1991 (the beginning of the war).[8] However, for a series of reasons that will be analysed in this chapter, it was the German initiative that incited the most hotly contested response from the international community, beginning with the five members of the UN Security Council (Britain, China, France, the United States and the former Soviet Union). Despite the war's chronological unfolding and all the empirical evidence showing that events had occurred independently from recognition, the myth of German responsibility for the war has remained. And despite the fact that Germany's role was greatly circumscribed, and indeed that international recognition strongly limited the human suffering brought about by the war, the accusations even increased as the war worsened, while the incapacity of Western governments to deal with the problem became more and more evident.

Why has this 'German-bashing' attitude and ideology been so readily and widely accepted by leading international politicians, by sectors of academia, and even by some members of the public? This chapter will try to find an answer to this bewildering question by identifying three main ingredients of the German-bashing syndrome. First, it will pinpoint the reemergence of anti-European trends, particularly in Britain. Second, it will analyse the perverse effects of German unification, which created a remarkable sense of threat among several European countries, reviving far-fetched memories of renewed German expansionism. Third, it will focus on the lack of Western expertise in Balkan security, and the supplanting and usurping role exercised in this sector by Belgrade's diplomatic circles, as well as by Serbian and other diaspora.

Before embarking on such a task, the chapter will start with a definition of German-bashing by identifying one of its sources in a persistent Anglo-Saxon isolationist and elitist tradition – as particularly evinced in the British tabloid press' 'anti-Hun' rhetoric. The two most extreme forms of this angst manifested themselves as veritable conspiracy theories: the myth of the purported reemergence of a Fourth Reich, and the ancillary conjecture of a Papist plot versus the non-Catholic world. It is argued that the manufacturing of such a political atmosphere inhibited and conditioned the debate over ongoing developments in the Balkans.

In this context, the term 'German-bashing' refers exclusively to international reactions to the break-up of Yugoslavia. I will not imply that it refers to other dimensions of Germany's foreign or internal politics. This chapter fully endorses the principle that the sense of guilt commonly associated with post-war Germany in the wake of the Holocaust has helped to shape and give direction to Western politics since the end of World War II. This sense of German guilt is central to the entire post-war effort of pan-European unification, and, indeed, of world peace. On the other hand, by chastening Germany for an excessive concern over human rights in the Balkans, as happened during the pre- and post-recognition debates, German-bashers have played into the hands of neo-revisionists and, in general, of those who argue that Germany has been unjustly blamed for past misdeeds. What characterises contemporary attacks likening Germany post-unification to a new Reich is the extreme unscrupulousness of the attackers. Neo-revisionists have been only too happy to use the cynicism of German-bashers against the bountiful evidence that points to the relative success of Germany's early initiative in the Balkans – as opposed to that of other Western partners. In other words, the attacks have risked rekindling a kind of petty wounded pride that had supposedly been laid to rest.

The revival of Britain's German-bashing tradition

As Britain was the key international protagonist during the early phase of the war, its role remains crucial in explaining the ensuing political attack on Germany. Since the initial phase of the negotiation process, Lord Carrington's accusations against Germany were widely disseminated as soon as they became public domain. Moreover, because at that time 'Germany' really meant 'Europe' for large sectors of the British elites, these attitudes blended well with a vigorous Euro-sceptic undercurrent. In a study rich in insights, the American sociologist Randall Collins noted that German-bashing represents a long-standing tradition among Anglo-Saxon intellectuals and ruling classes. Within the most conservative strands of British and American academic circles, the criticism rested on unfounded claims of 'retarded modernisation': that is, Germany was usually seen as backward and as lagging behind Britain and France in terms of intellectual and cultural development.[9] Such sentiments were often expressed against all evidence to the contrary, and disregarded the fact that several German scholars had anticipated their British counterparts in their respective fields and achievements.

German-bashing has traditionally struck a popular chord amongst the British public. As a fictional argument, it ideally stretches back to the times of the Huns and the Teutonic Hordes. This public attitude was dramatically exploited in the first decade of the twentieth century by newspaper magnates who, in order to increase their sales, emphasised their anti-German interventionist propaganda. 'The demand of the *Daily Mail* on 26 October 1914 to expel from the country people with German names, or its revengeful tone since the aftermath of the war up to the 1922 Versailles Treaty are classic examples.'[10] Paradoxically, 'Kraut-bashing' was not as prevalent in Britain during the Third Reich's expansion and Hitler's preparations for World War II.[11] The politics of appeasement were then reflected in a popular indifference to the fate of the Nazi victims. Several studies exist on the history of British appeasement in the face of Nazi aggression.[12]

In the past ten years, Germanophobia has staged a massive comeback in British politics. For instance, a survey carried out in June 1996 by the communication system company Gestetner – which paradoxically runs a project to encourage British children to make friends with their European counterparts – revealed that 'when Germany is mentioned, children immediately think of war – and a dictator with black moustache'.[13] All occasions, from football matches to the ban on British beef, are taken advantage of by the tabloid press to raise the level of Germanophobia and hence anti-Brussels rhetoric. 'Brick by brick, a European superstate is being created in which Germany and France wield the power and the rest of us are told what to do.'[14] This attitude is just ridiculous, as is the claim by the former Conservative MP Christopher Gill that 'it is Britain's historic destiny to champion the cause of freedom and guide our European partners away from the totalitarianism that threatens to engulf them'.[15] Was Serbia's campaign of ethnic cleansing a preferable vehicle for such a crusading task?

A new climax of anti-Germanism was reached when figures in the Tory establishment, including former Prime Minister John Major and Foreign Secretary Malcolm Rifkind, raised the argument of the European ban on British beef to provoke 'the biggest crisis in Anglo-European relations since Britain joined the European Union in 1973'.[16] Interestingly, this new jingoistic posture erupted only two days after the same Tory establishment suffered one of the greatest scandals in recent British history, the knowledge that the party had accepted at least £100,000 – that is the amount so far identified – from Serbian ultra-nationalists faithful to the war criminal Radovan Karadžić.[17] The atmosphere amongst top Tory ranks became so heated that Sir Bryan Nicholson, president of the Confederation of British Industry, expressed his deep concern in the following terms: 'In this pungent atmosphere of romantic nationalism and churlish xenophobia, I sometimes wonder if there are some among us who have failed to notice that the war with Germany has ended.'[18] Germany – and Europe – could function as a useful lightning-rod to externalise the internal tensions of the Tory regime at a moment when it was facing one of the greatest challenges in its recent history over the Serbian corruption scandal – a scandal which, for all its implications, was immediately quashed. An important clue to this Anglo-Serbian entente was already evident in the May 1995 parliamentary debate over Bosnia, when, following a trend common to the two major British parties, Germany served as an *explicans* for the war and a diversion for the unwillingness of the British establishment to protect Bosnia. Indeed, the British conflict with Germany seems to have been revived through the *interposta persona* of Serbian ultranationalists. As Cambridge historian Brendan Simms has pointed out, British academic and media elites seem to mirror their government's persuasion: 'Among British – and not only British – intellectuals, commentators and journalists, there is a tenacious myth which runs something like this: the war in Bosnia and Croatia is the more or less direct continuation of the second world war in Yugoslavia.'[19]

During the Cold War – and within the framework of NATO, the EC and other supranational organisations – xenophobic trends had been considerably restrained. In the public arena at least, dislike for Germany emerged only under particular circumstances. A notorious case was that of the former British secretary of state for trade and industry, Nicholas Ridley, who in 1990 remarked that Germany was planning to 'take over Europe'. These remarks were widely reported, created a huge scandal, and cost Ridley his Cabinet post. At a time of relatively benign polemics and timid concern for British sovereignty, Margaret Thatcher was often accused by rival Tory MPs of instigating Germanophobia. Yet, without

Thatcher, by the mid-1990s unbridled anti-German hysteria had become daily routine and nobody was forced to resign.

Britain's attitude and behaviour during most of the Yugoslav wars was subject to increasing scrutiny.[20] Accusations of British connivance with Serbia recurred in Eastern Europe, as well as in Germany, the Islamic countries and several Third World countries.[21] The pro-Serbian line in British politics had remained broadly uninterrupted since at least World War I.[22] It became stronger still after World War II, and, again, after the demise of communism. The Serbophiles were able to reabsorb lost elements of anti-fascist, Titoist, and otherwise leftist discourse, through an anti-Croat, more precisely anti-Tudjman, rhetoric.[23] The bottom line of this argument was that, rightly or wrongly, the Serbs were seen as the traditional allies against the Germans in two world wars.

During the House of Commons emergency debates on Bosnia in May 1995, Germany's recognition of Slovenia and Croatia was high on the target list. The entire parliamentary discussion was diverted into rapping Germany for virtually all misdeeds in the Balkans – an argument aped and parodied from Serbian propaganda.[24] Even the then leader of the opposition Labour Party, Tony Blair, could claim: 'Undoubtedly, there have been errors of judgement. The early recognition of Croatia without thinking through its evident impact on Bosnia is one example.'[25] Blair's more moderate approach nevertheless reflected a view which is far from being commonly accepted outside Britain. From the opposite end of the political spectrum, Ulster Unionist MP John D. Taylor echoed with sterner vigour: 'If the recognition of Croatia, Bosnia and the other states of the former Yugoslavia was wrong – if we were bounced into it – why is that now the basis on which we foresee a settlement being made? Recognition was wrong then and it is still wrong today.'[26] Similar analyses could be heard in the House of Lords special debate that same day.[27]

The fact that both Labour and the Conservatives shared a common language in which Germany's role was highlighted as a root cause of the war also points to the fact that both parties lacked competent advisors on the area. But there were more practical reasons: German-bashing was used to stave off any idea of firmer British commitment to Bosnia, particularly in the form of more decisive military intervention and a lifting of the arms embargo. Hence, it assumed a crucial function in the British, and as a corollary European, management of the conflict. Indeed, most MPs who fought against further British commitment in Bosnia, found in Germany's recognition a convenient scapegoat for upholding their line.

As sponsors of the South Slav state, Western politicians overlooked Serbian repression of other ethnic groups. When EC efforts to keep the country together foundered, Genscher vigorously pushed for diplomatic recognition ... Though Brussels and Washington eventually followed [Genscher's] lead, they were annoyed that he had forced their hand.[28]

The clash between new expectations of responsibility and old fears of hegemony placed the German government in a no-win situation. If it took the lead as in the recognition of Croatia, it was criticised as overbearing. If it held back as in the Persian Gulf War, it was attacked for shirking its duties.[29]

Germany's foreign minister at the time of the crisis, Hans-Dietrich Genscher, led the diplomatic initiative among his European partners.[30] Ominously, Kraut-bashing is a more popular sport amongst British and French elites than among the populations of these countries at large, which is a probable indicator that, rightly or wrongly, these elites see their dominant position challenged, at least after German unification. For instance, French elites were so anxious about their prospective loss of leadership in Europe, that political scientist Alfred Grosser protested that 'the French elite lags forty years behind the mood of the population'.[31] The French newspaper Le Monde also lamented that 'some politicians have lost all sense; the German colors wave on the title pages of magazines like on military command-posts; caricatures of the fat Mr. Kohl fill newspaper pages'.[32]

A fourth Reich?

The most extreme form of anti-Germanism turned into the belief in a 'Fourth Reich conspiracy' to dominate Europe and the world.[33] Is it possible to say that a new unified Germany was 'much more likely than its disunited parts to aspire to the hegemonic status it was denied in the past'?[34] This was the view that the conflict was premeditated by German political elites prodded by the experience of unification. Germany was now accused of trying to 'gain access to a warm Mediterranean port'. Parallels between pre-unification Germany and the Weimar Republic suddenly emerged.[35] As John Agnew and Stuart Colbridge point out, 'if the federal, liberal, and restrained West Germany could be cast in the role of the Weimar Republic, then reunification and its aftermath can be read as a re-play of the rise of Hitler and the Nazis. Only the new Hitler is missing so far.'[36]

Ironically, Germany's predicament was also linked to the peaceful nature of its foreign policy. In both the two main post-Cold War conflicts, the wars in the Gulf and in former Yugoslavia, German foreign policy – in contrast to that of the 1930s – has been shown to be 'neither bellicose nor effective'.[37]

Germany's policy of recognition was ineffective precisely because it could not be backed up by military support. For instance, Treverton observed that a united Germany in the post-Cold War world tried to launch its first bold international diplomatic initiative by recognising Croatia and Slovenia, 'but it did not have the military capability to back up its decisions'.[38] These analysts would seem to have preferred a militarised Germany with its own power of committing troops in war zones, rather than a peaceful Germany where public decisions in foreign policy matters are taken openly and without contemplating coercive measures. Thus, a foreign policy based on consensus was paradoxically rejected in favour of one based on coercion. Negative comments about Germany's lack of commitment during the First Gulf War can also be included amongst these pro-militarist exhortations.

It is also important to consider that Germany's relationships with the rest of Europe are crucial to its own socioeconomic development. Being so dependent on the continent's stability and security, it is unrealistic to assume that Germany would have taken an adventurist route in the Balkans. This is less the case for Britain, which has a powerful reserve of income and surplus labour from its former colonies in the Commonwealth.[39] Thus, Germany's choice reflected a considered balance between economic interests and political realism, as particularly manifested in the firm commitment to quickly re-establish democratic regimes in the region. Indeed, the defence of Germany's economic interests and respect for human rights are certainly not contradictory options.

Finally, the idea that the German attitude expressed a deliberate will to 'dismember Yugoslavia' was easily invalidated for the same reasons we have exposed above. First, the German government acted in response to public pressure. Second, this pressure was shared by other European countries. Third, Germany acted only after initial hesitancy and considerable distress. These three factors alone can dispel the idea of a 'deliberate plan to dismember Yugoslavia'.

Yet, the 'German conspiracy' theory became a popular myth in a Europe increasingly beleaguered by national frictions. In turn, it contributed heavily to fostering intra-European antagonisms. This idea bears close resemblance to Samuel Huntington's cognate theory of civilizational fault lines.[40] Indeed, it is part and parcel of it; instead of presenting a clash between Islam, Western civilization, and Eastern Christianity, it alleges an atavistic collision between the Teutonic world and the anti-Barbarian West.[41] It stretches back through the centuries to long-lasting rivalries between Britain (and France), and the Austro-Hungarian empire and its predecessors. Nazi Germany is but the last reincarnation of this enmity and the most fresh and useful in terms of offending memories.

The Vatican plot

Another variety of 'conspirationist' theory identifies Germany as lying decidedly within the Catholic orbit. Conjuring up civilisational fault lines between Papists and anti-Papists, this analysis speculates that, by favouring recognition, Chancellor Helmut Kohl wanted to avoid trouble with the Catholic-dominated Christian Social Union. These rumours brushed aside the fact that the most articulate proponent of the German decision was former foreign minister Hans-Dietrich Genscher from the liberal Free Democratic Party (FDP), rather than Kohl and his Christian Democratic Union (CDU). Both parties, moreover, represent the Protestant vote as well – although the CDU is particularly strong in Germany's Catholic heartland, Bavaria, where most immigrants from former Yugoslavia are also concentrated.[42] For instance, on 13 July 1991, the Bavarian partner of the CDU, the Christian Social Union (CSU), 'issued a call to the German Federal government to recognize Croatia and Slovenia, partially out of solidarity with fellow Catholics and partially out of indignation at the "brutal actions of the Yugoslav army which are unconstitutional and against the international law"'.[43]

The popularity of Croatian resistance in Italy also allowed for similar comparisons. In Catholic countries, the Church provided some backing for a spontaneous movement of humanitarian support. This was based on a Christian vocation of social solidarity with the downtrodden, who in the case of Slovenia and Croatia, happened to be fellow Catholics. However, the Pope's appeal to peace and his condemnation of Belgrade even increased once the Muslims, rather than fellow Catholics, became the new victims.[44] Bosnia turned into the epicentre of a new febrile humanitarian activity. This was in line with ecumenical principles that have emerged in the Church over the last thirty years – since at least Vatican Council II. These principles showed their most remarkable aspect when John-Paul II condemned the Allies' bombing of Iraq during the First Gulf War. Paradoxically, this 'neutral' attitude during the First Gulf War earned the Pope accusations of lack of 'loyalty' to the Allies' war effort, at a moment when the need for international cohesion was paramount. These accusations were made even more vigorously against

Germany, whose apparently non-responsive and 'pacifist' attitude was taken by German-bashers as a proof of Germany's weak commitment to common Western ideals – ignoring the fact that France played a much more decisive role in supporting Saddam Hussein until the last moment and tried to re-establish contacts with Baghdad even before the UN embargo could be called off.

Pope John-Paul II proposed to Kohl that Slovenia and Croatia be recognised simultaneously by Germany and the Vatican. Eventually, the Vatican recognized them two days earlier than the European Community. As the death toll mounted, France and the United Kingdom procrastinated over recognition, while Germany deemed it urgent. The movement of support for Croatia and Slovenia was particularly strong in Italy and Bavaria. This was often erroneously interpreted as a form of far-right support for Croatian nationalism and a revival of the wartime 'alliance', which the Axis power had established with Croat ultra-nationalists.

The Pope's appeals for peace in the Balkans and his reprobation of the Serbian treatment of minorities was regarded with suspicion in some Protestant countries, as well as in England. Here, a tradition of sodality between the Anglican Communion and the Serbian Orthodox Church was unexpectedly revived.[45] For Conservative British elites, the 'Papist conspiracy' had a remarkable aspect: the perceived similarity between the cases of Ireland and Croatia. The Serbs in Krajina were seen as replicas and copycats of Ulster's Protestants, Knin was imagined as a southern version of Londonderry, while a 'solidarity' movement between extreme Unionists and Serbian paramilitaries took shape. In every single debate in the House of Commons the Protestant Unionist MPs were among the staunchest Serbophiles (with the possible exception of fringe Labour MP Tony Benn).[46] Serbophile propagandists like Richard West seized upon these perceived similarities to press the case against recognition. West defined the Croatia's Ustashe regime during World War II as 'similar to an IRA terrorist regime'.[47] Yet, as if to disprove the weakness of the idea, the pro-Croatian movement was surprisingly feeble in Ireland. Parts of the Irish intelligentsia, traditionally influenced by their British counterparts, failed to take any serious action, or to draw salient comparisons between Croatia and Ireland.[48]

Finally, the proximity of Germany and Italy to the northern Balkans also relied on ties fostered by international organizations and economic links, such as the *Alpe-Adria* association.[49] This association was formed as an instrument of regional economic cooperation between Slovenia, Croatia, Austria, Hungary, parts of Northern Italy and Bavaria. Hence, strong ties had already been established between these neighbouring regions much before the trouble began.

German unification: ancient ghosts in a new bottle

The process of German unification was inarguably the main catalyst of this new fear of Germany, which disproportionately influenced British and French perceptions of the Yugoslav crisis. A parallel and deeply interconnected factor lies in the end of the Cold War. As it has been time and again observed, the end of the bipolar world allowed for hitherto suppressed tensions to resurface, while the glue provided by the common battle against communism and Soviet expansionism was melting down. In particular, German unification reawakened dormant ghosts.

German-bashers also claimed that German unification is the single international event which most influenced Yugoslavia's break-up. Post-1989 Germany was the first country to apply the principle of self-determination for itself. It is claimed, often arbitrarily, that its example directly or indirectly inspired nationalists in other parts of the world, from the Baltics to Moldova, and even Saddam's Hussein ill-fated invasion of Kuwait. The apologists of greater Serbia themselves often cited German reunification as a precedent, omitting to consider that it was achieved without a single shot. Yet, in international relations and political science, the 'domino effect' paradigm is far from being considered a real thing.[50]

Popular mutterings about Germany's secret ambitions in the Balkans were voiced particularly in Britain – as well as in other European countries – in the aftermath of German reunification. German unification took everybody by surprise. On the one hand, there was a genuine enthusiasm for the break-down of a barrier which had divided Europe's core for over forty years. On the other hand, the very idea that Germany could be *one* revived the ghosts of the past. People suddenly realized that, at least in terms of land mass (349, 520 kmq) and number of inhabitants (80, 767, 591),[51] Germany was now the dominant member of the European Union. This added to previous fears of economic domination, expressed particularly by Britain and other North European countries. In short, a united Germany induced instinctive fears and hence a widespread tendency to 'castigate' it at its weakest point, namely foreign politics.

In other words, although it was never verbally opposed, German reunification created a sense of apprehension amongst other European partners. This was particularly true for Britain, where a strong anti-European lobby found new legitimacy for its anti-federalist stance.

Likewise, Germany's chief neighbour, France, feared it could be treated as a smaller partner in the EU. It took a long time for these fears to dissipate. In the popular domain, they had been reinforced by massive media focus on racist attacks against asylum seekers and *gastarbeiter* in Germany.[52] Indeed, the sudden upsurge of attacks on foreigners by neo-Nazi gangs since 1990 contributed a great deal to spread an unprecedented sense of alarm. More distressingly, these attacks occurred in the wake of German unification and were mostly the work of East German youth who grew up under Socialist internationalism and were receiving the apparent benefits of the fulfilment of the long-time dream of democracy and unification. Similar attacks in France and other countries before the crisis attracted less public attention. It is possible that foreign policy analysis was affected by the simultaneous occurrence of German unification and the rise of xenophobia in the country. But this linkage ostensibly ignores the fact that Croatian refugees and Bosnians *gastarbeiter* were among those attacked, and even murdered, by skinheads and vigilante groups. Yet, the democratic strength of the German fabric could be noticed in the huge candlelight demonstrations and mass mobilisations against the xenophobic attacks which have impregnated German political life more than that of any other European country.[53]

But how was Germany's politics of recognition related to the country's unification? And why was Germany less inhibited than other European countries in dealing with momentous changes in Eastern Europe? Not bound to any neo-colonial empire, Germany did not share the same apprehensions as other Western powers. Moreover, Germany was a relatively 'homogeneous' country, which did not include territorial minorities posing a tangible threat to its own integrity – apart from the Danish-speaking community in Schleswig-Holstein, a small Slavic minority of Lusatian Sorbs, and an even smaller one of North Frisians.[54] This perception of a threat to the internal divisions of Britain and France will be discussed later, but it should be noted that this concern extended to virtually all non-homogeneous countries, from China, Burma and Iraq to Italy, Spain and Canada.

Finally, German unification was carried out according to much-acclaimed principles of self-determination. For some, the recognition of Croatia and Slovenia was a logical extension of the same principles applied to other countries which, like former East Germany, were moving through the birth-pangs of democracy. Thus, as soon as the conflict erupted in Slovenia, Helmut Kohl declared that it was 'unacceptable that suddenly the right of self-determination should no longer play a role'.[55] Indeed, for many political commentators, democracy and self-determination were inseparable concepts.

Conclusion

Within the European Union, there was unanimous support for the preservation of a united Yugoslavia. As we have seen, even Germany was initially opposed to the disintegration of the country. In the above investigation I have shown that the idea that Germany caused the break-up of Yugoslavia, and even that it caused the war, is largely a myth. Like all myths, it had its functions. For Western leaders, particularly in Britain, it served to justify their *impasse* and belated awareness of the causes of the conflict. For Belgrade's elites, it represented a conscious attempt to divert attention from their crucial responsibility in the war. The punctuality and timeliness of attacks against Germany reflected a typical diversion strategy. The idea of German responsibility was disseminated in particular moments of international debacle to excuse the West from its incapacity to coordinate a common policy on the war. The crucial turning points were chiefly the failure of Lord Carrington's peace plan, the beginning of hostilities in Bosnia, the Anglo-French opposition to lifting the arms embargo on Bosnia, and the failure of the Vance–Owen Plan. At the same time, Germany has been made accountable for breaking a taboo by recognising new states and acknowledging new international border changes.

In analytical terms, the German-centred explanation is also flawed, as it builds on another misguided interpretation, the idea that the conflict is basically a tug-of-war between Serbia and Croatia. This has turned out to be a major distracting 'decoy'.[56] As the ensuing war in Bosnia showed, it was folly to try to solve the Croatian conflict in isolation from Bosnia and from all other prey of the Serbian offensive.

After being censured and marginalised for recognising Croatia and Slovenia, Germany's pressure was more muted in respect of the need to recognise Bosnia. It was the United States which, after refusing for a long time to recognize Croatia and Slovenia, took the lead in recognizing Bosnia. But the US's original indecision was a forewarning of the coming tragedy.

As soon as Lord Carrington pointed the finger at Germany's initiative for seriously wrecking the leverage power of his plan, a kind of fever spread across Europe, chiefly in Britain.[57] Accusations of Germany 'manoeuvring behind the scenes' and images of an EC 'prodded by Germany' promptly circulated from Anglo-French ministries to the world media, feeding ancient prejudices and contributing to what has been cogently defined as the 'Balkanization of the West'.[58]

Among all countries, non-interventionism and German-bashing reached the greatest extremes in Britain and the US. Relying on popular

memories dating back from the time of Bismarck's competing colon-
ialism up until the Nazis, Anglo-Saxon elites constructed a framework in
which all otherwise unaccountable events in former Yugoslavia could be
conveniently placed. Germany's unification prompted a first muted
reaction which emerged in the open once the new German state took an
unprecedented initiative in foreign policy.

By blaming Germany, the United States and Britain were indeed
blaming Europe. Accordingly, Germany had been 'allowed' to 'steam-
roll' its European partners with an 'overhasty' recognition of Croatia
and Slovenia. For years, the adjective 'hasty' has bounced around in the
media like an uncontrollable squash ball whose momentum was unexpected even by its launcher. It was in turn reflected in popular perceptions, particularly in Britain. When international responsibilities
risked being identified, Germany provided an ideal target to divert all
potential criticism away from the West's mismanagement of the conflict.

The main argument of this chapter is that the policy of apportioning
blame on Germany for the Balkan crisis has been a fall-out from
German reunification. The latter not only came as a surprise, but many
Westerners reacted to it with alarm. Criticism was held back for a while,
only to explode once Germany ventured into the taboo area of foreign
policy, anticipating a move which most Western states frowned upon:
the recognition of Slovenia and Croatia. It is known that autonomous
initiatives in foreign policy matters are looked at with suspicion. They
are bound to be especially alarming if they involve an alteration of
existing boundaries. Obviously, Germany did not act without the official
support of other governments, but several leaders who accepted
recognition subsequently claimed *post facto* that they had not intended to
do so, and that they had acted under German pressure.

A major mistake was to confuse secession with instability. Events have
shown that instability was rather spurred by persistent counter-efforts to
uphold state integrity and the untouchability of frontiers inherited by the
Cold War. Indeed, Slovenia, the first country to leave Yugoslavia, was
also the first to join the European Union. Such principles can only work
with the agreement of both the governments involved and their subjects,
but we have seen how Belgrade itself had a separatist agenda which had
nothing to do with the international community's wishful thinking.

Finally, there was the persisting mistake of conceiving the current war
as having derived from secession and Balkanisation – an old Western
nightmare. Far from it, the tragic evolution of events was most likely
dictated by the major international powers' relentless attempts to keep
Yugoslavia together. In their futile effort to maintain the unity of the
country against powerful centrifugal trends, most Western governments

de facto adopted a pro-Serbian line. Moreover, implying that the conflict was basically a Serbian–Croatian one meant that one was forced to play down the harassment and persecution suffered by the other minorities.

The Croat and Slovene move did put Western governments under unprecedented pressure, a pressure which they were unprepared to tackle. This may be the only alibi for the West's politicians, their vacillations and shilly-shallies. All their subsequent moves do not absolve them.

I wish to conclude by stressing that German recognition had no discernible negative impact on the crisis. By recognising Slovenia and Croatia as international partners, Germany did indeed dissuade further Serbian aggression. The EC decision of 16 December 1991 to recognise Croatia and Slovenia was in fact followed by a Serb decision to stop the war in Croatia. If the same did not occur in Bosnia that was mostly due to the contrasting signals sent by the West to Belgrade and the *de facto* non-recognition of Bosnia as a single entity. Again, the tragedy of Bosnia had often been attributed to Germany's politics of recognition. The 'German conspiracy thesis' hence represented one of the cardinal myths supporting Western abnegation of responsibility. It also represented an easily available interpretation for those Western elites which, particularly in Britain, lacked substantial information on the background of the conflict, or decided to rely on information filtered by Belgrade-centred sources – even to the point of ignoring events as reported by the media.

Notes

1 Michael Libal, *Limits of Persuasion: Germany and the Yugoslav Crisis, 1991–1992*, Westport, CT: Praeger, 1997.
2 See Heinz Jurgen-Axt, 'Did Genscher disunite Yugoslavia? Myths and facts about the foreign policy of united Germany', in Günay Göksu Özdogan and Kemali Saybasili (eds.), *Balkans: A Mirror of the New International Order*, Istanbul: EREN, 1995 (for Marmara University, Department of International Relations). For a comprehensive legal analysis, see the Proceedings of the Symposium on 'Recent Developments in the Practice of State Recognition', *European Journal of International Law*, 4, 1 (Summer 1993), 36–91, 142–3.
3 Mihailo Crnobrnja, *The Yugoslav Drama*, London: Taurus, 1994.
4 Warren Zimmermann, 'Origins of a catastrophe: memoirs of the last American ambassador to Yugoslavia', *Foreign Affairs*, 74, 1 (1995); 4, 2–20.
5 David Owen, *Balkan Odyssey*, New York: Harcourt Brace, 1996.
6 Susan L. Woodward, *Balkan Tragedy: Chaos and Dissolution After the Cold War*, Washington, DC: Brookings Institution, 1995.
7 Beverly Crawford, 'Explaining defection from international cooperation: Germany's unilateral recognition of Croatia', *World Politics*, 48, 4 (1996), 482–521.

8 Belgium, Denmark, Hungary, Italy, Austria, Iceland and other Scandinavian states and several East European countries were voicing their approval for recognition before Germany and other countries could even act.

9 Randal Collins, 'German-bashing and the theory of democratic modernization', *Zeitschrift fur Soziologie*, 24, 1 (1995), 3–21.

10 On Britain's 'jingoistic' and 'warmongering' press, see Jean-Karim Chalaby, 'Nationalism as a discursive strategy', *ASEN Bulletin*, 4, 1 (1993–4), 19–25. On present-day Kraut-bashing tabloid hysteria, see Nick Cohen, 'And you thought the war was over', *Independent on Sunday*, 5 May 1996, p. 16.

11 'The British press was much more nationalist before World War I than World War II, ferociously anti-German in 1914 and forgiving in 1939, whereas the behaviour of Germany and the outcome of the interplay of alliances was much more predictable in the 1930s than the 1910s'. Chalaby, 'Nationalism as a discursive strategy', p. 21.

12 See Keith Robbins, *Appeasement*, Oxford and New York: B. Blackwell, 1988; M. Gilbert, 'The roots of appeasement' and J. Wheeler-Bennett, 'The road to appeasement', both in Kleine-Ahlbrandt and W. Laird (eds.), *Appeasement of the Dictators: Crisis Diplomacy?*, New York: Holt, Rinehart & Winston, 1970.

13 'Ve haf vays of making you hate ze Germans', *Evening News*, 12 June 1996, p. 23. When British children were asked what they most associated with other European countries, most replied 'frog legs and snails' for France, 'pizza and spaghetti' for Italy, 'sun and beaches' for Spain, 'kilts' for Scotland, 'dragons' for Wales, 'the Queen' for England, 'chocolate' for Belgium and 'IRA violence' for Ireland (John Carvel, 'Young Brits still bashing the Boche', *The Guardian*, 10 June 1996, p. 2).

14 *The Sun* (London), 23 April 1996, cited in Cohen, 'And you thought the war was over', p. 16.

15 *Ibid.*

16 Patrick Wintour, 'Major goes to war with Europe', *The Guardian*, 22 May 1996, pp. 1, 4, 8 and 9.

17 On the financial scandal involving top British Conservative leaders, see Tim Kelsey and David Leppard, 'Serbs gave Tories £100,000', *The Sunday Times*, no. 8/960, 19 May 1996, pp. 1, 24; 'The thief, the Serbian link and the financing of Britain's ruling party', *The Independent*, no. 1, 2, 990, 20 May 1996, pp. 1, 13; 'Tories probe Serb links to funding', *The Guardian*, 20 May 1996, pp. 1–2, 8.

18 Wintour, 'Major goes to war with Europe', p. 1.

19 Brendan Simms, 'The unknown accomplices in the Holocaust, *The Times Higher Education Supplement*, 4 October 1996, p. 25.

20 See Daniele Conversi, 'Moral relativism and equidistance: British attitudes to the war in former Yugoslavia', in Thomas Cushman and Stjepan Mestrovic (eds.), *This Time We Knew: Western Responses to the War in Bosnia*, New York: New York University Press, 1996, pp. 255–62; Brendan Simms, 'Bosnia: The Lessons of History?', in Cushman and Mestrovic (eds.), *This Time We Knew*, pp. 65–8; and Mark Almond, *Europe's Backyard War: The War in the Balkans*, London: Heinemann, 1994, pp. xv–xvii, 31–57, 91–103, 143–7, 240–62, 289–326.

21 In the Islamic world, the officialdom's muted reactions contrasted with widespread solidarity felt among ordinary Muslims, who 'tend to identify the fate of Bosnia with their own, and to see this war as a symbol of their destiny.' Tetsuya Sahara, 'The Islamic world and the Bosnian crisis', *Current History*, 93, 586 (1994), 386–9.

22 On Dame Rebecca West (1892–1983), the most famous English Germano-phobe and Serbophile, see Brian Hall, 'Rebecca West's war', *The New Yorker*, 15 April 1996, pp. 74–83. Her selective xenophobia targeted Germans and Turks as mainly responsible for all evils in the Balkans.

23 Milošević's able use and abuse of past memories, including the Holocaust, has proved to be highly effective in Serbia, and even abroad.

24 A mention of Germany in England customarily evokes the ghosts of the past. When this anti-German sentiment joins the anti-Europeanist strand, then the explosive mixture is translated into blaming everything on the Croats. This might explain why the idea of a German conspiracy is not correspondingly popular in Scotland, Ireland and Wales – except amongst Ulster Unionists.

25 Great Britain, Parliament, *House of Commons. Official Report. Parliamentary Debates (Hansard)*, London: HMSO (daily), vol. 260, no. 112, 31 May 1995, cols. 999–1102 (col. 1008).

26 Ibid., col. 1043.

27 Great Britain, Parliament, *House of Lords. Official Report. Parliamentary Debates (Hansard)*, London: HMSO, vol. 564, no. 96, Wednesday 31 May 1995, cols. 1117–72.

28 In Conrad H. Jarausch, *The Rush to German Unity*, Oxford: Oxford University Press, 1994, p. 206.

29 Konrad H. Jarausch and Volker Gransow, 'The New Germany: Myths and Realities', in Jarausch and Gransow (eds.), *Uniting Germany: Documents and Debates, 1944–1993*, Providence/Oxford: Berghahn Books, 1994, p. xxix.

30 For Genscher's version of events, see his memoirs: Hans-Dietrich Genscher, *Rebuilding a House Divided: A Memoir by the Architect of Germany's Reunification*, New York: Broadway Books, 1997 (Transl. of *Erinnerungen* [Memoirs], Berlin: Siedler, 1995, 1st edn.).

31 T. Klau, 'Angst vor dem bš sen "Boche" geht in Frankreich wieder um', *Bonner Rundschau*, 28 March 1990. Reprinted in Jarausch and Gransow (eds.), *Uniting Germany*: pp. 131–2.

32 Ibid., pp. 131–2.

33 A typical example of this view which blends radical Germanophobia, anti-Islamism and elements of anti-American discourse, can be found in C. J. Jacobsen, 'Washington's Balkan strategy: aberration or herald?', *South Slav Journal*, 17, 1/2 (1996), 67–70. Other pro-Serbian propaganda by the same author has been published by *European Security* and *Mediterranean Quarterly*. Though with much more sophisticated nuances, the Fourth Reich conspiracy is quoted uncritically in Crawford's article, 'Explaining defection from international cooperation'.

34 For a critique of this view, see John Agnew and Stuart Corbridge, *Mastering Space: Hegemony, Territory and International Political Economy*, London/New York: Routledge, 1995, 152ff.

35 Western commentators, their gaze firmly fixed on the past, failed to look at what was happening in the real world around them. They often disregarded the fact that Russia in the early and mid-1990s could much more appropriately have been cast in the role of the Weimar Republic, and that Russia's emerging xenophobic elites were much more tempted to assume the Hitler uniform – this time with thousands of atomic warheads.

36 Agnew and Corbridge, *Mastering Space*, 152.

37 David Marsh, *Germany and Europe: The Crisis of Unity*, London: Mandarin, 1994, p. 70.

38 Gregory F. Treverton, 'The new Europe', *Foreign Affairs*, 71, 1 (1992), 94–112.

39 The same may apply to a lesser extent to France.

40 Samuel Huntington, 'The clash of civilizations?', *Foreign Affairs*, 72, 3 (1993), 21–49.

41 This attitude has become widespread in the US, but even more so in the UK, where it has been championed by both Ulster Unionists and the far left (Conversi, 'Moral relativism and equidistance', pp. 255–62).

42 Protestants represent 45% of Germany's population and it is inaccurate and deceptive to claim that the Catholics (37%) could influence Genscher's decisions more than the former, although they were generally more vocal on the issue.

43 'Possible recognition of Croatia, Slovenia urged', *Deutsche Presse Agentur* (DPA), 12 July 1991, trans. in *Foreign Broadcast Service* (FBIS), *Daily Report* (WEU, Western Europe), 13 July 1991, p. 15. See also Jonathan Bach, 'One step forward, three steps back? Germany, the European Community, and the recognition of Croatia and Slovenia', paper presented at the German Studies Association Conference, Washington, DC, 8–10 October 1993.

44 Barbara Spinelli, 'Gli ipocriti mea culpa dell' Ovest: La fine della Bosnia', *La Stampa*, 30 June 1993, p. 1.

45 Conversi, 'Moral relativism', particularly pp. 250–1.

46 *House of Commons. Official Report. Parliamentary Debates (Hansard)*, London: HMSO [daily], vol. 260, no. 112, Wednesday 31 May 1995, cols. 999–1102.

47 Richard West, 'Yugoslavia really is one nation', *The Sunday Telegraph*, 30 June 1991.

48 This, notwithstanding the fact that historians like R. W. Seton-Watson had traced parallels between Croatia and Ireland as early as 1912, Robert William Seton-Watson, *Absolutism in Croatia*, London: Constable & Co., 1912.

49 On Alpe-Adria, see Liviana Poropat, *Alpe-Adria e Iniziativa Centro-Europea: Cooperazione nell'Alpe-Adria e nell'area danubiana*, Naples: Edizioni Scientifiche Italiane, 1993.

50 For a critical assessment of the 'domino effect' paradigm as applied to nationalist movements, see Daniele Conversi, 'Domino effect or internal developments? The influences of international events and political ideologies on Catalan and Basque nationalism', *West European Politics*, 16, 1 (1993), 245–70.

51 July 1993 estimate.

52 On the rise of neo-racism in unified Germany, see Sabrina Petra Ramet, 'The radical Right in Germany', *In Depth*, 4, 1 (1994), 43–68.

53 On the candlelight demonstrations against xenophobic violence which gradually changed the public mood, see Stephen Kinzer, 'Demonstrations for tolerance', *New York Times*, 13 January 1993, reprinted in Jarausch and Gransow (eds.), *Uniting Germany*, pp. 267–9. On foreign reactions to xenophobia, see Angelo Bolaffi, 'Foreign reactions to xenophobia', *Der Spiegel*, 14 December 1992, no. 51, 28–9, reprinted in Jarausch and Gransow, *Uniting Germany*, pp. 263–5.

54 On the Lusatian Sorbs, see Martin Kasper (ed.), *Language and Culture of the Lusatian Sorbs throughout their History*, Berlin: Akademie-Verlag, 1987.

55 *International Herald Tribune*, 1 July 1991.

56 Among the staunchest proponents of this view is Misha Glenny, who inspired Lord Owen and was one of the first to focus on Germany's alleged responsibility. For a more condensed example of the author's attitude, see Misha Glenny, 'Germany fans the flames of war', *New Statesman and Society*, 27 December 1991, pp. 145ff.

57 John Newhouse, 'The diplomatic round: Dodging the problem', *New Yorker*, 24 August 1992, p. 66. For Germany's 'crucial' influence see Nenad Ivankovic, *Bonn: Druga Hrvatska Fronta*, Zagreb Mladost, 1993. See also *FBIS-EEU-94-080*, 26 April 1994, p. 44, speech by Josip Manolic, Tudjman's former associate.

58 Stjepan G. Mestrovic, *The Balkanization of the West: The Confluence of Postmodernism and Postcommunism*, London/New York: Routledge, 1994.

6   From Bosnia to Kosovo and beyond: mistakes and lessons

Kemal Kurspahic

NATO's seventy-eight-day air campaign against Serbia confirmed much of the early analysis of Slobodan Milošević's ten-year drive for 'Greater Serbia' including the point some of my colleagues and I had been arguing since the beginning of the wars in the former Yugoslavia. That is, it takes international leadership – and not huge military risks – to stop the bloodshed in the Balkans. At the start of NATO's campaign, United Press International (UPI) invited me to write an opinion-piece on the intervention to stop Serbian 'ethnic cleansing' in Kosovo. Before I wrote the first sentence, the title jumped out at me – 'Air Strikes: A Decade too Late'. I believe that there was a moment in 1991 when just two F-16s could have accomplished what hundreds of fighter jets were trying to achieve in 1999 as they battled to put an end to Milošević's genocidal wars.

In fall 1991, the ancient walled city of Dubrovnik on Croatia's Adriatic coast was besieged and the target of Yugoslav Army shelling. Had the international community deployed some planes to strike even a handful of the JNA's tanks, Milošević would have received a powerful message that some things are impermissible and that Europe at the end of the 'Never Again' century would not tolerate such violence. I believe that had decisive action been taken then, some of the most gruesome atrocities since World War II could have been prevented, including the three and half year long siege of Sarajevo, the Serb takeover of the UN 'safe area' of Srebrenica, the genocidal massacres perpetrated there, and even the ethnic cleansing in Kosovo in 1998–99.

The outcome of NATO's intervention in Serbia proved the point: after only eleven weeks of bombing, NATO achieved all stated goals: Milošević capitulated and agreed to withdraw his forces from Kosovo. Afterwards, ethnic Albanians returned to their shattered homes, villages and towns, and NATO-led peacekeeping forces took over Kosovo. It should be stressed that this all took place without the deployment of ground troops and without any fatalities among NATO forces.

What was missing during the decade of Milošević's terror in the Balkans, which coincided with the jubilation of the end of the Cold War

76

and removal of the Berlin Wall, was the leadership and understanding of the destructive potential of the ultranationalist forces emerging from Yugoslavia. At the time of the attacks on Dubrovnik, and following his victory in the Gulf, US President George Bush distanced himself from events in the Balkans. Bush's secretary of state, James Baker, went on record saying, 'we don't have a dog in that fight', as if to stress that the United States was less than interested in the fate of Yugoslavia. According to Laura Silber and Allan Little, George Bush's national security advisor, Brent Scowcroft, recalled the president asking him on a weekly basis, 'Tell me again, what this is all about.'[1] It was obvious that Washington's reaction to the crisis was to let Europe handle events in its backyard, rather than exercise leadership on behalf of the United States. That was the original sin of American policy in the Balkans in the 1990s. This chapter describes the cost of America's inaction and offers some thoughts on lessons to be learned from this policy failure and steps to be taken in order to strengthen peace in the Balkans.

Letting Europe lead

Handing the case of Bosnia to Europe was a foreign policy oxymoron. In spite of the international conferences and desires of the political elites in Brussels, Europe as a single entity did not exist. Neither, however, had the European states managed to agree upon a set of principles that could guide a common policy. Low-level European mediators, ignorant of the roots of the Yugoslav conflict, resorted to the popular colonial game of divide and rule. It is hard to believe that anything but colonial arrogance, as illustrated in European efforts to assign land to one tribe versus another, explains the European mediators' obsession with maps.

The first maps were produced by Portuguese diplomat Jose Cutileiro and British Lord Carrington in Lisbon in March 1992. Summoning the leaders of the three Bosnian ethnic groups, they offered a map of Bosnia, divided into three cantons, one for Muslims, one for Serbs and one for Croats. They believed that such division would pacify the political agitators who sought to divide Bosnia on ethnic lines. Instead, the drive to partition the country – to create ethnically dominated territories in multiethnic, multireligious and multicultural Bosnia – was the source of Bosnia's problems in the 1990s and not the solution the mediators had thought. Before the war, there was not a town in Bosnia, and certainly not a region, that could be described as purely Muslim, Serb or Croat. Throughout the history of Bosnia, people of all three backgrounds lived together in the same apartment buildings, attended the same schools, and there was a large percentage of mixed marriages. Offers to divide the country were an invitation for bloodshed and not a recipe for peace.

But that is exactly what happened. Only two weeks after the map was introduced in Lisbon, the bloodshed began. The Serbian Democratic Party led by Radovan Karadžić started to 'cleanse' the 'Serbian' part of the map. First, towns along the Drina were attacked. Citizens were driven out, imprisoned, tortured and killed. The Muslim populations of Zvornik, Bijeljina, Foča and Višegrad were decimated. Then, Brčko, Banja Luka, Prijedor and Sanski. Most were overrun until 70 per cent of Bosnia fell under Serbian occupation.

A year later, another set of maps was presented in Geneva. New mediators, David Owen and Cyrus Vance, offered their political solutions in February 1993. The Vance–Owen Plan proved to be a direct encouragement for Croatia's President Franjo Tudjman to start 'cleansing' his part of Bosnia according to a pre-war agreement reached with Milošević. As with the creation of a 'Bosnian Serb Republic', the creation of a 'Croat Republic of Herceg-Bosna' was made possible by mass expulsions and war crimes. It is no exaggeration to say that the maps of partitioned Bosnia tragically introduced into Europe – the same Europe that had celebrated the removal of the Berlin Wall and the end of apartheid – provided additional motivation for war. In the end, these maps were drawn in the blood of more than 200,000 Bosnians killed and more than 1.5 million others expelled, as the Milošević–Tudjman plans for Greater Serbia and Croatia, respectively, were implemented.

Redistributing blame

The initial policy that emerged from Washington, so clearly illustrated in James Baker's remark on the United States not having 'a dog in that fight', delayed the prospect of serious involvement and leadership on the part of the United States. Both European and American politicians found convenient excuses for inaction. They adopted a theory of 'ancient hatreds' to justify their refusal to stop first Serbian and later Croatian aggression against Bosnia. Clichés such as the 'centuries-old conflict' and the accusation that the people of the Balkans habitually kill each other were readily offered up by apologists for Milošević's and later Tudjman's genocidal drive for partition. Even newly elected American President, Bill Clinton, who had criticised the Bush administration for its failure in Bosnia, initially subscribed to the line that Bosnians hadn't 'tired of killing each other' in spite of a leaked CIA report which indicated that 90 per cent of crimes were committed by Serb forces.[2]

For a long time, I myself had difficulty even calling Serbian aggression in Bosnia a war. For a war, you need two armies fighting each other. In our case, there was no army on the Bosnian side. Bosnia was attacked on the first day of its international recognition, 7 April 1992. With no army to defend itself, what took place was not a war – not a civil war – it was a war against an age-old civilisation of tolerance and coexistence between people of different religious and ethnic backgrounds. Bosnia is replete with monuments that are evidence of long-standing traditions of coexistence. Shrines of four major world religions– mosques, Catholic and Orthodox churches, and a synagogue – stand side by side in Sarajevo. These religious monuments were not attacked or damaged in World Wars I and II. But all religious heritage of the non-dominant groups, the 'others', was systematically destroyed in the Serb and later Croat campaigns for ethnic purity. Much later and to a lesser extent, Muslim extremists engaged in acts of blind revenge and vandalised monuments as well. For Bosnia, then, the ultranationalist phenomenon, demonstrated by hatred for other cultures and religions, is especially new. Ultranationalism has nothing to do with our history, as portrayed in many Western explanations and excuses for non-intervention.

The Powell doctrine

In the prevailing international climate of the early 1990s, which was defined by a lack of leadership, a special brand of American Balkanists – scholars and other writers who fell in love with former Yugoslavia – decided to blame its destruction on Slovenian, Croatian, Bosnian and Macedonian campaigns for independence rather than Milošević's quest for domination. In addition, there was another powerful voice against military involvement in the Balkans, the then chairman of the Joint Chiefs of Staff, General Colin Powell. Elaborating the 'Powell Doctrine', the general argued that US military should not be used except for the strictest of criteria. Only when America's vital national interests were affected should the military be prepared to act, with decisive force, clear goals and a well-defined exit strategy.[3] Powell made this doctrine clear in his autobiography, *My American Journey*.[4]

In 1991, I was asked why the United States could not assume a 'limited' role in Bosnia. I had been engaged in limited military involvements before, in Vietnam for starters. I said, 'As soon as they tell me it's limited, it means they do not care whether you achieve a result or not. As soon as they tell me 'surgical,' I head for the bunker.' I criticised the pseudo-policy of establishing a US 'presence' without a defined mission in trouble spots. This approach had cost the lives of 241 Marines in Lebanon.[5]

It was General Powell's theory that led both the Bush and early Clinton administrations to believe that it would take hundreds of thousands of ground troops to stop Serbian aggression and reverse 'ethnic cleansing' in Bosnia.

Seven years later, developments, both in Bosnia and Kosovo, proved Powell wrong. When NATO was finally shamed into intervening in Bosnia, after the Serbian takeover of Srebrenica and the subsequent extermination of much of its male population, it took only a few weeks of limited bombing to make Serb nationalistic leaders accept an American-brokered peace deal. And in spring 1999, air strikes – which had produced no fatalities among NATO troops – forced Milošević to do what he insisted he would never do: withdraw from Kosovo and leave the province to its 90 per cent majority Albanian population.

The UN's years of shame

While Serbian troops 'ethnically cleansed' Bosnia and erected concentration camps from Foča to Omarska, Bosnia's major cities, including Sarajevo and Mostar, fell under siege. The international community tried to wash its hands of any responsibility by sending to Bosnia a UN Protection Force (UNPROFOR). Even though the force helped establish some humanitarian corridors, providing Bosnia's besieged areas with life-prolonging supplies of food, the mission was a colossal failure. From the very beginning, it was designed as a peacekeeping operation in a country with no peace to keep. It was based on a distorted concept of neutrality between 'parties in conflict' – regardless of the fact that one 'party' was doing all the killing and the other all of the dying. It failed to protect even cities formally declared UN Security Council 'safe areas' to the point when Serb forces under the direct command of General Ratko Mladić entered the town of Srebrenica in July 1995 and slaughtered most of the male population in the presence of the Dutch 'peacekeepers' who had failed to obtain close air support from the UN headquarters in New York.

The history of the UN involvement in Bosnia produced some of the most damaging episodes in the history of that organisation. Former Secretary General Boutros Boutros-Ghali, in a visit to the besieged Bosnian capital of Sarajevo on the eve of the new year 1993, ignorantly said that there were many places on the planet in much worse condition. He effectively tried to diminish the magnitude of the tragedy that his organisation failed to address. A succession of UN generals – Canadian Louis McKenzie, British Michael Rose and French Bernard Janvier – made a habit of blaming the victims of Serb shelling almost as much as the aggressors in order to justify their inaction in the face of mass slaughter; and Boutros-Ghali's special representative to the Balkans, the Japanese diplomat Yasushi Akashi, was so accommodating to the Serbian leaders, now indicted for war crimes, that he denied air strikes against Serb forces, even while they trained their artillery on the positions of the Dutch 'peacekeepers' in hours leading to the imminent fall of the 'safe area' of Srebrenica in July 1995.

In addition, there were credible newspaper stories on then UN commander in Bosnia, General Janvier, even promising Serb General Mladić guarantees against any air strikes in exchange for the release of the UN 'peacekeepers' he held and humiliated as hostages.[6] Most of these facts were later substantiated in a devastating UN report by Boutros-Ghali's successor Kofi Annan. Ironically, the failure to prevent genocide in Bosnia coincided with the self-congratulatory celebration of the fiftieth anniversary of the UN in 1995.

Tying the victims' hands

To make the failure of international peacekeeping mechanisms complete, the United Nations imposed an arms embargo on the former Yugoslavia that decisively favoured the aggressors and tied the hands of the victims. Almost all weaponry of the former Yugoslav National Army – the fourth largest in Europe – ended in Serb hands. This monopoly gave the Serbian forces the power to terrorise Bosnia's cities with impunity while the Bosnians were left defenceless. With international reluctance to intervene militarily to protect the few remaining 'safe areas', the denial of arms to Bosnia amounted to the complicity in genocide.[7] The irony was complete: Bosnians were told that they couldn't be protected by air strikes nor were they allowed to protect themselves in self-defence because it might imperil those who came to protect them!

False representation

Having decided since the earliest stages of the crisis that it was more or less another tribal war, and having failed to recognise the international nature of the conflict, with Serb and Croat campaigns for ethnically pure states out of the UN recognised state of Bosnia Herzegovina – the international community made another fatal mistake. Instead of addressing the source of the tragedy, forces in Belgrade and Zagreb led by President Milošević and President Tudjman – who had plotted even before the war to split and seize Bosnian territories – international mediators were brought in to deal with the Serb and Croat leaders' proxies in Bosnia. By doing so, they gave them the legitimacy they never had. By organising their negotiations along tribal (i.e., Muslim–Serb–Croat, lines) international mediators promoted Radovan Karadžić (Serb Democratic Party–SDS) and Mate Boban (Croatian Democratic Union–HDZ) into legitimate and equal partners in all peace talks with Bosnian President Alija Izetbegović (Party of Democratic Action – SDA), even though he was the democratically elected president of an internationally recognized state, while Karadžić and Boban were self-appointed Bosnian Serb and Croat representatives who had never participated in any election. Over time, this tactic led to the delegitimisation of Izetbegović as a representative of the state since more and more he came to represent one of three interest groups, the interests of Bosniaks, instead of the whole country.

Dayton's 'construction error'

The Srebrenica massacre, the worst atrocity in Europe since the Second World War, shamed the international leadership into limited military action. After a few weeks of air strikes against Serb military targets, the stage was set for an ending to the war. American diplomat Richard Holbrooke was charged with that noble task. His mission was more to end a war – a gigantic undertaking by itself – than build foundations for lasting peace in the Balkans. Dayton was about ending the killings at any cost. And the cost was to have the two initiators of the destruction of Bosnia, the Serbian leader, Slobodan Milošević, and Croatian leader, Franjo Tudjman, dictate the terms for peace. Appeasement and the promotion of Balkan arsonists into firefighters created an irreparable construction error in the Dayton Agreement. Instead of providing constitutional guarantees for all ethnic groups and all citizens of Bosnia Herzegovina, it was based on territorial apartheid that recognized the results of 'ethnic cleansing'. Tudjman and Milošević got what they wanted: the first one received guarantees for the withdrawal of Serb forces from occupied Eastern Slavonia in Croatia and an arrangement for giving Bosnian Croats veto power in 51 per cent of Bosnian territory through the newly established Bosniak-Croat Federation; the latter was offered the Serb-held territory, 49 per cent of Bosnia, which became the Republika Srpska a newly created political entity with its own army and governmental institutions. Dayton left Bosnia Herzegovina partitioned along ethnic lines, with three armies, constitutionally two, but in reality three entities, and with ultranationalists holding on to territories they had 'cleansed' during the war. On top of this, the central government was left with only extremely weak institutions.

War criminals free to roam

With all elements that had led to the war still in place until late 2000, including the architects of 'Greater Serbia' and 'Greater Croatia', Milošević and Tudjman, whose cronies now had legal control over most of the territories they had seized from their rightful inhabitants, it was only natural that, years after Dayton, Bosnia would continue its dependence on the international community. The two indicted war criminals most responsible for genocide in Bosnia – Radovan Karadžić and Ratko Mladić – were still at large even after the anniversary of the Srebrenica massacre in 2005. They had been protected by the Serb population, including – for many years – by the authorities of both *Republika Srpska* and Serbia proper. The two basic conditions for the post-war healing and reconciliation, namely, a full acknowledgement of war atrocities and the apprehension and punishment of those responsible for war crimes, had not been met even ten years after the Dayton Agreement was signed.

Internationally sanctioned apartheid

The agreement itself, based on appeasement of the 'guys with guns', left almost half of the Bosnian pre-war population homeless. Bosniaks and Croats expelled from Serb-occupied territory remained abroad or displaced within the Federation. For years after Dayton, those who dared to return to their pre-war towns, especially in Serb-controlled and to a lesser extent in Croat-controlled areas of Bosnia, had to endure officially sanctioned harassment, including the orchestrated violence against the rebuilding of their religious heritage and ethnic segregation in the school system.[8] There is also increasing Muslim radicalism in territories controlled by the leading Bosniak SDA, including the once cosmopolitan capital of Sarajevo, best illustrated by the early 2005 election of a first City Council in the city's history without a single Serb representative. Following the example of Serb and Croat ultranationalists, Bosniak politicians increasingly embraced the idea of having their own share of unchecked power. Consequently, they too became part of the problem and have also made it more difficult for Serbs, Croats and others who escaped the war to return to territories under Bosniak control. These practices prevent reintegration even within the supposedly joint Bosniak–Croat federation and there is even less integration in Bosnia as a whole.

Having celebrated the end of apartheid in South Africa, the international community risks becoming the enforcer of a new apartheid in

Europe. Why not sanction partition, one might ask? The answer is simple: to do so would have violated the basic human rights of more than half of the pre-war Bosnian population, including not only Bosniaks, the prime victims of the war, but also hundreds of thousands of Serbs and Croats. Above all, the issue concerns their right and desire to return – Bosniaks to Banja Luka, Prijedor, Doboj, Jajce, Mostar, Stolac, Čapljina; Serbs to Sarajevo, Drvar, Sanski Most; Croats to Sarajevo, Travnik, Posavina, to name just a few areas. Violence and attacks against those expelled who tried to visit their pre-war towns on the occasion of religious holidays in post-Dayton years is just an illustration of the fears that some have of a future Bosnia, without international peacekeepers.

Instead of helping establish and enforce the rule of law, including the arrest of indicted war criminals and the creation of an environment for the unconditional return of rightful owners to their property, the international supervisors have – since Dayton – helped enforce a new apartheid. By holding a series of 'free elections' in 'ethnically cleansed' territories, they enabled ultranationalists on all sides to legitimise their hold on power. By allowing, and even imposing the 'privatisation' of social property throughout Bosnia, in the absence of hundreds of thousands of citizens who now live in exile, they made the prospects for return even more complicated, if not impossible. As we have witnessed over the past few years, the newly established ethnic elite is not likely to make any concessions to minorities, nor offer equal employment opportunities in companies seized by force and privatised through such distorted processes.

Leaving Kosovo unattended

While Dayton achieved an historic goal – ending the war in Bosnia – it was also a missed opportunity to do much more in the name of building a genuine regional peace. On top of Dayton's flaws, outlined above, the Accords failed to address the issue that had ignited Milošević's wars in the first place: Kosovo. Dayton was the last chance to address the legitimate grievances of Kosovo's Albanian population. A fruitless decade of peaceful, almost Ghandian resistance to the Milošević government's oppression, encouraged a section of the population to resort to guerrilla attacks against Serbian police and army patrols. This gave Belgrade an excuse for the wholesale terror, the 'ethnic cleansing', burning of entire villages...atrocities that finally led to NATO's intervention in 1999.[9]

Lessons to be learned

Early detection of upcoming storms – and early interventions – is the first lesson to draw from the Yugoslav experience of the 1990s. NATO's success in 1999 proves that the civilised world has means at its disposal to prevent or to stop genocide at an affordable cost.

Events after the victory in Kosovo suggest that the West has learned the basic strategic lesson from the Balkan wars of the 1990s: nationalism has the potential to set the whole region afire and the correct response to that must be the intensification of regional cooperation. The Stability Pact for Southeastern Europe summit, held in summer 1999 in Sarajevo, set the goals of helping to bring democracy, development and prosperity to the region with a view to connecting it to the rest of Europe. This institution has now been complemented by the growing involvement of the European Union in the Stabilisation and Association process. Europeanisation of the Balkans is undoubtedly the best prospect for a lasting peace to take root in this area. Once the region embraces the principles of democracy and human rights, as enjoyed in the rest of Europe including some former communist states, there will be less room for antagonistic notions of ethnic exclusivity, sacred borders and nationalist manipulations. After all, Europe – whole and united – is becoming a continent of open borders, free movement of people and goods, collective security, common currency and common institutions. To help the region move from the policies based on fear and antagonism to the prospects of joining the continent of open borders, based on the lessons of the past decade, the West needs to complete its tasks in the region. Bosnia – and to no less extent Kosovo – cannot enjoy peace and prosperity as long as ultranationalists, responsible for much of the suffering during the 1990s, remain unchecked.

Today, ten years after Dayton, and as the High Representative prepares to conclude his work in Bosnia, the international community faces a moment of truth. Ending the war was an accomplishment well deserving of Ambassador Holbrooke's memoirs.[10] But with the built-in obstacles to a functioning state; with five levels of government – for example – in the city of Sarajevo (municipal, cantonal, city, federal and joint institutions); with the veto power in the hands of ultranationalist parties that presided over the war, the country still can't survive the removal of a life-supporting international presence. There is a need for a bold move from the Dayton constitution, which anyway still hasn't been translated from English into Bosnian, to a constitution that will make Bosnia Euro-compatible. Unfortunately, there doesn't seem to be any international leadership at hand for such a move. Bosnians are repeatedly told they have to 'agree between themselves', which is a mission impossible with all of the paralysing Dayton-imposed powers entrusted to ethnic entities. Without a major international undertaking to assist the country in moving from the 'ending the war' to fully enjoying the benefits of peace phase, Bosnia will remain a country dependent on the life-supporting international presence, probably left behind its neighbours, Croatia and Serbia, in search for European acceptance.

Notes

1 Laura Silber and Allan Little, *Yugoslavia: Death of a Nation*, London: Penguin Books/BBC Books, 1996, p. 201.
2 President Clinton much later, during the Serb 'ethnic cleansing' of Kosovo – justifying his decision to now intervene – said he regretted initial acceptance of the killing-each-other theory. 'That was the excuse used by countries and leaders for too long', Clinton said on 23 March 1999 in a speech to the American Federation of State, County and Municipal Employees in Washington, DC, referring to the war in Bosnia as 'genocide in the heart of Europe'. Clinton said about Bosnians, 'It was an insult to them to say that somehow they were intrinsically made to murder one another.'
3 An antithetical view was published by Max Boot, editor of the *Wall Street Journal* who argues that the United States can and should engage in small wars and build nations as required. See Max Boot, *The Savage Wars of Peace: Small Wars and the Rise of American Power*, New York: Basic Books, 2002.
4 Colin Powell and Joseph E. Persico, *My American Journey*, New York: Ballantine Books, 1996.
5 Ibid., pp. 543–4.
6 James Geary, 'Politics and massacres: did France tacitly trade a Bosnian "Safe Haven" to the Serbs for the return of peacekeeper hostages?' *Time*, 147, 26, 24 June 1996.
7 President Clinton, coming into office in early 1993, had the right instinct when he announced his lift-and-strike strategy, which entailed a lifting of the arms embargo against Bosnia and an accompanying air campaign against Serbian strategic positions. He later abandoned the idea following European insistence that the strategy might endanger their peacekeeping troops on the ground in Bosnia.
8 These attacks have been extensively documented in reports issued by the Organisation for Security and Cooperation (OSCE) and US Department of State from 1996 to 2000.
9 Some critics of the intervention draw parallels between Kosovo and Rwanda and ask: Why was the West so quick to intervene in Europe but not in Africa? While the question is justified, the fact is that intervention in former Yugoslavia – following on from the genocide in Bosnia years earlier – came a decade too late.
10 Richard Holbrooke, *To End a War*, New York: Random House, 1998.

American cooperation with the International
Criminal Tribunal for the former Yugoslavia,
1994–1999

William A. Stuebner

In recent years, there have been several excellent studies of the International Criminal Tribunal for the Former Yugoslavia (ICTY) and its sister International Criminal Tribunal for Rwanda (ICTR) dealing with both the institutional development of those institutions and the influence that decisions issued by these bodies has had on international criminal law.[1] This chapter aims to complement those studies by focusing on the history of political cooperation with the ICTY. It reviews the role that the United States played during the early years of the ICTY when military intelligence was critical and includes some personal remarks from a former 'insider' seconded by the US government.

In the early days, the United States was the best friend of the ICTY. It provided more money, gratis personnel, in-kind donations and information to the Tribunal than any other country. The record is, however, less than perfect due to disunity of purpose among US Executive Branch agencies and within individual agencies; political considerations that put expediency above justice; and bureaucratic incompetence. Moreover, where problems occurred, they just as often were the fault of the ICTY's own confusion and lack of expertise and/or the peculiar characteristics of the UN bureaucracy. Sometimes, however, despite all the mistakes and reluctance to cooperate, individuals stepped forward to make things work and help the Tribunal to some very substantial successes.

Although Madeleine Albright has often, deservedly, been called the godmother of the ICTY and ICTR, American support began before the Clinton administration. Michael Scharf's book, *Balkan justice*, explains much of the early history of the idea for the ICTY in the Bush administration and points out in the introduction that it was largely a reaction to the impotence of the United States and the international community in dealing forcefully with the slaughter going on in the Balkans.[2] At the time, Scharf and other State Department attorneys, most notably Jim O'Brien, were engaged in bureaucratic battles to give birth to the ICTY while others in the field were given orders to begin the work of documenting atrocities in the former Yugoslavia. Several State Department officers rotated through the American Embassy in Zagreb, Croatia, in 1992–93 to take statements from the human flotsam that had washed up there from the notorious death camps of Bosnia – victims and witnesses of unimaginable cruelty.[3] Simultaneously, a UN War Crimes Commission established by Security Council Resolution 780 in October 1992 was engaged in a more systematic but underfunded and poorly supported effort to record atrocities.

As the Bush administration faded away and Clinton's first weeks as president stretched into months, those of us engaged in this gruesome and sometimes heart-breaking task began to question its purpose. Despite documentation of the horror, Washington diddled. Finally, in April 1993, the Security Council passed Resolution 827 establishing a war crimes tribunal for the former Yugoslavia. This is the period when Albright, then Permanent US Representative to the United Nations, began to win her reputation as the primary sponsor of the ICTY. She would soon be the first to acknowledge several subordinates who did most of the work to take the idea and make it a functioning reality. These include Jim O'Brien, who made the transition from the previous administration, David Scheffer, the first ambassador at large for war crimes issues, Foreign Service Officer Sheila Berry, and Albright advisor Laura Bowman who, altogether, worked the myriad practical issues of support for the Tribunal in the early days.

The establishment of the ICTY moved slowly despite pressure from Ambassador Albright. While judges were elected in 1993, it was not until early 1994 that an acting deputy prosecutor, Graham Blewitt, arrived at the Hague. He began work in part of an insurance company building and with almost no staff or equipment. Because of bureaucratic squabbling in the UN Secretariat, the Tribunal was in real danger of suffering the same lack of funding that had plagued the work of the earlier War Crimes Commission. The United States weighed in heavily on the modes of funding and secured the provision of a 'voluntary fund' to which donors could contribute to the ICTY outside the regular UN budget. This proved a valuable tool, especially for the prosecutor, when urgent needs were identified that had not been provided for in the regular annual budgets.[4] In March 1994, the US government also sent a team of attorneys and investigators to Bosnia under the auspices of the acting deputy prosecutor to demonstrate that war crimes investigations could be effectively conducted even in the midst of the ongoing conflict.[5]

The United States supported every early ICTY budget proposal, providing over $93 million as its share of the regular budget between 1994 and 1999 and more than $11.5 million in voluntary contributions from 1993 to 1999. It also gave the Office of the Prosecutor (OTP) a kick-start by providing twenty-four seconded or gratis investigators, attorneys, analysts and administrative experts and $2.3 million in computer equipment. Without this early contribution, the Prosecutor's Office would have taken years instead of months to bring its first indictments. Regrettably, due to UN bureaucratic animosity towards gratis personnel, by 1999 there was only one temporary official US secondee at the Hague.[6] It is estimated that the cost of one secondee, including all pay, allowances, housing and Embassy support costs, was approximately $250,000 per year.[7] In 1999, the US government also provided teams of FBI investigators and forensics experts to support OTP investigations in Kosovo. Additionally, an unknown number of intelligence personnel have worked on providing support to the ICTY since 1994.[8]

In the realm of diplomatic support, the United States was reasonably faithful to the ICTY. On most occasions, the US government stood up for compliance with the ICTY statute. There were times, however, when staff in the Office of the Prosecutor had reason for concern. For example, although Richard Holbrooke claims in his book, *To End a War*, that he worked hard to make sure the Tribunal's interests were protected at Dayton,[9] at one point I received a call from one of the international participants in the talks warning that immunity for Radovan Karadžić and Ratko Mladić was being seriously considered.[10] In response to this news, Judge Goldstone used a press luncheon the next day to announce that, if any immunity were granted for Karadžić and Mladić, he would have to consider resignation.

We will never know if the threat of immunity was real; nonetheless, I informed the State Department that if Goldstone quit, all the American secondees would also be at the podium with him announcing their departure and pointing fingers at those who had betrayed the cause of justice. The ICTY staff also worked around the clock for several days to complete the Srebrenica indictments against Karadžić and Mladić, making any grant of immunity politically untenable.[11] The end result was that the ICTY figured prominently in the Dayton Agreement.

At other times, American diplomacy, at least on the surface, appeared to undermine the Tribunal. Despite chronic non-cooperation by the former Croatian government of Franjo Tudjman, the Clinton administration was never as vocally critical of the Tudjman regime as it was of Milošević and his cronies in Belgrade. The US government was also extremely sensitive about even implicit criticism of the French forces in Bosnia for failing to arrest the many indicted war criminals living openly in their sector, and for making the ridiculous claim that they could not find Radovan Karadžić. However, the most obvious case of American diplomacy cutting deals at the expense of justice was the October 1998 agreement Ambassador Holbrooke made with Milošević regarding Kosovo. In that agreement, the ICTY was never mentioned, and the prosecutor and her subordinates continued to be banned from Kosovo by Milošević.[12]

Of course, the administration may have been hesitant in its criticism of the French because it too had a poor record. In the first two years of the Dayton era, the American army was the strongest force on the ground in Bosnia and Hercegovina but possessed the weakest will.[13] American soldiers were rarely allowed out from behind their sandbagged bunkers and they could travel only in convoys of four or more vehicles. While General Ratko Mladić lived in the American sector, not a finger was lifted to apprehend him. Nor were any other indictees arrested despite the boastful claims of some of them that they regularly passed through American checkpoints.[14]

Later, when SFOR finally started making arrests, there is some reason to doubt how actively engaged the Americans were even in their own sector. From 1998 onwards, the Americans became more aggressive. They deserve full credit for the arrest of Bosnian Serb General Radislav Krstić on 2 December 1998. Much of the criticism of previous American army timidity may now be moot; indeed there was no reliable evidence of any of the indicted living in the American sector during the first five years of the SFOR mission beginning in late 1996. Furthermore, American reluctance to be tough and proactive was characteristic in all areas, not just in pursuing indicted war criminals and supporting the Tribunal. Along with many other observers, I also believe the 'be all and end all' of American military involvement in Bosnia and Hercegovina in the early years was force protection.

At times, the American command's dread of 'mission creep' even went so far as to attempt to stop other national forces from providing assistance to the ICTY. In the spring of 1997, the Dutch army and the British who commanded their sector leaned over backwards to help ICTY investigators locate a suspected mass grave site. The British even agreed to bring in engineering equipment to de-mine a 2 kilometre path for our forensics experts to be able to access the site. The SFOR operations officer, an American brigadier general, exploded at a meeting called to plan this cooperation and would have forbidden the mission if it were not for the intervention of the SFOR chief of staff, a British major general, who overruled him. On another occasion, after the subject of a sealed indictment tried to turn himself in, the same American general kept Dutch forces from effecting a follow-up arrest and laid down such strict rules of engagement that he made a mockery of the supposed SFOR policy to arrest indicted war criminals whenever soldiers of SFOR encountered them in their 'normal course of business'. In the one area where American units provided substantial support, security and logistics for mass graves exhumations, odd restrictions continued to wreak havoc on operations.[15]

The question is, of course, about where within the US government to place the ultimate responsibility for lack of cooperation with the ICTY on the ground in Bosnia, especially regarding the capture of the most high-profile indictees – Mladić and Karadžić. On one occasion, I took prosecutor Louise Arbour to see the SFOR commander, an American four-star general, to request greater cooperation. He explained to her that, 'people far above my pay grade have drawn this box within which I am to operate and I was warned again just yesterday that I am not to step outside that box. And if you quote me on that, I'll deny I ever said it.' One has to ask exactly how many people in the chain of command are far above a four-star general's pay grade, and what, exactly, was their commitment to the success of the ICTY and Dayton implementation. After all, a favorite mantra of many senior Clinton administration officials was 'there can be no peace without justice'.

The young officers and the men and women who served under them displayed a burning desire to get the job done during the early years of SFOR would have preferred a more aggressive policy. Time after time, commanders on the ground and their subordinates exceeded their orders and overstepped the bounds of what they were allowed to do. In many cases, the ICTY could not have accomplished what it did without their help. When they could not help, because superiors had explicitly ordered them not to, they often apologised and confidentially expressed embarrassment.

The obvious question is that since the US government professed its unqualified support for the ICTY, why is it that cooperation was often not more forthcoming in the first five years of the Tribunal? Many have speculated that there was some kind of conspiracy to protect Milošević and Tudjman, or that a deal was cut at Dayton to the effect that certain persons would have *de facto* immunity so long as there were no attacks on NATO troops. Incompetence, however, is another possibility, along with the conflicts of interest that are commonplace in governmental bureaucracies. Within the US government policy establishment, there are, of course, many players with numerous opposing interests. In the case of the Tribunal, some, but not all, would have provided, if they could, almost unrestricted assistance. Some former players like the ambassador at large for war crimes issues, the assistant secretary of state for democracy, human rights and labour (DRL), and the special envoy for Dayton implementation were, without doubt, strong allies of the Tribunal and saw its mission and the need to arrest indicted war criminals as the *sine qua non* of the peace process in the Balkans.

Others with broader political responsibilities and different motivations saw the primary objective as protecting the president. In the case of Clinton, the concern was to shield him from controversy and criticism at all costs, including references to casualties in Bosnia. Still others thought narrowly and believed that any relaxation of the rules such as those protecting the security of classified information is a long-term threat to the security of the nation. The simple fact is that the Executive Branch of the USG does not speak with one voice on most issues, and when one does disagree with a policy, it is usually easy to find a way to block it or at least to ignore it.

A prime example of ignorance, incompetence, political influence, and in some cases recalcitrance, was the provision of useable intelligence to the Tribunal. Officials at the ICTY have told me that an improvement in the provision of US intelligence began in the autumn of 1998. Suddenly, it was like a dam broke and the investigators began seeing the kind of information they had always longed for – but only regarding Kosovo. There was almost no improvement on past requests for information regarding other theatres of the Balkan wars. It is interesting to speculate why this was the case, but the answer seems rather obvious.[16] Suddenly, for the first time, the informational needs of the Tribunal coincided with the political needs of Washington. The Clinton administration wanted to see Milošević indicted. It is probable that those who saw him as the major problem in the region finally won out over those who saw him as the guarantor of peace in Bosnia. This tilted the preponderance of policy weight towards overcoming the resistance of those in the intelligence community who were opposed to releasing sensitive information to the Tribunal.

During the Kosovo crisis, once the NATO bombing campaign started in March 1999 and there was a need to vilify Milošević as the principal enemy, the ICTY received even more information and, probably, more pressure to bring an indictment, which it did. The fact that Milošević's initial indictment was for crimes in Kosovo, and only later for crimes committed in Bosnia and elsewhere in the former Yugoslavia, bears out this conclusion as to why high-quality intelligence was not provided in the ICTY's early years.

The history of US intelligence sharing with the ICTY has not been a proud one. Of the original twenty-four persons seconded to the Tribunal in 1994, only one was dedicated to this task. The person chosen was unable to move to the Hague and so became the obvious candidate to work on the provision of intelligence from Washington. While the person had some expertise in the region, they were certainly not fully versed in intelligence collection and analysis and also had little or no background in legal matters. Also, the place of work chosen for American intelligence connection was in the Intelligence and Research Bureau at the US Department of State, not one of the major agencies in the Washington world of intelligence. The result was less than encouraging. Almost the only things the Tribunal received for months were hundreds of faxed pages of open-source media reports. It is accurate to say that in his first year as prosecutor, Justice Goldstone received almost nothing of value to the prosecution from the American intelligence community.

There are many reasons for the poor performance of the United States in providing worthwhile intelligence to the Tribunal. First, it is only fair to point out that the support of criminal prosecutions has never been part of the mission of the vast majority of the intelligence community. Most intelligence agencies are focused in one way or another on national security. Their job consists of safeguarding the country and, when necessary, helping the military destroy the enemy with the lowest possible cost in friendly casualties and resources. Those engaged in supporting policy-makers naturally emphasise predictive intelligence about threats to and opportunities for the United States and its allies. Unless specifically tasked, intelligence resources will never be directed towards what a criminal prosecutor needs. Otherwise, what is collected or produced will have only coincidental value to the prosecution of criminals. And even if resources are redirected at the request of an organization like the Tribunal, the intelligence community is unlikely to have the legal expertise necessary to make the end product truly fit the need.

Another problem is the OTP's wish for useable intelligence and information that can be used in court and is, therefore, accessible by at least the defence, if not the public at large. This raises the problem of compromising sources and methods, revealing to possible enemies American capabilities of spying and gathering intelligence, as noted by the United States District Court for the District of Columbia in the case of *Students Against Genocide* vs. *US Department of State*.[17] While often a legitimate concern, it can also be used to scare away policymakers who want information released if the powers in the intelligence community do not want to cooperate or fear setting a precedent for future requests from the *ad hoc* tribunals or embryonic International Criminal Court (ICC). This is especially true of many of the intelligence agencies that would be most likely to have the information the ICTY needs, since they belong to the Department of Defence, an enemy of the ICC if not the *ad hoc* tribunals. Sources at the ICTY report that on the rare occasions that they received good information prior to the conflict in Kosovo, it was always tightly restricted by provision under Tribunal Rule 70 and, therefore, could not be used in open court or even submitted to the judge confirming the indictment as back-up material. Even open source media reports have been provided under Rule 70 rendering them unusable; unless the Office of the Prosecutor analysts spent time returning to original sources, they could not have incorporated this information in prosecutorial material.

The ICTY itself is also not without blame in the intelligence-sharing problem. Often the main problem was, once again, an inability to communicate. Just as the US intelligence community remains largely ignorant of prosecutorial evidentiary needs, the Office of the Prosecutor failed to develop any detailed understanding of intelligence collection and analysis. During its first five years, the Office of the Prosecutor never hired an experienced intelligence officer with extensive and up-to-date knowledge of how to exploit national intelligence resources. This is to be expected, since the police and attorneys who largely make up the prosecutor's staff have no experience in this field. Thus, although staff in the OTP often knew what they wanted, they had no understanding of whether it might exist, how to ask for it, and what was necessary to get resources redirected. They really did not even have the ability to properly evaluate those on their own staff who claimed to be intelligence experts. Thus, despite regular meetings where the ICTY sent people to Washington or the intelligence community sent people to the Hague, very little real communication took place, and the Tribunal continued to receive little useable evidence except for some of the later information on Kosovo. One final point of blame for the prosecutor, which also helps to refute some of the conspiracy theorists, is that the Office of the Prosecutor is unlikely to receive specific intelligence unless it requests it. As it has been reported that Prosecutor Arbour did not even begin a case on Milošević until October 1998, it is no wonder she never received information that she did not request. As a matter of fact, if the US government had tried to force feed information about Milošević or other leaders, the prosecutor might well have accused it of improperly trying to guide or pressure the prosecution.[18]

As noted in the first part of this chapter, the US government was a consistent supporter of increasing budgets for the *ad hoc* tribunals. Given the fact that, in an age of UN cutbacks, the ICTY and ICTR saw their budgets increase on the order of 40 per cent per year between 1998 and 2000, it is reasonable to assess US government efforts as having been remarkably successful. This was, however, endangered when, in 1999, the US lost its seat on the 16-member Advisory Committee on Administrative and Budgetary Questions (ACABQ) because of its non-payment of approximately $1 billion in back dues. The US government had used its membership in this influential committee to support the Tribunal budget increases. Later, it had to rely on others to carry the water for this cause and many others. This was bad news for both the ICTY and the ICTR and made it difficult for them to even maintain what they had, let alone expand it further. Furthermore, as the ICC takes off, it will become a major competitor for resources, especially from European governments.

The question of how US policy towards the Tribunals would be formulated in the administration of G. W. Bush was a bigger question, especially given its stance on the International Criminal Court. The Office of War Crimes Issues was established by the personal initiative of Secretary of State Albright shortly after she replaced Warren Christopher in order to coordinate all issues related to war crimes for the USG. Such offices come and go as secretaries rotate. Previously, war crimes issues as well as support for the *ad hoc* tribunals fell primarily under John Shattuck as assistant secretary of state for democracy, human rights and labour (DRL). The creation of the new office somewhat diminished the responsibilities of Shattuck and his successor Harold Koh, but they continued to maintain an interest in the Tribunals and related issues like the ICC. DRL was also responsible for many of the voluntary contributions that have gone to the Tribunals.[19] Other offices like the geographic bureaus in State and the Office of the Special Envoy for Dayton Implementation have also weighed in for both good and ill in relation to Ambassador Scheffer's responsibilities. Even other Executive Branch Departments have interfered, sometimes causing policy confusion and promoting uncoordinated positions.[20]

In conclusion, the overall record of the United States in supporting the ICTY in the early years was fair to good. The bureaucratic problems encountered were much the same as with any other policy issue. There are always competing interests. To a great extent, the backing of the ICTY was personality-driven, but this is no different from the situation in any other democracy. A case in point is the British record. Under the Major government, support was almost non-existent and at times it appeared that the ICTY was seen as nothing but an irritant.[21] The situation changed overnight when Prime Minister Blair was elected in 1997, and this was, at least in large part, due to his choice of Robin Cook as foreign secretary. In the case of the USG, the choice of Madeleine Albright first as UN ambassador and then as secretary of state, made the

United States the leader in establishing and resourcing the Court. She was supported by key people on her own staff and by those who happened to be in the right place at the right time throughout the State Department. On the military side, where the US was at its weakest, the selection of General Wesley Clark brought great improvement to the overall support of the ICTY on the ground. On the negative side, the person in the US government who successfully resisted pressuring the French to do more in their sector of Bosnia and Herzegovina did grave injury to the cause of international justice and to sustainable peace in the Balkans.

Fortuitously, there were important people outside of the government who also helped to get the ICTY off the ground. Outstanding among these are philanthropist George Soros and the president of his Open Society Institute, Aryeh Neier, who were always ready to provide support both in resources and political influence.

Notes

1 See, for example, Howard Ball, *Prosecuting War Crimes and Genocide: The Twentieth Century Experience*, Lawrence: University Press of Kansas, 1999; Gary Jonathan Bass, *Stay the Hand of Vengeance: The Politics of War Crimes Tribunals*, Princeton: Princeton University Press, 2000; Yves Beigbeder, *Judging War Criminals: The Politics of International Justice*, New York: St. Martin's Press, 1999; Gideon Boas and William A. Schabas (eds.), *International Criminal Law Developments in the Case Law of the ICTY*, Leiden: Martinus Nijhoff, 2003; John Hagan, *Justice in the Balkans: Prosecuting War Crimes in The Hague Tribunal*, Chicago: University of Chicago Press, 2003; Pierre Hazan, *La justice face à la guerre: de Nuremberg à la Haye*, Paris: Stock, 2000; Rachel Kerr, *The International Criminal Tribunal for the Former Yugoslavia: An Exercise in Law, Politics, and Diplomacy*, Oxford: Oxford University Press, 2004; Geoffrey Robertson, *Crimes against Humanity: The Struggle for Global Justice*, New York: The New Press, 1999; Michael Scharf, *Balkan Justice*, Durham, NC: Carolina Academic Press, 1998; Paul Williams and Michael Scharf, *Peace with Justice? War Crimes and Accountability in the Former Yugoslavia*, Langham, MD: Rowman and Littlefield, 2002.
2 Scharf, *Balkan Justice*, p. XV.
3 As a contractor for USAID and the only quasi-official American working regularly in Bosnia early in the war, I was also tasked with taking statements and recording the locations of concentrations of internally displaced former camp inmates and others who had been subjected to war crimes and crimes against humanity.
4 Examples include US donations in 1998 ($1,075,000) for translation, Kosovo investigations, support for the Rules of the Road project, and to assist the president of the ICTY in establishing an outreach programme to the people of the former Yugoslavia in 1999 ($500,000).

5 I was tasked to take this multiagency team to Tuzla to investigate the notorious 'Luka' death camp in the town of Brčko.

6 The US would have continued the provision of gratis personnel, but UN bureaucrats killed the programme throughout the United Nations, claiming it was unfair to poor countries that cannot afford to second personnel. A very senior UN official once confided to me, however, that UN bureaucrats hate gratis personnel because they fear member countries might begin to question why the UN pays for what it can have for free, and this might eventually jeopardise their own jobs. This is further supported by the attitude of ICTY Registry career UN personnel who used to refer to the secondees as 'those illegal Americans'.

7 All figures in this paragraph are from an unofficial State Department source.

8 This includes probably fewer than a dozen persons at State and unknown numbers in the various intelligence agencies.

9 Richard Holbrooke, *To End a War*, New York: Random House, 1998.

10 I did not think this would happen with staunch friends of the ICTY such as Assistant Secretary John Shattuck and Ambassador John Menzies at Dayton, but I thought that if Holbrooke was taking real heat on this subject, we should give him some ammunition.

11 There is a long-standing argument over whether it is possible to negotiate an end to hostilities while, at the same time, attempting to render justice to the combatants. Dayton and the settlement of the Kosovo conflict after the indictment of Milošević would seem to answer this question in the affirmative.

12 A Bosnian Serb army colonel made this claim to Czech journalist Jan Urban who helped to orchestrate an effort in 1996 to find the men publicly indicted by the Tribunal after IFOR (NATO) said that they did not know the locations of any of the indicted. As Jan recounted the story to me, the colonel said, 'I used to worry about driving through the American checkpoint near my home, since my photo was on the poster in the guard shack. But now when I go through and show them my ID card, they just salute and tell me to have a nice day.' It is interesting to note that this effort by journalists and human rights activists located approximately 80 per cent of those indicted for crimes in Bosnia and Herzegovina after only two weeks of effort and found some of them living only a few hundred meters from NATO garrisons.

13 Two eyewitnesses to the arrest of Goran Jelisic in Bijeljina on 22 January 1998, told me that the men who jumped out of a van to grab him were wearing British camouflage. In the case of Stevan Todorović, who was arrested in July 1998, he told investigators in the Hague that he had been abducted by masked Serbs inside Serbia and then taken across the Drina River in a small boat to Bosnia where he was turned over to a US unit.

14 John Pomfret and Lee Hockstader, 'In Bosnia, a war crimes impasse; NATO differences with UN Tribunal mean few are arrested', *Washington Post*, 9 December 1997, sec. A, p. 1.

15 For example, the American Command in Sarajevo ordered that the area security provided for mass graves sites could only be provided when Tribunal personnel were physically on the site. Consequently, because we could not carry out detailed, painstaking investigations during the hours of darkness,

and to abandon a site at night would require expensive and time-consuming demining operations again every morning, we had to hire unarmed, retired French soldiers to sleep on the sites. Also, although American officers at NATO headquarters in Brussels had promised the deputy prosecutor round-the-clock aerial surveillance of suspected grave sites to detect possible tampering, this support was never forthcoming.

16 Oft-heard speculation is that Richard Goldstone and Louise Arbour were under pressure from the American government not to indict the likes of Milošević and Tudjman. I can say without reservation that this never happened during Judge Goldstone's tenure, and, if anyone had ever tried to put improper pressure on Justice Arbour, I believe she would have condemned him or her in public. If anything, pressure was put on Arbour to investigate Kosovo and Milošević much earlier, but she delayed for her own reasons.

17 *Students Against Genocide v. US Department of State*, 257 F.3d 828 (DC. Cir. 2001) – E.O. 12,958; the CIA demonstrated that release of withheld reconnaissance imagery in combination with other known information would risk intelligence sources and methods; exemptions were not waived when withheld photographs were displayed (but not distributed) by then UN Ambassador Madeleine Albright during a televised presentation to United Nations Security Council.

18 Raymond Bonner, 'Tactics were barrier to top Serb's indictment', *New York Times*, 29 March 1999, p. 9.

19 Foreign Service Officer 'Spence' Spencer did more than anyone else at State to find money for voluntary contributions to the ICTY.

20 The biggest villain on this score was the Department of Defense, which was always reluctant to support the ICTY in the field and even held a meeting for foreign military attaches shortly before the ICC talks in Rome to encourage them to lobby their governments against the treaty. Defense also sent a representative with the US delegation to the Rome talks who, as one diplomat told me, was 'strapped to Dave Scheffer's back' to make sure he wouldn't 'give away the farm'.

21 The first registrar of the ICTY, Theo Van Boven, summed up the situation with humour when a British journalist asked us at lunch how many pounds his government had provided to the Tribunal. Theo answered, 'About two pounds – of paper clips.'

8   The European Union's role in the Balkans

Fraser Cameron

Introduction

The Balkans have been the major testing ground of the European Union's (EU) developing international role and in particular its common foreign and security policy (CFSP). Few could have imagined, when the CFSP was agreed in 1991, that it would have such a baptism of fire. In the summer of 1999, Southeastern Europe emerged from yet another violent conflict in the region. NATO forces had just ended the bombing campaign against the former Yugoslavia and had taken control of Kosovo. Yugoslavia was still under international sanctions, with detrimental effects on the whole region. Albania and Macedonia were recovering from the refugee influx due to the Kosovo crisis, which aggravated the situation in Macedonia to a degree that led to ethnic violence in the summer of 2001. While fighting had ceased in Bosnia and Croatia with the Dayton Agreement in 1995, the situation resembled a more uneasy truce than a good neighbourly relationship. Bulgaria and Romania, while on the path towards EU accession, suffered severely from the blocked trade routes through neighbouring Yugoslavia.

In 2005 the situation in Southeastern Europe was very different. All the countries of the region had a clear European perspective. Bulgaria and Romania are set to join the European Union in 2007. The December 2004 European Council agreed that accession negotiations with Croatia would start in 2005. Macedonia's application for membership is under consideration by the European Commission. Albania and Bosnia are *en route* to a Stabilisation and Association Agreement (SAA). Only Serbia-Montenegro is still being held back by the difficult internal situation as well as the undecided status of Kosovo, but the direction is clear.

The catalyst for these positive developments has been the EU. The decision to make the new European commissioner in charge of enlargement, Olli Rehn, responsible for all the western Balkan countries in addition to Romania, Bulgaria and Turkey, is not just a bureaucratic measure, but also a political message that the future of the region lies within the EU. The EU is widely recognised as the most important actor in the region. It has poured huge sums of money into reconstruction, promoted regime change throughout Southeast Europe, agreed a roadmap leading to eventual EU membership, and is heavily engaged in conflict prevention and crisis management in the Balkans.[1]

Background

With the establishment of the CFSP in 1991 there were high hopes that 'the hour of Europe' had arrived.[2] Sadly, it took several more years of bitter experience, including the Kosovo conflict, before the EU began to develop the instruments and the political will to make an impact in the Balkans. The reasons for launching the CFSP were variously ascribed to the need for the EU, as the major actor in global trade and development assistance, to 'punch its weight in the world', to shoulder more of the transatlantic burden, and to develop externally apace with internal developments (single market, single currency, enlargement).[3] CFSP was also a popular endeavour. Opinion polls revealed (and continue to reveal) a high level of public support across the EU in favour of closer cooperation in foreign and security policy.[4] In a widely quoted article, one analyst suggested that there was a substantial 'capability-expectations gap' in terms of what the public expected the EU to deliver, and the capabilities it had developed in this area. Looked at from the perspective of the early 1990s, the EU 'was not an effective international actor in terms both of its capacity to produce collective decisions and its impact on events'.[5]

Today, despite the doubts and setbacks, the EU has become a much stronger external actor and even the CFSP has started to fly. After the disarray over the Iraq war in 2003, the new constitution agreed in the summer of 2004 that it should provide the EU with a more solid platform to play an increasingly important global role. The Balkans, however, will remain a key benchmark for assessing the EU's external performance.[6]

A tough learning experience

In the early 1990s the Europeans were sharply divided in their approach to the Yugoslav crisis, particularly on the issue of recognition and independence of Slovenia and Croatia. They lacked the cohesion, determination and instruments to bring the crisis under control. The United States had been quite reluctant to become engaged, as no important US security interests were at stake. Secretary of State James Baker famously remarked, 'We do not have a dog in this fight.' However, as the bloodshed worsened and in the absence of a credible European effort the United States became more involved. In 1995 the United States bombed Serbia into acceptance of a peace deal at Dayton. During the following years the overall division of roles between Europe and the United States did not change significantly. Europe still contributed the lion's share of soldiers, humanitarian assistance and international expertise, but its political influence was not commensurate.[7]

Four years later the EU again failed to play a determining role in the Kosovo conflict. The EU's cohesion had improved but it lacked the military capabilities to end the conflict and had to watch as NATO (read America) bombed Serbia into submission.[8] This second failure was to have a powerful catalytic effect in pushing Europe to develop its own military capabilities. After Kosovo, the EU's Balkans policy became more coherent and proactive and the US–European relationship in the Balkans shifted towards greater equality.

A number of factors were responsible for this development. First, the victory of democratic forces in Croatia and then Serbia made it possible for the EU to move towards the development of a comprehensive policy for the region. Second, all EU member states had learned lessons from the experiences of the early 1990s. In the course of the intensive work on Balkan issues throughout the 1990s, the EU had developed a common analysis and a shared interest in the stabilisation of the region. There was now sufficient agreement on the objectives to develop a more ambitious policy.

Third, the CFSP had been greatly strengthened with the appointment of Javier Solana as the EU's High Representative in 1999. He and Chris Patten, the European commissioner for external relations, formed a good team and devoted considerable effort to the region. The EU also began to develop its own military commitments enshrined in the Helsinki Headline goals, a target of deploying 60,000 troops in the field for eighteen months for crisis management purposes.[9] Even as these forces were being developed, the EU played a leading role in managing the ethnic crisis in FYROM and in mediating the constitutional dispute between Serbia and Montenegro. Over a period of several years three of the EU's seven Special Representatives dealt with Balkan issues. The EU had also begun to develop a civilian and military operational capacity that in the first instance was deployed in the Balkans. In spring 2003 the EU took over the police operation in Bosnia from the UN. In the summer of the same year it took over from NATO in Macedonia, which in turn was followed by an EU police mission in December 2003.

A year later, an EU force of some 7,000 replaced the NATO SFOR mission in Bosnia. While an outright military confrontation is almost inconceivable today, the challenges in the area of military security are issues of downsizing over expanded armies without causing social disruption, converting the military industry complex to civilian use, and building confidence between armies that in some cases fought each other only a few years ago. On the other hand, fighting organised crime still remains a formidable challenge to most of the countries, with direct implications for the rest of Europe.

Finally, while generally much poorer and further handicapped by the recent conflicts, the Balkan states shared many features with their eastern and northern neighbours. Throughout the 1990s the EU had accumulated vast know-how in promoting the integration of the central and east European countries into European structures. It was logical that this experience would strongly influence its developing approach to the Balkans.

A new approach

In 2000 the EU decided that the western Balkans needed a comprehensive new policy approach. They would continue to deploy their foreign policy and crisis management instruments in order to promote the stabilisation of the region, but they would also hold out the promise of association; integrating the western Balkan countries gradually into European structures. The policy provided for the conclusion of comprehensive treaties with each of the countries, and it deployed important policy instruments, in particular in the areas of trade and assistance. Most importantly, the Stabilization and Association Process (SAP) gave the countries the perspective of future membership in the EU. At first this commitment was expressed rather tentatively, but it gained greater clarity in the course of the following years. A decisive meeting was the EU–Balkans Thessaloniki summit in June 2003 which clearly stated that the future of the Balkans would be in the EU, and that progress in this direction would depend on the fulfilment of the same conditions and requirements that applied to other candidates. This was a reference to the 'Copenhagen criteria' setting down benchmarks for EU candidates relating to democracy, market economy and administrative capability. Moreover, Thessaloniki decided also to put several instruments of the enlargement process (partnerships, opening of Community programmes, administrative twinning, etc.) at the disposal of the west Balkan countries, thus further reducing the gap between the SAP and the pre-accession process.

The perspective of EU membership linked to the step-by-step implementation of the SAP has become the major source of the EU's influence in the region. In its practical application the SAP involves a series of steps, ranging from the establishment of task forces, feasibility studies on an SAA, the beginning, conclusion and finally the ratification of the Agreement. This in turn opens the way to application for membership, launching the candidate country on a similar process ultimately aimed at accession to the EU.

At each of the steps of the SAP, progress is made dependent on the fulfilment of conditions formulated by the EU. The annual reports by the Commission introduced in 2002 are a further way to regularly assess performance. In 2004, European partnerships were also concluded to commit the countries of the region to a set of reform priorities. The assistance offered within the framework of the Community assistance for reconstruction, development and stabilisations (CARDS) programme, much of which is now devoted to institution-building, is also designed to support the same reform priorities.

While important foundations have been laid to improve the economic situation in the region, economic development is probably the biggest concern remaining. Growth rates in Southeastern Europe have risen substantially, but the rates and sustainability of economic growth are still disquieting. This is exacerbated by high unemployment and in parts severe lack of investment. The EU has provided by far the lion's share of external finance, contributing some 6 billion euros to the region in the period 2000–5.

Stability pact

With its threefold aim of stabilising the region, enhancing regional cooperation and supporting the region on its path towards European and Euro-Atlantic integration, the Stability Pact, established in 1999, has supported these positive developments in Southeastern Europe. With two prominent donor conferences in 2000 and 2002 significant donor support could be secured for the region, particularly for upgrading the necessary infrastructure. The focus has subsequently moved towards facilitating regional cooperation and promoting FDI. Attracting foreign direct investments is not possible on a national level considering the size of the market, but the current network of free trade agreements establishes a market of 55 million consumers, clearly more attractive for investment. Regional cooperation in the energy sector is an example of pre-empted sectoral integration into the EU.[10]

Open questions

There are also several open questions in Southeastern Europe that need to be addressed before the region can reasonably become a part of the EU. This does not only apply to Kosovo, where a decision on its status clearly has to be taken before the province can become a part of the EU in whatever form. It is also impossible to envisage Bosnia joining the Union while it is still under the authority of Paddy Ashdown, the High Representative. Similarly, the internal situation of Serbia and Montenegro will have be clarified, an issue which is already holding back the country's progress towards European and Euro-Atlantic integration. Even Croatia, a candidate country by now, still has to address a number of outstanding issues in particular regarding its cooperation with the International Criminal Tribunal for the Former Yugoslavia (ICTY).

Of course, the question of when all of South Eastern Europe will be a part of the EU is still very unclear, and will probably remain so for several years. The EU has come a long way in outlining a roadmap for the region but the timeline is of course dependent on a multitude of factors. The EU itself is preoccupied with coming to terms with the enlargement of 1 May 2004, the largest in the history of the Union. A degree of enlargement fatigue cannot be denied, considering the difficulties ahead. The ratification process of the European Constitution during 2005–06 has also added to the inward looking tendency of the Union. A further complication is the heated discussion on Turkey's accession to the EU.

With the accession of Romania and Bulgaria in 2007, the western Balkans will be an island within the European Union. The EU therefore has a clear interest in ensuring that these outstanding problems are addressed and that Southeastern Europe continues on its current path of stabilisation. In this respect, the clear perspective of European integration is likely to continue to be the key reform incentive in the region. Nevertheless, the necessary steps can only be taken by the governments in Southeastern Europe themselves. The timetable for accession is therefore largely in their own hands.

It is something of a paradox that whereas the overall risk of conflict in the western Balkans has greatly diminished, the EU's involvement in hard security issues in the region is expanding rapidly. The paradox however, is, easily explained by the fact that the development of ESDP really began only at the end of the Balkan wars, and EU military and police operations only became possible at the end of 2002. In view of the important European security interests at stake in the Balkans, it was the logical theatre in which to undertake the first ESDP operations. While the EU may be a latecomer as an operational actor in security policy in the Balkans, there remains much to do. The era of large-scale conflict might be over but, in parts of the region, the potential for interethnic tensions and confrontation persists.

Assessment

In early 2005, the situation in Bosnia could certainly be considered to be essentially stable. In terms of consolidating the state structures and the return of refugees, progress over the past years has been remarkable. However, the reform efforts are not yet self-sustaining, and a significant security presence is still necessary to maintain the commitment to the Dayton Agreement. In Kosovo, the tragic events of March 2004, which caused 19 deaths, the destruction of 730 homes and 29 religious buildings as well as the displacement of over 4,000 people, illustrated clearly that this question remains the greatest challenge to security in the Balkans. Finding an agreement acceptable to both Pristina and Belgrade will be extremely difficult.

The third post-conflict area where the EU remains strongly engaged, Macedonia, has developed encouragingly over the past years. There has been important progress in implementing the Ohrid Agreement and the ethnically mixed government appears committed to multi-ethnicity and to progress towards EU membership. The residual risks in Macedonia are mostly related to the danger of a spillover of a renewed crisis in Kosovo.

Organised crime

While the EU remains deeply involved in seeking to resolve these open questions a new security threat has emerged in the region. As the risk of major conflict has receded, the focus has shifted from the military to the policing aspect. Organised crime, in particular trafficking in humans, drugs and weapons, is today the most pressing security issue, with a clear impact also on EU member states. Widespread poverty, weak state institutions and endemic corruption provide a fertile ground for criminal networks which exploit the traditional transit role of the Balkans into Western Europe. Combating organised crime and bringing war criminals to justice are therefore essential elements of the efforts to consolidate democracy in the western Balkans.

The EU's approach to tackling these problems is multidimensional. It ranges from strict conditionality regarding cooperation with the ICTY in the Hague, to visa bans against individuals supporting war criminals and crime figures linked with extremist political groups, to police operations in Bosnia and Macedonia, to many CARDS programmes in the areas of rule of law and border security. This is complemented by the activities of EUROPOL and EU-sponsored activities within the Stability Pact. The multiplicity of projects and activities, which are complemented by bilateral measures by individual EU member states, cannot hide the fact that the overall record in this field is not altogether encouraging. Nor only is there a distinct deficit in coordination among the various actors in this field but the resources and the manpower deployed are so far no match for the well-financed and smooth international and interethnic cooperation of criminal networks.

Uneven progress

Overall progress in the Balkans is very uneven. By far the most advanced country is Croatia, with Albania lagging far behind. There are several explanations for the marked differences in progress. Historical factors, differences in capacity, constitutional issues and political commitment all play a role. The success of the accession process in central Europe rested to a considerable degree on the fact that the political elites in candidate countries were largely united in their commitment to European integration. Whatever the political complexion of the government, the EU always found a partner willing to take the necessary tough decisions and to move forward on the accession agenda. This is not yet the situation in the western Balkans. The legacy of the wars and structural weaknesses make the political landscape even more volatile and unstable. While almost all political parties pay lip service to the objective of EU membership, the European idea clearly does not yet have the powerful uniting force that it did in Central Europe. All too often the political agenda is dominated by the nationalist past rather than the European future, with the settling of old scores rather than the tackling of concrete challenges.

The EU's promises

Despite the varying degrees of enthusiasm and willingness to take tough decisions, it is important that the EU remains credible in keeping the promises set out at Thessaloniki. At the same time, the perspective of EU membership, although a powerful motor for reform, will not work without significant institutional and financial engagement. This may mean a change in the approach to funding for the region. The original idea of turning the status of 'Associate' (following the conclusion of an

SAA) into an attractive longer-term option for the countries of the region has clearly not worked out as expected. Both Croatia and Macedonia submitted their applications for membership long before their SAA entered into force. The other countries of the region are likely to follow their example. An SAA is not seen as an objective in its own right, but merely as a stepping-stone towards pre-accession status.

This view is perfectly understandable, since EU accession remains the ultimate objective and every country wishes to move towards the next stage as quickly as possible. But it is also reinforced by the EU's current funding policy. Enjoying pre-accession status is much more attractive financially than the CARDS assistance open to SAP countries. Thus the most developed countries enjoy the most generous EU assistance, a situation that is questionable in terms of both fairness and the overall development of the region. In the future Financial Perspectives for the period 2007–12 the CARDS programme and the pre-accession instruments could be amalgamated in a single assistance programme that would serve both the pre-accession and the SAP countries. This would still allow for differentiation, but with greater flexibility than has been the case so far.

Conclusion

The EU now has a stronger profile in the Balkans than ever before. Five years of the SAP process have produced sufficient progress to validate the overall policy approach, but clearly not enough to allow complacency. During this time the western Balkans have undoubtedly become more stable and the EU has become an operational actor also in the area of 'hard' security. Opening the perspective of EU membership to the countries of the region has had some important successes, notably in Croatia and Macedonia, but has not yet had its full mobilising impact in other parts of the region. Economic growth in the western Balkans rose above 4 per cent in 2003 for the fourth consecutive year, but all the countries continue to face significant structural challenges, in particular the decline of the old industries and underdeveloped agriculture. High unemployment and severe social problems continue to overshadow an essentially positive macroeconomic picture.

Throughout the 1990s the western Balkans was nearly always the top priority of EU foreign ministers. Today, the Middle East, Iraq, Afghanistan, the struggle against terrorism and WMD proliferation sometimes have an equal or higher priority on the agenda. Competition for the attention of decision-makers, but also for the administrative and financial resources of the EU, has become fierce. Yet there can be no doubt that because of its geographical proximity and the EU's massive involvement over the past decade, the western Balkans remain a central challenge for the EU's external relations. The stability of the region is intrinsically linked to that of the EU. If Bulgaria and Romania join the EU as planned in 2007, the western Balkans will turn into an EU enclave on the Mediterranean. As Paddy Ashdown has stated, the EU will either succeed in absorbing this region successively into its own structures or risk importing instability in various forms, including through uncontrolled migration and illegal trafficking.[11]

The EU's credibility as an international actor thus depends to a large extent on its success in the Balkans. If it fails to ensure lasting stability in its immediate neighbourhood, it need hardly try elsewhere. Moreover, the time when it was possible to shift responsibility onto Washington's shoulders has probably gone for ever. The United States will continue to play an important role in the Balkans, but in view of its worldwide commitments and changed priorities it will no longer be prepared to assume the leading role.

Unlike 1991, the EU today has the experience, the instruments and the appropriate strategic concept to help the West Balkan countries meet the challenges at hand. What is now required, first and foremost, is the determination and staying power to build on the progress achieved and to bring – in close cooperation with its partners in the region – the 'Europeanisation of the Balkans' to a successful conclusion. The EU's involvement in the Balkans has thus pushed it to develop a greater range of external policy instruments. The 2004 constitution provides for further steps forward with the creation of a minister for foreign affairs and an EU diplomatic service. Although the EU's involvement in the Balkans has been a difficult learning experience, it has led the EU to become a much stronger foreign policy actor and the principal stabilising actor across the continent of Europe.

Notes

1 See the European Commission's website for full details http://www.europa.eu.int

2 The unfortunate phrase used by Luxembourg's foreign minister, Jacques Poos.

3 Fraser Cameron, *The Foreign and Security Policy of the European Union, Past, Present and Future*, Sheffield: Sheffield Academic Press, 1999.

4 The European Commission's Eurobarometer polls have consistently shown high support for CFSP. See also Richard Sinnot, 'European public opinion and security policy', Chaillot Paper 28, July 1997.

5 Christopher Hill, 'The capability-expectations gap, or conceptualizing Europe's international role', *Journal of Common Market Studies*, 31, 3 (1993), 305–28.

6 Assessments of the new constitutional treaty and its likely impact on the CFSP are to be found on the websites of the European Policy Centre, www.theEPC.be, the Federal Trust, www.fedtrust.co.uk, and the foreign policy network, www.fornet.info.

7 For different perspectives see Richard Holbrooke, *To End a War*, New York: Random House, 1988; Carl Bildt, *Peace Journey*, London: Weidenfeld & Nicholson, 1998; David Owen, *Balkan Odyssey*, London: Cassell, 1995; Sophie Clement, 'Conflict prevention in the Balkans', Chaillot Paper 30, October 1997.

8 Wesley Clark, *Waging War*, New York: Random House, 2001.

9 See Fraser Cameron and Gerard Quille, *The ESDP State of Play*, EPC Working Paper number 12.

10 See www.stabilitypact.org

11 Conversation with the author, November 2004.

9 The disintegration of Yugoslavia, Macedonia's independence and stability in the Balkans

Andrew Rossos

The declaration of independence by the Republic of Macedonia in September 1991, in the wake of the bloody disintegration of the Yugoslav Federation, provoked a dangerous political and diplomatic crisis.[1] Potentially, it posed a far greater threat to Balkan and European peace and stability than the war to the north in Slovenia, Croatia and Bosnia-Hercegovina. Saying this is not to minimise in any way the inhumanity and the tremendous suffering caused by the war in the north. However, at that time, a war over Macedonia would have been, from the very outset, a much wider conflict, an international war. It would have involved not only former republics of Yugoslavia, but all of Macedonia's neighbours and possibly Turkey, and since Greece and Turkey were certain to be on opposite sides, it would have become the first armed conflict between two member countries of the NATO alliance.

This crisis was the result of the determined opposition, in some cases direct and open and in others indirect and concealed, of the neighbouring Balkan states to the establishment of an independent Macedonian state. The reasons for it are obvious. All of Macedonia's neighbours either consistently or at one time or another chose to deny the existence of a Macedonian people, and hence its right to possess its own state and to claim Macedonia and the Macedonians as their own. Although their irreconcilably contradictory aspirations in Macedonia could not be fully or equally satisfied, all of them had benefited from the partition of Macedonia by force of arms in the Balkan wars of 1912–13. Since then they had shown great determination to safeguard and, if at all possible, expand their respective Macedonian territorial possessions. All of them viewed the establishment of the small independent republic as a threat to their past gains or future aspirations in Macedonia, and considered or rejected the new state as an artificial creation.[2]

The breakdown and collapse of the Yugoslav Federation did not create the Macedonian problem. This problem had been the central issue dividing the Balkan states at least since the 1878 Congress of

Berlin. The Macedonian problem was an essential issue in four wars – the first and the second Balkan Wars, World War I and World War II, in which Balkan states participated, mainly fighting each other over Macedonia.

In addition to that, it was also the central issue in numerous *coups d'états*, government crises, political assassinations, etc., in almost every Balkan country since the Congress of Berlin.[3] However, the declaration of Macedonian independence did force the so-called Macedonian question once again to the forefront of Balkan politics.

In this chapter, I shall argue first of all, that the establishment of the new independent Republic of Macedonia constituted the only viable solution of the Macedonian problem at the time; and second, that the acceptance, not just the pro-forma recognition, but the acceptance of Macedonia, of its right to exist, by its neighbours is the best and, indeed, the only genuine guarantee of stability in the southern Balkans.

Macedonia and the Macedonians did not play a decisive or even a major role in the bloody disintegration of Yugoslavia. Membership in the Federation provided the Macedonians with a sense of security against unfriendly, even antagonistic neighbouring states – Bulgaria, Greece and, to a certain extent, Albania – and a condescending and patronising partner or neighbour inside Yugoslavia, namely Serbia. However, the attack of the Yugoslav national army and the spilling of blood in Slovenia and Croatia forced the Macedonian leaders from the federal and republican levels to face reality and accept the fact that the federal Yugoslavia, which provided for them a balance of sorts between external security and a limited but clearly defined autonomy, had ceased to exist. They had to seek and consider alternative solutions to the question of national survival.

In the summer of 1991, several solutions of the Macedonian problem were rumoured or considered in the capitals of the neighbouring Balkan states. One called for the incorporation of Macedonia into a third, or what was sarcastically referred to at the time as a reduced, Yugoslavia. This was the preferred solution of Belgrade and Athens. Without Croatia and Slovenia to counterbalance the predominance of the Serbs, however, the Macedonians would have found themselves in an extremely weak and unfavourable position in the new so-called Federation. Consequently, this option was entirely unacceptable to the Macedonians and they rejected it from the outset. Another option, at one time or another ascribed to Athens and Belgrade, and to a lesser extent also Tirana and even Sofia, proposed a partition of the republic among the four neighbours. In view of their irreconcilably contradictory aims that have traditionally divided them, it is virtually certain that any attempt to partition the republic would have resulted in an international war. It would have been impossible for them to agree on the terms of such a partition. Bulgaria would have claimed important areas, especially the historic medieval places (Ohrid, Struga, St Naum), which are in the immediate vicinity of the Albanian frontier, and would have clashed with both Albania and Serbia. Serbia and Bulgaria would have struggled also for control of the north, including Skopje, the capital city. And Bulgaria and Greece would have fought over the south of the republic and the city of Bitola. It would have been impossible for them to agree on the terms of a peaceful partition; hence, an international war would have been unavoidable. In any event, neither of these two options, incorporating or forcing Macedonia into reduced Yugoslavia or partitioning Macedonia, was acceptable to the Macedonians. Instead of resolving the Macedonian problem, both of these rumoured proposals would have turned Macedonia more than ever before into the powder keg of Europe and the 'apple of discord' in the Balkans. They would have, in effect, institutionalised instability in the region.

The third option, the one that was considered most seriously inside the republic, was the declaration of complete sovereignty and independence. It was the only option acceptable to the Macedonian majority of the population, as well as to the overwhelming majority of the total population of the republic; this included the Albanians of Macedonia who, for other reasons, chose to boycott the actual referendum on independence on 8 September 1991. The establishment of the independent republic of Macedonia was then and remains today the only viable, realistic and practical resolution of the Macedonian problem. For the first time in the long history of the Macedonian question, the people of this part of Macedonia – both ethnic Macedonians and those belonging to the other nationalities – were free to decide democratically their own fate and future. This was and remains an indispensable precondition to any lasting settlement of the Macedonian problem, which in turn is indispensable for stability in the Balkan Peninsula.

This leads me to my second major argument, namely, that stability in Macedonia, and consequently peace in the region, could only be attained through the acceptance, not just formal recognition, of the existence of a Macedonian nation and the new Macedonian state by its neighbours. This is not to suggest that the new state does not face other internal, serious problems. It has major social, economic and educational problems, and faces serious tensions caused by the ethnic divisions within the republic. However, these internal or domestic issues and challenges can be tackled only in an atmosphere of external, or at least greater external, security as evidenced by the events in 2001 when violence in Kosovo spilled over into Macedonia.[4] This is particularly true of the greatest problem that the republic has faced over the past few years, namely the tensions that divide the ethnic Macedonian majority and the ethnic Albanians of the republic. From its inception as an independent state, Macedonia has been governed democratically, at least in Balkan terms. It met all the conditions for recognition imposed by the European community, now the European Union, already in the autumn of 1991, and apart from Slovenia was the first to enter into a Stabilisation and Association Agreement with Brussels. These included establishing policies towards national minorities, which is more than can be said about other former Yugoslav republics,[5] or the treatment accorded to Macedonian minorities in neighbouring Balkan states.[6] From the beginning, Macedonia accepted the existing borders and made no territorial claims against any of its neighbours. Even though some Macedonian nationalists or nationalist leaders may dream about or may voice the dream of Great Macedonia, the republic does not possess the means to threaten any of its neighbours, let alone to challenge the existing territorial status quo. It does not have the resources, the manpower or the will.

Nevertheless, even though this small republic does not threaten any of them, the neighbouring Balkan states responded to the declaration of Macedonian independence with hostility. In some cases this hostility was direct and open, as was the case with Greece and Serbia. In other cases, it was indirect and concealed, as was the case with Albania and Bulgaria. These hostile reactions and the resulting lack of international recognition, the isolation, the boycotts, the economic embargoes, etc. complicated Macedonia's transition from communism to democracy and from a dependent federal republic to an independent state, in the most difficult initial half decade of independent existence.[7] As a result, these reactions created further internal problems for the struggling state and set the stage for ethnic tension.[8] More than anything else, these factors also kept the so-called Macedonian problem as a potential flash point of an international conflagration in the region.

Since the troubles in Tetovo, Macedonia's position in the Balkans and internationally appears to have improved and much diplomatic ground has been recovered. The conclusion of the Interim Accord with Greece in New York in September 1995 and the establishment of diplomatic relations with Yugoslavia in early 1996, after the signing of the Dayton Accords, completed the formal recognition of the new state by its neighbours. This undoubtedly contributed to the easing of tensions in the republic and in the region as a whole until the Kosovo crisis spilled over in 2001.

However, a grudging, conditional recognition of the country, especially when achieved mainly as a result of strong international pressure, as was the case in both the Serbian and the Greek recognition, is not enough to ensure long-term stability. It is not the same as the acceptance of both the Macedonian nation and the country, and it is unfortunate that for most of Macedonia's independence its neighbours failed to accept Macedonia genuinely and unconditionally as a nation and a state. Bulgaria was among the first to recognise Macedonia as a state but continues to deny the existence of a Macedonian identity, a Macedonian nation, and considers the Macedonians to be Bulgarians.[9] Greece now recognises the existence of a country to the north, but for many years denied it the right to use its constitutional name, Macedonia, and thus denies also the existence of a Macedonian identity and nation.[10]

Having recognized the Macedonians officially for more than half a century, it would be awkward and difficult for Yugoslavia or, more specifically, Serbia to deny their national identity and existence now. However, it is not entirely clear how seriously certain elements in Belgrade accept the sovereignty and territorial integrity of the state. It is also worth noting that influential Serbian politicians such as the indicted war criminal Vojislav Šešelj refer to Macedonia as South Serbia and to the Macedonians as South Serbians, as their counterparts did in pre-World War II royalist Yugoslavia. Finally, the Albanian position is a little bit more ambiguous. It has fluctuated between recognition and questioning of the existence of both the nation and the state, reflecting Tirana's ambivalent and changing perception of the treatment of the substantial Albanian national minority in the Republic of Macedonia.

What is needed now, especially while Kosovo remains a source of insecurity and vulnerability, is the genuine acceptance by Macedonia's neighbours of the existence of a Macedonian identity, nation and state. The United States and European Union should work towards this goal, which will in turn contribute to greater internal stability and security – a necessary precondition for Macedonia's transition to democracy and a market economy, and for enlightened interethnic relations. As the events in 2001 demonstrated, as long as Macedonia's neighbours, the traditional claimants to the territory and its inhabitants, do not do so, Macedonia will remain a potential 'tinderbox' of the Balkans and of Europe.

Throughout this chapter, I have stressed that with the disintegration of federal Yugoslavia, there was no other and certainly no better solution of the Macedonian problem than the declaration of independence. The time has come for a historic accommodation between the Macedonians and their neighbours; the precondition for that is the genuine acceptance by the latter of a Macedonian identity, nation and state. Indeed, by now this has become a Balkan necessity. There is no other acceptable solution.

Historians have debated and argued and will continue to debate and argue questions relating to the formation of the Macedonian identity. It is a controversial issue and arguments continue. However, there is and there can be no doubt that a Macedonian nation exists. Denying the existence of the Macedonians did not help solve the Macedonian problem and did not contribute to Balkan stability in the past, and it will not do so in the future. Only a settlement that recognises the Macedonians and respects their national rights would be of lasting value and would contribute to stability and tranquillity in Southeastern Europe.[11]

Notes

1 Portions of this chapter have been incorporated in my lengthy overview of the Macedonian question since the nineteenth century, published in Norman Naimark and Holly Case (eds.), *Yugoslavia and its Historians: Understanding the Balkan Wars of the 1990s*, Stanford, CA: Stanford University Press, 2003. I have previously commented on some of the themes in this chapter in my earlier writings: Andrew Rossos, *Russia and the Balkans: Inter-Balkan Rivalries and Russian Foreign Policy 1908–1914*, Toronto: University of Toronto Press, 1981; 'The Macedonians of Aegean Macedonia: A British officer's report, 1944', *Slavonic and East European Review*, 69, 2 (1991): 282–309; 'The British Foreign Office and Macedonian national identity, 1918–1941', *Slavic Review*, 53, 2 (1994): 369–94; and more recently, 'Macedonianism and Macedonian nationalism on the left', in Ivo Banac and Katherine Verdery, eds., *National Character and National Ideology in Interwar Eastern Europe*, New Haven: Yale Center for International and Area Studies, 1995, and 'Incompatible allies: Greek communism and Macedonian nationalism in the civil war in Greece, 1943–1949', *Journal of Modern History*, 69, 1 (1997): 42–76.

2 Much scholarship on this theme covers the most important manifestations of the so-called Macedonian question since the 1878 Congress of Berlin: the Macedonian problem in general, the development of Macedonian nationalism, the partition of Macedonia in 1912–13, the situation of the Macedonians in divided Macedonia, the establishment of the Macedonian Republic in the Yugoslav Federation at the end of World War II, and the crisis surrounding the declaration of independence in 1991.

3 Duncan Perry, *The Politics of Terror: The Macedonian Revolutionary Movement, 1893–1903*, Durham, NC: Duke University Press, 1988. For an early account, see Elisabeth Barker, *Macedonia: Its Place in Balkan Power Politics*, London, 1950 (reprint, Westport, CT: Greenwood Press, 1980).

4 For a good account of the impact of the skirmishes, see Robert Hislope, 'Between a bad peace and a good war: insights and lessons from the almost-war in Macedonia', *Ethnic and Racial Studies*, 26, 1 2003, 129–51.

5 See Human Rights Watch, 'Human Rights in the Former Yugoslav Republic of Macedonia', 1994.
6 See Duncan M. Perry, 'The Republic of Macedonia: finding its way', in Karen Dawisha and Bruce Parrot, eds., *Politics, Power and the Struggle for Democracy in South-East Europe*, Cambridge: Cambridge University Press, 1997, 226–81 and Hugh Poulton, *Balkans: Minorities and States in Conflict*, London: Minority Rights Group, 1993.
7 For a review of the Greece–Macedonia struggles, see John Shea, *Macedonia and Greece: The Struggle to Define a New Balkan Nation*, Jefferson, NC: McFarland, 1997. See also Janusz Bugajski, *Ethnic Politics in Eastern Europe*, Armonk, NY: M.E. Sharpe, and Loring M. Danforth, *The Macedonian Conflict: Ethnic Nationalism in a Transnational World*, Princeton: Princeton University Press, 1995.
8 Hislope, 'Between a bad peace and a good war'.
9 Human Rights Watch / Helsinki Watch, *Destroying Ethnic Identity: Selective Persecution of Macedonians in Bulgaria*, New York 1991.
10 See Human Rights Watch / Helsinki Watch, *Greece: Free Speech on Trial: Government Stifles Dissent on Macedonia*, New York: 1993; and *Denying Ethnic Identity: The Macedonians of Greece*, New York: 1994. Also, Anastasia Karakasidou, 'Politicizing culture: negating ethnic identity in Greek Macedonia', *Journal of Modern Greek Studies*, 11 (1993), 1–28.
11 The scholarly writings below appeared in the last three decades and together cover the most important manifestations of the so-called Macedonian question since the 1878 Congress of Berlin: the Macedonian problem in general, the development of Macedonian nationalism, the partition of Macedonia in 1912–13, the situation of the Macedonians in divided Macedonia, the establishment of the Macedonian Republic in the Yugoslav Federation at the end of World War II, and the crisis surrounding the declaration of independence in 1991. Additional resources in English include Fikret Adanir, 'The Macedonians in the Ottoman Empire, 1878–1912', in Andreas Koppeler, ed., *The Formation of National Elites*, New York: New York University Press, 1992. pp. 161–90; and 'The socio-political environment of Balkan nationalism: the case of Ottoman Macedonia, 1856–1912', in Heinz-Gerhard Haupt, Michael G. Müller and Stuart Woolf, eds., *National Identities in Europe in the XIXth and XXth Centuries*, The Hague: Kluwer Law International, 1998 pp. 221–54; Ksente Bogoev, 'The Macedonian Revolutionary Organization (V.M.R.O.) in the past hundred years', *Macedonian Review*, 23, 2–3 (1993), 118–28; Victor A. Friedman, 'Macedonian language and nationalism during the nineteenth and early twentieth centuries', *Balkanistica*, 2 (1975), 83–98 and 'The sociolinguistics of literary Macedonian', *International Journal of the Sociology of Language*, 52 (1985), 31–57; Karakasidou, 'Politicizing culture'; Ivan Katardzhiev, AI. M. O. R. O., in two parts, *Macedonian Review*, 20, 1–2 (1990), 31–49, and 20, 3, (1990), 139–61; Horace G. Lunt, 'Some sociolinguistic aspects of Macedonian and Bulgarian', in Benjamin Stolz, I.R. Titunik and Lubomir Dolezel, eds., *Language and Literary Theory*, Ann Arbor, MI: Michigan Slavic Publications, 1984, pp. 83–132; Krste P. Misirkov, *On Macedonian Matters*, trans. Alan McConnell, Skopje: Macedonian Review Editions, 1974. This important

work was originally published in Macedonian, in Sofia, in 1903; Stoyan Pribichevich, *Macedonia: Its People and History*, University Park: Pennsylvania University Press, 1982; Sabrina P. Ramet, 'The Macedonian enigma', in Sabrina P. Ramet and Ljubica S. Adamovich, eds., *Beyond Yugoslavia: Politics, Economics and Culture in a Shattered Community*, Boulder, CO: Westview Press, 1995. and Stefan Troebst, 'Yugoslav Macedonia, 1944–1953: building the party, the state and the nation', *Berliner Jahrbuch für osteuropäische Geschichte*, 1 (1994), 103–39.

10   The war in Croatia

Branka Magas

In his *Origins of a catastrophe*, Warren Zimmermann[1] describes how in late 1989 Washington endorsed Yugoslavia's unity out of fear of war and betting on Prime Minister Ante Marković's ability to deliver salvation through economic reform. Already that bet, in a sense, was lost. The events of 1989 had already set the ground for Yugoslavia's disintegration. During this time Serbia was making itself a wholly independent state and the JNA was enforcing its claims through violence, by shooting demonstrators in Kosovo. At the same time, Slovenia was moving towards independence through constitutional amendments that sought to free it from the Socialist Federal Republic. However, the most decisive outcome of all was Croatia's decision to hold multiparty elections.

The policy of keeping Yugoslavia together, which was understandable, if extremely optimistic at the time, became unsustainable once the Yugoslav People's Army failed to pacify Slovenia. This was the case not only because of this army's humiliating defeat in Slovenia which set off an irreversible process of its fragmentation into national components and the Serbianisation of essential structures, but also because the outcome of the war in Slovenia spelled the end of Yugoslavia.

After June 1991, there were only two options left: a 'peace option' and a 'war option'. The peace option involved immediate and unhesitating international support for the independence of Yugoslavian constituent states under lines established by the European Union's Badinter Commission. Delaying recognition, on the other hand, meant waiting for new political borders to be established by further use of armed force.

The United States, by insisting on Yugoslav unity at this point in time, inexplicably chose the latter – the war option. In other words, the future of what remained of Yugoslavia and Bosnia-Hercegovina in particular was left to be determined by war – that is, by the outcome of the war in Croatia. Although the start of the war in Croatia formed a seamless unity with a subsequent one in Bosnia-Hercegovina, in the strategic and operational senses alike, it was the Croatian operation that set the stage for what was subsequently to happen in Bosnia-Hercegovina.

In July of 1991, it was already clear that the military defeat of Croatia would result in a drastic revision of political borders leading to the emergence of a greater Serbia, and it was equally clear that a Croatian victory would put a stop to that project. In order to judge the American attitude at that point in time, it is necessary to describe Serbian and Croatian war aims.[2] Norman Cigar's work, which draws extensively on press sources in former Yugoslavia, illustrates just how transparent were these approaches in Zagreb and Belgrade to the issues of war and peace.[3]

Starting with Serbia first as the party which initiated the war, its proclaimed aim was to protect the Serbs in Croatia or, rather, to act as guarantor of their rights to self-determination and secession in accordance with the broader aim of bringing all Serbs within the confines of a single state, a greater Serbia, which its leaders for various important reasons continued to call Yugoslavia. To give tangible expression to that right, the Republic of Srpska Krajina was proclaimed on Croatian territory.

Serbia's real war aim, however, was quite simply to expand westward over a territory whose ethnic make-up was of secondary importance. In this expansion, the main prize was sought. What was sought was the occupation of most, if not all, of Bosnia-Hercegovina. The extent of the territory to be taken from Croatia itself was, for various reasons, never clearly specified and it was left to the war, to the course of the war, to determine its size. In its early days there was much talk about the Virovitica-Karlovac line being the new western border of Serbia which would have taken the whole of Slovenia and the whole of Dalmatia and added it to Serbia. At all events, much of the territory Belgrade intended to seize from Croatia contained an ethnically mixed population. Given the chosen ideological justification for the war, the Serb people's right to secede and join Serbia, the territory's exclusively Serb character had to be constructed *post facto* by the practice of what came to be called 'ethnic cleansing'.

The establishment of a new state frontier involved from the start the drawing of a new ethnic border. It was therefore not necessary to wait for the war in Bosnia-Hercegovina to realise that Milošević was waging war in ethnic terms and that any delay in recognising the existing political borders would only serve to encourage solutions relying on ethnic separation in an area in which this could be achieved only by relying on genocidal means. I wish to emphasise here that Belgrade's war against Croatia did not enjoy much support among Serbs either in Serbia or in Croatia, and a description of it in the Western press as an ethnic war between Croats and Serbs simply parroted Milošević's propaganda.[4]

Croatia's war aims were more complex. The Croatian leaders were also engaged in two parallel wars; one of which was very much a public concern while the other one was kept secret. To say this is not to argue that there was a complete symmetry between the positions of Croatia and Serbia or that one was confronted by two equally blind nationalisms. Serbia's war was one of aggression. Croatia's primarily one of national survival. By contrast with the situation in Serbia, the Croatian state had no problem in mobilising its population for the war. The Croatian people were motivated by the desire, indeed the need, to defeat the JNA, liberate all of Croatia and win international recognition.

However, the Croatian leadership, and here I mean first and foremost the former president, Franjo Tudjman, had an additional war aim that was kept secret from public knowledge. This was to annex a significant part of Bosnia-Hercegovina under the pretext of uniting all Croats. This plan of territorial enlargement did not include parts of Vojvodina settled by Croats. These people, these Croats, were instead offered resettlement in Croatia which, as a matter of fact, they refused. Greater Croatia as envisaged by Tudjman was likewise conceived as an ethnically pure state, to be realised, for its so-called humane exchange of populations that would also entail the removal of most, if not all, Serbs from Croatia. The Croatian Serbs both outside and inside of the Republic of Krajina became hostages in this way to Milošević's and Tudjman's secret war policy.

As the war intensified, after August 1991, so did the Croatian state's acts of terror against Serbs living under its control. The policy was there before but the incidents and scope of this terror increased significantly after the war intensified in the second half of 1991 and continued throughout 1992. It hasn't really stopped to this very day.[5]

It was after meeting with Milošević in Karadjordjevo in March 1991 that Tudjman became convinced that the partition of Bosnia-Hercegovina was a practical proposition, that it would provide the basis for a peaceful settlement of the conflict between Serbia and Croatia, and that this resolution would be acceptable to the international community. It must be said, there was nothing in the leaders' subsequent behaviour that left any room to question this conviction.

Unlike Serbian war policy, Croatia's was thus essentially contradictory. On the one hand, it involved the defence of western borders and Serbia's defeat. On the other hand, for Croatia to expand into Bosnia-Hercegovina, cooperation with Serbia was necessary – not war or a full Serbian defeat – particularly as Serbia, unlike Croatia, had the military means, or so it seemed in 1991, to enforce Bosnia's partition. This contradiction had a direct and lasting impact on Croatia's defence effort.

For much of 1991, Croatia's entire self-defence effort was over-shadowed and hampered by Tudjman's pursuit of a negotiated settle-ment with Milošević, for which much of the cost was to be borne by Bosnia-Hercegovina, and a considerable part of it also by Croatia itself. It was only in September 1991 when Croatia was faced with outright military defeat that the country's defence gained priority over the pursuit of Bosnia's partition. When this did happen, however, within two months the war turned to Croatia's advantage, particularly in Slavonia. Even during this period, Tudjman never broke off negotiations with Milošević, signing a string of cease-fires that caused great consternation, indeed sometimes outright disobedience among Croatian military commanders. His seemingly irrational behaviour at that fateful time for the country can be explained only by the desire to keep open the question of the borders in preparation for the coming war in Bosnia-Hercegovina.

In November 1991, Milošević, with his army in disarray and fearing a total defeat, broke with his previous policy and asked the Security Council for UN troops to be sent to what was described as Serb majority areas but which were, in reality, simply all those areas which the JNA held at that point in time. Despite the fact that the Croatian army was by now capable of liberating the whole of the country, Tudjman accepted a proposal for a permanent cease-fire, the deployment of UN soldiers in Croatia and the terms brokered by US envoy Cyrus Vance which left open the question of Croatian borders.

The JNA was permitted under the terms of the Vance plan to move the bulk of its forces out of this part of Croatia into Bosnia-Hercegovina. What was to appear as a peace option, stopping the war in Croatia, was in reality nothing but a green light for the war to move to Bosnia-Hercegovina, which could not happen as long as the JNA had yet to disengage from Croatia. The JNA was permitted to move its forces and weapons into Bosnia so the transfer of war from Croatia into Bosnia was in fact remarkably swift. Republika Srpska was proclaimed on the 9 January 1992, just one week after the cease-fire was signed by Gojko Susak and Veljko Kadijević in Sarajevo, of all places. Five days later, Tudjman told Zimmermann something that the US ambassador already knew, namely that he and Milošević had agreed to Bosnia's partition and that Croatia would be happy with less than 50 per cent.

War thus came to Bosnia well in advance of the 24 January decision of its parliament to conduct a referendum on the basis of which it would ask for recognition. It did that, in fact, against the express advice of the American ambassador. The United States instead backed the European plan for an ethnically based division of Bosnia even though it was well aware, to judge by Zimmermann's account, that an equitable settlement even on those terms was unlikely in view of Serbia's intention to tear away two tiers of Bosnia and incorporate them into Serbia. It was only after Slovenia and Croatia were recognized by the European Community against American wishes at the time, and after Karadžić predictably had rejected the Cutileiro plan, that the United States took the decision to recognise Bosnia-Hercegovina.

Why Washington recognised Bosnia in principle while in practice condoning deals made at its expense is something that requires an explanation. Any explanation of the United States' state of mind must derive from the way in which the war had ended in Croatia – the Vance plan did not simply accept a situation created on the ground by successful aggression. On the contrary, it helped freeze the existing situation on the ground even though from the military point of view Serbia's armed presence in Croatia had become untenable.

It may be safely maintained that an outright Croatian defeat of Serbia in 1991 would have minimised the chances of the war spreading into Bosnia-Hercegovina but, for some reason, Washington avoided that outcome. It remains to be seen, therefore, why the United States, after letting Serbia break the political impasse by going to war against first Slovenia and then Croatia, intervened to stave off a Serbian defeat at Croatia's hands. It was as if this outcome, the freezing of the established front lines in Croatia, permitted both Serbia and Croatia to pursue, sometimes in opposition but on the whole cooperatively, their annexationist aims in Bosnia and Hercegovina.

It is possible, indeed likely, that Washington had come to accept Milošević's and Tudjman's dubious views that peace in former Yugoslavia could be achieved and built upon on the basis of pre-drawing political and ethnic borders in Croatia and Bosnia-Hercegovina. However, since a peaceful partition of Bosnia-Hercegovina was always impossible, the only question remaining unanswered at the start of 1992 was just how much violence such a partition would entail. Moreover, it seems that everyone counted on an early Bosnian surrender.

Bosnian powers of resistance were not part of the American policy equation. However, as in the case of Croatia, and Bosnia too, it was the formation of a large and motivated defence force that completely altered the situation.[6] The Washington Agreement terminating the war between Croatia and Bosnia followed an effective Croatian defeat. The Dayton Agreement was reached after Serbia's forces in Bosnia-Hercegovina had been brought to near defeat. Nevertheless, and this is the curious thing, whether Washington and the Dayton Agreement, just like the Vance plan before them, were dropped in a way that helped weaken the existing political borders in favour of the newly forged ethnic ones, American policy at least up to now appears to have involved a surprisingly persistent underestimation of just how important the established political borders between the successor states of former Yugoslavia are for peace and stability in the region. More than that, in view of the JNA's poor performance in Slovenia and then Croatia and then Bosnia-Hercegovina, and if anything an even worse performance of the Serbian and Croatian proxy armies in Bosnia-Hercegovina, where they acted together against an initially unarmed and isolated Bosnian defence, indeed against civilians to begin with, they failed to subdue Bosnia. In view of all of this, it would be fair to conclude that the US indecision in regard to the continuity of the Bosnian state was a decisive factor in the extension and perpetuation of the war in the Balkans.

Notes

1 Warren Zimmermann, *Origins of a Catastrophe*, New York: New York Times Books, 1996.
2 Here I would like to acknowledge my debt to Professor Norman Cigar for his invaluable analysis of the war in Croatia and Bosnia-Hercegovina.
3 See Norman Cigar, *Genocide in Bosnia: The Policy of Ethnic Cleansing*, College Station, TX: Texas A and M University Press, 1995.
4 The numbers of young people who fled Yugoslavia, rather than be conscripted into the military, was especially notable. Over 500,000 young professionals fled Serbia creating a lasting brain drain. For a good discussion of the effects of brain drain in the form of skilled and unskilled emigration from Yugoslavia and its impact on Western Europe, see Aleksandar Bogojevic, 'Brain drain project' http://www.braindrain.eu.org/objectives.htm and Thomas Straubhaar, *International Mobility of the Highly Skilled: Brain Gain, Brain Drain or Brain Exchange*, HWWA Discussion Paper 88, Hamburgisches Welt-Wirtschafts-Archiv (HWWA), Hamburg Institute of International Economics 2000. http://www.hwwa.de/Publikationen/Discussion_Paper/2000/88.pdf
5 Several human rights agencies have chronicled acts of violence and discrimination against Serbs in Croatia. See Minority Rights Group International, *Minorities in Croatia*, London: Minority Rights Group International (September 2003); *Human Rights Watch 2003: Broken Promises: Impediments to Refugee Return to Croatia*. (http://www.hrw.org/reports/2003/croatia0903/croatia0903.pdf); Organisation for Security and Cooperation in Europe, *OSCE Status Report No. 12, Assessment of Issues Covered by the OSCE Mission to the Republic of Croatia's Mandate since 12 November 200*. 3 July 2003; (http://www.osce.org/documents/mc/2003/07/450_en.pdf)
6 See Marko Hoare, *How Bosnia Armed*, London: SAQI Books, 2004.

11 Negotiating peace in Croatia: a personal account of the road to Erdut

Peter Galbraith

Of the three United States brokered agreements that ended the wars in the former Yugoslavia, the Erdut Agreement stands out for its relative success in recreating a multi-ethnic society in a war-ravaged region. Signed 12 November 1995, the Erdut Agreement ended the war in Croatia by peacefully reintegrating Serb-held Eastern Slavonia into Croatia's constitutional and legal order. Solving the Eastern Slavonia issue was an essential precondition to the peace agreement for Bosnia-Hercegovina that was concluded in Dayton nine days later. The Erdut Agreement also provided the legal basis for the United Nations Transitional Administration for Eastern Slavonia (UNTAES), one of the UN's most successful peacekeeping operations and one that helped restore the organization's prestige in a region where it had been badly battered by its perceived ineffectiveness in halting the worst abuses of the Yugoslav wars.

From the start of his administration, President Clinton based US policy in the former Yugoslavia on three principles: (1) the territorial integrity of the successor states of former Yugoslavia; (2) the right of refugees and displaced persons to return to their homes, to recover their property, and to live in security; and (3) justice for those who were victims of war crimes. These principles are at the core of the three US-negotiated peace agreements: the 1994 Washington Agreement ending the Muslim–Croat War in Bosnia by establishing the Federation of Bosnia-Hercegovina, the Erdut Agreement, and the Dayton Agreement.

Early on, the Clinton administration recognised the potentially decisive role Croatia could play in ending the war in Bosnia-Hercegovina. This recognition lay behind the 17 February 1994 proposal Special Envoy Charles Redman and I put to Croatian President Tudjman: If Croatia would give up its ambition for a separate Croat republic in Bosnia-Hercegovina – an ambition that was fuelling a three-sided conflict in Bosnia that seemed to be irresolvable – the United States would support generous power sharing for ethnic Croats in a Muslim-Croat Federation, would support Croatia's goal of closer relations with the West, and would work diplomatically for a political solution within Croatia's internationally recognised borders of the Serb-occupied territories.

After some hesitation, Tudjman accepted our proposal with dramatic results for the Bosnian War. Almost instantly, the Muslim-Croat War ended and in its place came an alliance among Croatia, the Bosnian Croats and the Muslim-led Bosnian government. Within eighteen months this alliance (aided by NATO airstrikes) reversed Serb military gains in Croatia and Bosnia, paving the way to the two peace agreements (Erdut and Dayton) that ended the war.

The day President Tudjman and I returned from the signing of the Washington Agreement, I began work as the principal US negotiator charged with finding a political settlement in Croatia. The 1991 war had left Belgrade-backed Serbs in control of 27 per cent of Croatia's territory in three geographically distinct areas: (1) the Krajina, a sparsely populated Serb majority region in the west extending from Dalmatia to the outskirts of Karlovac; (2) ethnically mixed western Slavonia around Pakrac; and (3) a plurality Croat, ethnically mixed sliver of land along Croatia's Danube border with Serbia comprising parts of eastern Slavonia, Baranja, and western Srijem, and commonly referred to as Eastern Slavonia. In 1991, the Yugoslav Army and Serb paramilitaries brutally expelled ethnic Croats from all these territories creating a vociferous domestic lobby for a speedy solution.

Since January 1993, there had been a low-intensity conflict over the demarcation line between the Serb-held territories and the rest of Croatia.[1] My first task was to co-sponsor ceasefire talks initiated by Russian Deputy Foreign Minister Vitaly Churkin at the Russian Embassy in Zagreb. Two all-night negotiating sessions produced an agreement in the early hours of 30 March 1994.

Following this success, the talk's co-sponsors (which also included the European Union and the United Nations) decided to continue in the same format in a second round aimed at confidence building and economic cooperation between the two sides with the ultimate view of proceeding to a third stage on a political settlement. Because of the four-party sponsorship beginning in Zagreb, the talks became known as the Zagreb-4, or Z-4 talks. While an economic and confidence building agreement was concluded on 2 December 1994, the process of getting there proved frustrating both to the Croatian government and the international mediators. While both sides played elaborate games, often cancelling negotiations for the most trivial reasons, it became clear that the Serbs were not prepared to engage on the core issues and that Croatia might soon opt for a military solution.

Long before the economic agreement was finished, I came to the conclusion that time for peaceful settlement was running out. Therefore, in early fall 1994, EU envoy Gert Ahrens, Russian Ambassador Leonid Kerestedzhiyants and I decided to jump to the final stage of the process and put forward a proposed political settlement. Ahrens, Kerestedzhiyants and I prepared a comprehensive thirty-page proposal that provided extensive self-government to Serbs living in those parts of the Krajina where they had been a majority in the 1991 census. Under the plan (which the Croatian press promptly dubbed the Z-4 Plan) the Krajina would have its own parliament and president, would control its local police, would have exclusive jurisdiction over domestic issues such as education, culture, the environment and the local economy, and would have exclusive power to raise and spend revenues within the self-governing area. (The political autonomy provisions for Kosovo proposed at Rambouillet were almost a carbon copy of the Z-4 plan.) Our idea was to demonstrate in detail just how much self-government was possible for Serbs within Croatia and thus induce their leaders to engage in serious negotiations.

Unfortunately, the Serb leadership refused even to receive the plan. When the sponsoring ambassadors travelled to the Serb capital Knin on 30 January 1995 to present the plan to the Krajina Serb leadership, the self-styled President Milan Martić refused to touch the document. President Tudjman, who intensely disliked the plan for giving too much autonomy to the Serbs, was shrewd enough to agree to negotiate on the basis of the document.

Martić's intransigence sealed the fate of the Krajina Serbs. Six months later, Martić's forces joined Bosnian Serb General Ratko Mladić in an assault on the Muslim-held Bihac enclave. Frustrated with the absence of any serious negotiations and unwilling to allow the Serbs to consolidate their position by eliminating Bihac, Croatia mobilised its army to retake the Krajina. The United States declined to stop Croatia as its army seemed the only available force that could spare Bihac the fate of Srebrenica, which had fallen two weeks before with the massacre of its men and boys.

On 4 August 1995, President Tudjman launched Operation Storm, which retook the Krajina in just four days. Nearly all of its 180,000 ethnic Serb population fled in advance of the Croatian Army.[2] Thus, by the second week of August, the Serbs controlled only eastern Slavonia. (Croatia had taken back western Slavonia in May 1995 in a two-day operation code-named 'Flash'.) Following Operation Storm, President

Clinton prepared an American peace initiative for Bosnia. One part of the initiative addressed eastern Slavonia: 'There must be a long-term plan for resolving the situation in Eastern Slavonia ... based on Croatian sovereignty and the principles of the Z-4 plan (e.g. Serb home rule, the right of refugees to return, and the other guarantees for Serbs who live there).' Richard Holbrooke, the Bosnia negotiator, delegated the issue to me and I started a shuttle diplomacy between Zagreb and local Serb leaders, whom I met in a yellow villa in the Danubian village of Erdut. While the other Z-4 sponsors no longer had a role, I asked UN envoy Thorvald Stoltenberg to join me in the mediation effort. With very different temperaments and styles we complemented each other well in our role as mediators.

Much more than Krajina, eastern Slavonia was an extremely emotional issue for the Croatian public. Prior to the war, ethnic Croats had enjoyed a slight plurality in this ethnically mixed region (in addition to Croats and Serbs, it is also home to Hungarians, Slovak Protestants, Czechs and gypsies) and these Croats were almost all expelled in 1991 in the war's first large-scale ethnic cleansing. Vukovar, the largest town in the region, withstood a (two-month) siege in 1991 and became the symbol of Serbia's aggression against Croatia.

My goals for the eastern Slavonia negotiations were modest. I sought an agreement that would peacefully reintegrate the region into Croatia in such a way that its Serb population could safely remain while enabling Croats expelled from the region to return to their homes. Although featured prominently in President Clinton's plan, Serbian home rule of any kind proved unattainable. In my first draft for an eastern Slavonia settlement, which I previewed to the Croatian negotiator Hrvoje Sarinic, I proposed limited autonomy for the local Serbs in those municipalities where they were a majority. The language I used describing the autonomy came entirely from a provision of the Croatian constitution granting special rights to ethnic minorities who are a local majority. (I did not label it as coming from the constitution to make the provision look more attractive to the Eastern Slavonia Serbs.) This draft never got to the Serbs as Sarinic sent a diplomatic note warning that Croatia preferred a military solution to applying this part of its constitution to eastern Slavonia.

By late September 1995, it was clear that Serbian President Milošević would not assist the local Serbs militarily thus depriving them of any leverage in the negotiations with the Croatians. (Milošević continued to instruct the Serb negotiators, however.) Even so, the Serb negotiators were surprisingly passive and barely engaged on the critical issues of how to protect ethnic Serbs as Croatia resumed control over the region.

On 3 October, at the first and only productive face-to-face negotiation between the Croatian and Serb sides, Stoltenberg and I secured agreement on eleven articles. These included agreement that the area would be governed by an international authority with suitable military force for a transitional period, that there would be an ethnically mixed transitional police, and that local elections would be held at the end of the transitional period.

The two sides accepted human rights language guaranteeing all refugees and displaced persons the right to their homes, to recover property that was unlawfully taken from them, and to be compensated for property that could not be restored. Most important, these rights were to be available to both Serbs and Croats without regard to ethnicity, and the language was carefully crafted to encompass the right of Croats expelled from eastern Slavonia in 1991 to get their homes back as well as the right of Serbs in Eastern Slavonia and Serbia to return to homes in government-controlled parts of Croatia.

The human rights provisions are the core of the agreement and are critical to the goal of restoring the multiethnic character of Eastern Slavonia by enabling Serbs to remain after the Croatian takeover. However, the Serb negotiators (almost all of whom left the region before Croatia assumed full control) showed almost no interest in the provisions. They exist in the final agreement because I wrote them into all the drafts and insisted the Croatian government accept them.

Although Stoltenberg and I had hoped to wrap up the eastern Slavonia negotiations prior to the start of the Dayton talks on 1 November, Serbian President Milošević preferred to keep the issue open for tactical reasons of his own. When he was finally ready to settle, former secretary of state, Warren Christopher, brokered a deal at Dayton over the final issue in disagreement between the two sides: the length of the transition period. The Serbs wanted two years; the Croatians one. Christopher's compromise specified one year that could be extended to two if requested by either side.

The final text that came out of Dayton was virtually the same as the 3 October text, except that the Croatian government managed to weasel out of a commitment in the earlier draft that gave Croatian Serbs who were refugees in Serbia the same right to return to their original homes that was given to Serbs living in eastern Slavonia. It was an unfortunate change, apparently made by one of my colleagues at Dayton (at this stage Stoltenberg and I had resumed our shuttle in the region) who did not understand the significance of the original commitment.

At 1 p.m. on 12 November 1995 the Agreement was signed by the Serb negotiator Milan Milanović in the yellow villa in Erdut and at 4 p.m. by

Sarinic at Zagreb's presidential palace. Stoltenberg and I signed as witnesses, and as he said, it was 'the beginning of the end of the war in the former Yugoslavia'.

The structure of the Erdut Agreement is relatively simple. The agreement provides for a one to two-year United Nations administration of eastern Slavonia as the region transitions from Serb to Croatian control. (Ultimately it turned out to be two years.) During this period the United Nations was to establish and train a multi-ethnic police force (reflecting the ethnic composition of the area), demilitarise the region and organise local elections. Seven of the Erdut Agreement's fourteen points relate to human rights.

Although not without flaws, I believe the agreement and its implementation must be judged a success. The two-year transition period permitted the passions generated by the war to cool and gave both the Serb and Croatian communities time to adjust to the new realities. The UN administration forced Serbs and Croats to work together on common problems for a full eighteen months prior to the handover thus establishing elements of trust and patterns of cooperation.

The police play a critical role in enabling communities to live together. Because the police were often the shock troops of the ethnic cleansers in the former Yugoslavia, the creation of a professional neutral force was especially important. The UN did establish and train a multi-ethnic police force, carefully screening out those accused of human rights violations and working to instil a sense of professionalism that transcends ethnicity. While the final result was far from ideal, the police in eastern Slavonia were (and remain after the transition) a force for stability.

Local elections became the defining event of the reintegration process. Because the United Nations insisted that local Serbs acquire Croatian citizenship documents in order to vote, the desire to vote (and maintain Serb control of as many municipalities as possible) proved a powerful incentive for the Serb population to accept their status in Croatia. In the end, elections left approximately half the region's municipalities in Serb hands with the other half going to Croat parties. The two largest municipalities, Vukovar and Beli Monastir, worked out power sharing arrangements with Vukovar having a Croat mayor and Serb city council president, and Beli Monastir, a Serb mayor and Croat council president.

Ultimately the test of the Erdut Agreement was whether ethnic Serbs remained in the region after Croatia assumed control. Two years after the UN mandate ended in January 1998, most Serbs who were from the region remained in the region. To be sure, it has not been easy for them and there have been isolated acts of ethnic violence as well as official discrimination. Nonetheless, it is significant that a sizable part of the region's Serb population considered it a better future to remain in Croatia.

The reasons for the success of the Erdut Agreement are several. Partly, the certainty of outcome – i.e., that the region would become a full part of Croatia – forced the Serb population to accept the reality of Croatia in a way the Bosnian Serbs have not been forced to accept that country. The agreement design, with its extended time period for the changeover and concrete benchmarks, such as elections, played a role in reassuring the local population, as did the agreement's extensive human rights provisions. The Croatian government deserves credit as its ability to fulfil its obligations became a source of pride for the officials involved in the transition. Finally, very significant credit is due to the United Nations mission and its energetic chief, Jacques Klein, who understood the extensive powers granted to the United Nations under the Erdut Agreement and used them.

The long-term prospects for ethnic reconciliation in Eastern Slavonia cannot be separated from the treatment of Serbs in the country at large. In 1991 Croatia's Serb population was 600,000, or about 12 per cent of the total population. Between 1991 and 1995, 300,000 Serbs left the country, nearly 200,000 fleeing the Croatian military offensives in western Slavonia and the Krajina in May and August 1995 respectively. In the aftermath of Operation Storm, the Croatian government took the view that the Serbs had left voluntarily, and by so doing had 'opted out' of their right to Croatian citizenship. Laws were then passed confiscating the property of anyone who did not claim it within thirty days (later extended to ninety). The Serbs who had fled had no possibility of filing such claims. These actions violated numerous European and United Nations human rights agreements to which Croatia was a party. The systematic burning and looting of Serb homes in the Krajina following Operation Storm, as well as the murders of several hundred Serbs who were left behind, made a mockery of Croatia's claim that the Serb exodus was voluntary.[3]

The Clinton administration made it a top priority that Croatia reverse its discriminatory legislation and that it permit Serb returns. Under intense American diplomatic pressure, Croatia in December 1995 repealed its laws confiscating Serb property. In July 1997, in a deal brokered by US ambassador to the United Nations Bill Richardson and myself, President Tudjman agreed to 'accept the return of all Croatian Serbs who wish to return and accept the rights, responsibilities, and legal obligations of Croatian citizenship'. Since then, there have been tens of thousands of Serb returns to Krajina and other parts of Croatia.

Nonetheless, bureaucratic obstacles remain to returning and to the ability of Serbs to reclaim lost property.

Leonid Kerestedzhiyants, the Russian ambassador who was my collaborator in designing the Z-4 plan, observed that the treatment of Serbs in Croatia was not just about the rights of an ethnic minority but rather the defining issue as to the character of Croatia itself. Will Croatia join the mainstream of European democracies by espousing a political culture of tolerance or will it remain on the fringe, imbued with a racist nationalism that excludes other ethnic groups?[4] The Erdut Agreement was the first step away from an ideology based on ethnic homogeneity, but even as Croatia advances on the path to joining the European Union, on the larger question the verdict is not yet in.[5]

Notes

1 For a contemporary history of Croatia, see Marcus Tanner, *Croatia: A Nation Forged in War*, New Haven: Yale University Press, 1997.

2 See P. K. Rakate, 'The shelling of Knin by the Croatian Army in August 1995: a police operation or a non-international armed conflict?', in *International Review of the Red Cross*, 840 (31 December 2000), 1037–52.

3 For an historical account of the legal instruments brought in by the Tudjman government and the discriminatory effect they had on Croatian Serbs, see Brad K. Blitz, 'Refugee returns in Croatia: contradictions and reform', *Politics*, 23, 3 (2003), 181–91; Human Rights Watch, 'Croatia: human rights in Eastern Slavonia during and after the Transition of authority': http://sol;www.hrw.org/reports/1997/croatia/Croatia-04.htm, 1997; Human Rights Watch, 'Broken promises: impediments to refugee return to croatia': http://www.hrw.org/reports/2003/croatia0903/croatia0903.pdf, and Human Rights Watch, 'Croatia fails Serb refugees – ethnic discrimination slows refugee return', 3 September 2003: http://sol;www.hrw.org/press/2003/09/croatia090203.htm.

4 Although the HDZ returned to power in December 2003 parliamentary elections, the new government of Prime Minister Ivo Sanader has repeatedly stressed its commitment to the return of Serb refugees and, in 2004, expanded housing and social care schemes for returnees. These measures were deemed inadequate by the OSCE and international agencies who feel more is needed to pave the way for sustainable returns.

5 For a critical account, See Brad K. Blitz, 'Refugee returns, civic differentiation, and minority rights in Croatia 1991-2004', *Journal of Refugee Studies*, 18, 3 (2005), 362–86 and Internal Displacement Monitoring Centre, 'Croatia: reforms come too late for most remaining ethnic serb IDPS', 18 April 2006. http://www.internal-displacement.org/8025708F004BE3B1/(httpInfoFiles)/5A32E9EC172B9AC125714F00538ED1/$file/Croatia_overview_April2006.pdf.

12   The fall of Srebrenica

David Rohde

The fall of Srebrenica, the world's first United Nations declared safe area, is widely considered one of the darkest hours in United Nations history. An estimated 7,300 Bosnian Muslim men are still missing and presumed dead, the victims of a series of ambushes and mass executions carried out by Bosnian Serb soldiers.[1] Several years after the town's fall, exhumations of mass graves around Srebrenica, a small mining town nestled in the hills of eastern Bosnia, continue and additional evidence has been discovered.[2] The exact role of the United States in the tragedy remains unclear. Fairly or unfairly, the world's lone superpower is viewed as having had the ability to save the enclave if it wished, but chose not to. I believe American policy in the southeastern Balkans played a pivotal role in the creation of a 'Safe Areas' policy in Bosnia that, in essence, doomed Srebrenica and its people. In the days just before Srebrenica fell on 11 July 1995, a period when decisive action may have saved the town, the United States also failed to act boldly.

The Bosnian Serb attack on Srebrenica was launched on 6 July. As a small column of Serb tanks advanced into the enclave on 8 July, Dutch peacekeepers in Srebrenica made the first of what would be six requests for NATO air attacks to defend the safe area. Over the next four days various UN commanders repeatedly turned down the Dutch requests.[3] The United States and its allies made public statements condemning the Bosnian Serb attacks, but they did not pressure UN officials to aggressively defend the enclave, as they did when other safe areas were attacked in the past.[4] Something was different when it came to Srebrenica.

The most glaring denial of a Dutch request for NATO air attacks came on the evening of 10 July, the day before the fall of the town. After weighing the Dutch request for two hours, the French commander of UN forces in the former Yugoslavia, General Bernard Janvier, turned it down, saying he believed a promise he had received from a Serb general that the attack would halt. When the Serb attack continued the following day, General Janvier approved an air attack. But the effort was too little too late. Discouraged and lightly armed Dutch peacekeepers and Bosnian Muslim soldiers, who had been waiting days for NATO air attacks, were already retreating. Bosnian Serb forces swept into the town. An estimated 15,000 Bosnian Muslim men tried to walk through 30 miles of Serb-controlled territory to reach Bosnian government controlled central Bosnia. They were systematically attacked and ambushed by Bosnian Serb forces along the route. Those who surrendered were killed in mass executions.[5] After the bloodletting ended, 7,300 Bosnian Muslim men were missing and presumed dead.

In an even more glaring failure to act, the United States and its allies made no effort to use NATO air strikes to halt a subsequent attack on the safe area of Žepa, just south of Srebrenica. Bosnian soldiers in Žepa held off the Bosnian Serb attack for two full weeks, but no effort was made by the international community to halt a Serb attack on an enclave of 15,000 people. American, British and French officials vowed at the London Conference on 21 July 1995 to defend only Gorazde, the third and final enclave in eastern Bosnia.[6] Žepa and its people were ignored. Four days later, Žepa fell.

Since the war in Bosnia ended in November 1995, the fall of Srebrenica and Žepa has emerged as one of the most hotly disputed events of the three-year conflict. Many telling historical accounts of this massacre have been produced, as well as a vast historical record of testimonies from survivors, documentation and other evidence from war crimes trials in the Hague. A damning UN report[7] on the fall of the town has also been produced.

But many questions still remain as to why Srebrenica fell so quickly and why so little was done to protect it. While two other enclaves, Bihac and Gorazde, were able to withstand earlier Serb attacks, Srebrenica was overrun in a mere five days. Various theories exist as to why the town fell so easily.

Shortly after the attack, many Bosnian Muslims from Srebrenica blamed a vast, international conspiracy led by the United States for the fall of the town. UN and Bosnian government officials, they argue, intentionally sacrificed the town as a way to simplify the partitioning of Bosnia in a peace settlement.

The hesitation of the UN commander in Bosnia at the time, French General Janvier, to approve the use NATO air attacks to defend the town stemmed from secret orders he had received to sacrifice the town, they claim. This story has been extensively reported.[8] According to this theory, American and European leaders, realising that the existence of the enclaves complicated any effort to end the war through a *de facto* partition, decided to eliminate the enclaves and hoped for minimal bloodshed.

In another version of the theory, General Janvier's hesitation stemmed from a secret deal he or French officials struck with Bosnian Serb officials a month before the fall of Srebrenica. The French, according to this theory, agreed to block the use of NATO air power against the Bosnian Serbs in exchange for the release of hundreds of French peacekeepers taken hostage by the Bosnian Serbs in early June. The deal endangered the enclaves but saving the lives of French peacekeepers was a priority, according to the theory, and the fall of the enclaves would simplify a peace deal.[9]

General Janvier and other French officials deny that they made any deal with the Serbs or that he had any secret instructions to sacrifice Srebrenica. The general said NATO air attacks alone would not have saved the town and questioned why Bosnian government soldiers in Srebrenica did not do more to protect the town. They argue that the Bosnian government may have intentionally sacrificed the town as part of a territorial exchange and that Bosnian officials secretly negotiated with Serbian leaders. According to that theory, the Serbs received Srebrenica and Žepa in exchange for the Serb-controlled suburbs of Sarajevo.[10]

The theory I subscribe to is that the US, UN and Bosnian government officials all engaged in a tacit conspiracy to allow Srebrenica and later Žepa to fall. There was no overt conspiracy, no secret agreement by the various players to allow the two safe areas to fall, according to this theory. But all of the parties, for their own reasons, had an interest in allowing the town to fall.

UN, US and Bosnian government officials reacted slowly and then repeatedly delayed the use of NATO air attacks that might have slowed the Serb advance on the town because they wanted it to fall. A tacit conspiracy, I believe, explains why so little was done to protect the enclaves. Those who participated in it, I believe, did not expect such bloodletting and were stunned by what occurred.

A final possibility is simply sheer incompetence. Unable to agree on even basic policy issues, the United States and its European allies cobbled together a compromise Bosnia policy in the spring of 1993 that proved totally unworkable. They created civilian 'safe areas' in Bosnia without enough peacekeepers to adequately protect them. The policy allowed the United States and its allies to appear active in Bosnia, but not risk the political fallout of suffering high Western casualties in Bosnia. When the attack began, the same indecision and inability to agree on a course of action prevented a bold response from the West. The safe areas were shown to be the bluff they had always been. Disaster ensued. Srebrenica fell, this theory argues, not due to a vast conspiracy, but due to faulty policy.

Early American policy towards Srebrenica and other Bosnian Muslim enclaves during the war is well documented.[11] To greatly simplify events in the spring of 1993, the United States, France and Britain, after months of dispute, agreed on a compromise course of action in Bosnia as Srebrenica appeared on the verge of falling that April.[12]

A divided United Nations Security Council enacted Resolution 836 on 16 April 1993 declaring Srebrenica the world's first UN declared civilian safe area. Over the next several weeks, five more Bosnian-Muslim controlled towns and cities, including Sarajevo, were also declared safe areas. But while the Clinton administration supported the creation of the safe areas, they refused to commit US ground troops to defend them. When UN Secretary General Boutros Boutros-Ghali requested 34,000 peacekeepers to defend the newly created safe areas, he found few takers. A second proposal, sarcastically referred to as 'safe areas light' by UN officials, was adopted and only 7,600 peacekeepers were sent to the six safe areas. First Canadian, then Dutch peacekeepers were deployed in Srebrenica. In July 1995, 750 lightly armed Dutch were expected to protect the enclave's 40,000 Bosnian Muslims.

The vaguely worded UN resolution that created the safe area gave the Dutch little military backing and scant guidance. Skittish of an outright promise to protect the enclaves, the United States, Britain and France had agreed on a vaguely worded compromise resolution that called for peacekeepers to 'deter' attacks on the safe areas. The tools they had to deter the attacks were also circumscribed for diplomatic reasons.

A US fear that the lives of American pilots would be unnecessarily risked, expressed by then chairman of the Joint Chiefs of Staff, Colin Powell, led to a limiting of the type of NATO air attacks that could be used to defend the safe areas. Attacks known as Close Air Support, which involved retaliatory attacks on specific Serb targets that had just fired on peacekeepers, could only be used in the safe areas. Far broader 'air strikes', which involved large numbers of planes attacking a variety of targets across Bosnian Serb territory, were ruled out for protecting the safe areas.

For the next two years, the safe areas, despite intermittent Bosnian Serb attacks, stood. A combination of ground opposition by Bosnian government soldiers and limited NATO air attacks helped halt Bosnian Serb attacks on the safe areas of Bihac and Gorazde in 1994. But by the summer of 1995 the Clinton administration was growing increasingly wary of the UN mission collapsing, and American failure in Bosnia becoming a potentially major embarrassment in the 1996 presidential election.

The three eastern enclaves, Srebrenica, Žepa and Gorazde, were particularly troublesome. President Clinton had promised British Prime Minister John Major and French President François Mitterand that if the UN mission collapsed, 20,000 American troops would participate in a NATO-led pullout of UN peacekeepers from Bosnia. American forces, according to the plan, were responsible for withdrawing peacekeepers from the eastern enclaves. In a highly dangerous and politically humiliating mission, helicopter-borne American troops were to pull Dutch, Ukrainian and British peacekeepers out as they abandoned women and children in the three 'safe areas'. For obvious reasons, resolving the problem of the enclaves before the 1996 election season was in the Clinton administration's interest.

In late June 1995, National Security Adviser Anthony Lake met with a small group of advisers to develop an 'endgame' strategy for the war in Bosnia. Part of the strategy was the elimination of the eastern enclaves. According to administration officials, the enclaves were to be traded for Serb-controlled territory around Sarajevo as part of a final peace settlement. They vehemently denied any conscious decision by the United States to let Srebrenica or the other enclaves fall. Their plan, they said, was that the enclaves be peacefully traded.

Former Secretary of Defence William Perry, in a June 1997 interview, said he called for air attacks to defend Srebrenica as the town fell, but European officials blocked him. Perry denied that Žepa was also sacrificed. He said it was the Pentagon's honest military assessment that Žepa could not be defended by air attacks. He said the second enclave was not intentionally sacrificed to make negotiating a peace agreement easier. Richard Holbooke, in his 1998 book on the Dayton Peace Accord, also said the United States did not sacrifice the enclaves. He blamed the Dutch government for blocking his request for air attack to save Srebrenica before it fell. American officials are still unsure, he said, whether or not French officials or General Janvier made a secret deal with the Bosnian Serbs that led to Janvier's hesitancy to use NATO air attacks to defend the town.

Supporters of the theory that the United States intentionally sacrificed Srebrenica and Žepa scoff at these explanations. They cite the existence of Lake's endgame strategy as the explanation for the US's failure to aggressively intervene.

In their defence, administration officials who spoke on condition of anonymity contend that Washington's failure to act aggressively was due to a massive intelligence failure. When the Bosnian Serb Army carried out its attack on Srebrenica between 6 July and 11 July, the

Central Intelligence Agency consistently misjudged Serb intentions in Srebrenica, according to administration officials.

Up until the day before the town fell, the CIA assessment was that the Serbs were punishing the enclave for a raid carried out by Bosnian Muslim soldiers from Srebrenica in mid-June. The CIA predicted that the Serbs did not intend to shrink the enclave, nor eliminate it. The CIA assessment on the day before Srebrenica fell, 10 July, according to an administration official, was that the Serbs would not want to deal with the large number of civilians in the enclave.

Supporters of the theory that Srebrenica was intentionally sacrificed contest this view and argue that it is not plausible that the CIA could make such a massive mistake.

One other document sheds some light on the situation. A cable obtained through a Freedom of Information Act request filed by Robert Silk, an attorney in New York, and the group Students Against Genocide,[13] illustrates the raw information officials in Washington were receiving as the attack on Srebrenica intensified. Mr Silk believes more incriminating cables are being withheld by the government. It is not clear whether he is correct.

The cable was sent by the US Embassy in Sarajevo to Washington an hour after Serb forces had taken Srebrenica itself. The Embassy was apparently unaware that the town had already fallen. The cable was from the Embassy's *chargé d'affaires* and recounted a meeting he held with Bosnian Prime Minister Haris Silajdžić, who expressed the government's fear that Serbs intended to take the enclave and expel its Muslims. The final section of the cable appears to show that even the US Embassy in Sarajevo was unclear about the true intentions of the Bosnian Serb Army in Srebrenica. The cable states:

No consensus has formed among government and diplomatic contacts here as to the ultimate Serb military strategy in Srebrenica, but most think it is interactive. That is, the BSA (Bosnian Serb Army) probes resistance and pushes until it locates opportunity. GOBH (Government of Bosnia & Herzegovina) officials now fear the Serb aim in Srebrenica is to expel and occupy, the former being pursued with brutality.[14]

The final two sentences of the cable were blacked out by State Department officials before it was released publicly. The cable concludes with the words 'and other contacts sum up the Serbs' objective: they want it all'. While the cable warns that there is a strong possibility that the Serbs intend to take Srebrenica, it is clearly not a dramatic warning. It is impossible to know what intelligence information officials in Washington were receiving, but the cable suggests that American officials, intentionally or unintentionally, misjudged the intent of the Serb attack until Srebrenica had actually fallen.

American policies enacted that spring in Bosnia further limited the meagre military tools UN peacekeepers had to defend the town. After General Janvier finally approved a NATO close air support attack request from the Dutch, a new American policy slowed it. In the wake of the downing of US pilot Scott O'Grady on 2 June 1995 by a Serb anti-aircraft missile, NATO officials required all groups of NATO planes flying over Bosnia to include planes with more sophisticated electronic jamming equipment. Assembling the larger groups of planes over the Adriatic Sea before they entered Bosnian airspace was more time consuming. On the day Srebrenica fell, the assembly of the new, larger group of planes created at least a three-hour delay. On the day the town fell, an American desire to maximise the security of the US pilots hampered the UN effort to protect Srebrenica.

An incident that occurred after Srebrenica fell further demonstrates the Clinton administration's true priorities. On the day after the safe area fell, officials in Washington contacted the US Embassy in the Netherlands, according to diplomatic sources. They urged American diplomats there to encourage the Dutch government to tell their surrounded peacekeepers in the fallen safe area to 'stand tall'. At that point, American officials feared that the Dutch would call on the earlier promise by US officials to use American helicopters to withdraw NATO forces from the enclaves. American officials were afraid of having to risk casualties. As Bosnian Muslim men were being hunted by Serb soldiers around Srebrenica, the Clinton administration's priority remained minimising American casualties.

Bosnian officials, meanwhile, continued to warn of disaster. Former Prime Minister Haris Silajdžić and former Bosnian ambassador to the United Nations, Muhammad Sacirbey, both warned American officials that they were receiving accounts of mass executions just outside Srebrenica. The reports of executions focused on a soccer stadium in a town just north of Srebrenica called Bratunac.

According to American officials, the CIA did check its aerial photographs of Bratunac after receiving the warnings, but found no evidence of mass executions. But no effort was made to check other nearby areas or trace the path of 15,000 Bosnian Muslim men fleeing through the woods, they said. The CIA'S priority remained tracking potential surface-to-air missile sites that could shoot down American and NATO planes.

Some openly question that explanation. The central thrust of the Freedom of Information Act filed by Mr Silk and Students Against

Genocide was to force the US government to disclose all of the aerial photos it has of the area around Srebrenica in July 1995. Mr Silk and others believed the Clinton administration had photographic proof of the mass executions, but waited to release them until a full month after the town fell. The delay allowed the administration to avoid, they argued, being forced to act to halt the killings.

Administration officials have denied the allegations and said that US spy satellite and spy planes were focused on anti-aircraft missile sites at the time. They say a cable sent by US Ambassador to Croatia Peter Galbraith, to Secretary of State Warren Christopher in late July prompted a second effort to find evidence of atrocities around Srebrenica. Mr Galbraith had heard via a UN official the detailed account of a survivor of a mass execution in a village outside of Srebrenica called Nova Kasaba. He relayed the account in a cable to Washington.

While Galbraith's cable alerted Washington to atrocities in Srebrenica, its real focus was to save Žepa, which had not yet fallen. 'The London declaration implicitly wrote off Žepa', Galbraith writes. 'In view of the numerous accounts of atrocities in Srebrenica and the possibility of a major massacre there, I urge reconsideration of air strikes to help Žepa.' Galbraith then gives a detailed account of the man's story. The cable concludes with: 'Again, it is not too late to prevent a similar tragedy at Žepa. Žepa's defenders valiantly continue to hold on. Undoubtedly they realize the fate that awaits them. They should not be abandoned.'[15]

Galbraith's recommendation was ignored in Washington. Instead of moving to protect Žepa, the administration dispatched John Shattuck, the assistant secretary of state for human rights, to interview refugees from Srebrenica about atrocities. In a trip in late July, Mr Shattuck found survivors of mass executions and pinpointed the location of mass graves in Nova Kasaba and other towns near Srebrenica. After his return to Washington, CIA officials checked photographs of the area and found a half dozen mass graves in Nova Kasaba and other towns named by survivors. In a dramatic presentation to the UN Security Council on 10 August, then US ambassador to the UN Madeline Albright publicly unveiled the photos, calling them clear evidence of Bosnian Serb atrocities. US intelligence officials later said they did not see the graves sooner because they had not reviewed photos of the area. They said US satellites and spy planes take far more photographs than can be reviewed by analysts. Without a pinpoint location to focus on, they said, analysts can miss evidence.

What, then, explains the fall of Srebrenica? What responsibility for the tragedy, if any, lies with American policy in the southeastern Balkans? I believe the fall of the town was neither a terrible mistake that resulted simply from incompetence and poor policy-making. Nor was it the result of a vast international conspiracy agreed upon by the American, French and British governments.

Instead, the most likely explanation for the fall of Srebrenica and Žepa is that the tacit sacrifice of the two safe areas was in the interests of all of the parties – American, British, French and Bosnian officials. The conspiracy was a passive one. No leader wanted to be seen openly sacrificing the two enclaves. Instead, each sat back on their own, and for their own reasons, paid little attention to events in Srebrenica and Žepa, or intentionally misread them. These 'errors' allowed them to not intervene. The responsibility is widespread.

The French most likely did broker a tacit deal to halt air strikes in exchange for the release of the hostages in June 1995 in order to free their peacekeepers. The deal endangered Srebrenica and Žepa, the two smallest and weakest enclaves, but the two safe areas held no French peacekeepers and were not a French priority.

Bosnian government officials had the Bosnian Army do little to aid to Srebrenica and Žepa for their own reasons. They had already likely decided they would trade the two enclaves as part of a peace settlement, but knew openly abandoning the enclaves would be politically unpalatable.

Senior UN officials in Bosnia at the time also did little to intervene, for their own reasons. Yasushi Akashi, the civilian head of the UN mission, and General Janvier, the military commander, did not aggressively defend the towns because avoiding casualties among peacekeepers was their top priority. The loss of the two enclaves, which were difficult to supply and the source of frequent problems, also simplified the United Nation's struggling mission in Bosnia.[16]

Finally, the American government's inaction, particularly in the case of Žepa, strains credulity. The idea that the fall of the two safe areas was the result of simply poor policy and bad luck is too simplistic. I believe American officials initially paid little attention to, and later grossly misread, the situation in Srebrenica and Žepa because the fall of the two safe areas furthered the administration's goals in Bosnia at the time. The existence of the two enclaves greatly complicated any effort to negotiate a peace settlement before the 1996 presidential elections. Their fall made a partition of the country easier.

That is not to say that the United States, Britain and France engaged in a vast conspiracy to sacrifice the enclaves. I do not believe France, for example, issued secret orders to General Janvier to turn down the Dutch requests for NATO air attacks. I also do not believe that the United States covered up aerial photos of atrocities for one month.

But I do believe that as the Bosnian Serb attacks on the two towns intensified, there was a decision in Washington to sit back and allow events on the ground to run their course. If the two enclaves fell, it would simplify peace negotiations. If they held their own, so be it. American officials probably did not expect so much bloodshed. They were probably genuinely stunned and horrified by what ensued.

The creation and fall of the two enclaves reflected the dynamic of American policy in the Balkans during the war in Bosnia. American officials compromised and cobbled together weak, unworkable policies that gave the impression of action, but were hollow at their core. When political imperatives called for a change in policy, the policies and the safe areas, were discarded.

Notes

1 These figures are derived from ICRC sources. See the UN Report on Srebrenica for further discussion of these figures. *The Fall of Srebrenica: Report of the Secretary-General pursuant to General Assembly resolution 53/35*, United Nations General Assembly Document A/54/549, 15 November 1999. Hereafter *UN Srebrenica Report*: http://ods-dds-ny.un.org/doc/UNDOC/GEN/N99/348/76/IMG/N9934876.pdf?OpenElement

2 In June 2004, the Bosnian Serb government acknowledged that their forces committed the massacre in Srebrenica, and revealed the location of a further thirty-two mass graves. See Maja Zuvela's Reuters Report, 'Bosnian Serbs reveal 31 new Srebrenica mass graves', 4 June 2004: http://www.alertnet.org/thenews/newsdesk/L04568018.htm

3 See *UN Srebrenica Report*, 11 July. Initial confusion over air support; Srebrenica falls, 67–71.

4 On 10 July, Nicholas Burns, former spokesman and principal deputy assistant secretary for public affairs at the US Department of State provided the following assessment. 'We do understand that the Dutch have formed a defensive line just outside the city; that the United Nations has threatened NATO air strikes if the Bosnian Serbs attempt to pierce that line. NATO, of course, could launch air strikes or provide close air support to UN forces if requested to do so by the UN, but NATO has not yet received any such request by the United Nations': http://dosfan.lib.uic.edu/ERC/briefing/daily_briefings/1995/9507/950710db.html

5 For a detailed account of atrocities committed during the fall of Srebrenica, see Human Rights Watch, *The Fall of Srebrenica and the Failure of UN Peacekeeping*, New York: Human Rights Watch, 1995.

6 See the author's book, *Endgame, the Betrayal and Fall of Srebrenica: Europe's Worst Massacre since World War II* for a detailed account of the way the London Conference was perceived by the Bosnian government.

7 See *UN Srebrenica Report*; Jan Willem Honig and Norbert Both, *Srebrenica: Record of a War Crime*, London: Penguin, 1997; Eric Stover and Giles Peress,

The Graves: Srebrenica and Vukovar, St Louis, MO: Scalo Publishers, 1998; and Patrick McCarthy, Tom Maday, David Rohde and Lejla Susic, *After the Fall: Srebrenica Survivors* in St. Louis, MO: Missouri Historical Society Press, 2001.

8 For a detailed account of the complicity between United Nations commanders and officials, Serbian President Slobodan Milošević, and Serbian Army General Ratko Mladić in the Srebrenica massacre, see Bianca Jagger, 'The betrayal of Srebrenica', *The European*, 15 September – 1 October 1997, pp. 14–19: http://www.haverford.edu/relg/sells/srebrenica/BiancaJagger1.html and http://www.haverford.edu/relg/sells/srebrenica/BiancaJagger2.html.

9 See Roy Gutman, 'UN's deadly deal', *New York Newsday*, 29 May 1996, pp. A7, A24–A25, A31.

10 For an astute analysis of why Bosnian forces in Srebrenica failed to mount a more effective defence, see Chuck Sudetic, *Blood and Vengeance: One Family's Story of the War in Bosnia*, New York: W.W. Norton & Company, 1996.

11 For a fuller account, see Rohde, *Endgame*.

12 For a more detailed description and excellent analysis of the development of the safe areas policy, see Honig and Both, *Srebrenica*.

13 For the final ruling on this case, see *Students Against Genocide, et al., Appellants v. Department of State, et al., Appeal from the United States District Court for the District of Columbia* (No. 96cv00667), decided 7 August 2001; http://www.ll.georgetown.edu/federal/judicial/dc/opinions/99opinions/99-5316a.html

14 Rohde, *Endgame*, p. 400.

15 Ibid., 331.

16 See Jagger, 'The betrayal of Srebrenica'.

they started shooting indiscriminately at buildings they passed, killing an Albanian school teacher in his classroom. A crowd of 20,000 Albanians gathered for his funeral; among them were a few men in military dress, who said they represented the Kosovo Liberation Army. This was the self-styled army's first public appearance.

Who were, or what was, the KLA? Albanian villagers thought it was a local resistance movement, aimed in theory at 'national liberation' and in practice at protecting their villages against Serb attacks; and because enough of them came to think so, that is what it turned into. The structure and leadership of the organisation in its early stages were, however, wrapped in mystery. Outside Kosovo, radical groups among the Albanian diaspora claimed to be directing its activities and issued 'communiqués' on its behalf. Chief among these groupings was the LPK (Levizja Popullore e Kosoves: The Popular Movement of Kosovo), which combined Albanian nationalism with Marxism-Leninism, having campaigned for Kosovo's unification with Albania since the early 1980s, when that country was under hard-line communist rule. Yet the left-wing ingredients of this ideological mixture held little attraction for ordinary Albanians inside Kosovo; and, as the KLA grew in numbers during 1998, it would acquire local leaderships from a variety of backgrounds, including former army officers and members of the moderate political movement of Ibrahim Rugova. At this early stage, however, Rugova's own attitude to the KLA was quite uncomprehending. When the first KLA attacks on Serb policemen took place in 1996 and 1997 he became convinced that the whole thing was a chimera, invented by Serb *agents provocateurs*. It would be well into 1998 before he changed his mind.

In the eyes of Rugova's critics, this was just another sign of his increasing inability to keep up with the reality of developments in Kosovo. His political reputation had already been damaged in October 1997, when the Albanian student movement in Pristina planned a large demonstration, protesting at Milošević's failure to fulfil his promises to restore educational facilities to them. Rugova publicly called on the students to postpone the protest, and they ignored his request. (In the event, the march was halted by a Serb road-block, and the leaders of the demonstration were beaten up by the police.) This issue caused an open disagreement between Rugova and his own prime minister, Bujar Bukoshi. Among the general Albanian population Rugova's personal standing remained high; at unofficial elections for the self-styled Kosovo government on 22 March 1999, he was returned unopposed as president. But among members of the political class the growing dissatisfaction with his policy was evident, with several prominent defections from his party; and the reason why he was elected unopposed was that the main opposition parties boycotted the election, arguing that it was inappropriate at such a time of political crisis.

What had caused the crisis was a huge escalation in the use of military force by the Serbian authorities. Attacks by the KLA on the Serbian police and other targets had continued during the winter of 1997–98, but on a very limited scale: in the two years up to mid-January 1998, the KLA claimed to have killed five policemen, five other Serbian officials and eleven Albanian 'collaborators' with the Serbian regime. Other European countries had experienced similar small-scale campaigns of politically-motivated violence, and had dealt with them using normal police methods. But the response of the Serbian authorities in this case was hugely disproportionate; and it was the nature of this response which, more than anything else, pushed Kosovo into war.

On 28 February 1998, after a fire-fight between Kosovar rebels and Serb police in which four policemen were shot dead, the Serbian authorities launched an attack on two Albanian villages, using military helicopters and armoured personnel carriers. In one village, Likoshani, sixteen Albanians were killed; the police also looted the houses they raided there. A few days later a similar military assault against the village of Prekaz left fifty-one people dead; the main target of this attack was the family house of Adem Jashari, a local strongman who was said to be a commander of the KLA in that region. The Serbian forces killed not only Jashari but also most of his family; nearly half the victims were women, children and old men. This action turned Adem Jashari into a hero and martyr in the eyes of the local Albanians, and encouraged large numbers of them to join the KLA. Further attacks on other villages in the Drenica region of central Kosovo during the next few weeks had a similar effect, while also creating a flood of refugees. The process by which Milošević's policy acted as the recruiting-master for the KLA was now fully under way.

Western governments reacted hesitantly and ineptly to these events. Many observers believed, indeed, that Milošević had actually been encouraged to launch this campaign by the comments of an American diplomat, Robert Gelbard, who had denounced the KLA as a 'terrorist group' on 23 February. On 9 March the 'Contact Group' (USA, Russia, Britain, France, Germany and Italy) threatened a limited package of sanctions, such as visa restrictions and the blocking of investment credits, if Milošević did not change his policy within two weeks; when that deadline was reached, they then extended it by another month. Milošević's only response was to widen the attacks on Albanian villages and increase his military build-up in the region. The threatened sanctions were eventually introduced at the end of April. Meanwhile a resolution of the UN Security Council had imposed an arms embargo, aimed at cutting off supplies to both Yugoslavia and the KLA. (Yugoslavia was, however, a major arms producer, and had recently made a large purchase of arms from Russia; the KLA was equipped mainly with small arms acquired from people who had stolen them from weapons stores in Albania in 1997.)

While the Western politicians debated these measures, Milošević was strengthening his own political position inside Yugoslavia. In March he invited the radical nationalist politician Vojislav Šešelj to join his government. Šešelj was known for his extreme views on the Kosovo question, having publicly advocated a policy of infecting Kosovo Albanians with the AIDS virus. Most of the political spectrum in Serbia (with the exception of the tiny Civic Alliance party) was in any case hostile to the Albanians; a typical example was the commentator Aleksa Djilas (someone regarded in the West as a liberal intellectual), whose main contribution to the debate in Kosovo in April 1998, published in the Belgrade nationalist magazine *Argument*, was entitled 'Whatever Israel Does to the Palestinians, We Serbs Can Do to the Albanians.' During that month Milošević organised a referendum on the question of whether 'foreign representatives' should be allowed to mediate in the Kosovo conflict. The majority, not surprisingly, voted 'no'.

While international political pressure on Milošević to change his policies was non-existent, Western leverage on him also seemed extremely limited. A display of military force was made on 15 June, when NATO jets flew along the southern borders of Kosovo; and on the following day European governments issued what was described as 'a strong final warning' to Milošević. This warning, like the previous ones, was ignored. Military actions by Serb forces were intensified in two areas: the Drenica region of central Kosovo, and the south-western border areas running down from Pec to Gjakova. The official reason for concentrating on this second area was to stop the smuggling of arms to the KLA from Albania; but the tactics used by the Serb forces were aimed mainly at civilian population centres not at military supply lines. Towns such as Decanci and Junik were shelled by heavy artillery, and in early June there were reports of villages being bombed by Serbian aircraft. A similar campaign was conducted in central Kosovo, with the ostensible purpose of eliminating the strongholds of the KLA (which had abducted and killed a number of Serb civilians, and was claiming that it controlled a large area of 'liberated territory'). By means of random shootings and artillery bombardments the Serb forces emptied village after village of their inhabitants; the houses were then looted and burnt, and in many cases livestock were killed and crops destroyed in the fields. Over a period of six months, from April to September 1998, more than 300 Albanian villages were devastated in this way; aid agencies estimated that between 250,000 and 300,000 were driven from their homes. The majority moved to the major towns while some left Kosovo altogether and others (up to 50,000) sought refuge on hillsides. From the nature of the systematic destruction of houses and livelihoods, it was clear that the main purpose of this entire campaign was not military but demographic: nothing less than the permanent uprooting of a significant proportion of the rural population of Kosovo.

During the summer months the Western powers, despite the urgent 'final warnings' they had issued, remained curiously inactive. Some Western officials apparently believed that the Serbian campaign would increase the chances of an eventual negotiated settlement, by reducing the self-confidence of the KLA and thus forcing the Albanians to climb down from their demand for outright independence. Such a view was gravely mistaken, not only in its acceptance of the idea that the Serbian forces were engaged in a normal 'counter-insurgency' operation, but also in its failure to understand the psychology of the Albanians, whose determination to throw off Serbian rule could only be strengthened by these experiences. While the Albanians became more radicalised, however, they did not become more united politically; criticism of Rugova's moderate policy was intensified, but the KLA failed to put forward any coherent political programme, or to offer any convincing leadership at the political level. American diplomats made several fruitless attempts to persuade the Albanians to come together and form a unified negotiating position. Yet, the overall failure of this diplomacy was not very surprising, as the only thing on which all Albanians agreed – the need for full independence from Yugoslavia – was the one option that Western governments ruled out. The Western policy was aimed merely at the restoration of 'autonomy', which meant local self-government under the continuing rule of Belgrade.

At the end of September 1998 world opinion was shocked by the discovery of a massacre near the village of Obrinje in central Kosovo. Sixteen Albanian civilians, including ten women, children and old men, had been killed on a hillside; one elderly man had been left with his throat slit, and with the butcher's knife carefully placed on his chest. The Western powers now renewed their efforts to put pressure on the Yugoslav government, threatening air strikes within days if it refused to halt its campaign. On 16 October the US envoy Richard Holbrooke finally persuaded Milošević to sign an agreement; the text was never made public, but the key provisions included a promise to scale down the Serbian deployment in Kosovo to its pre-February levels, an agreement that all Kosovar refugees could return to their homes, and an acceptance of the presence of an international force of observers to make sure that these pledges were fulfilled.

The Holbrooke–Milošević deal looked, on the surface, like a success for Western diplomacy; but the American envoy had been forced to make important concessions. He had failed to secure free access for investigators from the International War Crimes Tribunal at the Hague, and had conceded that the observers sent to Kosovo should neither be directed nor protected by NATO, but should consist instead of an unarmed 'Verification Mission' under the direction of the OSCE (Organization for Security and Cooperation in Europe). His frequent return visits to Belgrade during these negotiations, and the equally frequent postponements of threatened air strikes, had served merely to illustrate the weakness of the Western negotiating position. The fundamental problem was the West's commitment to autonomy as the maximum that the Kosovo Albanians could be allowed. For Western governments to threaten the military destruction of Serbian forces in Kosovo, while proclaiming that the long-term aim of any such action was to return Kosovo to Serbian rule, was patently illogical. Milošević seems to have recognised this, and therefore to have supposed that whatever pledges he made could later be broken with virtual impunity. Indeed, his willingness to scale down his operations in Kosovo probably reflected nothing more than the fact that his campaign was drawing to a close anyway as the winter approached.

The next two months did see a major reduction in the fighting. Many Serb units were withdrawn at the end of October, and thousands of Albanians were able to return to the burnt-out shells of their homes (which, in some cases, were found to have been booby-trapped with grenades by the Serb forces as they left). The Verification Mission began to operate, though the number of 'Verifiers' fell far below the total of 1,800 agreed in October: there were only 600 of them in Kosovo by the end of the year. During the last week of December, however, the Serb military forces launched a new offensive against KLA positions near the northeastern town of Podujevo; the battle group used in this attack then remained in place, in further breach of the October agreement, and during the next few weeks an additional force of 15,000 Serbian troops was assembled at staging-posts just outside the Kosovan border. Western monitors concluded that the Serbs were preparing for a new spring offensive against the KLA – which, for its part, had also been re-arming and training since October. However, other evidence suggested that the Serbian authorities were preparing a campaign of destruction and expulsion against the local Albanian population that would be even more far-reaching than the scorched earth policy of the previous summer. In January and February, for example, it was reported that they were seizing official documents and land-ownership registers from Albanian villages, and removing Serbian Orthodox icons and artefacts from museums in Kosovo for 'safe keeping' in Belgrade.

In mid-January 1999 Western diplomacy was jolted once more into action. The immediate cause was not the Serb military build-up, but the discovery of a massacre at the village of Racak, where forty-five Albanian civilians, including children, had been murdered. Most had been shot in the head at close range with a single bullet, and some of the bodies had been mutilated. When the head of the Verification Mission publicly condemned the Serb forces for this atrocity, the Belgrade authorities demanded his removal; they also refused entry to the chief prosecutor of the International War Crimes Tribunal. Two weeks later the six-nation Contact Group announced that it was summoning the Serbian and Albanian leaderships to a conference at Rambouillet, near Paris, on 6 February, at which they would be required to agree to a negotiated settlement on the political future of Kosovo.

The basis for this negotiation was a proposal which had already been in circulation for many months: known as the 'Hill plan', after the US ambassador to Macedonia, Christopher Hill (who had been trying to negotiate with the Serbian and Kosovo Albanian sides throughout the previous year), it consisted of a detailed set of constitutional arrangements for an autonomous Kosovo. These included an elected Assembly, a president and a Constitutional Court. In some respects this plan restored elements of the autonomy enjoyed by Kosovo before 1989, but at the same time it introduced new principles which would significantly weaken the power of the Kosovo government. The people of Kosovo were to be divided into so-called 'national communities', which would hold quotas of official posts and would have the power to block any measures in the Assembly that they deemed contrary to their national interests. Also, many governmental powers were to be transferred to the level of local communes; in 1989 only one out of the twenty-two communes of Kosovo had had a Serb majority, but a subsequent gerrymandering of communal boundaries by the Serbian authorities had created several more, which would now be given substantial powers in areas such as policing. During the second half of 1998 the Albanian politicians had objected to many aspects of this plan; and the Serbian authorities had, in any case, remained hostile to the whole idea of restoring Kosovo's autonomy.

The most important feature of this proposal, however, was its status as a so-called 'Interim Agreement'. In the original versions of the Hill plan, a final clause declared that the agreement would be reconsidered in three years' time; but the phrasing clearly implied that this would be only an 'implementation review', not a rethinking of the fundamental question of Kosovo's status. The Albanians would not accept this, as it appeared permanently to rule out any further moves towards independence. In the version of the plan discussed at Rambouillet in February, this clause was significantly revised: 'Three years after the entry into force of this Agreement, an international meeting shall be convened to determine a mechanism for a final settlement for Kosovo, on the basis of the will of the people . . . ' But the Albanians hesitated to accept this as a promise of eventual independence, given that the stated policy of all the Western powers was still set firmly against the independence option. The political representatives of the KLA were also opposed to another key provision of the Rambouillet proposals, the complete disarming of their forces. The Belgrade authorities, for their part, objected to the demand that they withdraw all their troops from Kosovo (with the exception of a small number of border guards); but most of all they opposed the demand of the Western powers that a peacekeeping force of NATO troops be stationed inside Kosovo to police the agreement.

After two weeks of inconclusive negotiation, the Albanian representatives at Rambouillet reluctantly announced their 'conditional' acceptance – the condition being that they needed more time to discuss the proposals with various political and military leaders inside Kosovo. In mid-March the peace talks resumed in France, and on the 18th of that month the Albanians finally signed the agreement. The Yugoslav delegation, on the other hand, boycotted the ceremony and declared its continuing opposition to the plan.

Within Kosovo, meanwhile, the build-up of Serbian military forces had intensified throughout February and early March. New army units and large numbers of tanks had been brought into the province; paramilitary forces controlled by the gangster-politician 'Arkan' were established at a site near the northern Kosovo town of Mitrovica, together with other groups known for their work as 'ethnic cleansers'. Milošević had installed one of his most loyal army commanders, General Nebojša Pavković (a relative by marriage), to direct these forces, and Pavković had immediately begun to integrate his army units with the local special police forces, a move which clearly indicated that something other than a normal military operation was being planned. By 20 March, when the international Verification Mission withdrew from Kosovo, there were more than 26,000 Serbian troops inside the province and another 15,000 stationed just beyond its eastern border. According to some reports, their deployment was in accordance with a strategic plan known as Operation Horseshoe, aimed at 'solving' the Kosovo problem. The nature of the plan was not known in detail, but the code-name itself indicated the principle on which it would work: a controlled near-encirclement, designed to force people inside the 'horseshoe' to exit in one particular direction. 'Exit', in this case, would turn out to mean leaving Kosovo altogether, and the aim of the Serbian policy was to ensure that they would never come back.

On 24 March 1999, after the failure of one more attempt at negotiation by Holbrooke and a final rejection of the Rambouillet proposals by the Serbian parliament, NATO forces began their campaign of air strikes against strategic targets inside Yugoslavia. In effect – *de facto* but not *de jure* – the NATO alliance was now at war with Milošević's state. It seemed a classic example of how nations can stumble into war. Milošević, fortified by the knowledge that the Western alliance was still committed to keeping Kosovo as an integral part of Serbia, apparently assumed either that the NATO threats were an outright bluff, or that they would amount, in the event, to no more than a few days of symbolic air strikes. The NATO governments, conversely, seem to have thought that Milošević himself was bluffing, and that a brief period of bombing would force him to climb down – or perhaps even give him a secretly welcome excuse for compliance with their demands. They were not planning a long war; had they done so, they would have not announced, at the outset, that they had no intention of deploying ground forces. Indeed, it would have been hard to get the nineteen-member military alliance to agree to any long-term military commitment at this stage; consensus on the need for immediate air strikes was the most that could be achieved. Although the justification for this action in international law was reasonably clear – on the basis of customary principles of humanitarian law, which permit intervention in cases of extreme humanitarian necessity – some NATO governments were unhappy about the lack of an explicit authorisation by the UN Security Council. If Milošević had halted all anti-Albanian actions in Kosovo when the first bombs were dropped, and if he had then concentrated on opening up diplomatic divisions among the Western allies, it is conceivable that NATO's political will might have been dissipated within a week or two. Instead, he decided on a very different policy.

During the first few days of the air strike campaign, while NATO confined itself to the use of cruise missiles and high-altitude bombing, the Serbian forces inside Kosovo embarked on a massive campaign of destruction, burning down houses and using tanks and artillery to reduce entire villages to rubble. At first their actions were concentrated in three areas: in the northeastern corner of Kosovo (securing a wide corridor for the introduction of more forces into the province), in the Drenica region (where KLA had its main strongholds), and in a broad stretch of southwestern Kosovo, near the Albanian border. The significance of this third target soon became obvious; the strategy was to clear a path for the mass expulsion of the Kosovo Albanian population. Two days after the air strikes began, the first waves of deported people began flooding over the southern borders of Kosovo, into Albania and Macedonia. Most had similar stories to tell, of a coordinated operation of 'ethnic cleansing' on a hitherto unprecedented scale. Armed men had arrived at their houses – sometimes special police, sometimes paramilitary gangsters, in many cases accompanied by local Serbs – and had ordered them to leave within minutes. An atmosphere of terror was created by random killings of civilians in the streets; some houses were set on fire as the population was leaving, and the rest would be first looted and then demolished when they had gone. As they left the village they would be funnelled through a cordon of troops, who would rob them of their money and possessions. Finally they would be told which route to take to the border. In many cases, however, not all the inhabitants were allowed to leave; in a development chillingly reminiscent of the seizure of Srebrenica in 1995, men were separated from their families and taken away by Serb forces. By the third week of April the US government was reporting that it had satellite images of many newly dug mass graves; the American diplomat with special responsibility for war crimes issues, David Scheffer, calculated that up to 100,000 men were unaccounted for. Some of these, no doubt, had managed to flee to the hills, where pockets of heavily outgunned KLA fighters were putting up a limited resistance.

The scale of this cleansing operation, and the coordination it displayed between Serbian military and police forces, indicated a high degree of planning. This was clearly not a spontaneous response to the NATO bombardment – though the air strikes may well have given Milošević a welcome opportunity to accelerate and extend the actions he had already planned. The main way in which this campaign of expulsion went beyond the ethnic cleansing of the previous year was in its application to the major towns; the inhabitants of cities such as Pristina and Mitrovica, whose lives had been largely untouched by the 1998 campaign, were now subjected to the same methods of intimidation and deportation. Thousands of people were forced to board trains at Pristina, which then took them to the Macedonian border; they were packed so tightly into the wagons that several elderly people died during the journey. By 20 April 1999 it was calculated that nearly 600,000 refugees had left Kosovo in the previous four weeks: 355,000 were in Albania,

127,500 in Macedonia, 72,500 in Montenegro and 32,000 in Bosnia. This was in addition to an estimated 100,000 who had left during 1998. And inside Kosovo, according to NATO spokesmen, there were five large pockets of 'displaced' Albanians, representing a total of 850,000 people.

One especially sinister aspect of the deportation was the confiscation of passports and identity papers; it was reported that municipal registers of births and deaths, and of land ownership, were also being destroyed, and refugees who were allowed to leave the country in cars or tractors were ordered to remove their registration plates before crossing the border. The thinking behind this policy emerged when, after the first week of the NATO campaign, Russian Prime Minister Yevgeni Primakov obtained a 'peace proposal' from Milošević; this included an offer to allow refugees to return to Kosovo, 'so long as they are Yugoslav citizens'. The idea, clearly, was to eliminate any proof of such citizenship, and then deny these 'non-citizens' re-entry. Serb nationalist propaganda claimed that hundreds of thousands of Albanians had crossed into Kosovo from Albania during and after World War II; the claim was baseless, but the physical evidence was now being adjusted to fit. In practical terms, this meant that Milošević was preparing a fallback position; even if he were eventually forced to accept the return of the Kosovars, he would limit their numbers to whatever total he found acceptable. In the last week of April, diplomatic sources in Belgrade reported that Serbian officials were now magnanimously saying they could 'manage' a population of 600,000 Albanians in Kosovo – less than one third of the previous population.

What those Serbian officials failed to appreciate was that the very nature of the campaign they had launched against the Kosovar population had radically transformed the resolve of the Western powers, making them much less willing to compromise with Milošević and much more determined to break his military machine. The aim of their action, they announced, was to make Milošević withdraw all his forces from Kosovo and permit the return of all refugees. The air campaign continued without pause, and the definition of strategic interests was enlarged to include oil refineries, factories, television transmitters and even Milošević's house in Belgrade. Public opinion in the major NATO countries, shocked by television pictures of hundreds of thousands of destitute refugees, moved firmly behind the bombing campaign; polls suggested that in the United States more than 50 per cent were in favour of sending in NATO ground troops, and the figure was above 60 per cent in both Britain and France. Officially, the governments of those countries remained strongly opposed to such a move; but all military commentators agreed that the conflict could not be decided by air power alone. Given that the Western governments were also reluctant – for reasons that were less clearly explained – to supply arms to the KLA inside Kosovo, it seemed that there was a gap between the announced ends of the NATO campaign, which were absolute, and the apparent means, which were uncertain.

One other (and greater) uncertainty concerned the ultimate political aims for the NATO actions. At the outset, the stated purpose had been to force Milošević to accept the terms of the Rambouillet accord – a document which, though it restored some degree of autonomy to Kosovo, still affirmed that it was an integral part of Yugoslavia. Once Milošević had launched his terror campaign against the entire Albanian population, it became abundantly clear that the Rambouillet plan was dead: the Albanians would never return to Kosovo on such terms. Western politicians still shied away, however, from the obvious con- clusion, which was that only independence would work. The most commonly stated reason for this reluctance was the claim that granting independence to Kosovo would set a dangerous new precedent; it was argued that if one country's borders were redrawn to reflect ethnic realities, other countries might be forced to do the same. Many states with ethnic minority areas within their borders also feared the con- sequence of such a policy.

This whole argument rested on a misunderstanding of the nature of Kosovo's claim. Independence for Kosovo would involve not setting a new precedent, but following an old one – the precedent of Slovenia, Croatia, Macedonia and Bosnia, which gained their independence in 1991–92. In legal terms (according to the Badinter Commission, a committee of experts advising the European Union at that time), what happened when those states became independent was not secession, not the breaking away of a few branches from a continuing trunk; rather it was the dissolution of the entire Yugoslav Federation into its constituent units. (This post-1992 self-styled Yugoslavia, often wrongly described as 'rump Yugoslavia', is not the continuation of old Yugoslavia but a new state, formed by the coming together of two ex-Yugoslav units, Serbia and Montenegro.) Unfortunately, the Badinter Commission had never specified which entities were the constituent units of the old Yugoslavia, and Western governments had simply made a policy decision to regard only the six republics as such – thus treating Kosovo as a wholly owned subsidiary of Serbia. Possibly they were influenced by the fact that, by the time Yugoslavia broke up, Kosovo's autonomous status had already been revoked by Milošević, but this was an act of dubious legality, pushed through the Kosovo Assembly under blatant duress. Kosovo had in fact been a unit of the federal system, with virtually all the powers of a republic and with its own direct representation on federal bodies. When the entire federation dissolved, therefore, Kosovo should also have been given the right to independence. An independent Kosovo would thus set no new precedent. Its claim would be based on constitutional principles, not ethnic geography, and other countries would become liable to the application of this precedent only if they were federal states in a process of complete dissolution – an extremely rare event in modern history.

Note

1 This chapter first appeared in slightly longer form as a preface to Noel Malcolm, *Kosovo: A Short History*, London: Macmillan, 2002. It is reproduced here with permission.

14   Kosovo and the prognosis for 'humanitarian' war

Mark Bartolini

A prelude to war

Susan Sontag, in the *New York Times*, wrote of the war in Kosovo: 'It's complicated, but it's not that complicated. There is such a thing as a just war.'[1] Given that over 800,000 Kosovar Albanians were brutally driven from their homes and forced into camps in Albania and Macedonia, that thousands were summarily executed inside Kosovo and that hundreds of thousands more were displaced from their homes and families, Sontag's critique appears irrefutable. But from the early days of the war a debate arose among human rights advocates and humanitarians about the legality of going to war and the morality of methods which were used to prosecute the war. Some, the strict constructionists, argued the merits of this case based unwaveringly on the norms of international humanitarian law (IHL) which forbids military action, even non-lethal action, against civilians. Yet, others, the pragmatists, argued that context, and an overriding concept of necessity, must be considered in NATO's performance in Kosovo.[2]

Many in the human rights movement claimed at the time that NATO overemphasised force protection and, in the process, forsook the original aims of the intervention, protecting Kosovar Albanians from Serb aggression. Some critics of NATO's intervention, in addition to charging violations of IHL, also charge NATO with the primary responsibility for Kosovo's humanitarian crisis. They claim that it was NATO's air strikes that triggered widespread violence directed at Albanians. Where the responsibility for Kosovo's humanitarian crisis lies may never be definitively apportioned. But as others argue in this volume, a compelling case can be made that it was Serbian nationalism, and not NATO air strikes or NATO's flawed strategy, that led to the humanitarian crisis.

All wars, even 'just wars' are the result of failed diplomacy. The case of Kosovo is a particularly egregious example of such a failure. The wars in Croatia and Bosnia telegraphed to Western leaders the scale and form of tragedy that could be expected should they fail to peacefully resolve the growing crisis in Kosovo: the unleashing of Serbian government forces and their state-sponsored paramilitary death squads.

The failure of Serbian authorities to amend their 1989 revocation of autonomy in Kosovo, despite years of primarily non-violent struggle by Kosovar Albanians relegated to live in an apartheid state, led to a nascent movement of militant nationalist Albanians. Even though this movement failed to garner broad public support, its mere existence would be used by ultranationalists in Belgrade as cover for the solution to their Kosovo problem: a massive shift of Kosovo's demographics and transference of Albanian wealth in favour of Serbians under the guise of liquidating the Kosovo Liberation Army (KLA). This intent was evidenced by the Serbians' widespread plundering of Albanians and the confiscation of hundreds of thousands of Kosovar Albanian identity documents as they were forced across international borders.

Belgrade's conviction that this strategy of ethnic cleansing would ultimately prevail – the Bosnian war had produced the Republika Srpska, and the West had demonstrated that its interests in the region were not vital enough to challenge Belgrade – left President Clinton in an unenviable position in the spring of 1999. Two confirmed genocides, Bosnia and Rwanda, had already occurred under his watch. All signs pointed to Kosovo becoming the third. Making the situation even worse was the fragility of neighbouring states. A destabilised Macedonia was considered the trigger for a wider Balkan war that could draw in Greece and possibly Turkey. Kosovo, therefore, was the 'line in the sand' drawn by President George Bush who despite never summoning the will to intervene in the other Balkan wars warned in 1991 that Serbian military action in the province would provoke US intervention.

The long list of geopolitical concerns raised by intervention in Kosovo included the UN problem. The pro-Serbian sentiments of Russia and China in the Security Council, and the disastrous legacy of the mandate-less UN intervention in Bosnia resulting from that configuration, made UN legitimacy a non-starter in resolving Kosovo. If intervention was the only option, it would have to be an intervention in a sovereign country without the imprimatur of the UN. This decision continues to divide scholars on international law.

The days leading up to the bombing, and the early days of the bombing, were marked by colossal intelligence failures. US government officials were confident that Milošević, facing NATO bombing, would relent and agree to the principles laid down at Rambouillet. When this did not happen, they convinced themselves that Milošević would capitulate after a few days of NATO bombing 'light'. Hindsight, and the recovery of documents, suggests that NATO faced a Belgrade determined to brutally solve the Kosovo problem through: 'Operation Horseshoe'. The plan called for destabilising neighbouring states by releasing a population bomb from Kosovo's borders while simultaneously permanently altering the provinces' demographics in favour of Serbians.

Some have argued that Belgrade drew up the plans for 'Operation Horseshoe' as a contingency plan should NATO begin bombing and that NATO, knowing of the existence of this plan and deciding to intervene, had a duty to tailor its response to best protect Kosovar Albanians threatened by the plan. It was clear after the first days of air strikes that bombing from 15,000 feet was not going to deter the abuses being committed against Kosovar Albanians. Acknowledging that frustration, one American commander leading the air war commented 'you can't stop a guy from burning down a house at 15,000 feet'. Therefore, according to this school of thought, NATO should have launched a ground war.

While it is not certain that a ground war would have resulted in any fewer casualties than occurred, it is also not clear that the political environment in which the NATO alliance was operating would have allowed for a ground war. And those who argue that Belgrade would not have acted on 'Operation Horseshoe' had NATO not intervened, fail to acknowledge ten years of precedents. Along with the genocide that took place in Bosnia, the year prior to NATO's response saw nearly 500,000 Albanians driven from their homes by Serbian aggression.

Those of us who witnessed the war in Bosnia were not surprised by what was taking place – we had seen it before. The same actors, the same denials and obfuscation. The fact that in March of 1999 President Clinton faced only nightmarish options in Kosovo was due in large part to the fact that three successive administrations failed to vigorously address Kosovo and the Balkan's building tensions. The Dayton Agreement ended the formal war in Bosnia, but a low-level war continued, prosecuted by some of the same actors responsible for the original war. One such actor, Slobodan Milošević, viewed the weakness of the West on Bosnia as a sign that no matter how brutal his tactics, NATO would opt for a face-saving deal on Kosovo. He failed to calculate NATO's resolve in making the return of refugees to their homes (which meant no partition) the *sine quo non* of its continued existence.

The decision to use NATO force demonstrated both leadership, and an acknowledgement of the administration's past failure in Bosnia. It would have been easy to continue the Bosnia lie and treat Kosovo as a humanitarian problem when, like Bosnia, it was fundamentally a political problem requiring a political solution. The decision to use military force to effect that solution was an acknowledgement that the man ordained as a guarantor of peace at Dayton, Slobodan Milošević, was in fact the progenitor of four successive wars in the past decade. To further legitimise him through negotiations would, as it did in Bosnia, only result in continuing instability and suffering in the region.

War in Kosovo

After numerous miscalculations leading to war in Kosovo, perhaps the most criticised aspect of NATO's strategy was its failure to position troops in front-line states prior to commencing the bombing campaign. Milošević knew it would take NATO from six to twelve weeks to deploy troops and material necessary for a ground war. With this in mind he had ample time to try and crack NATO resolve by absorbing the air strikes, create regional chaos by expelling nearly a million Kosovar Albanians, and in the process change Kosovo's demographics. A ground war that might threaten to roll into Serbia, an option NATO considered a last resort, could be avoided by negotiating a settlement as preparations for such an attack began. After two months of bombing, NATO had not yet begun such a deployment and Milošević continued his brutal campaign despite suffering severe losses from nightly bombing raids.

The tactics used by NATO to end the war were clearly aimed more at forcing a political solution to the Kosovo problem, rather than addressing the immediate humanitarian concerns of the Kosovars. Despite all the 'smart bombs' dropped on Kosovo, the Serbian paramilitary and police forces operated with brutality and near impunity throughout the crisis. A visual survey of Kosovo after the June agreement suggests that NATO, while very proficient at hitting fixed targets, may have exaggerated their effectiveness against tanks and heavy artillery. Buildings hit by precision-guided munitions were clearly in evidence, while the hulks of tanks and heavy artillery were few and far between. Immediately following the cessation of hostilities, aid workers describe massive traffic jams as Serbian forces pulled out what some described as 'more tanks than were said to be in all of Kosovo'.[3] And one Turkish journalist who lived through the war in Pristina described elaborate camouflage and 'inflatable tanks and artillery'[4] as methods Serbian forces used to mislead NATO surveillance.

One commentator, when asked the biggest danger facing NATO during the air campaign, remarked 'haemorrhoids'. While this witticism fails to take into account that NATO pilots were at risk and that planes were indeed shot down, some critics wrote that the emphasis on force protection leading to a zero casualty war was tantamount to racism. The statistics were most telling: approximately 10,000 Albanians killed, tens of thousands injured, and nearly a million forced to flee their homes. 'Those people are not worth the life of one American', a sentiment heard uttered in some corners of Capital Hill and the media had been translated into a battlefield strategy. The fear of political fallout, including the fear that Americans would abandon their tenuous support for the war should Americans begin to be killed, quickly changed NATO's goals from protecting Kosovar Albanians, to ensuring that they would one day be able to return home.

Was there a possibility for a more aggressive intervention that would have saved lives and resulted in fewer traumas to the people of Kosovo and their culture? Early preparations for a ground invasion might well have forced Milošević to capitulate and have saved lives. A ground invasion, or the threat of one, in the early days of the war may also have resulted in less loss of life and suffering for all sides. However, in the time it would take to assemble such a force, the same scenario of cleansing and killing could have occurred. Moreover, such an action would have created additional political problems with Russia and China and would have bitterly divided NATO allies, threatening an already tenuous alliance. And should a ground invasion actually have occurred, it is likely that a large number of Albanians would have been killed, being used as human shields by Serbian forces. In summary, the pre-positioning of substantial NATO forces capable of carrying out a ground assault against Serb forces prior to NATO bombing might have saved lives. But it is not clear that political realities facing key NATO countries including the United States, France and Germany would have allowed for such a deployment.

Another criticism was the altitude and composition of the air strikes. Would the use of low flying A-10 'tank killers' and Apache helicopters have brought a quicker resolution? As reported by Dana Priest in the *Washington Post*,[5] this was a heated debate within the NATO command structure. According to military experts, such tactics would also have resulted in NATO casualties.[6] But these same experts also claim the use of low-flying aircraft would have sharply curtailed the ability of Serbian forces to commit atrocities against Albanians by inflicting serious casualties on Serbian forces. Given the number of civilian casualties that occurred in Kosovo as a result of a combination of NATO mistakes and the brutal Serbian use of civilians as human shields, it was likely this tactic would have further exacerbated the political strains in the NATO alliance. Belgrade never failed to capitalise on civilian deaths by allowing television crews in to film the carnage. But whether the losses to Serbian forces would have broken the resolve of Belgrade before NATO and civilian casualties broke the resolve of NATO remains an open question.

The Clinton administration deserves tremendous credit for making the difficult decision to take action. But they failed to make any but a tertiary case to the American public of why Kosovo was important and why military action was the only way to respond to Milošević's aggression. Part of the reason that President Clinton found it so difficult to make the case for Kosovo, was because of his obfuscation on Bosnia. At one point he claimed that his failure to act in Bosnia had been unduly influenced by a book describing the war in Bosnia in a historical context (despite the fact that the author of the book was publicly urging intervention during the Bosnian war). But now he understood that carnage in the Balkans was not necessarily ordained by history. Going back through the record of statements on Bosnia by candidate Clinton reveals a politician who asserted that the only appropriate moral response to genocide was intervention. But the actions of President Clinton reveal obfuscation in the face of the political costs of intervention.

Only a handful of politicians in Washington stood out during the Balkan crisis. Chief among those taking a stand was former Senator Bob Dole who championed the cause of US engagement as the only road to peace in the Balkans. In Congress an odd coalition of pacifist Democrats joined forces with newly reconstructed isolationist Republicans. At times such Republicans seemed bent more on discrediting a president they deemed illegitimate due to domestic scandal, rather than supporting what in years past might have been deemed a 'meat and potatoes' Republican issue: the credibility of NATO. Again, there were notable exceptions to this isolationist shift as evidenced in the critical support for NATO given by Senator John Warner and Senator John McCain.

Whatever the reasoning behind the intervention, much criticism, even from human rights groups and humanitarians, was aimed at the administration for the perceived results of the bombing campaign – the refugee crisis. But if one considers the history of the Balkans in the past decade, and the preparations being made prior to NATO's bombing by Serbian forces in Kosovo, it is simply a failure to understand Balkan politics that leads to the assertion that NATO bombing drove the Serbians to brutally and forcibly drive nearly a million Albanians from their homes, all the while destroying mosques and historic Turkish districts, burning homes and looting possessions.

In a 1999 article in *The National Interest*, entitled 'For the Record', the authors assert that the depopulation of Kosovo was a 'military tactic designed to restrict the [KLA] base of support and cover'.[7] It goes on to say that 'students of "low intensity" conflict will recognize the similarities between the counterinsurgency tactics of the Serbs in Kosovo and those of the French in Algeria, the British in the Boer War and the Americans in the Philippines'.[8] Such an argument fails to recognise the character of Serbian actions in cleansing Kosovo of its Albanian population.

Despite a few stories in the press in which Albanian refugees were quoted as saying they were fleeing Kosovo because of NATO bombing, the vast majority of Albanians fled because they were forced out by Serbian forces. This was confirmed by the overwhelming nature of responses in the Albanian and Macedonian camps, as well as by statistical surveys, one of which was conducted by Physicians for Human Rights.[9] The specific events leading to individual flight vary considerably. Some were warned that they had to leave or they would be killed. Some were helped by Serbian neighbours or even local police who offered advice on how to avoid the MUP (Serbian military police) and paramilitary forces. Others witnessed Serbian neighbours they had known all their life murdering, raping and robbing Albanians. In rural areas many fled the shelling which preceded advancing paramilitary units used to cleanse a village. A majority of refugees were robbed at some point in their exodus and very few were allowed to leave Kosovo with their identity documents.

It seems a denial of the history of the previous ten years to think that Milošević would not have depopulated much of Kosovo had air strikes not occurred. The cleansing of Kosovo began in 1989 when Milošević revoked autonomy for the province. That was when Albanians began to leave. Stage two was accomplished in the summer of 1998 when over 350,000 internally displaced persons and refugees were driven from their homes. The spring of 1999 was the final stage in the Milošević solution to the Kosovo problem: 600,000 internally displaced, over 800,000 refugees, perhaps more than 10,000 killed, and much of the country, especially its historic Turkish districts, destroyed.[10]

The command and control necessary to logistically complete the deportation of such huge numbers of people could not have occurred spontaneously. Refugees described preparations made prior to the air strikes that also foretold the cleansing of Kosovo. The stories told by refugees coming across the border mirror in many ways the methodology of 'ethnic cleansing' employed in Bosnia. In fact many of the same individuals and paramilitary groups (including those operated by Arkan's 'Tigers' and Seselj's 'Franky's Boys') participated in the cleansing of Kosovo. The Serbian VJ (Yugoslav army), MUP and paramilitary forces orchestrated a systematic campaign of terror that included murder, rape, torture and larceny. As in Bosnia, money was the fuel driving the juggernaut of ethnic cleansing. It created a kind of frenzy among those doing the cleansing. Before houses were blown up, they were looted of everything valuable including TVs, stereos, VCRs, even major appliances.

Then the people themselves were robbed. There were numerous stories of masked men entering homes holding a knife or gun to a child and demanding money from the parents. There were also refugees whose children were killed in front of them when they had no money to give. And there were new twists to the process. Refugee women in several Albanian refugee camps told of how baby bottles were system-atically snatched from their hands and smashed in front of them. These women then had to travel several days, sometimes on foot, to leave Kosovo. Why would soldiers do such a thing? Did they know that traumatised women are often unable to lactate and so would have no other means of feeding their babies? The fact that these were not iso-lated incidents (the two NGOs working to replace these bottles pur-chased thousands of bottles) is evidence of the intent of Serbian forces.

In addition to this general mayhem, there was a more orchestrated process. The intellectuals, the doctors, and those who worked with international organisations were targeted. Numerous mosques and other vestiges of Muslim culture were destroyed. By eliminating the societal leaders, creating terror in the population, destroying their homes and businesses, and eliminating cultural, religious and historical sites, the Serbians attempted to erase a culture.

Virtually all the refugees when they were forced out were told that 'Kosovo is Serbian, it is for Serbians.' All identification documents were stripped from Albanians at the border by Serbian police. It seems illo-gical to conclude, given all these details, that it was NATO's bombs that led Serbians to drive Albanians out of Kosovo and Albanians to flee. It was ethnically based greed and hatred fuelled by a political structure seeking to reverse decades of demographic shifts in favour of Kosovar Albanians.

Did NATO air strikes hasten this process? Unquestionably. 'Opera-tion Horseshoe', the Serbian military document reported to describe planning for the cleansing of Kosovo, appears to have calculated NATO bombing into the equation of the mass expulsion of Kosovar refugees. Especially in the opening weeks of the bombing campaign, the cleansing was accomplished at much swifter rates than experienced in Bosnia. Some military experts speculated that the Serbians feared that after the initial days of bombing took out their air defences, their mobility would be curtailed by low-flying attack aircraft and thus the haste to cleanse.

The speed with which the cleansings occurred may have actually saved lives. There are two areas of Bosnia where similar, in terms of numbers, cleansing occurred. Northern Bosnia around the Banja Luka region and eastern Bosnia around Visegrad. Approximately 800,000 Muslims and Croats were cleansed from northern Bosnia in 1992–93. The cleansing continued for well over a year. During that time death camps were operating, rape camps were operating, and tens of thousands of people were killed. A similar scenario unfolded in eastern Bosnia.

We know from refugee stories in the early days of the Kosovo conflict that the pace of cleansing was so chaotic that many men were able to slip into the throngs of those fleeing. Who is to say what is a bigger humanitarian disaster: 800,000 fleeing out of Kosovo in one month or 800,000 fleeing in six months or a year? If one takes Bosnia as the example, it is possible to argue that the cleansing of northern Bosnia in relation to what was done in Kosovo demonstrates that lives might have actually been saved because of the rapid rate of expulsions.

Almost from the start of the air war, many humanitarians called for ground intervention as the only possible measure to end the suffering of the Kosovar population. While it will never be known whether an early ground invasion or a more aggressive air campaign would have resulted in fewer casualties and less suffering, it is clear that the Pentagon's long-held maxim that air power alone could not win a war was wrong. While there is some evidence to suggest that only when NATO allies began to edge towards a ground war did Milošević capitulate, it was air power alone that ultimately fulfilled NATO's goal of returning over 800,000 refugees to their homes.

Human Rights' groups and humanitarians have raised serious questions about the type of ordinance and specific targets of NATO air strikes. Some warned that NATO was subject to the jurisdiction of the International Criminal Tribunal in the Hague (ICTY). They claimed the deliberate bombing of Yugoslavia's electrical grid and the use of cluster bombs violated IHL. While the use of cluster bombs against civilian targets was denied by the Pentagon, there is evidence that such attacks occurred, although it is unclear whether the possibility of civilian casualties was given an appropriate review, or were the result of unintended 'collateral damage' or malfunctioning munitions. Nevertheless cluster bombs pose a long-term hazard to civilians in the region almost at the level of Serbian laid land mines. Thousands of these small bomblets lie unexploded, but still potentially lethal, in Kosovo and Serbia, and are thus a major challenge for the de-mining missions.

The decision to bomb Serbia's electrical grid was another contentious violation of IHL. Writing in *The New Yorker*, Michael Ignatieff argued that bombing Serbia's transformers turned out to be the 'single most effective military strike of the campaign...'[11] But the most effective strike of the war was also the most morally problematic. Hitting the grid meant taking out the power for hospitals, babies' incubators, water-pumping stations and steam heating systems. It meant that many civilians in Serbia would pass a very uncomfortable winter, although without the sniper fire and shelling that – in addition to no heat – characterised winter for Sarajevans during the Serb nationalist four-year siege of that city.

Hitting the grid also meant that almost a million people would not have to spend the winter in makeshift shelters and tents in Albania, Macedonia and Montenegro because they were able to return to their homes. It meant that no more cluster bombs would be dropped. It meant that a parent would not have to watch a child killed before their eyes by Serbian paramilitaries; nor would Serbian parents have to fear for their children being hit by a NATO bomb. In short, bombing the power grid, while in violation of IHL, had a predominantly non-lethal impact on Serbian civilians, yet likely saved countless lives. And it is one reason that while attempts to regulate war are worthy and necessary, war is by nature such a horrific and unpredictable facet of man's existence that strict observance of IHL may not in all cases be the *sine qua non* for mitigating suffering and saving lives.

Nonetheless, the human rights movement must stand fast to its purist adherence to the principles of IHL. The assertion of a moral justification to countenance any act of war no matter how barbaric is a slippery slope. (Serbian snipers shooting children in Sarajevo claimed it as a way to bring the war to a quicker end, firebombing entire cities, using nuclear weapons to save soldiers' lives, etc.). It is necessary for the guardians of IHL to practise strict constructionism.

So while it is both laudable and necessary to advocate principles of war that protect civilians, it is unlikely to be clear-cut how the principles of IHL, if adhered to by only one side in a conflict, will impact the civilian population. This in itself is not a reason to abandon principles. The human rights community performs an invaluable and heroic service by reporting on human rights abuses in complex emergencies, such as those that have occurred in Chechnya, Afghanistan, Iraq, Chad and Sudan. But, at least in part due to their concern over how a war might be conducted, they are loath to call for military intervention. If, as Sontag suggests, 'There is such a thing as a just war',[12] then the reluctance, and often outright inability, of such groups to call for intervention works against the victims of aggression.

A division of labour between the human rights and the broader humanitarian community would help to ameliorate this problem. The International Crisis Group (ICG), an organisation with the requisite regional knowledge and mandate to raise these complex issues is an example of an attempt to bridge this gap. However, human rights groups and humanitarian agencies hold a capacity for moral suasion that is infinitely more influential among policymakers than any group currently trying to bridge the gap between purists and pragmatists. The inherent limitations on advocating for military intervention to resolve conflicts makes human rights groups and humanitarian agencies subject to the same failings the United Nations recently admitted to in Bosnia:

Through error, misjudgement, and the inability to recognize the scope of evil confronting us we failed to do our part to save the people of Srebrenica from the Serb campaign of mass murder ... These failings were in part rooted in a philosophy of neutrality and non-violence wholly unsuited to the conflict in Bosnia ... The cardinal lesson of Srebrenica is that a deliberate and systematic attempt to terrorize, expel or murder an entire people must be met decisively with all necessary means.[13]

Failing the ascendancy of more non-governmental organisations like the ICG, whose voice can rise to the level of the most influential human rights and humanitarian agencies, the humanitarian and human rights community may be guilty of safeguarding the principles of IHL to the last victim of a Rwanda or Bosnia-like genocide.

The post-war conundrum

The West has had time to discuss the moral dimensions of tactics used and not used during the war in Kosovo, but the people of the Balkans have had to live with the results. There is much discussion of collective responsibility among Serbians for instigating four wars over the last decade. Some will doubtless have to reconcile their own silence or support for what was being done to the Albanians with their own suffering. But there should be a great deal of remorse and support for those Serbians who did not support the cleansing of Kosovo and who nonetheless suffered from NATO strikes or Albanian reprisals. As Batim Haxoi, the editor of Kosovo's independent daily *Koha Ditore*, (having fled from Kosovo into Tetovo, Macedonia) noted, when asked why Americans should die for Kosovars, the issue was more than Kosovo. Haxoi remarked: 'NATO is not fighting for Albanians. It is fighting for the ideal that this [the cleansing of Kosovo] is not acceptable at the dawn of the 21st century.'[14]

NATO assumed a responsibility when it intervened in Kosovo that it is failing to meet. Serbians, some of them too young or too old to have been involved in Kosovo's cleansing, have been murdered. In 1999, in Pristina a 70-year-old Serbian man was nailed to his door and then had his throat slit. Others were shot through their doors. Some of the Serbians remaining in Kosovo assisted their Albanian neighbours; yet, in the aftermath of the war, they were indiscriminately targeted. There seems to have been a conviction among many in the international community that reprisals were tolerable, given what the Albanians endured. But there is a question as to whether these incidents are best described as random acts of revenge or organised attempts to cleanse Serbians from Kosovo in the misguided belief that this would lead to independence. In either case, it is incumbent on the international community to address the issue of human rights violations as a political problem – something they did not do publicly until the disturbances in early 2004.

The Kosovo experience highlighted the imperfect and complex nature of military intervention on humanitarian grounds. It forever dispelled the 'big lie' used in Bosnia that air strikes alone could not win a war. (In fact proponents of air strikes in Bosnia were not looking for them to 'win' the war, but to alter the balance of power enough to bring the parties to a negotiated settlement.) But, unlike the recent campaign in Iraq, it also highlighted the complex process of prosecuting a war based on humanitarian goals rather than vital national interests. In the end it was not the Kosovars for which the war was fought, but the need for NATO to prevail.

In summing up the lessons of Kosovo, President Clinton claimed that when it could, regardless of state sovereignty, the United States would intervene when masses of people are being killed. He further asserted that the United States had a clear national interest in ensuring that Kosovo was where the trouble must end.[15] However, the continuing bloodshed in parts of Africa and the Caucasus demonstrates that Kosovo, like Iraq, was the exception, not the rule.

One administration official, when commenting on comparisons between US government policy on Bosnia and Kosovo remarked: 'We won't make the same mistakes we did in Bosnia. We will make new ones.' To a great extent this intended witticism has proved to be the case. Unlike in Bosnia, the correct decision to use force in Kosovo was made. But the emphasis on force protection to the point that NATO took minimal risks to safeguard the victims and suffered no combat casualties itself has rendered concepts of humanitarian intervention infinitely more problematic and set the bar impossibly high for future humanitarian interventions on the scale of Kosovo.

Notes

1 Susan Sontag, 'Why are we in Kosovo?' *New York Times Magazine*, 2 May 1999, p. 52, col. 1.
2 One of the most engaged advocates of the war in Kosovo was Michael Ignatieff who claimed that the war in Kosovo broke new ground and could be declared a humanitarian war. see Michael Ignatieff, *Virtual War: Kosovo and Beyond*, New York: Henry Holt, 2000.
3 International Aid worker, interview with the author Pristina, Kosovo, July 1999.
4 Sharif Targut, interview with the author, Washington, DC, 5 September 1999.
5 Dana Priest, 'Kosovo land threat may have won war', *The Washington Post*, 19 September 1999, p. A1.
6 Interview with Apache helicopter commander.
7 Christopher Layne and Benjamin Schwarz, 'For the Record', *The National Interest*, Fall 1999, p. 13, col. 1.
8 Ibid., col. 4.
9 See Physicians for Human Rights, *War Crimes in Kosovo: A Population-Based Assessment of Human Rights Violations of Kosovar Albanians by Serb Forces*, 15 June 1999: www.phrusa.org/past_news_kexec.html.
10 For a detailed account of the abuses carried out by Serbian forces against the citizens in Kosovo, including documentation of 5,000 individual and mass grave killing sites and revenge attacks conducted against Serbs, Roma, Gorani and others, see *Erasing History: Ethnic Cleansing in Kosovo*, US Department of State, May 1999. www.state.gov/www/regions/eur/rpt_9905_ethnic_ksvo_toc.html.
11 Michael Ignatieff, 'The virtual commander: how NATO invented a new kind of war,' *The New Yorker*, 2 August 1999.
12 Sontag, 'Why are we in Kosovo?', p. 52.
13 Barbara Crossette, 'UN details its failure to stop '95 Bosnia massacre', *New York Times*, 16 November 1999, col. 8, 12.
14 Batim Haxoi, interview with the author, Tetovo, Macedonia, April 1999.
15 Clinton Foreign Policy Speech, San Francisco, 26 February 1999.

15 The international administration of Kosovo since 1999

Bryan Hopkinson

Introduction

The riots which broke out in mid-March 2004 brought Kosovo back onto the international agenda and into the headlines.[1] Until then it had been considered a modest success of the international presence that an area which so dominated international politics in early 1999 had barely featured since, allowing hard-pressed foreign and defence ministries to address other problems. But the international presence had always struggled with difficulties in attempting to turn Kosovo into a pluralistic liberal Western open society. Was this job done badly, or was it always impossible? This chapter concentrates not on the performance of UNMIK, but on the factors that made it so difficult to administer Kosovo despite the quasi-sovereign powers enjoyed by the special representative of the secretary-general (SRSG).

The difficulties of conception

The concept of the international administration of Kosovo was created in a few days in June 1999 in a climate of emergency.[2] Kosovo at the time was perceived as a war-torn society where the most difficult problems would be to manage the return of the 800,000 or so Albanian refugees mostly in Macedonia and Albania; and to enforce authority against the main enemy, Belgrade under Milošević. The structure created was a tribute to quick thinking, and looked like an improvement on the loose international family which moved into Bosnia in 1996. There was at least a unified international structure, the four-pillar UNMIK. However, the environment into which UNMIK deployed was not the environment foreseen in UNSCR 1244 – instead of remaining in refugee camps outside Kosovo, the Albanian population returned in a mass, while the ethnic-Serb population, together with all authorities, left – or at least consolidated themselves in areas where they had always formed a majority. Not the Yugoslav Army – which departed in an orderly manner, as set down in 1244 – but the KLA emerged as the most powerful indigenous armed force. Not officials loyal to Belgrade, but rusticated Albanians who had been kept out of public life for ten years, occupied the positions of government and started to entrench themselves. The assumptions underlying UNSCR 1244 were out of date before the international administration even started to deploy. Although UNSCR 1244 would never hobble successive SRSGs as badly as the absurdities of Dayton hobbled their near peers holding the post of High Representative in Bosnia, yet like them they were stuck with an instrument designed for another purpose. Against this, it should be noted that both officials have used their rigid mandates as a policy basis to block unwelcome indigenous initiatives in their areas. But either way, the mandate has been a brake, not a motor.

The difficulties of arrival

The refugee Albanian population moved back into Kosovo far faster than the arriving international authorities.[3] There had been no masterplan for staffing the emergency, and there were no trained cohorts of administrators waiting for the order to deploy. UN career staff and UNVs were deployed as quickly as they could be made available, but needed to be supplemented by specialists who took time to recruit. The EU, OSCE and others, all with their own separate recruitment mechanisms, coped with varying degrees of success with the need for a rapid build-up of suitable staff. Self-establishing Albanian authorities had no such problem: it was an easy matter to walk into town halls and take possession. For them the problem was resources; with no functioning industry or employment their role as self-appointed governors could be little more than titular. Mostly they waited for the UN officials to arrive, to enter into partnership with them.

The absence of any police force, and the unfitness of international police who started to arrive, was a particular difficulty. The UN authorities were dependent on individual member states of the UN to send them policemen. At first, the difficulty was that member states acted too slowly, and for several critical weeks Kosovo was an unpoliced society. Organised crime quickly moved into the gap, the self-established Albanian provisional authorities ran their own unofficial police, and there was open season for persecuting those few Serbs who had not fled the moment SCR 1244 was passed. KFOR soldiers at this time attempted basic policing with degrees of enthusiasm and success which varied wildly between national units, but in general felt aggrieved at having to do the civilians' job in addition to their own. Later, police flooded in from all corners of the world, creating a new problem – how to police an alien society with an impenetrable language. Once arrived, the international police were faced with the self-created difficulty of dealing with the local interests who had started to carry out their own policing. Were these people thugs to be suppressed or potential colleagues to be co-opted?

Against these manifold difficulties of the arriving civilian presence, the multinational force KFOR quietly and effectively established itself. KLA units were surprised to be treated by arriving KFOR units with suspicion rather than as allies, but nowhere did KFOR meet opposition; everywhere it was welcomed as a liberator by the population. The contrast between military and civilian performance has often been noted. Perhaps, indeed, the military performed a simple task well, the civilians a complex task badly – but pro-military analysts fond of contrasting the successes of KFOR with the failures of the civilians seldom ask how KFOR would have fared if it had had to recruit all its personnel only after SCR 1244 had been passed.

The difficulties of trust-building

Some did, some did not, accept UNMIK as a legitimate authority. At the political level two different sets of Albanian authorities claimed legitimacy: the KLA by right of conquest, superior organisation and a presumption of popular acclaim (though they never enjoyed quite the degree of popular support they thought they had); and Ibrahim Rugova's prewar parliament and government which existed only in theory (but which in elections later on proved to have much more genuine popularity). As UNMIK tried to assert its authority over these two groups, at the same time it tried to bring them into dialogue. For months the SRSG was a sad but valiant figure, promoting an ideal of dialogue and compromise which seemed to find no echo in his interlocutors. Finally, after half a year of unsuccessful attempts, the UN managed to establish a working mechanism for dialogue and cooperation which brought together all major local interests, and this survived until elections at the end of 2001.

With the remaining Serbs there was a different difficulty. They tended to insist on a literal interpretation of SCR 1244, negotiate toughly, be very ready to take offence, and always liable to resort to boycotts. Meanwhile, in the areas they inhabited, they tried to live like ordinary Serbians in a parallel society which ignored UNMIK attempts to govern it. The Belgrade government cooperated in this, making available to them what services it could.

In general, any attempt to promote 'multiethnicity' in Kosovo (the avowed objective of the international community) was doomed to failure.[4] The intercommunal rioting in March 2004 showed just how deep that failure had been. It was not necessarily that reconciliation activities could not work – quite the contrary, reconciliation was a crowded field where minor successes were being reported all the time – but that the forces in society working to keep relations hostile were stronger and more ruthless than those working to improve them.

The difficulties of delivery

Under the bad-tempered surface of political life, the UN gradually imposed some normality on everyday life, using donations from any source. In the summer of 1999 towns choked on the smell of burning rubbish-heaps in the street; gradually garbage collection was put in place. At first there was no public transport – second-hand buses began to arrive, donations from German cities. Daily life and expectations for ordinary people began to return to the rather drab normality which had always been the lot of Kosovo's inhabitants. Institutions were created, staffed at first mostly by international experts (many of whom were admittedly not very expert, but at least understood how to function within an organisation). A combination of dogged perseverance by international officials, and cheerful resilience on the part of the population, schooled to take care of themselves during years of neglect by much less palatable authorities than those they now lived under, re-established a society of sorts, poor but functioning.

But UNMIK laboured under the burden of unrealistic expectations, on the part of the populace and of its own officials. Much of the population seemed to think Kosovo would be given a Western-type society and economy as a donation, and many of the officials prepared to volunteer for uncomfortable post-war jobs were idealistic rather than practical. And yet, by any measure, Kosovo was a poor and backward part of Europe. Even as an economy in transition from communism it was handicapped by its recent history and its present dilapidation. Democratic pluralism could not be created by legislation, unfortunately, and the societal changes, which alone could create it, were probably a generation away. Even that timetable depended on economic growth and the creation of a critical mass of citizens with some financial interest in the rule of law – rather than a small number of influential people doing very well out of the opposite.

Yet what no one could create out of nothing was a new economy. Kosovo had never been rich, and had lived for years by exporting its young men to work in blue-collar jobs in Germany and Switzerland. Now even those industries which had existed were either obsolete rusting factories or destroyed by war and the departing authorities; for example the famous Trepca mines, once among the richest in Europe, had become an environmental liability rather than an industrial asset. This difficulty of foreseeing a future livelihood for Kosovo under any political dispensation was never overcome. Kosovar politicians claimed dubiously that investment would follow independence, but meanwhile, the only investments were chic restaurants and bars for the use of international officials, and shiny hotels and shopping centres with the smell of money-laundering hanging around them.

The difficulties of handover

By the end of 2002 many Albanians felt that they could now do without the international civilian presence – though all still wanted the NATO protection provided by KFOR. For different reasons, mainly to do with budgetary pressures and new priorities elsewhere, the international side was also anxious to accelerate a process of Kosovarisation – a process which had always existed, but had previously gone at a snail's pace. Even in 2003 many in the international presence considered that locals were not yet qualified or competent to take over, but the hand-over of an ever-growing range of responsibilities continued, excepting only competences which would remain reserved to the SRSG as long as SCR 1244 remained in force.

Although Albanian politicians demanded ever-increasing control over their own society, their overriding preoccupation was still to achieve independence for Kosovo. This was something the SRSG could not deliver even if he wanted to – the arrangement set up in UNSCR 1244 could only be changed at the same level. The issue of independence stupefied political life among Albanians, making it impossible to discuss any other topic sensibly, making it indeed impossible to have any normal political life in the sense of a debate between different parties on policy.

Many Serb areas were running their own affairs much as they always had done. Handover was for them, if anything, unwelcome, since it appeared to them to promote a drift towards independence, an unacceptable result. While details of Serb arguments constantly changed, their general position was that Serbs should not be required to live under Albanian rule. It was hard to see how this could ever be squared with the policy of the international presense, which was to promote a multiethnic society within a unitary Kosovo. And the unforgiving attitude of most Albanians did nothing to help reconcile Serbs to the new reality.

The difficulties of exit

From its first days, UNMIK had always had one eye on the exit door. It was hoped that Kosovo would be a much simpler task than Bosnia, and not nearly such a terrible drain on resources. Exit seemed to depend on two open questions: what status would Kosovo have when UNMIK left (an explicit condition in UNSCR 1244), and when could the job of society-building be said to have been achieved?

Status was always going to be problematic. Kosovo remained part of Serbia. UNSCR 1244 had not changed its status, only hinted that its status might change. Serbia claimed to want to keep it. The entire Albanian population wanted independence. Getting the two sides to talk to each other might possibly help – except that if any compromise at all was possible between them it must involve ethnic division of some sort, and so complete defeat for the ideal of multiethnicity in which the international community had invested so much. Moreover, it would reopen the question of inconvenient frontiers elsewhere in the Balkans. In limbo, the status of Kosovo gave little trouble except to the frustrated officials in the field; any new solution risked destabilising, yet again, a region which the world's chanceries really did not want to spend any more time on.

The creation of a sustainable society was by comparison an easier task, at least to understand. Once it was clear that UNMIK was not aiming to leave behind a new Denmark or Luxembourg, but rather something more in keeping with the immediate neighbourhood, the exit door seemed less firmly shut. UNMIK from 2002 judged the progress of Kosovo society against a series of 'benchmarks' representing acceptable minimal standards of modern democracy. Even against these minimum standards Kosovo was easily seen to be unsatisfactory – but Kosovars asked how many of their neighbours would pass such a test. 'Standards before Status' was at first the slogan, designed to show that a good society was more important than an abstract idea, but it failed to capture hearts and minds. As a result, the slogan was quietly dropped, and by 2004 had become simply 'Standards for Kosovo', accompanied by an epic-length Implementation Plan. A new feature was a half-promise from the international community to begin a process for resolving Kosovo's final status by mid 2005 if progress towards Standards was satisfactory – naturally enough, this created a belief among Albanians of 'Independence in 2005'. But following the riots of mid March 2004, an orderly withdrawal by UNMIK, leaving behind a stable multiethnic society and a job well done, still seemed a remote prospect.

The difficulties of assessment

State-building in the modern era is still a new field. Between 1999 and 2003, a sort of state was constructed in Kosovo despite its limbo status, though many international officials believed that not even minimum standards of public service and law and order would be maintained if they all left. Kosovo had never before been a state, it had always been part of someone else's empire. What could reasonably have been expected of an international administration whose members could not even read the billboards in the street? The daily agenda tended to be driven by the personalities of the leading actors; could different personalities have produced better results, or were they just floating on the surface of events they could really control very little? Certainly mistakes were made. Certainly money was wasted or embezzled but was any of this crucial? Could the multiethnic democracy have been created in five years with a skeleton and mostly amateur government?

Lessons learned

This observer believes that if the NATO bombing had not been followed up with a civil administration, however imperfect, Kosovo would in 1999 have transformed itself from a totalitarian dictatorship run from Belgrade into a similar one run from Pristina, with warlords and criminals at the top. Avoiding that result has been a triumph in itself, and it is hard to see how a military presence alone would have managed it. But the positive achievements of UNMIK have been disappointing when set against its ambitions. Perhaps such a task cannot be done perfectly, but it can be done better:

- Deployment must be quicker. The loss of the first few post-war weeks in Kosovo gave the international deployment an initial disadvantage which took months to redress – if indeed it was ever fully redressed.
- Of course it is difficult to put together mandates for international operations, and we cannot expect perfection in the midst of crisis. But both the Dayton peace agreement and UNSCR 1244 have become untouchable commandments for those implementing them on the ground; however, out of sympathy they later become with real conditions. Cannot mandates be a bit more flexible?
- Internationals must take local languages more seriously. However difficult the language, three weeks' intensive training can make the difference between understanding and ignorance. And the difference is

important, as anyone who has worked both with and without interpreters will confirm.

- Law and order are the first priority, but the international community has no police force of its own, while its component members do have armies they have been ready and able to deploy quickly. So, the military must be trained and prepared to carry out emergency policing, however much they hate it.

Finally, some homilies. Organisations are led from the top and their performance, and the relations between them, are a question of personalities – but societal change comes from the bottom and is a question of education; confusing the two is bound to lead to frustration. Peace can be imposed when people are weary of war, but minds cannot be changed by order, even if the changes are seen as desirable by all parties. Economic development is both a cause and result of increasing pluralism and openness, but breaking into this virtuous circle is trickier than it looks. Elections do not create democracy, but the people who win them think they do.

Notes

1 See Organisation for Security and Cooperation Mission in Kosovo, *Human Rights Challenges Following the March Riots*, May 2004: http://www.osce.org/documents/mik/2004/05/2939_en.pdf
2 For a good historical account of the development of UNMIK as a lead agency, see Kurt R. Spillmann and Joachim Krause (eds.), *Kosovo: Lessons Learned for International Cooperative Security*, Studies in Contemporary History and Security Policy, vol. 5, Bern: Peter Lang, 2000.
3 Within ten days, 300,000 refugees returned. *UNHCR Briefing Note: Kosovo*, 25 June 1999: http://www.reliefweb.int/w/rwb.nsf/0/3ea3e43e357094-ba8525679b00488f6e?OpenDocument
4 Subsequent proposals to create Serb enclaves in Kosovo have also weakened the prospect for a genuinely multiethnic state. See the recent European Stability Initiative Report, *The Lausanne Principle: Multiethnicity, Territory and the Future of Kosovo's Serbs*, European Stability Initiative, Berlin/Pristina, 7 June 2004: http://www.esiweb.org/pdf/esi_document_id_53.pdf

16 After the storm: Greece's role in reconstruction

Thanos Veremis

The disparate record of Balkan states in attaining independence throughout the nineteenth century and even as late as the twentieth century and their intermittent efforts at constructing administrative and parliamentary institutions, were never free of European politics. Their irredentist wars against Ottoman rule and the resultant borders were closely supervised by foreign patrons and regulated by the principles that governed European relations. If the First World War restructured the boundaries of the Balkans and afforded a period of relative freedom from great power involvement, the communist era that followed the Second World War imposed Soviet influence and impeded Balkan development along Western lines.

Of all the Balkan states, Greece alone escaped the fate of being engulfed by communism. The victory of anti-communist forces in the civil war of 1946–49 secured the country into the Western camp, and made it, along with Turkey, the bulwark of NATO's defence in its southern flank. Throughout the Cold War period Greece's major security concerns on its northern frontiers focused on Bulgaria, a loyal Soviet ally, and Yugoslavia, whenever its relations with Moscow improved. The Greek provinces of Macedonia and Thrace constituted the apples of discord in the Yugoslav, Bulgarian and Greek triangle.

The concept of a territorial unification of the three Macedonias (Greek, Bulgarian and Serb) into an autonomous whole was expounded by Bulgarian communist leaders at the Comintern Congress of 1924. During World War II the idea was appropriated by the pro-Axis Bulgarian forces that annexed both Greek and Yugoslav territory. After liberation, it was Tito's turn to usurp the plan and put it to use in Yugoslavia.[1] The Vardar province of Serbia was renamed the Socialist Republic of Macedonia and was deemed a rump state with irredentist claims on its neighbours. Although Tito, as a non-aligned communist, maintained the strategic value of Yugoslavia for the West, the claims of his federated republic on Greek territory could not prevail over a NATO ally. The collapse of communism altered the rules of the game and Eastern Europe's prodigal sons were greeted without prejudice by the Western family. It was during this period of transition that the Greek government of 1992–95 committed a mistake that tarnished its Balkan credibility.

Having acquired a reputation for anti-Western sentiments due to Andreas Papandreou's maverick politics, official Greek positions on the new Macedonian question were greeted with suspicion by the Western community. The official Greek view that the Federated Socialist Republic of Macedonia should not be recognised as an independent state with the term 'Macedonia' in its new designation, proved impossible to defend in a post-communist environment. Unfortunately both Athens and Skopje persisted in a policy that had ceased to be relevant.[2] The former insisted on its Cold War fixation with the Slavo-Macedonian irredentist threat, patronised by a powerful Yugoslavia, while the latter still cultivated its foundation myths that appropriate Greek and Bulgarian cultural elements which consider the Greek and Bulgarian provinces as 'occupied territories' and promote the 1924 Comintern map of the united Macedonia (see The schoolbook of FYROM).[3]

The Greek nationalist outburst had spent itself by the summer of 1995. On 13 September of that year the Interim Accord was signed by foreign ministers Karolos Papoulias and Stevo Crvenkovski, and Cyrus Vance as a special envoy of the UN secretary general. Although the Accord was a temporary agreement to be followed by a permanent settlement of Macedonia's name, relations between Athens and Skopje improved considerably and no major relapse has marred them since.

Greek responses to the disintegration of Yugoslavia and the case of Kosovo

Of all the EU states, Greece resisted the dissolution of Yugoslavia with the greatest tenacity. Yugoslavia not only offered the quickest land route to the West, but any turbulence in that state was sure to have an effect on neighbouring Greece. Furthermore, the creation of an independent Macedonian entity harbouring the irredentist designs of a new nation made the prospect of dissolution less palatable to the Greeks. Greece's initial sympathy for Serbia was partly based on having fought on the same side during two world wars and also for sharing the same religious denomination. The warmth of the relationship, however, was exaggerated by foreign and domestic media, because in fact good will between the two states had dissipated in the post-war years due to Tito's

Macedonian policy. Milošević's recognition of Macedonia as the 'Republic of Macedonia' was the beginning of a cooling in Greek–Serb relations.

Greek politicians and diplomats, well versed in regional politics and past irredentist struggles, warned the EU of the violence that a break-up of Yugoslavia would unleash. The Greek prediction was that recognition of secessionist unitary states, in which preponderant ethnic forces held sway over their own minorities, would provoke a chain reaction of further ethnic claims until the process of disintegration led to a plethora of ethnically pure but unworkable neighbourhood entities. It should be noted that the consequences were felt well beyond the former Yugoslavia.

Western policy *vis-à-vis* Kosovo was prompted by the Bosnian precedent, and the Dayton Accord. Unlike Bosnia, however, Kosovo has been a province of Serbia since the Balkan wars of 1912–13 and a territory replete with Serbian history and religious shrines. Whereas Dayton confirmed a *fait accompli* in the field, Kosovo had remained under firm Serb administration, until the Kosovo Liberation Army (KLA) began to challenge the authority of Belgrade. Some argue that the goal of the KLA was to provoke the Serb authorities into violent reprisals that would capture the attention of the West and compel it to act. In the cat and mouse game that ensued between the Serb forces and the KLA, outside intervention could only keep them apart by committing ground troops of the SFOR type. At that particular juncture (April 1998) a Greek NGO proposed a solution of the Kosovo problem that would evolve in three stages: (a) autonomy with Albanian and Serb cantons; (b) membership as a Republic in the Yugoslav Federation without the right of secession; and (c) a referendum among the cantons with longer periods of incubation separating each stage.[4]

The agreement reached between US Special Envoy Richard Holbrooke and Slobodan Milošević in October 1998 for a partial Serb withdrawal from Kosovo failed to resolve the issue of ground troops that could ensure a peaceful withdrawal and prevent the KLA from filling the vacuum in the field. Milošević was averse to the presence of foreign troops in what he considered to be Serbian sovereign territory unless Russians were included and the United States refused Russian participation. OSCE unarmed observers proved a poor substitute. The West came to Rambouillet in December 1998, without exhausting the possibility of committing an SFOR type of contingency to supervise the October 1998 agreement. The Rambouillet ultimatum to Serbia, which presumed control of its entire territory by NATO forces, left little margin for further negotiations.

If deeds are not to be judged by intentions but by outcomes, then the entire operation of bombing Serbia was a grand mistake. NATO devastated a centrally located Balkan state in order to rid its people of Milošević, to save the imperilled Kosovar Albanians and to secure multiethnic coexistence in an autonomous province. However, it succeeded in achieving the opposite on all counts. Milošević became the rallying point of the Serbs and was therefore allowed to remain in power long enough to undermine Serbia's transition to liberal democracy.

The Kosovar Albanians became the scapegoats of NATO's attack and were left to the tender mercies of the advancing Serb army. The OSCE report on the conflict[5] provides a chronological account of all human rights violations committed in Kosovo and produces evidence that killings before the bombardment were much fewer than those following the event. Whereas 496 Albanians were killed before 24 March 1999, a total of 5,504 died after that date and up to the end of hostilities in June. Needless to say that only a few were victims of the bombs. After Bosnia, Kosovo emerged as yet another ethnically cleansed protectorate of the West. A residual Liberation Army (KLA) gradually proceeded to lay claims on the neighbouring Presevo valley and Tetovo. In March 2004 Albanian paramilitary forces caused the death and displacement of many Kosovar Serbs.[6]

In the ethnic antagonisms over territory, NATO took sides and made its presence a determining factor in shaping the future of the region. The paradox in this exceptional Western involvement in an ever-growing number of Balkan protectorates, throughout the 1990s, is that unlike the Cold War period, the region did not constitute a US, NATO or EU priority. It did however become a net exporter of illegal immigrants and crime to Western Europe. Moreover, it is argued that the Serb vacuum in a region which has always been an important junction of trade and travel, may well have played its part in the economic stagnation of the western Balkans up to this day.[7]

Greek opposition to the bombings included an array of political positions. The Communist Party and a populist offshoot of the socialists constituted a small percentage of the political spectrum. Along with nationalists and those who sympathised with the Christian Orthodox Church of Serbia, the vociferous opposition may have covered 20% of public opinion. Most of the rest reflected, in varying degrees, views aired in this chapter. Official policy was steadfast in its resolve not to impair Greece's position either in NATO or the EU and therefore the government fell in line with the unanimity of the two institutions. Having walked the tightrope by facilitating the movement of NATO troops through the port of Thessaloniki, the Simitis government was much relieved by the war's end. Given the concern of both major parties in parliament (PASOK and New Democracy) that NATO's importance in the troubled region would not be diminished, there were concerted efforts to boost its credibility.

Reconstruction and the EU's legacy in the Balkans

The answer of the West to the crisis in Kosovo and the former Yugoslavia has been a plethora of state and non-governmental pacts, initiatives and processes, structured after the bureaucratic tradition of public institutions. Despite their *raison d'être*, competition rather than cooperation has prevailed between them, and the resources that they consumed would have produced better results if they had been ploughed into regional projects.[8] The former High Representative of the international community in Bosnia, Carl Bildt, produced his own outline for a Stability Pact in 1999: (1) Military security: initially NATO, but gradually acquiring a European character; (2) economic integration: free trade, then customs union, then a single market within the European Economic Area, with a New Balkan Reconstruction Agency; (3) political security and integration: structures to move into the European Union during the next decade. Reconstruction was originally planned for 2005, with full European integration at 2010.

Based on a similar plan of incorporating the southeastern European states into the EU, was the Working Document (No. 131) of the Centre for European Policy Studies in Brussels 'A System for Post-War South-East Europe' (3 May 1999, Revision 4). Its premise was that the only realistic solution entailed integrating the whole region into the EU once and for all, including post-Milošević Yugoslavia (p. 3). Of its nine EU innovations of policy, the proposals on market regime and money were the most controversial. Michael Emerson, as the chief architect of this innovative proposal, suggested a multilateral, pan-European, zero-tariff free trade agreement. Concerning monetary measures, he proposed to exploit new potential for a wider euro, both for economic value and as a symbol for inclusion in modern Europe.

The liberal optimism of Emerson was countered by the realism of the former finance minister of Romania, Daniel Daianu. He believed that Balkan economies could not profit from shock therapy but required treatment commensurate with their stage of development. Daianu emphasised the need for infrastructure projects of regional importance which would link Southeastern Europe with the EU. The European Investment Bank would have a major role to play in this process.[9] His blueprint of regional assistance included: (1) humanitarian aid for the return of refugees; (2) macroeconomic support in order to deal with balance of payments gaps, budget deficits, the impact of labour dislocations, trade disruptions and the loss of markets; (3) infrastructure projects, such as building pontoon bridges over the Danube and water supplies facilities in Albania; (4) the strengthening of local banks.[10]

The 'Stability Pact for South Eastern Europe' was the product of a meeting in Cologne, on 10 June 1999, between foreign ministers of the EU, the Balkans (minus Serbia and Montenegro), NATO members and Japan and a number of representatives from international and regional organizations. The mechanisms of the pact included a Southeastern Europe Regional Table, which coordinated working tables: on democratisation and human rights, economic reconstruction, development and cooperation, and, security issues.

Of all the goals set out for the Stability Pact, the most difficult was democratisation. Democracy has had a chequered life in interwar Yugoslavia and evocations of the free market are often synonymous with a mafia *laissez faire*, rather than with free enterprise. Soft (private armies, prostitution, contraband and traffic of drugs, arms and illegal immigrants), rather than hard, security considerations, are still among the most daunting tasks of the reconstruction and integration process.

The leaders of the forty states that joined the Stability Pact summit in Sarajevo, on 30 July 1999, were aware that the span of international attention was running out and would soon be diverted towards other trouble spots in the globe. The outcome of the summit was full of declarations of good will, but also recorded little determination to put up the several tens of billions of dollars required for rebuilding Serbia and Montenegro.[11]

Whereas US attention in the Balkans was focused on questions of security, the interest of the EU was more comprehensive. Southeastern Europe's inertia may bear no consequence on the distant American continent but it affects the fortunes of the rest of Europe. France, Germany and Britain, therefore, have sought to combine regional stability with a transformation of the western Balkans that will facilitate their signing of association agreements. Qualifying for EU accession constituted a strong incentive for reform and in 2000 the Stabilisation and Association Process (SAP) was dedicated to this purpose. Three years later, at the Thessaloniki summit, the future of the Balkans in the EU was clearly spelled out.

Most of the developments in the western Balkans since 2000 can be assessed from the stabilisation and association perspective. Human rights violations at the expense of the Serb minority in Kosovo and irredentist claims by the Kosovo Liberation Army (KLA) and its offshoots in southern Serbia (the Presevo valley) and the Former Yugoslav Republic of Macedonia (FYROM) have been met by an EU resolved to impose 'Standards before Status'. In other words, the EU demanded that human rights would be secured before the final status of Kosovo was considered. In the autumn of 2003 the Contact Group and the UNMIK decided to evaluate progress in meeting the standards by June 2005.[12]

The prudence of the post-Milošević Serbian leadership in the Presevo valley conflict did not allow the KLA to bait the Serbs into a bloody repetition of 1999. On 21 May 2001 the Albanian guerrillas came to terms with this reality and agreed to disarm under KFOR supervision. Another offshoot of the KLA, the National Liberation Army (NLA) made FYROM the target of its irredentism. Throughout April and May 2001 the rebels launched their attacks against the north-west of FYROM in order to alleviate their Albanian Macedonian kin from the hardships of Slav rule. On 3 May the government of FYROM unleashed helicopter and artillery fire against Albanian villages suspected of complicity with the rebels. Prime Minister Ljubco Georgievski was warned by European officials not to play into the hands of the NLA by answering rebel provocations with violence. On 13 August delegates from the Slav Macedonian majority and the Albanian Macedonian minority concluded an agreement on Ochrid which provided for constitutional amendments and reform that improved the status of Albanians in FYROM.[13] The EU in cooperation with the United States and NATO made significant contributions in conflict management and in post-conflict stabilisation. In 2003 an EU police force replaced the NATO and EU military presence in FYROM.

In 2001 the government of Kostas Simitis introduced a five-year Reconstruction Plan for the Balkans (ESOAB, Greek acronym), which provides 550 million euros for bilateral investment projects between 2002 and 2006. More precisely, 79% of the amount is earmarked for public infrastructure projects, and 20% is directed to investment in the private sector. Serbia has received the largest share. Kosovo is also included in the Reconstruction Plan (74 million euros) as a separate entity. By the end of 2003, twenty-nine investment projects were funded by ESOAB, most located in Bulgaria and Romania.[14]

The 21 June 2003 Summit in Thessaloniki between the EU (and candidates) and the five states of the western Balkans brought the region onto the screen of European attention. The EU made a strong commitment to the future membership of the five Balkan states and participants welcomed the reinforcement of the Stabilisation and Association Process and affirmed their resolve to fight organised crime and corruption. Regional cooperation was also at the forefront of the Greek presidency's watch. The Thessaloniki declaration included the following excerpt: 'We reiterate that rapprochement with the EU will go hand in hand with the development of regional cooperation ... We support the regional cooperation initiatives such as the South-East European Cooperation Process (SEEC) ... which is gradually becoming the voice of the region.'[15] The creation of regional markets for electricity and gas, visa-free movement within SEE, coordinated environment and water management and parliamentary cooperation, were also mentioned. The Greek EU presidency highlighted some of SEECP's capabilities and paved the way for future memberships for the western Balkans.[16]

The economic picture

Peace has benefited the region, but no state, except Slovenia, has yet attained its 1989 level of GDP. Bosnia-Hercegovina, Serbia and Montenegro and FYROM are still behind, while Croatia is approaching that goal rapidly. The Commission's view is not altogether negative. Since 2000 there has been an average of 4.5 per cent growth per year, but that along with trade liberalisation have spurred the deficits in trade balances. The region's exports cover only a quarter of the imports. In Bosnia-Hercegovina most enterprises are still public (except for the banking sector) and the market is segregated between the Republika Srpska and the Muslim-Croat Federation. Foreign direct investment has shirked this turbulent part of Europe which has not yet rid itself of nationalist reflexes. Given the dependence of the successor states of Yugoslavia on foreign capital, the Stability Pact has been their main source of support; 80% of this went to infrastructure, while the rest was allocated to institution-building, internal security and the development of democracy.[17]

In Bosnia the multilayered public administrations and bureaucracies absorb the bulk of international aid. Unemployment is 42 per cent in Bosnia and 45.3 per cent in FYROM, while social security is devoid of funds in both states. Legal unpredictability also causes low inflow of foreign capital with the concomitant effect on foreign investors.[18]

Greek business ventures have played a leading role in foreign direct investment in the Balkans. Geographic proximity and knowledge of the region and its idiosyncrasies have made Greek companies an important influence in the transition of Balkan economies. Throughout the past thirteen years a total of 7 billion euros was invested in the region. Greek private business and state-owned enterprises have appeared since the beginning of the transition in Bucharest, Sofia, Tirana, Skopje and Belgrade. Although there was always a percentage of opportunists who sought quick gain among the investors, those with a long-term per-spective made a significant contribution to development and stabilisa-tion. Follow-up investments that introduce new inputs in business ventures constitute a solid criterion of success. In Bulgaria there are at least 1,500 active Greek companies, of which the Biohalco metal industry acquired in 2001 the majority holdings of a Bulgarian firm for 12 million euros. The subsequent investment funds of Biohalco were five times the original amount, dispersed over five years. In the food industry, 3E Coca Cola, Delta dairy products and Chipita croissants, made their early mark in the region. These companies have successfully extended their activities in Slovenia, Croatia and Moldavia. The deci-sion to invest is usually prompted by low wages, availability of an abundant workforce, semi-skilled labour, and also the proximity of universities.[19]

Future prospects

The SCG operates in the confusion of the two economies of Serbia and Montenegro. As in Bosnia, bank reforms and trade liberalisation are positive developments but have caused deficits in the trade balance. The Serbs, even after Milošević's electoral defeat on 24 September 2000 and his subsequent deportation to the Hague Tribunal did not fully come to terms with their recent misadventures and their present predicament. The two politicians who dominated Serbian politics after Milošević, Vojislav Kostunica and the late Zoran Djindjic, spent valuable time on personal quarrels.[20] A self-inflicted malaise continues to hound Serb politics. Furthermore the ongoing disintegration of the rump Yugoslavia into the precarious Serbia and Montenegro union and Serb refugees from Croatia, Bosnia and Kosovo, estimated at 600,000, have made transition to normality the more difficult. The influx of refugees, or internally displaced people, has offset the drain caused by a similar number of able-bodied people who migrated abroad in the 1990s in search of a better life, but added an economic burden on Serbia. Yet parliamentary democracy is operating and the economy, although with many problems, is slowly moving ahead.

Kosovo is a serious impediment to regional progress. A zero-sum game between Serbs and Albanians preserves the time warp of past irredent-isms that mesmerises the adversaries. After five years of UNMIK administration, intercommunal relations have made no progress. The Kosovo-Albanian media played an inflammatory role in relations leading to the March 2004 riots. Albanian parties are still divided between moderates and radicals, the latter backed by Kosovo Liberation Army supporters. Furthermore, religious shrines of the Orthodox Church have become objects of attack and destruction throughout the post-1999 period. One way of addressing Serb sensitivities and preserving medieval monuments of great value, would be to confer a status of protected autonomy on the surviving shrines, in line with the Mt Athos monasteries in Greece.

Regarding the future of Kosovo, the West will have to play the honest broker by invoking principled solutions. Upholding the integrity of a segregated Bosnia-Hercegovina while considering the independence of Kosovo, will enforce Serb bias about Western inconsistent behaviour. Equally, failure of the US and the EU to guarantee human rights will undermine their credibility in the region.

Notes

1 For a detailed analysis of the Macedonian question from the interwar period to the late sixties, see Stephen E. Palmer Jr and Robert R. King, *Yugoslav Communism and the Macedonian Question*, Hamden, CT: Archon Books, 1971.

2 In his exposé of the issue Kyril Drezov offers a convincing analysis of the misconceptions of both sides. 'Macedonian identity: An overview of the major claims', in James Pettifer (ed.), *The New Macedonian Question*, London: Macmillan, 1999, pp. 47–59.

3 See study on public documents of FYROM by Vlassis Vlassidis, 'We and others: the Greek image in the mass media and the educational system of FYROM', in *Athens-Skopje*, Athens: Papazissis, 2003, pp. 297–366.

4 E. Kofos and T. Veremis, 'Kosovo: efforts to solve the impasse', *The International Spectator*, 33, 2, Rome, April–June 1998, 131–46. For proposals on conflict prevention in Kosovo (early 1998) see ELIAMEP, *Kosovo: avoiding Another Balkan War*, Athens: ELIAMEP, 1998.

5 OSCE, *Kosovo/Kosova: As Seen as Told*, Warsaw, 1999.

6 Chris Hedges, 'As UN organizes, rebels are taking charge of Kosovo', *The New York Times*, 29 July 1999; and Carlota Gall, 'NATO soldiers fire on Kosovo Albanians', *The New York Times*, 8 March 2001.

7 Martin Sletzinger, 'The consequences of the war in Kosovo', in *Kosovo & NATO: Impending Challenges*, Washington, DC: The Woodrow Wilson International Center for Scholars, East European Studies, pp. 3–5.

8 The EU Council 1994–95 Stability Pact, The European Council decision of 14 April 1999, the Balladur Plan, the Royaumont Process for Stability and Good Neighbourliness in SEE, the South-East Cooperation Initiative (SECI), the Balkan Conference of SEE states, the OSCE Round Table for the region, the Association for Democracy in the Balkans, along with the British, the German and the Greek proposals, are some of the better known.

9 Daniel Daianu, 'Reconstruction in Southeastern Europe', *The Southeast European Yearbook 1998–99*, Athens: ELIAMEP, 1999. This issue includes papers delivered at the 20–26 June 1999 Halki International Seminars.

10 Ibid.
11 'For Balkan stability', *International Herald Tribune*, 4 August 1999.
12 Stefan Lehne, 'Has the "hour of Europe" come at last? The EU's strategy for the Balkans', in Judy Batt (ed.), *The Western Balkans: Moving On*, Institute for Security Studies, Chaillot Paper No. 70, October 2004, pp. 111–24.
13 Thanos Veremis, 'The ever-changing contours of the Kosovo issue', in D. Triantaphyllou (ed.), *What Status for Kosovo?*, Institute for Security Studies, Chaillot Paper No. 50, October 2001, pp. 85–7.
14 Jens Bastian, 'Knowing your way in the Balkans: Greek foreign direct investment in southern Europe', *Journal of Southeast European and Black Sea Studies*, 4, 3 (Sept. 2004), 463–4.
15 EU–Western Balkans Summit, Thessaloniki, 21 June 2003: Declaration; <http: //www.eu2003.gr/en/articles/2003/6/23/3135/index.asp>
16 Andrew G. Hyde, 'Seizing the initiative: the importance of regional cooperation in SEE and the prominent role of the Southeast EU Cooperation Process', *Journal of Southeast European and Black Sea Studies*, 4, 1, (2004), 18–19.
17 Franz-Lothar Altmann, 'Regional economic problems and prospects', in Batt (ed.), *The Western Balkans*, pp. 69–74.
18 Ibid., pp. 75–85.
19 Bastian, 'Knowing your way', pp. 458–90.
20 Ognjen Pribicevic, 'Serbia after Milošević', *Journal of Southeast European and Black Sea Studies*, 4, 1 (2004), 107–18.

17 Turkey, Southeastern Europe and Russia

Ali Karaosmanoglu

During the Cold War, the Balkans were considered in terms of the inter-bloc rivalry between the superpowers. Nevertheless, the bipolarity had introduced into the region a certain degree of stability. Contrary to the Cold War era, today the region is viewed in its own terms and is described as such by many commentators.[1] Since the end of the Cold War, the causes of instability have also shifted from external to internal. In addition to this shift, there has been a marked increase in projects that promote regional cooperation on every level in the hope that the Balkan states will open up to the West and follow the example of Eastern Europe by becoming an integral part of NATO and the EU.

This chapter begins with a review of Turkey's foreign policies during the first decade after the end of the Cold War, policies which have become increasingly complicated by Turkey's geopolitical position and historical alliances.[2] I then consider the situation of Turkey's neighbours, on which it has historically exerted much influence, namely Albania, Macedonia and Bulgaria. Finally, I would like to review the role of the United States, the European Union, NATO and Russia as guarantors of Balkan security.

Turkey's foreign policy calls for a number of clarifications. Turkey has no vital interest in the former Yugoslavia; it only has major interests in the Balkans west of Greece. During the wars in Bosnia and Kosovo, there was undoubtedly some sensitivity surrounding the conditions and the fate of Muslim and Turkish populations in the Balkans. Public opinion was extremely sensitive on this matter and it did exert an influence on the government, especially through the associations created by refugees and immigrants arriving from other Balkan countries.[3] Whenever there is instability and conflict in the Balkans, there is always a migratory pressure on Turkey.

In other respects, however, it is important to underscore the fact that the Balkan peninsula is a region between Turkey and Western Europe, a region of great interest to Turkey. Turkey has always had European ambitions, and thus it is important from its perspective that the links between Western Europe and Turkey should remain open and be consolidated. Whenever there has been instability and conflict in the Balkans, these links have been endangered, which is not in Turkey's interest. In more practical terms, there are nearly 4 million Turks living in Western Europe and Turkey's trade with Western Europe has seen a marked increase, with more than 60 per cent of Turkey's foreign trade destined for the European Union.[4]

There is a widespread opinion that conflicts in the Balkans tend to spread and could draw Turkey in. However, since the interests of Turkey in the area are not vital, it is hard to imagine that any conflict west of Greece would draw Turkey into a Balkan conflict, except in multilateral interventions such as in the former Yugoslavia. In fact, as a consequence of the secondary and indirect nature of its interests in the Balkans, Turkey has preferred, after the Cold War, to follow its European allies and adopt a multilateral approach to Balkan affairs. This multilateralism led to very serious contradictions, confusion and inconsistencies in Turkey's policy in the former Yugoslavia but, at the same time, its cooperative approach and multilateralism enhanced its position within NATO, the Partnership for Peace, and also in the West in general. This has been particularly important in a period when Ankara was isolated from the European integration process and was forced to watch other states move closer to its own goal of joining the European Union in the 1990s.

It is important to understand these inconsistencies before judging the actions of the United States and its European partners. Such inconsistencies in policy direction are not peculiar to the United States nor to the Western European nations. Right in the beginning of the Yugoslav crisis, Turkey was in favour of preserving the territorial integrity of Yugoslavia. This quickly changed and, once Slovenia, Croatia and Bosnia-Hercegovina were established, Turkey recognised these states without delay.

More important, however, were the inconsistencies in Turkey's support for Bosnia's right to self-defence. Turkey never considered the conflicts between Serbia and Slovenia, Serbia and Croatia and Serbia and Bosnia-Hercegovina as ethnic conflicts or religious conflicts, but defined them very clearly as flagrant aggression on the part of Serbia. From the perspective of Ankara, the Yugoslav crisis was never primarily a humanitarian problem, but rather the result of a war of aggression that had to be dealt with by adequate means. Specifically, this meant applying Article 51 of the United Nations charter which grants victim states such as Bosnia the right to individual and collective self-defence. However, in spite of its belief in the application of Article 51, Turkey actively participated in the application of an arms embargo on Croatia and Bosnia-Hercegovina by sending a frigate and a submarine to the Adriatic where it prevented arms from getting through. Turkey's active participation in the imposition of the embargo continued throughout the worst stages of the conflict in Croatia and Bosnia until November 1994, when the United States instructed its ships in the Adriatic not to impose the embargo. After the American decision, Turkey took an identical decision, following the United States by asserting its support in favour of the 'lift and strike' option and trying to convince the allies that this would be the best means of solving the problems in former Yugoslavia.

Another contradiction was the fact that Turkey was in favour of a multicultural and pluralistic Bosnia-Hercegovina and it always clearly voiced this. On the other hand, it actively contributed to the negotiation and conclusion of the Dayton Agreements which ensured that Bosnia would be divided along ethnic lines. After 1993, Turkey showed less and less interest in playing an active role in the Balkans, because of increasing domestic problems and various regional conflicts in the bordering areas, such as northern Iraq, the Black Sea basin and the Caucasus.[5] Nevertheless, the rise of tension over Kosovo induced Turkey to take an active interest in the Balkans again.

Turkey's inconsistencies reflected, on the one hand, the legacy of Cold War alliance behaviour and, on the other hand, its dramatic experience with nineteenth-century Balkan nationalism. While the latter induced it to voice its indignation as regards the Serbs' genocidal policies, the former restricted Ankara's post-Cold War activism to allied multilateralism. Nevertheless, one consistent aspect of Turkey's policy has been its persistent emphasis on regional cooperation. While being aware of the Balkan states' and its own limited capabilities, Ankara promoted cooperation as a fundamental element of conflict resolution and regional stability, and always welcomed cooperative projects of the Western states. This policy of cooperation ruled out the formation of regional alliances that could lead to new tensions, and exacerbate the old ones.[6]

From the mid 1990s, Turkey also paid particular attention to regional security cooperation. Its interest in regional multilateralism extended from participation in peace operations in the former Yugoslavia to initiation of regional arrangements, such as the Black Sea Economic Cooperation and a standing peacekeeping force in the Balkans. It undertook the responsibility of establishing a Partnership for Peace (PFP) Training Centre in Ankara and proposed the creation of a Multinational Peace Force in South-East Europe (SEEBRIG). The principal objective of the PFP Training Centre, which was inaugurated in June 1998, is to provide training and education support to military and civilian personnel of partners in order to prepare them for NATO standards. The Multinational Peace Force in South-East Europe came into effect by the establishment of its headquarters in Plovdiv, with the aim of contributing NATO-led peace operations which proved useful in enhancing peace and stability in the Balkans, and which, by promoting collective security, also served as an important confidence building measure.[7] Ankara also set the agenda for a Black Sea Naval Cooperation Task Force (BLACKSEAFOR) and has generally been keen to lead on such multilateral efforts.

Furthermore, Turkey, like its European allies, actively participated in peace operations in the Balkans. The Turkish Land Forces were assigned to UNPROFOR in Bosnia at the brigade level, and in December 1995 it was assigned to SFOR. The Turkish Navy participated in Operation 'Sharp Guard' with frigates, submarines and tankers. In the air the record was also noted. In April 1993, the Turkish Air Force Command joined Operation 'Deny Flight', launched by NATO to enforce the 'no-flight zone' over Bosnia with a squadron of F-16 operating from Italy's Ghedi air base. In 1995, these duties were transferred to SFOR. When the Kosovo crisis worsened, Ankara expressed its willingness to make available to KFOR a mechanised infantry battalion as well as headquarters personnel. Moreover, three Special Operations Teams were assigned to the Hostage Rescue Force and four F-16s based at Ghedi, as well as Turkey's fourteen 'on-call' aircraft, were assigned to Operation 'Allied Force'.

It also has to be noted that, since 1990, Turkey's relations with Bulgaria have undergone a significant improvement. This process was highlighted by the conclusion of a series of military cooperation and CSBM agreements. These agreements have been effectively implemented and have greatly contributed to the dissipation of the tension that had been created by the oppression of the Turkish minority in Bulgaria under the communist regime.

Turkey also established friendly relations with Macedonia. In Macedonia, there is a strong and demanding Albanian minority, which constitutes about 35 per cent of the population. This minority has a high birth rate and is mostly concentrated in the areas bordering Albania and Kosovo. This, by itself, creates a very risky situation and, as demonstrated by the recent skirmishes of past years, it is sometimes perceived as a threat to Macedonian territorial integrity from within Macedonia. Nevertheless, there are signs that Macedonia is now taking successful measures to respond to the needs of its Albanian minority and that the country is moving closer to Europe as well.

Although Albania's transition to democracy was slow and problematic in the mid-1990s, the situation has improved considerably since 2001, and its foreign relations are even more encouraging. Albania's relations with Greece have improved since 1995. Albania's relations with Turkey have always been good, and have also been strengthened in the military field, since Albania has emerged as a key NATO partner in the Balkans. Its close ties with the Alliance are very important for NATO because of the country's key strategic location. Albania was one of first nations to join Partnership for Peace in February 1994. Since then, Albania has been very active in the Alliance's Partnership for Peace programmes. On the other hand, NATO has contributed to the rebuilding of Albanian's armed forces. The key issue for Albania, however, remains the Kosovo problem and its security within the region. Naturally, Albania has a strong interest in the fate of the Albanian population in Kosovo but has so far shown remarkable restraint in dealing with that issue. Instead, even during the worst phases of the conflict, it offered shelter and assistance to Kosovar refugees and carefully refrained from being provocative.

Russia's interest in the Balkans diminished considerably after the Cold War. The reason for Moscow's residual concern with the region is not Russia's religious or historical affinity with some of the regional states. Ideological bonds have faded away as well. Today, there are two major reasons behind Moscow's interest. In the first instance, Putin's Russia worked hard to prevent NATO from gaining more strength and influence in Europe's new security order. This was especially the case during the mid-1990s when Russia felt increasingly isolated from Europe as a result of NATO's continuing enlargement process. The second reason for Moscow's interest is that the geopolitical rivalry in the Caucasus and Central Asia has important implications for the Balkans. These regions are becoming geopolitically interlinked. This includes Turkey, Bulgaria, Romania, Moldova and the Black Sea countries, as well as the Balkan countries. They have a role to play not only in Balkan security affairs but also in the security of the Black Sea basin.[8] Moreover, regarding the issue of transporting Caspian energy to the West, some might claim that the Balkans are becoming as important as the Black Sea and the Turkish Straits.[9]

During the Kosovo conflict it once more became clear how difficult it was for the allies to arrive at and maintain a consensus over an effective out-of-area NATO action. Although all NATO allies recognised the need for an air operation to deal effectively with the Serbian forces in Kosovo, little unanimity existed as regards subsequent dangers or responses in general terms. As the war in Iraq has demonstrated, out-of-area operations remain a matter of dispute for most of NATO's members and the increased number of new NATO members is likely to complicate this problem even further. Moreover, again as a consequence of NATO expansion and the enlargement of the European Union, the involvement of the Euro-Atlantic institutions in the southern region has given rise to competition with Central and Eastern Europe for the allocation of limited resources.

Stabilisation and development in the Balkans cannot be dealt with in isolation from the larger issues of European security and NATO. As the events in Macedonia revealed, failure to maintain stability in the Balkans not only complicated NATO's policy but also postponed the development of a European Security and Defence Policy.

In the management and resolution of conflicts, the role of the US, NATO and the European Union will remain crucial. To the extent that conflicts are resolved and tensions dissipated, the objective has shifted to economic reconstruction.[10] Without sustained economic growth, democratisation can hardly become successful and peace cannot be maintained. NATO still has an important role to play in the region. Most of the former Yugoslav republics are unlikely to become NATO members in the near future. However, an enhanced Partnership For Peace provides an important instrument for promoting closer military cooperation in the region, and also introduces a significant element of internationalism into national armies, contributing to regional stability. Until now, the presence of NATO has also served as a guarantee to prevent the recurrence of conflicts in the region. NATO's various cooperative projects which include non-member states, as well as its open-door policy, will continue to promote regional stabilisation. Turkey's support of Bulgaria's and Romania's NATO membership and its general activism within the framework of the PFP should be viewed from this perspective.[11] The end of the Cold War has opened a window of opportunity for the Balkan nations to cooperate effectively and to integrate in the Western world.[12] The former communist states and Yugoslav republics such as Slovenia have already benefited from this opportunity. Now, the southern Balkan states, following Slovenia's example, should not fail to seize this opportunity.

Notes

1 The 'Balkans' became especially popular as a term for describing insecurity and featured in the titles of hundreds of books, including those by leading commentators who emphasised insecurity as the root of the 1990s conflicts, such as Misha Glenny, *The Balkans: Nationalism, War and the Great Powers 1804–1999*, London and New York: Granta Books, 2000; David Owen, *Balkan Odyssey*, London: Victor Gollancz, 1995; and Susan L. Woodward,

Balkan Tragedy: Chaos and Dissolution after the Cold War, Washington, DC: Brookings Institution Press, 1995.

2 For a recent discussion of Turkish foreign policy, see Idris Bal (ed.), *Turkish Foreign Policy in Post Cold War Era*, Universal Publishers/BrownWalker.com, 2004; Ali Çarkoglu and Barry Rubin (eds.), *Turkey and the European Union, Domestic Politics, Economic Integration and International Dynamics*, London/ Portland: Frank Cass, 2003; and, Philip Robins, *Suits and Uniforms, Turkish Foreign Policy since the Cold War*, London: Hurst & Company, 2003. The complexities of Turkish foreign policy have been analysed by F. Stephen Larrabee and Ian O. Lesser, *Turkish Foreign Policy in Age of Uncertainty*, Santa Monica: RAND, 2003, and Nasuh Uslu, *Turkish Foreign Policy in the Post-Cold War Period*, Hauppauge, NY: Nova Science Publishers, 2003. For a review of Turkish–American relations, see Morton Abramowitz (ed.), *Turkey's Transformation and American Policy*, New York: Century Foundation Press, 2001; and 'The complexities of American policymaking on Turkey', *Insight Turkey*, 2, 4 (2000), 3–35; see also Nasuh Uslu, *The Turkish–American relationship between 1947 and 2003: The History of a Distinctive Alliance*, Hauppauge, NY: Nova Science Publishers, 2003.

3 See Brian Beeley, 'People and cities: migration and urbanization', in Brian Beeley (ed.), *Turkish Transformation: New Century New Challenges*. Huntingdon, UK: Eothen Press, 2002, pp. 36–58.

4 For an account of the impact of trade between the EU and Turkey on economic growth over the past decade, see Mina Tokgöz, 'The economy: achievements and prospects', in Beeley (ed.), *Turkish Transformation*, pp. 141–64.

5 Turkey's interests in the Caspian basin and the Caucasus have received less attention than they deserve. See Barry Rubin and Kemal Kirisci (eds.), *Turkey in World Politics: an Emerging Multiregional Power*, London: Lynne Rienner, 2001; and Ali Karaosmanoglu, 'Turkey's objectives in the Caspian region', in Gennady Chufrin (ed.), *The Security of the Caspian Sea Region*, Stockholm International Peace Research Institute, Oxford: Oxford University Press, 2001.

6 Ali Hikmet Alp, 'Balkan region in Turkey's security environment', in Ali L. Karaosmanolu and Seyfi Taşhan (eds.), *The Europeanization of Turkey's Security Policy: Prospects and Pitfalls*, Ankara: Foreign Policy Institute, 2004, pp. 190–1.

7 For a comprehensive review of the Southeastern Europe Multinational Peace Force, see Dimitris Bourantonis and Panayotis Tsakonas, 'The Southeastern Europe Multinational Peace Force: problems of and prospects for a regional security agency', *Politics*, 23, 2 (2003), 75–81.

8 Rubin and Kirisci, *Turkey in World Politics*.

9 Karaosmanoglu, 'Turkey's objectives in the Caspian region'.

10 On migration and citizenship, see Carl-Ulrik Schierup (ed.), *Scramble for the Balkans: Nationalism, Globalism and the Political Economy of Reconstruction*, New York: St Martin's Press, 2000.

11 Alp, 'Balkan region', pp. 203–4.

12 For a good discussion of Turkey's future prospects, see Beeley (ed.), *Turkish Transformation*.

18   In search of Bulgaria's new identity: the role of diplomacy, 1989–2005

Philip Shashko

> We should remember that individuals and parties come and go, Bulgaria stays. Let us be, and I am sure we will only be true European citizens if we are true Bulgarians.[1]
>
> Georgi Parvanov

A conscious choice: striving towards a Euro-Atlantic identity

The fundamental agenda of the Bulgarian elite during the 1990s was designed to solve the crisis of Bulgaria's post-communist political identity and orientation by finding the best means to make Bulgaria's transition to democracy a successful entry point into NATO, the European Union (EU) and other Euro-Atlantic structures. In the process of reconstruction and integration into Euro-Atlantic structures, the majority of the Bulgarian elite consciously redefined itself ideologically in order to present a broader view of the evolving national interest. This chapter explores the endeavours of Bulgarian policy-makers to convince themselves and their people of the necessity for a national reorientation, and the integration of their country into the political, economic, social and cultural structures of the European Union and NATO. This was a complicated process because it had to be done simultaneously with domestic transformations. The study of Bulgaria's diplomacy during the last fifteen years shows that the process of internal democratisation and the vision of a new order went hand in hand with the formation of a new political identity and Europeanisation. To accomplish this, most Bulgarian politicians themselves had to adopt a pro-European mind-set and then work to reorient the population's ideas to the new political conditions created after 1989. The construction of this new political identity effectively necessitated that the Bulgarian elite and especially its politicians behave and act as diplomats. The acquisition of the new identity was a complex process that entailed the making and taking of domestic and foreign policy decisions that required interaction not only with the Bulgarian masses but also with politicians and institutions in the European Union, the United States and Russia as well as Bulgaria's neighbours. It must be emphasised that in the construction of the new Euro-identity were included both the Bulgarian political and cultural elite and internal and external policy-making institutions. This was, therefore, a two-way process. Without the explicit guidance and pressure exercised by the European Union and the USA, for example, the Bulgarians would not have been able to carry out all the necessary reforms needed to join the European structures.

This chapter further considers the ways in which Bulgaria promptly repositioned itself after the tragic ethnic policies and abuses against the Turkish minority that took place in the final months of the Bulgarian Communist Party rule.[2] In addition, Bulgarian political identity and reorientation was greatly influenced by the tragic developments in neighbouring Yugoslavia and in the entire Balkan region. In general, identity politics in Bulgaria during the transitional period shows that while conservative politicians focus more on immediately adopting a European political identity, most liberals and leftist, while claiming, like the conservatives that Bulgarians were always Europeans, were more careful in accepting Euro-Atlantic institutions at the expense of alienating the Russians and the traditional friendly relations between the two countries. It is because of such a balanced approach that political, economic and cultural relations were not interrupted. Furthermore, notwithstanding the right-wing propaganda against everything Russian, including designating them as the untrustworthy 'Other', and reinterpreting the past, the emotional ties between Bulgarians and Russians, especially among the intelligentsia, were consistently maintained.

Among the most immediate and dramatic changes that occurred after 1989 were the meltdown of Bulgarian subordination to the Soviet Union and the gradual establishment of new institutions, the creation of a multiparty system, and methods of exercising power that correspond more closely to those existing in Europe and North America. The first years in the transition to a multiparty and democratic system were gradual and cautious. Since the early 1990s, the Voice of America, Radio Free Europe, the BBC and *Deutsche Welle* have had a very significant impact on the transformation of the political landscape. Bulgarians were able to listen freely to these radio stations which provided them with alternative information and urged them to participate in public debates regarding the problems facing their country. The pre-term parliamentary elections held in Bulgaria in April 1997 marked the final stage of a momentous change that reshaped Bulgarian politics. The election of the non-communist, conservative coalition of the United Democratic Forces (UDF) showed that Bulgarians were demonstrating further a radical break with Bulgaria's communist past.

There is little doubt that the changes since 1989 have been slow and economically painful for the great majority of Bulgarians. Even the partial reconstruction, however, transformed the political scene of the country. Although the Bulgarian elite was slow to fully agree on solutions to fundamental questions of domestic reform facing the country, one constant, especially since 1999, has nonetheless been a greater agreement on the goals and conduct of foreign policy. Bulgarian politicians of all ideological orientations came close to consensus on foreign policy aims because of their desire to transform the image of their country and facilitate Bulgaria's road back to Europe and its acceptance into the Euro-Atlantic structures.

Bulgaria's political transformation began with changes among the top leadership. They encouraged the immediate reversal of many old policies, including the forced change of names of the Turkish minority (the Revival Process of the 1980s).[3] Besides the momentous removal on 10 November 1989 of Todor Zhivkov from power, the adoption of a new constitution and the decision to follow the path to democratic reconstruction, one of the immediate achievements of post-Cold War Bulgaria as conceived by politicians and scholars is the Bulgarian ethnic tolerance model which envisages the realisation of peaceful coexistence and cooperation between the Bulgarian majority and the ethnic minorities in the country. The end of the Revival Process and the restoration of their property and full citizenship rights, led to the formation of political parties representing the interests of the Turkish, Muslim and Roma minorities. Their unobstructed participation in political life is proof of the success of this model thus far. While former Yugoslavia saw the revival of nationalism, ethnic cleansing and war, Bulgarians were able to control extremists, to channel their nationalism to constructive purposes, and make them full partners on the road to Europe.

Bulgaria's qualified success in peacefully sustaining and managing relations among minorities has maintained relative peace and greatly advanced its image in the world. It not only ushered in positive changes in inter-ethnic relations within the country but also brought about significant improvements in Bulgaria's relations with its neighbours and especially with the EU, the USA, Greece and Turkey. Foreign observers, including many US commentators and officials, refer to Bulgaria as an island and anchor of stability in Southeastern Europe.[4] However, this does not mean that Bulgaria has completely solved its ethnic problems. There are dissatisfactions and problems among and with the Roma and

Macedonian minorities in the country. In addition, many Bulgarians do not like the fact that Turkish and Muslim politicians hold the balance of power in the struggle among the major parties for power in the National Assembly, and in the formation of coalition governments. Although the Bulgarian ethnic model thus far has kept the peace and is deservedly regarded by Bulgarians and foreigners alike as an integral element of Bulgaria's new image, it could backfire in the future if Bulgarian Turkish leaders do not take into consideration the demands of the majority and urge their followers to acquire a new, Bulgarian and European political consciousness and identity.

Shaking off the recent past: the break with Russia

To defend its new-found freedom, enhance its security, promote its interests and establish a positive presence on the international scene, Bulgaria had to rely upon acceptable Euro-Atlantic principles and conduct in its foreign policy. The first step for Bulgarian politicians was to distance themselves from the perception that Bulgaria was the most subservient satellite of the Soviet Union and Russia. There is no doubt that during the post-1989 period when the Bulgarian Socialist Party (BSP), the reconstituted former Bulgarian Communist Party, was in power, both elements of ideological continuity and fears of alienating Russia or Western dominance played an essential part in the country's foreign policy. Even though the former dogmatic ideological orientation, together with constraints and subservience to foreign interests and dictates, no longer existed when the BSP controlled the National Assembly and the government, there were still uncertainties about the speed at which to proceed with domestic reforms, foreign policy reorientations and in breaking with the socialist past.

President Zheliu Zhelev, who at first represented the Union of Democratic Forces (UDF) and was elected president by the National Assembly with Socialist support, realized that bringing about radical domestic transformations and making Bulgaria a respected partner in the world required, as far as possible, a complete a break with the country's recent past. He introduced significant foreign policy changes starting with the appointment of new diplomats. His presidency ended with Bulgaria applying to join NATO and the EU. Today, the majority of policy-makers are the products and representatives of the recent democratic changes.

From the start the elite realised the importance of coordinating domestic reforms and foreign policy and the need to introduce transparent moral principles in the conduct of public affairs. The major organ of the UDF, *Demokratsiia*, for example, reiterated an idea articulated by Konstantin Stoilov, a Bulgarian prime minister at the end of the nineteenth century, that 'the more rational or wiser a small state's domestic policy, that much better is going to be the conduct of its foreign policy'.[5] In 1998 work, former President Zheliu Zhelev expressed similar ideas when he wrote that 'the time of great domestic changes was also a time of immense discoveries and bold activities in foreign policy. It was a period when the new orientation was being defined, new goals and priorities, principles and norms as well as the inclusion of new personalities in diplomacy and a new style of making foreign policy were formulated.'[6] Such alterations were the harbingers of a new way of thinking and looking at the surrounding world by most of the Bulgarian elite.[7]

Overcoming the state's dependence on the Soviet Union and Russia was a revolution in Bulgarian diplomacy. The majority of Bulgarian politicians began a conscious campaign to eradicate the old image of Bulgaria as the most loyal satellite of the Soviet Union and at the same time not harm the traditional Bulgarian–Russian friendship which had brought liberation and economic cooperation. Immediately after the removal of Zhivkov from power, Bulgaria maintained fairly good relations with the USSR and Russia. During the attempted coup in the Soviet Union in August 1991, President Zhelev was the first foreign leader to establish communications with Boris Yeltsin, the president of the Russian Federation, and to offer his support and recognize the independence of the Russian Federation before the demise of the USSR. Furthermore, President Zhelev established a friendly relationship with President Yeltsin.

In 1991 the old treaty of friendship of 1967 between Bulgaria and the Soviet Union was denounced and Bulgaria 'took a step toward independence that would have been inconceivable two years before'.[8] Notwithstanding such pressures for a new treaty and better relations with the Soviet Union on the part of both the BSP and Russian communists and nationalists, Zhelev was able to bring some semblance of normality to relations. He convinced Yeltsin to accept the Bulgarian leaders' views on the need for a new basis of Bulgarian–Russian relations and the correctness of their stand on Macedonia. Yeltsin agreed with Zhelev and immediately recognised the newly independent Republic of Macedonia. The warming of relations led the two countries on 4 August 1992 to sign a Bulgarian–Russian 'Agreement for Friendly Relations and Cooperation'. This was followed by other agreements on military, economic, scientific and technical cooperation.

Sofia's persistent movement towards closer relations with the West, however, was not always welcomed in Moscow by Russian ideologues and nationalist hard liners. A number of problems between the two countries strained relations again. One such problem was Russia's inability to satisfactorily settle the issue of building a pipeline through Bulgaria for the delivery of gas to Bulgaria and the countries of Central Europe. This episode lead to what historian John Bell called 'energy wars' between Bulgaria and Russia and created mistrust in both countries not only among government officials but businessmen as well.[9] Bulgarian criticism of Russian domestic and foreign policies and especially Sofia's moves toward the West were seen in Moscow as almost a betrayal of the traditional friendship. During the 1993 political crisis in Russia, President Zhelev, Prime Minister Liuben Berov and UDF leader Philip Dimitrov supported Yeltsin, while the leaders of the BSP called for a 'solution based on a constructive dialogue and compromises acceptable to the Russian people. While it did not support Yeltsin directly, the BSP rejected any move away from democratic processes in both Russia and Bulgaria.'[10]

In 1997, after a short and disastrous term in office by Jean Videnov's Socialist Party government, a new UDF conservative government under the leadership of Premier Ivan Kostov took office and announced its desire to seek full membership in the EU and NATO. This bold step brought about a deterioration in Bulgaria's relations with Russia. Politicians in Russia watched in amazement every move made by Bulgaria toward the West. When in September 1997 Bulgaria called a meeting of regional defence ministers and invited the United States to participate but excluded Russia, officials in Moscow saw this as an affront and formally protested.

On 27 October 1997 the Bulgarian National Assembly, controlled by the UDF, passed a 'Declaration on the Development of Equal Rights and Mutually Beneficial Relations with the Russian Federation' that disclosed the attitude of the governing conservative political elite toward Russia. The aim of Bulgarian foreign policy, the declaration states, is the protection and furthering of 'national security and independence of the country, prosperity and fundamental freedoms' of the people and 'cooperation in establishing international order of justice'. It further states that the 'main objective' of the Republic of Bulgaria is 'integration and membership within European and Euro-Atlantic structures'. The declaration contends that Bulgaria 'is willing to develop friendly, equal rights and mutually beneficial relations' with Russia 'as one of its foreign policy priorities'. The primary interest in relations with Russia as seen from Sofia, however, consisted in the development of trade and economic ties and cooperation in energy and infrastructure projects on the grounds of strategic and mutually beneficial cooperation. Furthermore, the declaration asserted that Bulgaria was an equal partner and all relations should be developed 'on a mutually beneficial and equal rights basis, accounting for the sovereign rights of the two countries'.[11]

It is clear that the conservatives wanted a political restructuring and a minimizing of relations with Russia.

This act, of course, can be interpreted as a formal declaration of Bulgaria's foreign policy independence by asserting that the country would deal with Russia as with any other state, on equal terms. However, recent relations have not been always normal. The political estrangement between Bulgaria and Russia is reflected in the decline in trade. In 1989 Bulgarian exports to the USSR comprised 65.8% and the imports 53.6% of the total trade. By 1994 exports from Bulgaria to the former Soviet Union were 14.4% and imports 24% of the total commerce. This drastic shift in economic cooperation and deterioration of relations, of course, reflects also the changed economic conditions in both countries and the fact that much more trade is now directed within the European Union.[12]

Relations between Bulgaria and Russia became even more strained in 1999 during the war in Kosovo when the Bulgarian government sided with NATO, permitted the use of Bulgarian airspace by NATO forces while Russia was opposed to the use of force to settle the Kosovo conflict. Furthermore, when hostilities ceased and the Russians asked the Bulgarian government for the right for Russian airplanes to travel over Bulgarian airspace to join the KFOR peacekeeping forces in Kosovo, the Bulgarians did not respond in time to Russian requests and thus disagreements both on principle and details gave rise to a small scandal. Some people believe that the Bulgarians' protraction prevented the Russians in sending more troops to Pristina before NATO forces arrived in Kosovo. Academician Blagovest Sendov, vice-president of the Bulgarian Parliament at the time, in an interview with the newspaper *Monitor*, stated that what happened was 'something unexpected and inadmissible', and implied that Bulgarian foreign policy-makers may have been 'fulfilling some instructions' from abroad.[13] It must be remembered that there were Bulgarians who opposed the intervention and demonstrated against the war. However, the Bulgarian government could not have taken such an anti-Russian step without the backing of the European Union and the United States.

University of Sofia sociologist Petur-Emil Mitev pointed to the divided perceptions the Bulgarian public has toward Russia and the West when he stated that an

intense anticommunist political propaganda helped to produce a degree of Russophobia unknown in Bulgarian history. But all the same, the Bulgarian attitude toward Russia continues to be unique. Bulgaria is the only country among the East European candidates for EU membership in which more people think their future is linked to Russia rather than the USA ... The Bulgarian attitude toward Russia ... is not ideologized. Bulgarian public opinion ignores constructs of the 'Orthodox Arc' type or other Slavophile utopias, although each has a handful of advocates.[14]

President Zheliu Zhelev took a more balanced position toward relations with Russia. Commenting on Bulgaria's political orientation, Zhelev wrote that in 'our movement toward democracy and market economy we had to travel the road from the "Soviet Bloc" to the European Union and the USA, not against Russia but together with her and the other post-communist states ... and with President Yeltsin'.[15] In reality, Zhelev and Bulgarian politicians had to carefully manoeuvre between members of the pro-Russian faction of the BSP who desired respectful relations and pro-Soviet Communists, who wanted friendly relations with Russia on the one hand and the right-wing nationalists, conservatives and liberals of the UDF who wanted to distance Bulgaria from Russia, on the other. In time, they were successful because of changes in other parts of Eastern Europe and new friendly diplomatic moves by the United States and the European Union.

This new orientation in Bulgarian domestic and foreign policy, by distancing it from Russia, gradually but surely brought not only novelty but a new political identity and radically altered goals, directions and practices for Bulgarian diplomacy. That is why relations with the Soviet Union and then with Russia are so important in tracing the course of Bulgarian foreign policy and the assertion of a new political identity. Through the estrangement from Russia, Bulgarian diplomats endeavoured to change the old, primarily negative, images of their country and to supplant them with positive representations by means of different principles, novel personal behaviour and trendy rhetoric and measures. It seems that Bulgarian conservative foreign policy-makers believe that unresponsiveness toward Russian moves for closer relations result in positive responses from the Western powers. This was an ongoing process and is still being carried out by conservatives through various innovative approaches in the diplomatic arena and domestic publicity.

The attempt by the conservatives to distance themselves from Russia, although successful in portraying a positive image of Bulgaria in the West, did not fully succeed in isolating Bulgaria from Russia. The freezing of relations did not survive the conservative government of Kostov and the presidency of Petar Stoyanov. Most Bulgarians wanted to keep open and friendly relations with Russia. The former Tsar Simeon II, now usually referred to as Simeon Sakskoburggotski, returned to

Bulgaria in April 2001 and as leader of the National Movement for Simeon (NMSII), won the national election. On 24 July 2001, Simeon Sakskoburggotski became prime minister of Bulgaria and surprisingly, the former tsar followed a more liberal domestic policy and a pragmatic policy towards Russia than the conservatives. In February 2002, Solomon Passy, Bulgarian foreign minister in Simeon's government, visited Moscow. This was the first official visit by a Bulgarian foreign minister in ten years. Passy pointed out that his talks in Russia 'have opened some previously closed doors in bilateral relations'.[16] This visit was followed in June 2002 by that of Simeon, the first official visit by a prime minister since the Bulgarian Socialist Party was in power. He met with President Vladimir Putin, Prime Minister Mikhail Kasyonov and the Russian Patriarch Alexei II. While Simeon called for 'more creative relations' between Bulgaria and Russia, Putin voiced the hope that the official visit 'will mark a turning point in bilateral relations'. Both sides stressed the importance of improving relations and signed numerous treaties in the field of science, energy, technical cooperation and film coproductions.[17]

In an interview given by Simeon to the Russian magazine *Business Contacts* he emphasised that Bulgaria's future EU membership and Bulgaria's relations with Russia should not be seen as 'a confrontation'. Simeon underlined that idea that 'Bulgaria's interests are of the greatest importance to me … If we strive for some farther target more calmly and more pragmatically it may be reached sooner. We have to consider our country's interests and develop our relations both with EU and Russia.'[18] Simeon's attitude and policy toward Russia was supported by the majority of Bulgarians. A survey in June 2001 showed that more than 70% of Bulgarians considered that the official visit of Simeon to Russia was of benefit to the Bulgarian economy. Furthermore, about 55.3% of people interviewed were convinced that the development of bilateral relations with Russia was 'as important as our relations with the EU, NATO and USA'.[19]

In March 2003 President Putin visited Bulgaria and as well as bilateral relations the Russian and Bulgarians discussed foreign policy issues. Bulgarian Foreign Minister Solomon Passy said that in foreign policy both Bulgaria and Russia 'have clear positions within the framework of the (U.N.) Security Council and each respects the position of the other notwithstanding if they are similar or not'.[20] The change in the Bulgarian attitude was evidenced by the fact that Bulgaria asked to maintain six diplomatic missions in Russia in order to facilitate greater contacts between the peoples of the two countries.

Relations between Bulgaria and Russia improved further when Georgi Parvanov, leader of the Bulgarian Socialist Party, took office on

22 January 2002 as president of Bulgaria. In May 2002 he stated that Bulgaria's membership in NATO and the EU was 'a strategic choice. Bulgaria has always belonged to the European historic and cultural space. The Bulgarians have always felt Europeans at heart and that is why there is nothing more natural than seeking to regain our place in the European family as soon as possible.' Bulgaria's membership in the European Union should be seen not as a sign that they were against others but as an idea 'evolving around three main principles: legitimacy, openness and efficiency'. By these principles he meant the 'redressing the deficit of democracy, a clearer and more visible responsibility in decision making and a closer link between citizens and institutions'. Through openness the president wanted to see 'a greater transparency of the European political process' and by efficiency, the creation of 'a better system of governance and simplification of contracts, stronger institutions and a better balance between them'.[21]

With such an approach, Parvanov believed Bulgaria would be able to avoid taking sides not only between the EU and the USA but also among EU member states. Parvanov made a number of official trips to Russia and many times expressed his belief that Bulgarian–Russian relations have a different base than those in the past. Bulgaria, he asserted in January 2003 does not look at Russia 'as an alternative to the EU but as an irreplaceable part of an open, balanced, emancipated foreign policy, as a constituent part of the new architecture of European security'. President Putin, on his part, clearly stated that he 'respects the right of the Bulgarian people to make sovereign choice in its strategic orientation'. Parvanov believed that since relations between the EU and Russia were good and improving, then Bulgarian–Russian contacts should also develop in all fields. In addition, he was critical of those who called for an estrangement from Russia because they were going against the traditional friendship between the Bulgarian and Russian peoples.[22] Public opinion polls show that President Parvanov is the most popular politician in Bulgaria and brought a much needed moderation and guidance to Bulgarian political thinking.

US overtures: a momentous turn

Bulgaria's estrangement from Russia would have had little success without the transformations that have occurred in Eastern Europe and especially without the help the country received from the West, especially the United States. In February 1990 James Baker paid the first ever visit by a US secretary of state to Sofia and urged the then BSP government to hold free elections and democratise the country. There is no doubt that his presence in Bulgaria encouraged the opposition forces to resist the left. With the coming to power of the UDF in October 1991 Bulgarian–US relations took a turn that would have been unimaginable two years earlier. The United States promised to help Bulgaria and in a few years the country became a favoured contender for US good will and economic assistance. In time, the negative attitude of Bulgarians toward the USA changed radically and the United States image in the Bulgarian media replaced that of the former Soviet Union. Presently, the right wing and centrist politicians and journalists not only praise but portrayed the USA as the Bulgarians' 'Big Brother'.

Aware of the security vacuum that was created in Southeastern Europe as a result of the decline of Soviet power, and the dismemberment of Yugoslavia, the USA saw developments in Bulgaria as holding promise of establishing a new centre in the volatile Balkan–Aegean–Black Sea region. This became more expedient due to the ethnic and political wars in Yugoslavia.[23] Zhelev and Union of Democratic Forces (UDF) politicians looked at and expected the USA to aid them in satisfying their security concerns and reform their institutions. In the early 1990s, of all the East European states none sought after the United States more than Bulgaria because UDF politicians saw the USA, a superpower that was prepared to restrain Bulgaria's neighbours from any aggressive designs, and 'as the one country that could and would organize international defense of small countries victimized by aggressors and as the likeliest source of relief from Bulgaria's long economic decline ...'[24]

When former Vice President Dan Quayle visited Sofia in July 1991 Bulgaria was already on good terms with the USA. Viktor Vulkov, the then Bulgarian minister of foreign affairs, said that since the USA played such a significant role in world affairs and since relations in the past were 'extremely restricted', in democratic Bulgaria 'thanks to mutual efforts Bulgarian–US relations were not only rescued from the deadlock of the totalitarian regime, but were even considerably intensified and further developed'.[25] When the Warsaw Pact, the Soviet Bloc's military alliance system, ceased to exist, and the ethnic conflicts in Yugoslavia were gaining momentum, Bulgarians were rightly concerned with their national security and wanted to improve relations with the USA as soon as possible.

The USA had its own concerns and national interests in the region also. Since there was no real change in the Albanian and Romanian leaderships yet and events were taking a turn for the worse in neighbouring Yugoslavia, Bulgaria's geopolitical situation offered an opening and opportunity for American policy-makers. From the very start of the intensified relationship between Bulgaria and the United States, it was made clear to the Bulgarian side that the USA would support Bulgaria only if Bulgaria had free and fair elections and achieved further improvement in establishing a genuine civil society and market economy. When the UDF came to power, Washington put greater emphasis on improving relations and on not criticising the shortcomings of the immediate past. While the USA promised aid and from 1990 to 1998 sent 295 volunteers under the Peace Corps programme, Bulgaria supported the US policy and actions in the Gulf War. According to Zhelev, this moral support showed that Bulgaria, for the first time in fifty years, had an independent foreign policy of its own. When Bulgaria was invited to participate in the victory celebration, 'the world noticed Bulgaria's new foreign policy and gave us our due'.[26] Bulgaria was thus earning a positive image in the West.

Recognising the independent turn in Bulgarian policy, the USA helped the country meet energy expenses, lifted trade restrictions, and in 1996 accorded Bulgaria unconditional most-favoured-nation trade status. The USA also opened a commercial office in Sofia and concluded agricultural and other agreements between the two countries. To help establish a free market, American institutions included USAID financed business development programmes, offered direct loans, and sought to create other investment activities. American advisors in Bulgaria aided various institutions and patterned themselves on those in Europe and the USA.

Significant progress was also made in the cultural and public relations fields. The USIA invited Bulgarians to visit the USA, students were encouraged to study in American higher institutions, a Voice of America station was established in Sofia and – strikingly enough – American naval forces were welcomed in the port of Varna.[27] During the past seven years the United States has provided Bulgaria with $290 million in assistance under the Support for East European Democracy Act to aid political and economic reforms and the democratisation process. The USA is Bulgaria's sixth-largest trading partner and the third-largest source of foreign direct investment. The US investments in Bulgaria have reached a level of $58.4 million with major projects by AIG, American Standard and Sea Board. In addition, many American companies have invested in the Bulgarian market.[28] Through the years the Support for East European Democracy (SEED) provided Bulgaria with aid for various projects. In addition to direct aid from the USA, Bulgaria received loans from the IMF and other American and European agencies.[29]

Since 1997, relations with the United States have grown increasingly close. This trend has accelerated sharply since 2002. The general attitude in Bulgaria is pro-American and the Bulgarian market is very receptive to American goods and services. The NMSII government included ministers and deputy ministers and a large number of Western-educated officials. Some have studied and worked in the United States, and are very supportive of expanding US–Bulgarian trade relations.[30]

Following an older American–Bulgarian tradition, in September 1991 a US sponsored American University at Blagoevgrad opened its doors to students from the region and one year later the American College in Sofia – closed since 1947 – reopened its gates. The USA provided a 15 million endowment for the American University and this and other institutions received help from private donors. As with other American initiatives, not all Bulgarians were entirely happy about these developments. Bulgarian Socialist Party members accused the United States of interfering in Bulgarian internal affairs and of trying to Americanise the country. However, a majority of Bulgarians expressed a positive attitude toward the USA, seeing novelty in everything American.[31]

Under the presidency of Petar Stoyanov and the UDF government led by Ivan Kostov multilateral relations between Bulgaria and the USA and the EU have blossomed and have culminated in Bulgaria's formal application for membership to the European Union. This was due to the willingness of the Bulgarian leadership to continue the economic reform process, to act in agreement with most of the demands made by the EU and to its support for NATO actions during the Yugoslav crisis. In all of these endeavours Bulgaria showed its willingness and commitment to join Western initiatives and to take the necessary steps to demonstrate that it deserves entry into Western structures.

Former presidents Bill Clinton and Petar Stoyanov met on various occasions to discuss the further strengthening of ties between the two countries and 'committed themselves to building a partnership that reflects a new era in Bulgarian–American relations'. The former American president assured Bulgaria of America's 'commitment to NATO's "Open Door" policy' and support for Bulgaria's future membership in the alliance through its 'engagement in the Partnership for Peace, enhanced dialogue with NATO and the Euro-Atlantic Partnership Council'. In 1999, the United States provided Bulgaria financial assistance in such areas as criminal law enforcement training, and in developing a new education curriculum to promote democratic values, and is offering a $900,000 grant to train cadets in US military academies. In addition, US agencies gave Bulgaria another $3.2 million for a military liaison team resident in the Bulgarian Ministry of Defence to organise staff and information exchanges and modernise the military forces.[32]

Even before Bulgaria's acceptance into NATO and in anticipation of the visit of former president Clinton to Sofia on 21–23 November 1999, the Bulgarian media discussed the issue of the possible location of US military bases in Bulgaria. At the time Prime Minister Kostov and President Stoyanov denied that any official discussions had already taken place on this issue. However, Christopher Hill, the former American ambassador to the Republic of Macedonia and a member of the US National Security Council, said that former presidents Clinton and Stoyanov were expected to discuss the possibility of having US bases in Bulgaria.[33] Comments made by Stoyanov showed that the former Bulgarian president was not opposed to having US bases in his country even though the deployment of nuclear bases in Bulgarian territory 'was not on the agenda'.[34] It was reported that on 22 November 1999 Stoyanov and Clinton discussed the possibility of NATO's use of Bulgarian 'military objects' in Sofia. Under the NMSII government, the issue was discussed but no final decision has been made, up to 2006, even though the media supports what it calls American bases. Bulgarian right-wing and centrist politicians think that such American presence would make Bulgaria gain greater significance for the USA and, in turn, the country would benefit economically and politically. Bulgarian right-wing leaders have been well aware that one way to facilitate entrance into the European Union was by becoming a member of NATO as soon as possible and they have been actively seeking to advance the process of membership. This proposed move has recently been described as a 'success guarantee' for Bulgaria.[35] After waiting a few years and pre-paring its military, on 29 March 2004 Bulgaria officially joined NATO. Although there were Bulgarians who opposed entry, the majority approved of the Simeon Sakskoburggotski government move.[36]

It must be noted that, initially, Russian officials, as expected, reacted to Bulgaria's ambition of NATO membership negatively and treated it as an unfriendly act towards their country. Recalling that the Soviet Union had no bases on Bulgarian territory, Russian Foreign Ministry spokesman Vladimir Rakhmanin said that statements suggesting US and NATO bases might be set up in Bulgaria did not 'promote security and stability in Europe, particularly in its Southeastern part'.[37] Given the anti-American climate that exists in Greece, it is plausible that either the USA or NATO would like to establish some permanent presence in Bulgaria. Asked about this issue in May 2003 Secretary of State Colin Powell stated: 'We might want to put in place facilities that give us access to training areas in other countries or that facilitate the movement of our forces through Europe to other parts of the world, as we change the strategy of NATO not to deal with the Soviet Union but to deal with terrorism, to deal with regional crises in other part of the world.'[38]

The post-Cold War relationship between Bulgaria and the United States culminated with the visit of President Clinton, three United States Congressmen and a distinguished group of Americans to Sofia on 21–23 November 1999. The people of Sofia gave Clinton a warm welcome. Clinton praised the Bulgarians for standing with NATO during the Kosovo crisis and said that the USA and Bulgaria had reached agreements that would encourage more American companies to do business in Bulgaria and create jobs for both countries. He also noted that the USA was taking steps to help Bulgaria crack down on corruption 'once and for all'. Clinton reiterated what he told Stoyanov in Washington and what most Bulgarians wanted to hear most, that the United States strongly supported the Stability Pact for Southeast Europe and encouraged the expansion of the European Union to Southeastern Europe as well. He said specifically that NATO's doors would be kept 'open to those democratic nations here who are able to meet their obligations'. The president called on businessmen and investors to aid Bulgaria in building a better future and promised to work together with them.

Bulgarians took this as a commitment and expected the former president and the United States to lobby on their behalf and provide economic aid. As Krasen Stanchev, director of the Institute for Market Economy, wrote, 'Bulgaria received recognition not only for things it has achieved in its economy but also for its foreign policy pursuits.'[39] There is no doubt that Clinton's visit and praise of Bulgaria's achievements was a great public relations achievement for the country and, once again, strengthened the country's image as a prospering democracy.

During the last two to three years Bulgarian–American relations, in the words of Secretary of State Colin Powell, 'are the best they have ever been in all of the past one hundred years'. Bulgaria, following the democratic changes introduced since 1989, 'has proven to be a valuable friend of the U.S., committed to the principles of democracy, human rights, peace and free markets'. US Department of State Spokesman Richard Boucher claimed that 'Bulgaria is a pivotal country in Southeastern Europe' and therefore 'has been an important factor for tolerance and moderation in the region'. Bulgaria has been praised for promoting peace and stability in the Balkans through its support of such undertakings as the Stabilization Force in Bosnia and Hercegovina (SFOR) and to the Kosovo Force (KFOR) in Kosovo. In addition, 'in the international struggle against terrorism and extremism, Bulgaria has demonstrated its commitment through its significant support to coalition forces during Operation Enduring Freedom and Operation Iraqi Freedom. A 500-man Bulgarian infantry battalion is in Iraq now as part of coalition efforts to stabilize and rebuild Iraq.' For all the support Bulgaria has rendered to the USA in the war against terrorism, President G. W. Bush stated in May 2003 that 'Americans have always considered the Bulgarian people to be our friends, and we will be proud to call you allies.'[40] US Congressman Joe Wilson on 10 February 2005 stated before the US House of Representatives that Bulgaria 'is a thriving democracy which recognizes the importance of furthering freedom throughout the world', and spoke of 'the Bulgarian miracle: the establishment of a dynamic democracy and the restoration of economic freedom creating unlimited opportunities for the Bulgarian people'.[41] Prime Minister Simeon responded to these praises on the occasion of the 100th anniversary of the establishment of diplomatic relations between Bulgaria and the United States by saying that 'common human values unite us and on their basis I believe we will build our good relationship for many years ahead!'[42]

The road back to Europe: the crooked path set straight

Although relations with the United States are regarded by most Bulgarians as crucial for the development of the Bulgarian economy, the road back to Europe is probably more important for the majority. Philip Dimitrov, former prime minister of the first democratically elected government, former leader of the Union of Democratic Forces, was the first to place on the agenda the need for an accelerated move to enter NATO and the EU. A similar public relations effort was conducted nine years earlier with President Stojanov who courted Clinton. Dimitrov was the first to endorse 'a new face' for the conduct of foreign policy, Bulgaria's *Westpolitik*. Although Bulgaria sought to benefit by trading with the European Community as early as 1986 it was not until 1990 that the Bulgarian government seriously sought affiliation with the EU. Bulgaria was admitted into CSCE before the fall of Zhivkov but the process of integration accelerated during the 1990s when the country entered the Council of Europe, EFTA, IMF and other institutions. Bulgaria has since signed many multilateral and especially bilateral treaties with all the West European states. Since 1990, Germany has invested more than 250 million euro in Bulgaria.[43] At present, most of Bulgaria's commerce is with Western Europe and Bulgaria wants to expand further its political, economic and cultural ties with the EU member states.

Today, Bulgaria has developed good bilateral relations with all European countries, including post-Milošević Serbia. Bulgarians desire normal relations with their neighbours for the same reason they wanted

to make their country a normal state and create institutions and infra-
structures that will benefit all. Surprisingly, this has been achieved to a
greater degree than is usually recognised. Presently, relations between
Bulgaria and its neighbours are better than at any other time. Bulgaria
has established friendly bilateral relations with the countries of Central
Europe, the former Soviet republics and most of the developing countries, and actively participates in multilateral activities through the
Central European Initiative and the Black Sea Organization for Economic Cooperation.

Bulgaria has signed treaties of friendship, good neighbourliness and
cooperation with Albania, Greece, Macedonia, Romania and Turkey. In
addition, other specific treaties and agreements that deal with development of commerce and economic ventures, defence and diplomatic
consultation, education and culture, science and technology, health and
the protection of the environment are in effect. Treaties, however, do
not always solve the real problems that exist between states. For this
reason, Bulgaria's policy of open borders in the region aims at
strengthening relations between the peoples. In general, Bulgaria has
tactfully and perceptively followed an equidistant policy toward its
neighbours and, again, to a considerable degree, has achieved its aims of
friendly relations with all.

In 1995 the short-lived government of Prime Minister Zhan Videnov
altered Dimitrov's programme and gave priority to developing relations
with Bulgaria's neighbours rather than with European institutions. In
effect, he expanded Bulgaria's diplomatic capacity. By skillfully balan-
cing its policies, Bulgaria was to act as a bridge between Greece and
Turkey, while still deepening European ties to the West. The results of
this policy were remarkable. Relations with Greece are better than ever.
In 1992 Bulgaria signed a treaty of friendship and cooperation with
Greece followed by agreements on investment, security and travel.
Greek businessmen have invested in Bulgaria and additional border
routes have been opened. Working together, Russia, Bulgaria and
Greece are building a gas pipeline from the port of Burgas to the port of
Alexandroupolis. Bulgarian diplomats regularly consult with their Greek
colleagues regarding Balkan issues and Greece came out strongly in
support of Bulgaria's admission to the EU and NATO.

The maintenance of domestic ethnic tranquillity, especially the
improvement in the treatment of the Turkish and Muslim minorities in
Bulgaria, was crucial for the improvement of relations with Turkey.[44]
The intentions of the two countries, 'to be on good terms' were
embodied in the 1992 Bulgarian–Turkish agreement on friendship, good
neighbourliness, cooperation and security, which 'signaled an end to

tensions between the two states'. President Stoyanov, on a visit to Ankara, in 1999 apologised for the mistreatment of the Turks in Bulgaria during the Zhivkov regime. In addition, relations with Romania, as with the other Balkan states, remained good throughout the 1990s even though there are still issues to be solved, such as pollution and where to build a second bridge over the Danube. As both Bulgaria and Romania became EU candidate members the governments had to collaborate on many issues of common interest.

Bulgaria also took the initiative in creating the Balkan Conference of Stability and Cooperation in Southeast Europe and belongs to other regional associations such as the transport infrastructure development along main international routes, the interconnection of electric power systems and gas networks as well as environmental projects and the association of chambers of commerce. Since then, Bulgaria has hosted numerous Balkan ministerial conferences and in 1999 the city of Plovdiv became the headquarters of another all-Balkan initiative, the Multinational Peacekeeping Force Southeast Europe.[45]

After years of preparation and perspiration, Bulgaria was finally approved to join the European Union. 'The Treaty of Accession of Bulgaria and Romania to the European Union' was signed on 25 April in Luxembourg by Prime Minister Simeon Saxe-Coburg, President Georgi Parvanov, Minister of Foreign Affairs Solomon Passy and Minister of European Affairs Meglena Kuneva. When the government adopted a declaration on the ratification of the treaty it said that, 'With it, the dreams of a few generations of Bulgarians to come back to the world of democracy, freedom, solidarity and law and order came true. It fulfilled the fifteen-year efforts of politicians and governments, because if there was a consensus in Bulgaria on some issue, it concerned the country's EU membership.' The Bulgarian parliament overwhelmingly approved the treaty. Bulgarians hope that, notwithstanding the recent setbacks regarding the EU constitution, the country will join the union in January 2007 as a full member on schedule.[46]

Bulgarian–Macedonian relations: overwhelmed by the past

As the situation in Yugoslavia deteriorated, Bulgarian foreign policy-makers announced as early as January 1991 that in case Macedonia was to disassociate from Yugoslavia, Bulgaria would recognise its independence. On 8 September 1991 Macedonians voted for independence, and Bulgaria, insisting on the principle of self-determination, was on 15 January 1992 the first country to recognise the Republic of Macedonia under its constitution. Careful not to create an impression of having special designs on Macedonia, Bulgaria also recognised Croatia, Slovenia and Bosnia-Hercegovina. The recognition of Macedonia and the refusal to participate in any dealings at the expense of Macedonia's integrity were politically timely moves by Zhelev and the National Assembly for which Macedonians were grateful. Notwithstanding subsequent arguments between Bulgarians and Macedonians, the recognition of the Republic of Macedonia as a sovereign state helped strengthen Macedonia's national affirmation, and thus aid its autochthonous national development.

Bulgarian recognition of a separate Macedonian state, however, did not imply the recognition of the Macedonian people as a nation.[47] Moreover, Bulgaria's policy of conditionality prompted some intellectuals and the media in both countries to fight a protracted war of words about history, culture, the Macedonian minority in Bulgaria and Bulgarians in Macedonia, ethnic identity and language issues. These primarily artificial problems hindered speedy progress between the two states, and relations stagnated for years even though Bulgaria came to Macedonia's aid when the Greeks imposed an embargo over the constitutional name of the country. It is unfortunate that even though the former presidents, Kiro Gligorov of Macedonia and Zheliu Zhelev, visited each other's country, the elites failed to take advantage of their historical and cultural affinity and the new conditions created in Europe.

Distrust began to wane in 1999 when the Bulgarian government and the former Macedonian government of Prime Minister Ljubco Georgievski embarked on the task of finding satisfactory solutions to existing issues that divided their states. As a result, the two governments found a way to solve the so-called language dispute, that is, whether Macedonian is a dialect of Bulgarian or a separate language. The two governments agreed that accords should be signed in the official languages as determined by the constitution of each country. This simple formula permitted the two states to sign and put in force many treaties that had been ready for years. Even though this breakthrough did not satisfy nationalist extremists on both sides, it brought a radical change in relations. In addition to governmental ties, individual organisations and institutions have collaborated in economic development and in trade, science and technology, education and the media, transportation and many other fields. Credit for reaching such a satisfactory state ought to be given not only to politicians and intellectuals of both countries but also to the strong urging of European and American diplomats to find a way to solve the existing language and history issues.[48]

One result of warming relations between Sofia and Skopje was the Agreement on Free Trade between Bulgaria and Macedonia which entered into force on 1 January 2000. Accordingly, trade between the two countries will expand and almost 90 per cent of the trade in industrial goods will be tariff free. Businessmen from both countries held forums on establishing contacts and improving cooperation.[49] Relations between the two countries further improved under the presidency of Parvanov and the NMSII government. Both Bulgarian and Macedonian politicians make frequent visits to each other's country and exchange views.

There are, of course, many issues that remain unresolved. To both Macedonians and Bulgarians, for instance, it is inconceivable that the Bulgarian Orthodox Church has still not recognised the independence of the Macedonian Orthodox Church. Most important is the national question, that is, the recognition by Bulgarian intellectuals and politicians, in a fundamental way, that the Macedonians in the republic and in the Diaspora are a separate *ethnos*, ethnically different from the Bulgarians. The Bulgarian attitude of questioning the identity of the Macedonians has had a negative impact on both domestic issues and foreign affairs. When these issues are solved, greater economic and cultural integration between the two states will follow and only on this basis can the special relationship between the two states flourish. Bulgaria and Macedonia are two countries on the European continent that have much in common but thanks to extremists, they have failed thus far to establish a sound special relationship between their states and peoples.

Wars and the dissolution of Yugoslavia: Bulgaria's different course

The Yugoslav crisis of the 1990s had a pronounced impact on Bulgaria's economy and policies with its neighbours, the distancing from Russia and turning towards the West. The multiple problems created posed intricate issues for foreign policy-makers. They had to ensure the Yugoslav wars did not spill over, that the disintegration and ethnic problems did not affect Bulgaria's security, that the establishment of relations with the five new states in the region did not antagonise others, and that the consequences for the Bulgarian economy of the embargo and sanctions imposed on Yugoslavia would be minimised.

Events in the neighboring country caused much anxiety and Bulgarian society was divided in its attitude toward the wars and the government's policy and strategy. Throughout the Yugoslav crisis, Bulgarian political parties and public opinion was polarised along ideological and nationalist lines. While the BSP was for the preservation of the Yugoslav federation and took a pro-socialist and pro-Serbian position, and on occasion some even supported Slobodan Milošević, the UDF and nationalist parties took anti-Serbian, anti-Yugoslav stands, supported anti-communist groups, and called for the immediate recognition of the new break-away republics of Yugoslavia. Bulgaria, concerned about stability in the region and its own security, took the position that no Balkan states should become directly involved in the Yugoslav conflict. During the war in Bosnia, the former Bulgarian foreign minister, Stoyan Ganev, stated, for example, that non-involvement would help 'in overcoming a historical build-up of suspicion and in achieving durable stability in the region'.[50]

In reality, Bulgarians could do little but react to the events in the neighbouring country and the policies of the powers. The Yugoslav conflict created instability in the region and postponed regional cooperation and jeopardised economic reforms. While Bulgaria successfully developed bilateral and multilateral links with Greece, Romania, Albania, Turkey and Macedonia, relations with Yugoslavia usually had to follow Western initiatives, and foreign policy-makers faithfully adhered to the policies of expediency and the strategic measures of the EU and NATO. Notwithstanding that the country suffered greatly from the sanctions imposed on Yugoslavia, Bulgaria demonstrated its commitment to the West by being 'very clear on its intent to follow the dictates of the United Nations – even when those dictates quite clearly are not to Bulgaria's advantage'.[51]

While Bulgaria always called for a peaceful solution of the conflicts in Yugoslavia and made it clear that it was not going to become directly involved in the war, many Bulgarian politicians supported the EU and NATO policies and actions. During the Kosovo crisis the Bulgarian government called for autonomy for the Albanians within Yugoslavia. Nadezhda Mihailova, the minister of foreign affairs, visited Belgrade to offer Bulgaria's services to mediate between the Yugoslav government and the Albanians and NATO, while at the same time Bulgaria fully aligned with the Western powers in support of the Rambouillet Agreement. However, the Bulgarians, again, opposed changing the borders of Yugoslavia or any other territory in the region.

On 19 April 1999, Kostov stated that 'Bulgaria supports NATO only because it is in this country's own interest to return peace to the region and to return the deported people to their homes.' Bulgarian leaders argued that 'to refuse support to NATO would also mean turning its back on the only countries from which Bulgaria could possibly hope for assistance to overcome the heavy economic price to be paid for the conflict'.[52] During the war there were mass demonstrations in Bulgaria against the war and Bulgarian intellectuals debated issues of human rights, the principle of sovereignty, and the practicality of intervention in the internal affairs of states. At present, Bulgaria supports the United Nations presence in Kosovo and has a fifty-member police unit participating in the KFOR mission in charge of the protection of public order and crime control.[53]

In addition to the problems created by the wars, Bulgaria had other concerns. As Yugoslavia was crumbling, Bulgarian nationalist organisations requested that their government demand from Yugoslavia that Bulgarians living in the 'Western Borderlands', that is, in regions of eastern Serbia, be granted human rights, Bulgarian schools and ethnic institutions. Moreover, Bulgarian ethnic organisations from Yugoslavia appealed to the Bulgarian government and to human rights organisations to come to their aid. Bulgarian nationalist groups and the reconstituted Internal Macedonian Revolutionary Organization – Union of Macedonian Societies even 'argued that the post-1918 borders were open for revision after the disintegration of Yugoslavia'. While supporting the demands of the Bulgarians in Yugoslavia, the Bulgarian government stressed that it opposed any border changes in Yugoslavia and the Balkans. Yugoslav politicians, however, reacted nervously and have consistently refused to recognise the official Bulgarian term for the Bulgarian-inhabited Yugoslav borderlands as the 'Western Borderlands'. Moreover, Serbian officials denied that the Bulgarian minority was oppressed and refused to even discuss the issue with Bulgarian foreign ministry officials. This problem was only one of many others that still continued to hinder the establishment of good relations between the two neighbours.[54]

The overthrow of President Slobodan Milošević and his regime brought a radical change in relations between Bulgaria and Serbia and Montenegro. During the last two years normal relations have been established between the two states. Foreign Minister Passy in a meeting in May 2005 stated that 'The regional cooperation is a fundamental priority of Bulgaria's foreign policy. However, we never considered it an alternative to our integration into the European and Euro-Atlantic structures. During these years of transition we have always regarded our regional policy as an essential part of the strategy towards EU and NATO integration.' He said that Bulgaria's emphasis on good neighbourly relations and regional cooperation was part of the country's strategy to join the Euro-Atlantic structures: 'Our foreign policy caters not only for the Bulgarian interests but also the interests of the whole region, since the Euro-Atlantic perspective is a common goal for all countries in South Eastern Europe.' He believed that after 'centuries of divisions and violent conflicts, today South Eastern Europe has a unique historical chance. For the first time in their history all countries in the region are united by a common geopolitical goal and a common future in the Euro-Atlantic structures.'[55]

Bulgaria, following the line of the EU is normalising relations with Serbia and Montenegro. On 21 June 2005, Solomon Passy conferred with his counterpart Vuk Draskovic in Dimitrovgrad, a city which is predominantly populated by Bulgarians. The Bulgarians said that the meeting was 'an expression of the fine relations' between the two states. The two diplomats signed a Joint Declaration on Balkans without Border, as well as a Programme on Cooperation in the Field of Education, Culture and Sports for the 2005-7 periods. Minister Solomon Passy solemnly declared that their meeting 'showed that the road of Serbia and Montenegro to Brussels passes through Sofia',[56] Minister Passy believes that the two states have established European-type relations far ahead of their formal membership of the European Union.

Problems ahead: the need for domestic peace and full European integration

The dilemma in Bulgarian foreign policy that started with the demise of the Soviet bloc still mirrors the earlier East–West Cold War confrontation. Now, however, it is replaced with the Russia/Europe/USA and poor versus rich dialogue among Bulgarians over the future development of Bulgarian polity and society; some of the public look toward the concept 'the common European home from the Atlantic to the Urals', which includes Russia as part of Europe; others focus on Bulgaria and Europe's relationship with the United States.[57]

Divisions among Bulgarians do not strictly divide over Russia versus the West. Relations between Bulgaria and its neighbours are, to a large degree, dependent on public perceptions of 'the other'. At present the Balkan peoples' views of each other are not as good as they should be. There is still ignorance of each other, mistrust, hatred and even enmity and these real and imaginary perceptions determine how the Balkan peoples see each other. All have to work for common regional objectives which would diminish and eliminate such negative notions.[58]

Without diminishing the success achieved, Bulgaria still has important problems to solve before it can become a full member of all the Euro-Atlantic structures. Ahmed Dogan, leader of the Movement for Rights and Freedoms, stated after the local elections in October 1999, that in the future his party will demand quotas for participation of ethnic

Turks in all state structures. Such demands, most Bulgarian politicians agree, are not provided for in any of the European conventions on treatment of minorities and therefore are not an acceptable policy for Bulgaria to follow.[59] Should other groups seek to enforce such policies, then it could further imperil minorities and the future of the Bulgarian ethnic tolerance model as well as political developments in the country and in the whole region. As with its Balkan neighbours, the condition of the Roma minority in Bulgaria still needs improvement if the minority tolerance model is to succeed and Bulgaria's image is to advance.

As the recent local and parliamentary elections showed, Bulgaria has too many political and social divisions. In the 1999 and 2005 elections, an astonishing 96 and 14 parties, coalitions and movements respectively competed for influence and power. The potential of ethnic tensions and even social conflicts are still present. Although serious Bulgarian politicians have long since distanced themselves from nationalist ideas of 'Greater Bulgaria', the 'San Stefano Syndrome' is still the dream of extreme nationalists. Unemployment and poverty seriously affect the lives of the majority of Bulgarians. With the entry of Bulgaria into the Euro-Atlantic structures and the creation of a market economy, some politicians and intellectuals believe that the transition period has come to an end. Certainly, this might be true but there are still dangers because both old and new elements in society are competing. Most Bulgarians must ask how they can live without ideological and even moral absolutes, and ethical foundations in the absence of guidance or the supposed certainty of a better tomorrow. An honest debate about the pros and cons of membership in the EU, the Roma problem and other ethnic issues, criminality, corruption, unemployment and the demographic crisis are real questions waiting for resolution by the new politicians who brought Bulgaria into the EU.

In remaking the country in the Western image it is necessary for Bulgaria to have stronger functioning institutions such as checks and balances, legality, a working free market, respect for human and civil rights, diversity and a social justice safety net. Moreover, the elite must understand that it is necessary to solve the country's problems through dialogue and compromise. Although there is openness and some public dialogue, greater citizen input and participation in the formulation and implementation of policy is necessary. Issues of the interplay between domestic and foreign policies are also the domain of the NGOs and politicians should give greater weight to their work.

Official conferences and treaties with regional neighbours or distant friends would not have the desired intent and impact if problems such as unemployment, corruption, social divisions and public security are left unresolved. To make treaties meaningful to the masses and viable in the international community, the benefits of change and prosperity should be extended to a broader spectrum of the population. People want to see growth in their economy but they also want opportunities with equity and equality. Freedom and democracy, most Bulgarians believe, are inseparable from equality and justice for all.

The EU should not set out too many stiff preconditions in the next few months and should permit Bulgaria to become a full member as agreed. It is crucially important to prove to the peoples of the area that they too are treated equally and that they would not be marginalised again. Since economic progress is the key to stability and democratisation, the Western community ought to address the Balkan's specificity within European/American context as soon as possible in order to reduce the wide gap that exists between rich and poor within the country and between the countries of Southeastern and Western Europe.[60]

The long-term success of Bulgarian foreign policy since 1989 aimed at helping make the transitional period into a real transformation of the country's economy and image. Bulgaria's Europeanisation has led to the democratisation of politics and society, and the building of a civil society. It must be said that transformation of the elites has succeeded beyond the expectations of many. Future success depends first and foremost on the Bulgarians themselves and then on the policy demands and aid that the EU, NATO and the United States provide for Bulgaria in order to successfully continue the changes to build not just a political but also an economically viable democracy.

In spite of Bulgaria's new self-consciousness and pro-Atlantic identity, it is not yet equal to other Western European states, including some of the East European states that have recently joined the European Union. To make the deadline of 1 January 2007 as a full member of the EU, Bulgarians must work hard in order to bring about all the necessary changes, especially in the judiciary and in fighting corruption. Hopefully, the incomplete victory in the 25 June 2005 parliamentary elections of the Coalition for Bulgaria, led by the Bulgarian Socialist Party, will produce a government of national unity capable of successfully leading the country to full membership in the EU. When in it, Bulgaria and its citizens would be treated as full members and as Europeans only if they participate in the European economic, political and social structures, on an equal footing with all other Europeans, and as active partners with the United States, Russia and the world community.

Notes

* The author wishes to express his gratitude to the Bulgarian journalist Chavdar Kisselinchev, colleagues Ronald J. Ross, Bruce Fetter, and Alexander P. Shashko, doctoral candidate at the University of Michigan and Tanya D. Shashko of Stanford University for their help and constructive suggestions.

1 'Inauguration Speech by Georgi Parvanov President of the Republic of Bulgaria' http://www.president.bg/en/news.php?id=7&st=0

2 For a comprehensive review of relations between Muslims and the Bulgarian majority, see Mary Neuburger, *The Orient Within: Muslim Minorities and the Negotiation of Nationhood in Modern Bulgaria*, Ithaca, NY: Cornell University Press, 2004; also, Antonina Zheliazkova, Bozhidar Aleksiev and Zhorzheta Nazurska, *Miusiulmanskite obshtnosti na Balkanite i v Bulgariia: istoricheski eskiz*, Sofia: Mezhdunaroden tsentur po problemite na maltsinstvata i kulturnite vzaimodeistviia, 1997.

3 Bulgarian ideologies of Marxism sustained its nation-building myths during the twentieth century, see Roumen Daskalov, *The Making of a Nation in the Balkans: Historiography of the Bulgarian Revival*, Budapest: Central European University Press, 2004; Philip Shashko, 'The past in Bulgaria's future', *Problems of Communism*, 39 (1990), 75–83.

4 There are many studies on ethnic problems and nationalism in the Balkans. On Bulgaria, see Daskalov, *The Making of a Nation*; Tom Gallagher, *Outcast Europe: The Balkans 1789–1999: from the Ottomans to Milošević*, London: Routledge, 2001; Emile Giatzidis, *An Introduction to Postcommunist Bulgaria: Political, Economic and Social Transformation*, Manchester: Manchester University Press, 2002; Lila Perl, *Yugoslavia, Romania, Bulgaria: New Era in the Balkans*, New York: EP Dutton, 2000; Antonina Zheliazkova, (ed.), *Relations of Compatibility and Incompatibility between Christians and Muslims in Bulgaria*, Sofia: International Center for Minority Studies and Intercultural Relations Foundation, 1995; Antonina Zheliazkova, 'Bulgaria's Muslim minorities', in John Bell (ed.), *Bulgaria in Transition*, Boulder, CO: Westview Press, 1998, pp. 165–87.

5 See 'Vnushnanta politika e tolkova po-dobra, kolkoto e po-razuman', *Demokratsiia*, 2 September 1992.

6 Zheliu Zhelev, *V goliamata politika*, Sofia: Knigoizdatelska kushta Trud, 1998, pp. 9–10.

7 He further wrote that 'in order to build an independent foreign policy solely in accordance with the national interests of the Bulgarian people, and in concord with the principles and norms of international law, the Bulgarian state had, first and foremost, to free itself from the economic, political, and military structures which strongly tied it to the international Communist system'. By this he meant Bulgaria's exit from reliance on the now-defunct Council of Mutual Economic Assistance (CMEA), the military Warsaw Pact and Soviet control generally. See Zheliu Zhelev, *V goliamata politika*, p. 9.

8 Oscar W. Clyatt, Jr, *Bulgaria's Quest for Security after the Cold War*, Washington, DC: The Institute for National Strategic Studies, 1993, p. 24.

9 On this complicated issue, see John Bell, Bulgaria's Search for Security', in Bell, ed., *Bulgaria in Transition*, pp. 314–15.

10 S. Lefebvre, 'Bulgaria's foreign relations in the post-communist era: a general overview and assessment', *East European Quarterly*, 28, 4 (1995), p. 465.

11 See 'Declaration on the Development of Equal Rights and Mutually Beneficial Relations with the Russian Federation', Bulgaria, Ministry of Foreign Affairs. http://.www.mfa.bg/policy/Russia_e.htm

12 Economist Intelligence Unit. Country Report: *Romania, Bulgaria, Albania*, no. 1 (1991), 5 and no. 4 (1994), p. 57.

13 *http://www.omda.bg/news.html* Review of the Bulgarian press for 14 July 1999.

14 Petur-Emil Mitev, 'Popular attitudes toward politics', in Bell, *Bulgaria in Transition*, pp. 57.

15 Cited from the inside cover of Zhelev's work, *V goliamata politika*.

16 'Solomon Passy: The visit to Russia is one of the most successful I have ever made' http://www.government.bg/English/Priorities/ForeignPolicy/2002-02-01/223.html

17 'Time for more creative relations between Bulgaria and Russia', http://www.government.bg/English/2002-06-03/637.html and http://www.government.bg/English/Priorities/ForeignPolicy/2003-02-27/1134.html

18 'Simeon Saxe-Coburg Gotha: Bulgaria's interests are of greatest importance to me', http://www.government.bg/English/Priorities/ForeignPolicy/2003-02-17/1103.html

19 'Bulgarian society supports Prime Minister Simeon Saxe-Coburg Gotha in his new policy towards Russia', http://www.government.bg/English/Priorities/ForeignPolicy/2002-06-24/691.html

20 'Prime Minister Simeon Saxe-Coburg Gotha and President Putin conferred for almost an hour', http://www.government.bg/English/Priorities/ForeignPolicy/2003-03-02/1141.html

21 'Bulgaria's European Future – Lecture before students at the Sofia University "St. Kliment Ohridski" ', http://www.president.bg/en/news.php?id=12&st=20

22 Nationalniyat interes ne se izmerva na prezidenta privanor za vestnik 'Duma', http://www.president.bg/news.php?id=648&st=30

23 Clyatt, Jr, *Bulgaria's Quest*, pp. 27–8.

24 Ibid., pp. 29–32.

25 Cited in ibid., p. 36.

26 Zhelev, *V goliamata politika*, pp. 39, 42.

27 'Bulgaria', http://gaia.info.usaid.gov/country/bulgaria.html

28 'Joint Statement U.S.–Bulgarian Partnership for a New Era', http://www.mfa.bg/policy/Usa_e.htm and 'Bulgaria and the United States,' http://bulgaria-embassy.org/bulgus.htm

29 *Sam Vaknin, God's Diplomacy and Human Conflict: The Costs of Coalition Building*, published by United Press International (UPI) http://samvak.tripod.com/brief-trade01.html

30 STAT-USA Market Research Reports, http://strategis.ic.gc.ca/epic/internet/inimr-ri.nsf/en/gr121081e.html

31 Clyatt, *Bulgaria's Quest*, pp. 44–5.

32 'Joint Statement U.S.–Bulgarian Partnership for a New Era', http://www.mfa.bg/policy/Usa_e.htm

33 'Bulgaria–US–Military Bases-PM Kostov', 2 November 1999, http://www.bta.bg/cgi-bin/hotnews

34 'Bulgaria–USA–President-Bases', 2 November 1999, http:/www.bta.bg/cgi-bin/hotnews

35 'Membership: Trade and Investment Opportunities in Southeast Europe' Deputy Prime Minister Plamen Panayotov pointed out that membership would not only improve Bulgaria's security but would also have a positive effect on the country's economy. 'Bulgaria's NATO Entry "Success Guarantee"', Sofia News Agency, 1 July 2004.

36 'In 2004 Bulgaria Became a NATO member', http://www.government.bg/English/2015.html

37 RFE/RL Newsline, vol. 3, no. 192, part I, 1 October 1999.

38 'Collin Powell: Bulgaria despite its relatively small size is playing a big role in the trans-Atlantic alliance', http://www.government.bg/English/Priorities/ForeignPolicy/2003-05-15/1318.html

39 Krasen Stanchev, 'Sega sa nuzhni usloviia za investitsii', http://www.eu-net.bg/bgnews/show_story.html?issue=158232609&media=1523776&class=2414656&story=158235712 [Demokratsiia, 24 November 1999].

40 'Bulgaria is a pivotal country in Southeastern Europe, reads a statement of the Spokesman of the US Department of State', http://www.government.bg/English/Priorities/ForeignPolicy/2003-09-19/1654.html

41 'Statement by the U.S. Congressman Joe Wilson before the U.S. House of Representatives', http://www.government.bg/English/2005-02-11/2201.html

42 'Common Human Values Unite Us and on Their Bases We Will Build Our Good Relationship for Many Years Ahead', http://www.government.bg/English/PrimeMinister/Statements/2003-05-17/1324.html

43 The 1998 two-way trade between the two countries reached DM 2,500 million. 'Bulgaria–Germany-Investments', http://www.bta.bg/cgi-bin/fnews_e.pl?newsid=5336443

44 See Neuberger, *The Orient Within*.

45 For a good review of the Multinational Peacekeeping Force, see Dimitris Bourantonis and Panayotis Tsakonas, 'The Southeastern Europe Multinational Peace Force: problems of and prospects for a regional security agency', *Politics*, 23, 2 (2003), 75–81.

46 'The Government Adopted a Political Declaration on the Forthcoming Ratification of the EU Accession Treaty of Bulgaria', http://www.government.bg/English/2538.html and Simeon Saxe-Coburg, 'I have no doubt that Bulgaria will join the EU as scheduled in 2007'. http://www.government.bg/English/Priorities/ForeignPolicy/2005-06-20/2672.html

47 For a discussion of this issue see Duncan M. Perry, 'The Macedonian question revitalized', RFE/RL, *Report on Eastern Europe*, I, No. 34, 24 August 1990, pp. 5–9.

48 On Macedonians in Bulgaria see John Bell, 'The 'Ilindentsi': does Bulgaria have a Macedonian minority?' in Bell, *Bulgaria in Transition*, 189–206, and for a Bulgarian perspective of the Macedonian question see Nauchen

Tsentur, Za Bulgarska Natsionalna Strategiia, *'Bulgariia prez dvadeset I purviia vek' Bulgarska natsionalna doktrina*, Sofia, 1997.

49 On the conference see http://www.bta.bg/cgi-binhotnews_e.pl?id-490453
50 'Ganev Assesses Results of London Conference', Foreign Broadcast Information Service, *Daily Report, East Europe*, 10 September 1992, 34, 92 and Kjell Engelbrekt, 'A vulnerable Bulgaria fears a wider war', *RFE/RL Research Report*, No. 12, 19 March 1993, pp. 7–12.
51 Luan Troxel, 'Bulgaria and the Balkans', C.P. Danopoulos and K. Messas, (eds.), *Crises in the Balkans: Views from the Participants*, Boulder, CO: Westview Press, 1997, 195–210. p. 203.
52 'Prime Minister, President, Speaker Unanimous: Bulgaria supports NATO because it wants lasting peace in the region', http://www.govrn.bg/eng/search/index.html
53 See 'KFOR-Bulgarian Police', http://www.bta.bg/cgi-bin/fnews_e.pl?newsid=5309956
54 K.D., 'Bulgaria' in John B. Allcock, Marko Milivojevic and John J. Horton, eds., *Conflict in Yugoslavia: An Encyclopedia*, Santa Barbara: ABC-CLIO, 1998, pp. 35.
55 'Regional Table of the Stability Pact, Sofia, 18 May 2005. Address of Solomon Passy, Minister of Foreign Affairs of Bulgaria' http://www.mfa.government.bg/index.php?tid=43&item_id=10083
56 'Minister Solomon Passy Confers in Dimitrovgrad with Foreign Minister of Serbia and Montenegro Vuk Draskovic' http://www.mfa.government. bg/index.php?item_id=11360 For a recent view of the different paths to Euro-Atlantic structures see John R. Lampe, 'Working toward the EU: Bulgaria's progress and Serbia's struggles', *EES News*, May–June 2005, pp. 9–11.
57 Mitev, 'Popular attitudes', in Bell, *Bulgaria in Transition*, p. 58.
58 On perceptions for the second half of the 1990s see the studies by Mariana Lenkova, 'Positive and negative stereotypes in the media of seven Balkan countries', http://www.greekhelsinki.gr/english/media/GHM-Media%20Monitoring-Bulgaria.html, and Mariana Lenkova, *Hate Speech in the Balkans*, Vienna: International Helsinki Federation for Human Rights, 1998.
59 See the article in *Demokratsiia* by Liliana Filipova, 'Sus siuzheta za kvotite Dogan se muchi da tushira krizata v sobstvenata si partiia', http://www.eunet.bg/bgnews/show_story.html?issue=149208535&media=1523776&class=1946720&story=149209911
60 For a Bulgarian perspective see Chavdar Kisselinchev, 'A world divided and polarized', in *Sofia Western News*, no. 44, September 1999, http://www.mobikom.com/sofia_westnews.main.html

19 Albania, Italy and Greece: some geopolitical considerations

Carole Hodge

The political scene in Albania since it gained its independence in 1912 has for the most part been beset by the attempts of one or a combination of the neighbouring states to dominate or dismember it. In fact, the only period in its history when Albania was effectively able to fend off incursions from its neighbours was during the austere dictatorship of Enver Hoxha. With the opening up of Eastern Europe after 1990, Albania's self-imposed isolation also ended and Europe's poorest state once more found itself struggling to assert its sovereignty, as the aspirations and agendas of its neighbours, Greece, Italy and, indirectly, rump Yugoslavia again came to the fore, aided unwittingly at various stages by internal political friction.

Over the past decade, Italian and Greek interests in Albania have extended from humanitarian to infrastructure projects, from banking to communications, from health to cultural institutions, and from peace-keeping activities to military alliances. By February 1999, sections of the Italian press and, reportedly, the Farnesina were discussing the possibility of Albania becoming an Italian protectorate.[1] Albania itself, after decades of deprivation as a minor satellite of successive communist powers, recognised the benefits of Western initiatives, and welcomed all external investment. Such initiatives also fall within the broad framework of EU and transatlantic programmes, such as the Stability Pact, which encourage regional cooperation as a stepping stone to integration into the EU and membership of international financial and military institutions. The potential implications of much of Albania's economy, security and infrastructure becoming dominated by neighbouring states remains to be assessed, however, in regional terms as well as in the context of shifting European allegiances and interests since the end of the Cold War.

Albania's extreme poverty, along with its isolation from mainstream European development throughout the Cold War era, often acted to obscure the country's economic potential as a source of oil, natural gas and other minerals, and, more crucially, its geostrategic importance, not only regionally, but within the framework of Europe's overall power balance. For many years, there was something of a paradox between, on the one hand, Albania's destitute, politically splintered reality, reducing the country to little more than a pawn in the regional power game and, on the other, its potential in the longer term to become an active partner in its own right in the wider European community. This paradox is gradually being resolved as successive Albania governments since 1997 have worked with the European Union, United States and an array of international institutions such as the Council of Europe, to establish democratic institutions and the rule of law. That said, Albania's longer-term destiny may ultimately hinge, as in the past, primarily on external factors outside its control.

The geostrategic significance accorded to the area that constitutes present-day Albania was already well in evidence during the process of its establishment as an independent state in late 1912. At the time, Durres was still occupied by Serbian troops, Shkoder under bombardment by Montenegro, and Greeks and Italians tussled over the Bay of Vlore, with Greek gunboats shelling the fortified area. At the international Conference of Ambassadors, the Serb delegate, strongly backed by Russia, insisted on Serbia acquiring an Adriatic port[2] while Montenegro, concerned that it might be forced into union with Serbia, declared that if Shkoder could not be secured by diplomacy, then it would be won militarily. It was not until 1925 that Albania's present borders were fixed through the Florence Protocol, Greece finally abandoning its claims to northern Epirus.

Today, Albania has not surprisingly moved once more into the orbit of neighbouring, and particularly Italian, interests but now with an economic and commercial orientation, as opposed to the gunboat diplomacy of earlier days. Italy is one of a number of countries which, in the politically more elastic environment of contemporary Europe, has sought to develop a higher international profile. Although a leading world industrial power, it has often tended to be regarded mainly as the repository of Europe's cultural heritage, and relegated to permanent fourth place ranking in the EU hierarchy. Mindful, however, of its major contribution to NATO's air strikes on Serbia in the spring of 1999 as a frontline base, Italy made renewed efforts to flex its international muscle in search of a new global role through a more focused foreign and defence policy, appealing for support in this to its extensive 'diaspora'.[3]

Albania is not the only Balkan country in which the Italians have taken a special interest over the last decade, but its territory plays a crucial part in Italy's ambition to achieve a higher profile on the world stage. Located just 45 miles away, across the Otranto Straits, with a vital strategic position at the mouth of the Adriatic, Albania is a prize for any power wishing to play a dominant role in the Balkans. For Italy, a controlling interest in Albania is almost a prerequisite to the success of its new *Ostpolitik* which has gradually evolved since the downing of the Berlin Wall.

Italy's involvement in all aspects of Albania's political, military and economic structures is in many ways a positive step, enabling it to work towards addressing the growing arms and drugs traffic and, not least, curbing the exodus of large numbers of immigrants to EU countries, with Italy in the front line.[4] Indeed, the crowning point of Italy's post Cold War international activity was considered to be its leadership of the military operation 'Alba' in the spring of 1997, when it picked up the reins following the failure of the European Union to muster a cohesive policy to address the crisis and restore order in Albania after the collapse of the pyramid schemes, and with it Albania's political and social structures. It was the first initiative in the Balkans in recent times in which Italy took a leading role, virtually walking into an EU policy vacuum and gaining a *bona fide* military foothold in Albania; 1997 may have marked an abyss for Albania, but it was a vital turning point for Italy on the European stage.

Perhaps the most important multinational project for both Albania and Italy is Corridor No. 8, involving the construction of a motorway, with an oil pipeline running parallel to it, from the Black Sea and Sofia, through Skopje and Durres on the Albanian coast, to Italy. At a meeting between Macedonian officials and Italian ministers and businessmen in Skopje in January 1998, including former premier, Romano Prodi, and his deputy foreign minister, Piero Fassino, Prodi pointed out the importance of the corridor as a strategic link between the southern Balkans and Italy.[5] It would also bring a considerable geopolitical dividend for Italy as the entrance point to the EU for commercial traffic and oil from Asia and the Black Sea. But the direct benefits to Albania from such a venture are debatable if viewed in the historical context of Italy's track record there, not least in regard to Italy's oil industry.[6]

To assess some of the wider implications for Albania of these various developments and proposals, it is important to consider the role of Serbia as envisaged by Italy in Southeastern Europe, a key issue both in terms of reconstruction and development and in regional stability and security. The fundamental divide between Italy and the United States on the question of Serbia is an issue that did not, in the final count, disrupt the NATO operation in Kosovo, but it suggested that future differences between the two countries in the Balkans, particularly where they involve NATO operations, may be less easily resolved.[7] In so far as it stresses the importance of integrating Serbia and Montenegro into the region in current reconstruction programmes, Italy parted company with not only the United States but also with some of its European allies on several occasions. Despite the accent on regional reintegration in the late 1990s, countries such as Croatia and Bosnia Herzegovina were marginalised in Italy's foreign policy line.[8]

Italy's relations with Serbia in the late 1990s demonstrated a marked rapprochement. In 1997, Italy was the now defunct Federal Republic of Yugoslavia's second trading partner, with a 22 per cent increase in trade from the previous year.[9] This fact should have raised eyebrows in Washington, given that the United States long resisted European-inspired attempts to relax sanctions and facilitate international trade while Milošević was in power. But the most explicit manifestation of Italian–Serbian relations was the purchase in 1997 of 49 per cent of Serbia's telecommunications system by the Italian telecom, STET, together with the Greek OTE, a move which helped to shore up the Serbian economy, drained by the Kosovo policing operation and years of UN sanctions. That move arguably sustained Milošević's regime as it faced growing domestic opposition.[10] The Italian government also sought to acquire Kosovo's electricity plants from EPS through ENEL, the Italian state electricity company. The EPS plants in Kosovo were of great strategic importance, producing nearly all the electricity for that area, including Macedonia.[11]

Some of the above actions were initiated by Italy's former foreign minister, Lamberto Dini, whose ministry also took a direct part, both through its membership of the Contact Group and unilaterally, to argue the Serb case in the build-up to the war over Kosovo. At Rambouillet in February 1999, Dini openly blamed the Albanian delegates for not reaching accord in the talks, prompting Albanian President Pandeli Majko to issue a press statement refuting reports that the Albanian delegation had been mainly to blame for the alleged intransigence at the peace talks. The Italian foreign minister also conducted a number of unilateral initiatives with Belgrade to secure a deal in an attempt to bring NATO air strikes to a halt.

One of the organs through which Italy's pro-active foreign policy was debated was the geopolitical journal, *LiMes*, established in 1993 with an all-Balkans first edition, and listing as editorial and scientific consultants a number of prominent figures from across the spectrum of Italy's political, religious and diplomatic fraternities. In the aftermath of the Dayton Peace Agreement, *LiMes* launched the *Euroslavia* project which proposed a reconciliation of Italian interests with those of former Yugoslavia and South Eastern Europe, starting with Albania, with the purported purpose of stabilising the Balkans.[12] The project advocated that Serbia should be assisted as a bastion against German hegemonism,[13] Serbia being perceived as the only regional power strong enough to prevent a German sphere of influence taking root in the Balkans. The American-led policy which excluded Serbia from international institutions through an 'outer wall' of sanctions was regarded by a number of Italian analysts and politicians as a threat to the stability of the whole region.

Italy's position with regard to Serbia was not only of direct longer-term concern to Albania, but also had wider strategic dimensions. For, while the 1999 NATO air strikes demonstrated that Italy could be harnessed into Alliance policy,[14] they also exposed the fragility of consensus amongst NATO member states, with Italy and Greece emerging as the weakest links.With a controlling interest in Albania, on the other hand, and strengthened political, economic and commercial links with Serbia, Italy was arguably better placed to influence the terms and nature of future Alliance policy in the region. Even the democratic opposition in Serbia – now the government – predicted that its relations with Albania would be hostile in the light of Albania's role in the Kosovo war and its support for Kosovo's independence.

Greece also sought to establish a new role in Albania since the end of the Cold War, a move which may be seen partly in the light of Greece's reduced role in the region and the EU after the fall of communism, and its relative isolation from other EU states, resulting from hostilities in former Yugoslavia. Supported by the EC's Europartenariat programme, Greece sought cross-border cooperation, in which it would act in an intermediary or advisory capacity. From Albania's point of view, the pooling of resources and expertise with an EU member state had, as with Italy, distinct advantages. But again, Greece's track record in Albania, both historical and contemporary, should have given pause for thought.

Ever since independence, Albania has been in dispute with Greece which has had irredentist claims over the southern provinces which it regards as Greek territory (Northern Epirus) due to the Greek minority living there.[15] This territory was awarded to Greece in 1915 in the secret Treaty of London and in 1919 Greece, together with Italy, the other main beneficiary of the Treaty, strove to defend its legacy at the peace conference, but without success.[16]

Since the end of the Cold War, a number of issues have further clouded Albania's relations with Greece, not least the actions of the powerful Greek-American lobby which has had a distinctly negative impact on Albania's relations with the United States. Apart from the long-festering issue of minority rights for Greeks living in Albania,[17] the periodic mass deportations of illegal Albanian immigrants to Greece stoked old fires, as did the ambivalent position of the Orthodox Church in Albania.[18] At first, Greece also took a negative view of Albania's relations with Turkey, Albania being regarded as a possible conduit for expanding Muslim influence in the region.[19] Macedonia was another factor exacerbating tensions with Greece, Albania being amongst the first countries to recognise its independence in April 1993, to offset Serbia's growing alliance with Greece after the disintegration of Yugoslavia.

In broader terms, however, of greater concern in Greece's multi-faceted programme in Albania may be the former's traditional close ties with Serbia which were rekindled since the end of the Cold War. Apart from the Greek government's appeasement of the Milošević regime throughout the Bosnian war, and its tacit support of Belgrade's policy in Kosovo, Greece's response to the NATO air strikes in 1999 provided explicit evidence of its Serbian sympathies, despite the importance Greece attached to its membership of NATO. In an opinion poll taken in Athens during the second and third weeks of the strikes,[20] 96 per cent of Greeks were opposed to NATO action against Serbia, 64 per cent of whom supported Milošević, 53 per cent Evgeny Primakov, then Russian foreign minister, as opposed to just 5 per cent support for British Prime Minister Tony Blair, who was seen as having taken the leading role in the NATO action.[21] Despite the more conciliatory foreign policy position of the former Greek premier, Costas Simitis,[22] this did not alter public opinion, largely fired by 'nationalist indignation' and the media.[23]

Greece also quickly established a stake in the Serbian economy. The Greek holding company, Mitilineos, reportedly signed an agreement with the RTB Bor copper mines for $1 billion worth of business, and as well had contracts with the Trepca mining conglomerate in Kosovo, the axis of Kosovo's economy.[24] In Serbia and Montenegro, Greek exports before the NATO campaign resulted in $243 million which surpassed the pre-war level for the whole of Yugoslavia.[25]

Greece's links with Russia are also worth noting in this context. As a Russian politician put it, Russia and Greece had one key priority, to put in place a common credible security system, resting on the economic interest of all regional states in close cooperation,[26] and Russia and Greece took an active part in building the energy structure of a common Balkans economic complex, a prospect which many in the Balkans, including Albanians, fear would, in the longer term, facilitate the renewal of Serbian domination in the region, and the strengthening of the 'Orthodox axis'.[27]

Following the War in Kosovo, Greek initiatives in Albania increased substantially, extending to all sectors of society. Relations between the Greek and Albanian armies were also placed on a firmer footing, with officers of the Kastoria division visiting Korce. The Greek military is also assisting Albania with logistics and joint activities in culture, sport and training.

Greek financing pledged for Albanian officers and students in Greece, and cooperation between the two countries, has been promoted in the field of military health, including a 480 million drachma deal to construct a new army hospital in Gjirokaster (southern Albania). Greek banking activities in Albania were extended, with the Greek government financing three Greek banks to the tune of 5 billion drachmas in 1999,[28] while the Greek ambassador promised the opening in Gjirokaster of an affiliate of the National Bank of Greece.

Despite some of the positive aspects of Greek investment in Albania which appear to be encouraging sustainable growth, institutional reform, the development of light industry and other commercial benefits, a number of concerns remain in this unequal bilateral arrangement which are not allayed by the mass expulsions of illegal Albanian immigrants to Greece which continue to occur[29] and, despite the welcome remittances brought in by Albanians working in Greece, Greece's overall position on human rights and minorities is likely to impact on Albania, as the two countries become further integrated.

Albania forms an essential element of Greece's overall strategy for Southeastern Europe. In its bid to establish itself as the leading player in the reconstruction of the region, Greece cannot afford to leave Albania out of the loop and risk a potentially hostile neighbour on its northern flank, in respect not only to its historical record in Albania and the ongoing minorities dispute, but to Albania's geostrategic position at the conflux between the Adriatic and the Ionian Seas, and its traditional (although mainly unstructured) links with Turkey. Through various ventures, not least in the energy section, Greece has put itself in a position to exercise a measure of control over its weaker Balkan neighbours, including Albania. In early 1997 a trans-Balkan pipeline for natural gas from Russia became operational in Greece, with an extension planned via Greece to Macedonia and Albania, with support from the European Commission.

Some may fear that Albania once again risks being exposed to much of the regional 'imperialism' it endured during the first decades of its existence as an independent state, as its neighbours intensify their efforts to dominate the country politically, economically, militarily and cultu-rally, often with the encouragement of Albania's leaders and the Eur-opean Union. In fact, during much of the last decade, Albania's main political protagonists battled amongst themselves as to who should be Albania's 'natural ally'. The Socialist Party regards Italy as a bulwark against Albania becoming a pawn of the US Balkans' policy, while the Democrats sought throughout their term in power, but with less success, to forge stronger ties with the United States and the wider European community.

The United States, recognising Albania's critical geopolitical role in the region, has committed considerable sums towards humanitarian needs and political and economic transition,[30] as well as much diplo-matic capital. In 1993 it signed a memorandum of military under-standing with Albania outside the NATO framework, whereby Albanian officers were trained in the United States and US military advisers became attached to the Albanian General Staff. Joint military exercises took place, and US reconnaissance missions were conducted over Bosnia from Albania. In 1994, however, this bilateral arrangement was shaken by Albania's refusal to release five ethnic Greeks who were members of the Omonia organisation,[31] arrested and sentenced on charges of espionage, resulting in the US postponement of plans for a $30 million American–Albanian Enterprise Fund, a move in which both Athens and the American Greek lobby were said to have played a considerable role, and on which the two main Albanian political parties clashed openly. This was compounded by the collapse of state structures following the pyramid scam in 1997,[32] when virtually all foreign investors withdrew, leaving a vacuum into which Italy moved.

During the NATO campaign in Kosovo, many of Albania's weak-nesses were graphically exposed. The relative inaccessibility of Kosovo, in geopolitical terms, to NATO troops was one of the factors which shaped that campaign (as it had undoubtedly shaped Milošević's Kosovo policy throughout the previous decade). Although supportive of the proposed NATO action, Albania's mountainous terrain, combined with its poor communications and infrastructure, reduced its effectiveness to a temporary sanctuary for Kosovo's refugees, reinforcing the general image of Kosovo as a virtual non-player in any future European order. In the immediate aftermath of the NATO campaign, however, Albania seemed momentarily to be on the crest of a wave. Viewed as one of the moral victors of the war, especially for its handling of the 500,000 refugees from Kosovo, and with the moderate socialist leader, Pandeli Majko, at the helm, Albania looked set to enjoy a period of rapid economic expansion and relative political stability. The country was courted by potential investors and appeared to achieve some recognition as a political entity in its own right.

But this vision was soon to fade as the scandal surrounding the Italian Arcobaleno Missione (Rainbow Mission) hit the headlines. Over 5 million Italians had contributed to the victims of the war in Kosovo, estimated at around 128 billion Italian lire ($82 million), much of which was reportedly misused, blocked in Italy, or had ended up in Albania, where over a thousand food containers were plundered by Albanian citizens. According to many Albanian politicians at the time, including Democratic Alliance President Neritan Ceka, plunder was encouraged by Italian troops. Whatever the truth of the incident, the much-anticipated visit of then US Defense Secretary William Cohen, scheduled for just three days later on 13 July, was cancelled on security grounds.

By the Autumn of 1999, the multinational NATO force, which had occupied Albania since the onset of the air strikes, was replaced by a smaller pan-Italian force, and the once and future prime minister, Fatos Nano, was returned as chairman of the Socialist Party, ousting Majko from power, to be succeeded by Ilir Meta, a close ally of Nano. Since that time Italy and Greece have strengthened their respective positions in Albania where both have much to gain in establishing their respective zones of influence. This also gave Greece the opportunity to recover from its identity crisis which resurfaced with the collapse of Yugoslavia, while an Adriatic corridor would link Italy directly with other Balkan states and the Black Sea, thereby enhancing its role within NATO and the EU.

In Albania, however, some fear that Italian and Greek infiltration into its economy and military structures may be reminiscent of the client–patron relationship with Italy of the 1920s and 1930s which ended in Albania becoming an Italian protectorate, and that it may help to realise Greece's longstanding irredentist claims on southern Albania which could lead to its eventual partition.

Until the European stabilisation process for the region was re-energised, with new Stabilisation and Association Agreements for Albania, Macedonia as well as other former Yugoslav republics, the complexities of Southeastern Europe bedevilled most of the attempts to restructure relationships both at geopolitical and economic levels. Each of the countries shares some of the history and contemporary problems ensuing from the new terms of reference that emerged after the collapse of communism. The struggle to achieve a balance of power within the region and the relationships which would emerge from this are amongst the major current concerns of leading world powers, not least the European Union. This balance is only partly contingent on the relations between individual states, due to overlapping interests in the creation of the new spheres of influence which have contributed in no small measure to the short-term, stopgap solutions characterising much of the international community's involvement in Southeastern Europe since 1991, evidenced not least in the Srebrenica report by the UN Secretary General,[33] and in the teething problems encountered by the Stability Pact for Southeastern Europe in its first few years.

One of the main stumbling blocks to restoring peace and stability since the onset of war in Yugoslavia in 1991 was undoubtedly the dichotomous positions of major world powers on the role of Serbia in the region, where perceived national interests often prevailed over, while claiming to defend, the interests of regional, and indeed, European security. While some international players viewed a strong, well-armed (even 'greater') Serbia as a factor of stability, and a counterbalance to Germany's ascendancy in Europe since the downing of the Berlin Wall,[34] others perceived it as the root *cause* of the regional instability. These divergences over the previous decade led to a perceptible weakening of international institutions, including the United Nations, the Western Alliance, the European Union and the OSCE, as member states have struggled to come to terms with their polarised positions. They have also threatened the welfare of smaller Balkan states such as Albania,[35] as major powers sought to establish common ground through the adoption of a minimalist 'lowest common denominator' policy on the region, which was often ineffective and at times counter-productive.

Since Milošević's removal and subsequent death, the question remains – can Serbia be counted on as a force for stability in the region as we move into the twenty-first century? In this context, Serbia's track record over the last century is worth examining from both military and political standpoints, starting with the Balkan Wars of 1912–13 and World War I, to the Kingdom of Serbs, Croats and Slovenes (the First Yugoslavia) led by Nikola Pašić and Serbian King Alexander, World War II,[36] Tito's Socialist Federal Republic, to the rogue state of Serbia under the rule of Slobodan Milošević and now a new democratising state of Serbia and Montenegro. Also relevant is the output of some of Serbia's leading intellectuals, including Garasanin, Stojanovic, Cvijić, Čubrilović and Ćosić[37] and his colleagues at the Serbian Academy of Arts and Sciences (SANU) from where the 'Memorandum', a document which laid the theoretical groundwork for the Milošević rule, emerged in 1986, where the pervading goal has been the creation of a 'Greater' Serbia, or a wider Balkan confederation in which Serbia is *primus inter pares*. From this, a further question arises – can peace and stability in Southeastern Europe be sustained in circumstances where *any* regional power commands a dominant role? Evidence to date seems to suggest not.[38]

All these are factors to consider in the international community's efforts to re-establish enduring peace and stability in the region, as the origins of the nine-year war, and the necessity for the NATO action in 1999 are forced into the background by new international imperatives not least of which is increased integration into European structures. They are also germane to Albania's survival as a sovereign state, as it becomes once again encircled by neighbouring states enjoying varying degrees of alliance with non-Albanian friendly states such as Serbia. In order to ensure Albania's inclusion in the broader European integration processes, this poor Balkan state would benefit from an encompassing and coherent approach to the region. In view of the many and continuing internal conflicts, as well as intra- and inter-regional imbalances, both political and economic, a global approach is called for, with commitment from European countries across the board and from the United States, based on lessons learnt, in order to avoid a repetition of the misguided policies built on flawed national agendas which have permeated international attempts to bring about stability in the region over the past decade.

Notes

1 A debate on returning Albania to protectorate status under Italy was initiated in the Italian press at the beginning of 1999, on the basis that the Albanians had shown little capacity during the transition period to develop a state structure.

2 He pointed out that it was 'not a case of conquest but of recovery of what belonged to us between the 10th and 15th centuries' Durres. Russian interest in acquiring a foothold in the Adriatic dates back to the time of Peter the Great.

3 Estimated at between 30–60 million people of Italian origin, and 3–4 million Italian citizens, living abroad.

4 Between July 1990 and June 1991, approximately 100,000 Albanians fled the country, with a further 20,000 crossing to Italy in August 1991. Elez Biberaj, *Albania in Transition: The Rocky road to Democracy*, Boulder, CO: Westview, 1999.

5 Macedonian ILS, 22 January 1998. This initiative was originally proposed in the 1930s by Mussolini, but abandoned for financial reasons, and due to competition from Nazi Germany.

6 Albania's oil industry dates from World War I. In the interwar period exploratory concessions were granted to British, French, Italian and US oil companies. But when fascist Italy acquired a dominant position in Albania, the petroleum and other mining concessions became an Italian monopoly.

Lacking fuel resources of its own, Italy invested capital and technology into Albania's oil industry, building a 49 mile pipeline linking the Kucove field with Vlore, with most of the crude oil being processed in Italy, forcing Albania to import from Romania the finished oil products it required at elevated prices. Italy intensified oil production during World War II, producing 250,000 tons by 1942. But by 1948 output had dropped to a fifth of that amount, under an Albanian–Yugoslav joint company. When the industry passed over to Soviet management after Tito's break with the Cominform, production increased considerably, although Russia was not prepared to raise production beyond a certain amount, due to its own large oil surplus.

7 Various ways of addressing this, including the construction of a European 'pole' of equal strength to that of the United States, are discussed in *Kosovo: L'Italia in Guerra, Revista Italiana di geopolitica (LiMes)* special edition, April 1999, editorial, pp. 5–10.

8 See, for instance, the *LiMes* article on Italian/Croatian relations ('Roma e Zagabria, partner per forza?' *LiMes*, 1.98, pp. 261–72).

9 *Nasa Borba*, 22 January 1998.

10 One prominent Italian diplomat noted that the 800 billion lire from Italian telecom, transferred to the exhausted coffers of Belgrade in 1997, was aimed at preventing the collapse of Serbia. (*LiMes*, 1 (1998), 241).

11 Balcani, *Notizie Est*, no. 16, 11 February 1998.

12 The Euroslavia project was outlined in *LiMes*, no. 4 (1995), 7–10, and expanded on in later articles, as well as in the Italian and international press. The project was also intended as a geopolitical alternative to Maastricht. See for instance *Gli assi euroslavi'*, *LiMes*, 1 (1996), 253–66.

13 See 'What's Germany looking for in Yugoslavia' by Lucio Caracciolo, March 1994, a thesis which also inspired British government policy in Yugoslavia and the successor states between 1991 and 1997.

14 Italy's relatively limited military potential has precluded an expansionist policy, at least in the short term, although in recent years there have been debates on how to address this. See *LiMes*, 4 (1999).

15 Southern Epirus had been incorporated into Greece in 1881, and the acquisition of Northern Epirus (which Greece had occupied for a time in World War II) was part of Greece's *Megali* idea, constituting an attempt to reconsolidate under Greek control the territories of the Byzantine Empire at its apex. The size of the Greek minority in southern Albania ranges between 58,000 (according to the Albanian census of 1989) or 2% of the Albanian population. (RFE Background Report 142. Albania, 8 August 1989), and 300,000–400,000, the figure maintained by Greece. Hugh Poulton, *The Balkans: Minorities and States in Conflict*, London: Minority Rights Group, 1991, pp. 195–8.

16 The Albanians, however, encouraged by the principle of self-determination laid down in Woodrow Wilson's Fourteen Points as a basis for settlement, announced at Versailles that they would fight to secure their territorial sovereignty and independence. Their borders were later confirmed, with minor concessions to Yugoslavia.

17 Including Greek schooling in Albania which the Greeks allege is limited to minority zones, while the Albanians retort that it is of a much higher standard than the Albanian educational system, which is largely due to Greek subsidies. It should be remembered that during the Hoxha regime the Greeks suffered serious human rights abuses. Although some provision was made for Greek tuition in schools, and a few Greeks rose to high positions, especially in the army, it was not until 1990–91 that religious and press freedom was restored, and confiscated property restituted. In 1993, CSCE Commissioner Max van der Stoel, in two visits to Albania, praised the Albanian government commitment to granting full CSCE rights to its Greek minority.

18 Among Albanians 17–20 per cent are orthodox and, in 1992, Anastasios Yanulatos, a Greek citizen, was installed as head of the Albanian Orthodox Church by the ecumenical patriarch, apparently contrary to church statutes which decreed that the leader of the church must be an Albanian citizen. The appointment was allowed to stand, but the following year the Albanian government expelled another Greek Orthodox cleric who was allegedly promoting Greek separatism. Greece responded by rounding up 25,000 illegal Albanians in Greece and deporting them.

19 There are 120,000 ethnic Turks in Thrace alone. Greece's suspicions grew when Albania joined the Organisation of Islamic Countries (although it later withdrew its membership).

20 Published in daily *Ta Nea*, 17 and 19 April, poll by V-PRC.

21 AIM, Athens, 30 April 1999.

22 Compared with his predecessor, Andreas Papandreou.

23 In Spring 1993, an EU-wide Eurobarometer poll showed only 21% of Greeks considered 'tolerance and the respect of others' as an especially important quality to encourage in their children (compared with 42–62% in other EC countries). See contribution by Thanos Vermemis in this volume.

24 Trepca by 1998 was allegedly in debt to the tune of DM 20 million and late in its deliveries to its Greek partner. The contract with Mitilineos included a clause in which it was confirmed that the Greek company has first option in the acquisition of the company if it privatises, and foresees the possibility of the Greeks obtaining stock from Trepca in lieu of debt repayments. The same clause may apply to Bor, one of FRY's top five exporting companies. Mitilineos and the National Bank of Greece were also to animate a consortium for the purpose of acquiring 90% of the stock of the Slavija Bank in Belgrade, as well as other mines and chemical companies on Serbia's privatisation list.

25 T. Veremis, 'The Greek approach to the Balkans', *Southeast European Yearbook 1997–98*, D. Triantaphllou, ed., Hellenic Foundation for European and Foreign Policy, p. 208.

26 For instance, in 1994 Russia, Bulgaria and Greece began working on a project to build an oil pipeline from Burgas to Aleksandropolis, capable of ensuring the stable transportation of substantial volumes of oil from Russia, the Transcaucasus and Central Asia to Western Europe.

27 See Michas Takis, *Unholy Alliance: Greece and Milošević's Serbia*, College Station: Texas A&M University Press, 2002.

28 Alba News, 1 September 1999.

29 In October 1999, during the Albanian elections, 1,500 illegal Albanian immigrants were deported from Greece in the space of seven days by bus. In August 1996, more than 7,000 illegal, mainly Albanian immigrants were apprehended and summarily expelled from Greece, some visibly abused by police, and in 1994 over 100,000 Albanians were expelled, following the Omonia trial. In both cases, it was documented in Greece that many immigrants were abused and even robbed by police, and not even allowed to take their personal belongings or collect their paychecks. *Greece: Albanian Immigrants for Hire or Expulsion*, Panayote Elias Dimitras, Greek Helsinki Monitor.

30 Over $200 million between 1992 and 1996. Biberaj, *Albania in Transition*, p. 232.

31 Set up in 1990 for the promotion of Greek minority rights, with a radical wing which called for *enosis* and border revision.

32 With liabilities estimated by a World Bank study to amount to almost 50% of Albania's GNP.

33 Report of the Secretary General Pursuant to General Assembly Resolution 53/35 (1998). *Srebrenica Report*.

34 The premise of, *inter alia*, the Major government in Britain which led international policy in former Yugoslavia for over four years. See Carole Hodge, 'Slimy Limeys', *New Republic*, 9 January 1996, pp. 21–2, and 'The Hurd mentality', *New Republic*, 7 August 1995, pp. 18–19.

35 Romania, Bulgaria, Hungary and other states were affected by years of sanctions against the FRY, and the fallout resulting from the NATO air strikes of 1999.

36 At the beginning of World War II in Yugoslavia, Četnik leaders drafted a plan for a Greater Serbia stretching over most of Yugoslavia and Albania, and parts of Bulgaria, Romania and Hungary. [Norman Cigar, *Genocide in Bosnia: The Policy of Ethnic Cleansing*, College Station, TX: Texas A&M University Press, p. 18].

37 Ilija Garasanin, a Serbian minister in the Karadjordjevic dynasty in 1844 wrote Nacrtanje (An Outline), a program for Serbian domination of a substantial area of the Balkans. Nikola Stojanović (1880–1965) wrote *Do istrage vase ili nase* [Until your or our extermination], on Croatian assimilation: 'The Croats ... cannot be a separate nation, but they are on their way to becoming Serbs.' Any mention of Croats at this time referred to them as Serbs of Catholic faith. See Philip Cohen, *Serbia's Secret War*, College Station: Texas A&M University Press, 1996. Jovan Cvijić (1865–1927), promoted the thesis that areas which Serbs had abandoned, or that contained even a small Serb minority, were Serbian ethnic territory. Vasa Čubrilović, a political adviser to the Royal Yugoslav government, wrote a memorandum called *Iseljavanje Arnauta* [The Expulsion of the Albanians] in 1937 which argued that 'if Germany can evict hundreds of thousand of Jews ... a few hundred thousand evicted Albanians will not provoke a world war'. Dobrica Cosic, a noted Serbian writer, considered the father of the SANU Memorandum, wrote in 1961: 'Today, the form of Serbian nationalism is often "Yugoslavism" ... They [Serb Yugoslavs] are for unification. Unification is for them a creation of privileges for their language, and the

assimilation of smaller nations ... ', quoted from Mark Almond, *Europe's Backyard War*, London: Heinemann, 1994, p. 168.

38 Croatian resistance to Serbian hegemony in the 'first' Yugoslavia (1918–41) led to the murder in the Yugoslav Assembly of the Croatian Peasant Party leader, Stjepan Radić, along with a number of his deputies, leading to the Serbian dictatorship under King Alexander, his death in 1934 and laying some of the groundwork for the establishment of the genocide Ustaša regime in Croatia, responsible for amongst the worst atrocities of World War II. It might also be said that, without Milošević, President Franjo Tudjman would have had difficulty in retaining his authoritarian rule throughout the 1990s in Croatia, while sustaining a genocidal regime in parts of Bosnia and Hercegovina.

20 New beginnings? Refugee returns and post-conflict integration in the former Yugoslavia

Brad K. Blitz

Introduction

Ten years after the Dayton Peace Agreement, the demographic situation in much of the former Yugoslavia bears the scars of war-time patterns of occupation and displacement. Even though the return of refugees has been a major plank of international policy, UN High Commissioner (UNCHR) estimates that by the end of 2004, there were almost 1 million refugees and displaced persons living within the borders of the former Yugoslavia who were still in need of a 'durable solution'. Over half of these are internally displaced persons (IDPs) who still cannot return to their homes as a result of political divisions in their countries.[1] While some refugees have returned, for example, over 1 million have returned to Bosnia, another million are still living as refugees abroad or have opted for integration in third countries.[2] When compared against the pre-war demographics, the return project has produced rather mixed results and failed to satisfy the ambitions of millions of refugees who may have once wanted to return home.

There are several possible explanations for the limited success of the return project in the former Yugoslavia. In the first case, many refugees cannot resolve the trauma they endured during the pre-flight phase – the prospect of returning to sites of abuse is simply too much to entertain. In the second case, conflicting agendas and divergent motivations for return among the refugees and various stakeholders including the countries of the former Yugoslavia; the United Nations, European Union, and United States and the service delivery organisations in the form of NGOs and specialised agencies have also influenced the return process and have undoubtedly contributed the mitigated result.

This chapter assesses the return project from the standpoint of sustainability. It explores the possibility for former refugees to carve out a new beginning by re-establishing themselves in their home states and considers three primary motivations: *justice*, which is understood to include the redress of past grievances; *development*, where the return of

239

skills is seen as a positive influence on post-conflict stabilisation and economic growth; and, finally, the *burden-relieving* argument where refugees are returned by third countries both to appease domestic interests and justify policies of foreign intervention, aid and investment in the region. This chapter notes the relative difficulties in achieving return based on the three ideals above and instead advocates an approach to return founded on the notion of sustainability defined in terms of full access and participation in the home state.

The first part of this chapter considers the concept of return and motivations for return programmes before examining the historical development of return programmes in Croatia, Bosnia, Serbia and Montenegro and Kosovo. It analyses the legal bases for return in each of the countries and evaluates the way in which return programmes have been implemented with specific reference to housing repossession. It concludes by assessing the impact that conflicting policies on return have had for those migrants who have returned and are currently trying to integrate in post-conflict society.

The concept of return

The concept of return includes both voluntary and non-voluntary transfers of refugees back to their countries of origin. Under ideal conditions, the notion of voluntary returns should raise the prospect of agency and decision-making based on individual motivation. In this context, the decision to return may be motivated by the accommodation of important psychosocial needs, including a sense of belonging, a secure identity, and emotional and patriotic attachments that are often difficult to establish in a foreign environment. In practice, however, refugees are rarely placed to make individual decisions free of external influence, including pressure from host governments.

In contrast to the individualistic account for return, the concept of return is often associated with post-conflict stabilisation based on macro-political considerations. Human rights monitoring agencies such as the Organisation for Security Cooperation in Europe (OSCE), in addition to refugee agencies such as UNHCR, have been contracted to further the return project by developing and monitoring specific pro-grammes.[3] These tend to be based on narrow criteria, mainly con-cerning the assessment of the numbers who have taken up the schemes. Although repatriation has a distinct legal meaning in international law, often the mere presence of former refugees back on home soil is counted as return and for the purposes of the Dayton process the manner in which refugees return has not always been afforded the significance that refugee advocates would wish. In the process, monitoring agencies often conflate *return* with *repatriation*, which is involuntary and is forced on migrants by political authority. For example, forced removals initiated by Western governments[4] have sometimes been described as returns, falsely suggesting that they are the outcome of individual choices.[5]

Common to both voluntary and forced returns, however, is the notion of sustainability which may be defined by the absence of re-migration (staying put), the realisation of certain living standards, and in terms of a rights-based approach where access to public and social services is seen as the key measure of sustainability. In addition, it is important to conceive of sustainability as the absence of dependency where return is achievable without undue influence from external actors. For example, migrants may be dependent on remittances from abroad and their economic viability may be considerably less secure than it appears to the outside observer. For this reason, Black and Gent recommend using a 'sustainable livelihoods' framework in which 'livelihoods are considered "sustainable" if they can be maintained without external inputs and are sufficiently robust to withstand external shocks'.[6]

Walpurga Engelbrecht has further developed the notion of sustainable returns by focusing on guarantees of safety and dignity which are essential to the integration of the former refugees in the home state. She offers three essential guarantees: (1) the guarantee of physical safety, including the right to freedom of movement, protection from harassment and attack and access to areas free of mines; (2) the guarantee of legal safety, including non-discriminatory access and exercise of civil, economic, social, political and cultural rights; (3) the guarantee of material safety, including access to food, potable water, shelter, health services and education.[7]

In practice, however, return programs tend to fall short of the ideals of sustainability, dignity and safety described above. Rather, it has been suggested elsewhere that there are three primary motivations for promoting return which are not people-centred and in their current form contrast with the ideal of sustainability. First, there are justice-based claims often voiced by human rights organisations, where return is seen as the end of the refugee cycle. Second, there are the claims made by refugee agencies that the return of skilled migrants is linked to economic development. Third, and most influential, are the domestic arguments put forward by third countries where return is linked to repatriation and is seen as relieving the burden on host states.[8]

Justice-based arguments

The justice-based argument considers return as a means of post-conflict stabilisation. It is based on the belief that outstanding claims of injustice, that might otherwise spark new conflicts, can be put aside through returns. This policy is seen as furthering the goal of reconciliation and transition from war to peace. Thus refugee returns represent the 'end of the refugee cycle'. The logic behind this view is that refugees have certain material needs and that, if these are adequately addressed, the propensity for conflict will disappear. The antecedents for the justice-based approach may be found in the 1951 United Nations convention on the status of refugees which recognises that once a migrant returns, he (*sic*) is formally no longer a refugee and thus his claims and rights can be addressed by the home state. Since 1951, the principle of allowing refugees to return home has been written into every major peace agreement. For this reason, some describe returns as a 'counter-refugee crisis policy'.[9]

There are several limitations with the justice-based argument as suggested above. First of all, the concept of justice is exceptionally hard to operationalise. A well-developed notion of justice should include participation and consultation with victim groups who are best placed to define what justice means to them. Second, the emphasis on material claims, above all housing, does not address the broader issues of political security which entail the arrest of war criminals and others abusers. Finally, there is considerable empirical evidence to suggest that in war-affected societies past conflicts are not simply resolved but institutionalised in political factions and that rather than resolve conflict, it is simply transformed into non-democratic processes of governance.[10]

It is important to recognise that the vast majority of refugees never actually return to their previous home. Returnees, many of whom may have lost essential documents during periods of conflict, are often subject to the same constraints as new arrivals and must re-establish themselves in their home country. Those seeking to return are thus faced immediately with the challenge of asserting their rights in the face of social opposition. Returnees may be associated with previous regimes and attached to former ethnic and political elite structures, and thus be the subject of hostility and jealousy. Returnees are often resented for having left, and for the opportunities they received while abroad, or for the incentive grants that they receive upon return. In most post-conflict situations where the International Organisation for Migration (IOM) and its related agencies are working to facilitate returns, the experiences of war and exile have served to intensify divisions between ethnic groups. Such divisions may be deepened by the actions of current political groups and leaders.

Development-centred approaches

The policy of returns has also been promoted on the grounds that returnees may have acquired skills that can be invested in their home countries and that their return may address shortages due to a brain drain. This view underlies many of the current return programmes, and is prominent in the intergovernmental and non-governmental organisations promoting return. For example, the International Organization for Migration (IOM) advertises its assisted return programmes under the banner, 'Your knowledge for your country'. Return programmes targeted at elite groups are being replicated in several post-conflict situations, including Afghanistan and Iraq where the return of qualified professionals is an important target for refugee organisations.[11]

The human development approach has a number of weaknesses. Such return programmes assume that one can match skills with needs on the ground, a claim which has been challenged by the results of the IOM's return of qualified nationals programmes in much of Africa and South-Eastern Europe.[12] More important is the assumption that refugees are in a position to make deliberate choices regarding their own future despite the fact that most return programmes take place against the backdrop of repatriation and peace agreements negotiated at the international level and involve the returnees being subject to pressure from host countries.[13] Many of those forcibly returned are refugees who never developed the social and educational connections that enable them both to flourish economically in the host country and to navigate successfully through the immigration appeals system. Indeed, many of those targeted for return are among the least skilled.[14]

Burden-relieving arguments

Finally, the burden-relieving argument is derived from an implicit reference in the refugee convention, where it states that an influx of large numbers of refugees could undermine delicate domestic arrangements and therefore returns should be encouraged as a means of protecting the internal order of vulnerable states. National policies of temporary protection, dispersal and eventual repatriation were developed to counterbalance this perceived threat. Oliver Bakewell describes how different stakeholders may interpret the practice of return according to their own interests:

Voluntary repatriation can be seen as an ideal solution to the refugee problem as it brings the refugees back under the protection of the state of origin, it restores them to their homes and it relieves the burden on the host society. This assumes that the conditions which have caused them to flee have substantially changed to enable refugees to come under the protection of the state, that their idea of home remains related to a particular place even a generation or more after leaving, and their presence has continued to be a burden on the host society.[15]

As refugee receiving countries tighten their controls on entry to appease domestic populations, the burden-relieving argument is gaining ground.[16]

A comparison of return policies

Croatia

The return project in Croatia was initially marred by the protracted conflict between the government of Croatia and rebel Serbs and the introduction of discriminatory laws which fostered the Tudjman regime's goal of ethnic homogenisation. The notion of return was imposed on the Croatian government by international authorities and until 2003 there was great reluctance to tackle the issue of returns in a consistent manner.

Croatia saw two major refugee flows which significantly altered the demographic composition of the state. The first was in 1991 and followed the initial attack and occupation of Eastern Slavonia and Krajina by the combined forces of the Yugoslav National Army and rebel army of the Serbian Republic of Krajina which expelled the majority of the ethnic Croat population. At the same time, a large number of Serbs were expelled from Croatia proper and sought refuge in Serbia and the Krajina region. By 1994, there were approximately 120,000 Serbs in the Krajina region. The second refugee flow was four years later when the Croatian government reclaimed three-quarters of the territory under Serb control during two rapid military operations, Flash and Storm, in May and August 1995, respectively. Eastern Slavonia, the final pocket of Croatia controlled by Serbian forces was transferred to the United Nations by means of the Erdut Peace Agreement of 1995 and was formally transferred to Croatian control on 15 January 1998.

Official sources estimate that during the first refugee flow, approximately 84,000 Croats fled from areas under Serbian control and another 70,000 ethnic Serbs, who had been displaced, settled in the Danube region. According to the Croatian government's former Office of

Displaced Persons and Refugees (ODPR),[17] approximately 300,000 Serbs had fled by the end of the war in 1991. Others left once territory around the Danube was transferred to the United Nations to administer in 1995 and then when this region reverted to Croatian government control in 1998 (OSCE, 2001a). By 2001, the Serbian minority in Croatia had been dramatically reduced from 12.6% of the overall population (approximately 4,334,142) to just 4.5%.[18]

The ethnic nature of the conflict from 1991–95 was reflected in many of the policies and laws introduced by the government of the newly independent state which introduced a host of laws that discriminated against Serbs and served to prevent them from returning. In 1991, the government of Franjo Tudjman introduced a law that sought to deny returning refugees citizenship in the new state. This law negatively addressed the issue of returns by barring habitual residents from returning to their homes, on the grounds that residents needed to show five years continuous residence prior to application, and thus deterred those who had been displaced from returning. Those most affected were Serbs, Roma and Bosniaks. In addition to the residency requirement, minorities were also subject to language proficiency tests administered in police stations where there was potential for abuse. Croatia's first responses to the challenge of repatriating thousands of people thus contravened international conventions to which the state was a signatory.[19]

The first mechanism for the organised return of displaced persons was established by the Agreement of the Joint Working Group on the Operations Procedures of Return in 1997. Rather than regulating the movement of all displaced persons and refugees from third countries, the 1997 provision facilitated two-way returns from and to the Danube region, thus limiting the right of return to a fraction of the population. According to this agreement, all displaced persons were permitted to remain in the houses they temporarily occupied before they could return to their homes or were provided with alternative accommodation. However, this return mechanism was short-lived and broke down with the departure of the UN administration, when thousands of Croats returned spontaneously to reclaim their homes. Of the 90,000 people who had been displaced from the Danube region prior to 1995, only a handful of Serb returns were facilitated by the two-way return mechanism. According to the OSCE, the majority of Serbs displaced to the Danube region left for third countries as a consequence of harassment and psychological pressure.[20]

After restricting returns to residents of the Danube Region, the Croatian government introduced further regulations that limited the right of return to ethnic Croat citizens and residents married to Croat nationals. It was only international criticism that forced the government to adopt new revisions to the 1998 law. And yet, the new legislation, known as the 'Mandatory Instructions', continued in the same vein by describing Serbs as persons who had 'voluntarily abandoned the Republic of Croatia', even though many fled during periods of intense human rights abuses.[21] Under the threat of international sanctions, new laws were introduced but they did not supersede the old discriminatory laws. Critics within the humanitarian sector claimed that Croatia 'ended up with a confusing mix of contradictory laws that continued to stymie refugee and displaced person return'.[22]

After introducing laws that denied minorities their basic right to return, the Tudjman government adopted institutional policies that left non-Croats further disadvantaged. The most obvious form of discrimination was in housing policy. The war had destroyed approximately 195,000 homes and it was therefore imperative that a solution be found to ease the burden on the transitional state. To this end, the former Tudjman government passed many laws regarding the take-over of private property and denied others the right to former state-owned property. The most notable of these was the Law on Temporary Take-Over and Administration of Specified Property (LTTP) of 1995.[23] Legal owners faced additional barriers and saw their rights curtailed by the 1996 Law on Areas of Special State Concern which created the term 'settlers' and gave ethnic Croats private or state-owned property for their use. In contrast, many Serbs were dispossessed by the Law on Lease of Apartments in Liberated Areas, which had come into effect just after Operation Storm and gave the original owners a ridiculously short window of 90 days to return and reclaim their property. Court hearings conducted *in absentia* enabled the administration to dispossess tens of thousands of Serbs, approximately 50,000–60,000 households were affected

In 1998, the House of Representatives approved a Return Programme that established procedures for the repossession of property that had been allocated to temporary users. New municipal housing commissions were created to administer the procedures but their decisions could only be enforced on the basis of prior court decisions. According to the OSCE, more than 21,000 properties, mostly Serb-owned, were handed over to housing commissions. Accounts of abuse against non-Croats were widespread and included the ridiculous. One story concerned a Croat who had occupied a Serbian home which he used to house a flock of sheep. The housing commission concluded that the sheep's owner needed a reasonable amount of time to find alternative accommodation and that the original owner could not return to his house at this point.[24] The argument that evictions could not take place without the provision of alternative accommodation was used repeatedly by the Croatian government and local authorities to protect sitting tenants of Croatian origin and deny minority landowners access to their pre-war homes. Such practices led international agencies to speak of 'double-standard cases' and to describe such actions as institutionalised discrimination on the grounds of national origin.[25]

With the election of Stjepan Mesić as president in 2000, Croatia appeared to be turning the corner. Following the 'Knin Conclusions', a series of meetings in March 2001, the government committed itself to addressing key social and economic problems, including the issue of return. A number of important reforms were introduced between 2001 and 2003, including a new Constitutional Law on National Minorities (CLNM) which introduced clauses regarding the representation of minority groups in the Parliament as well as educational provisions, and a Law on Areas of Special State Concern (LASSC) that altered the way in which returnee issues were to be administrated. The housing commissions that had frustrated the return of property to former refugees and displaced persons were abolished and instead claims were to be heard by the ODPR which was instructed to prioritise owners' claims of repossession over tenants' rights. As such, on paper, the LASSC appeared to break with the traditions established during the Tudjman era which discriminated in favour of ethnic Croats (from both Croatia and Bosnia) over the Serbian population.

In addition, Croatian President Mesić and former Prime Minister Račan went on record, urging Serbs to return and insisting that conditions were ripe for the reintegration of Serbs into Croatian society. 'We have to ensure the return of people and enable them to dispose with their property. Only then can we become a serious state', claimed Mesić.[26] He further acknowledged that at least part of the motivation for the reforms was the prospect of admission to the European Union by 2007. From 2002–03, Mesić publicly challenged the previous governmental attitude towards returns and introduced some key reforms that gave the semblance of a revolutionary new approach. Evictions of Bosnian Croats who had occupied Serbian homes in the Krajina region started to take place in Spring 2002, and in 2003, Zagreb adopted a public housing programme where public funds would be used to rebuild Serbian homes.[27]

In practice, however, the government was slow to introduce these reforms and, for this reason, the European Commission considered that the progress made by the Račan government was largely limited to the establishment of a legal framework. In the meantime, the pace of returns also slowed and even those who remained have been unable to establish a sustainable existence. According to the Office of Displaced Persons and Refugees (ODPR), as of 1 January 2005, there were forty-six collective centres still operating in Croatia. Of these, ten have been categorised as IDP/refugee accommodation facilities and the number of occupants is estimated to be less than 1,700.

In other areas, Mesić was exceptionally slow to react – for example, in the refusal to arrest Ante Gotovina for crimes committed during Operation Storm. Human rights authorities noted that during the first Mesić presidency, the government wanted to have its cake and eat it; the government of prime minister Račan was a fragile coalition and there was serious public opposition to a number of unpopular measures regarding minority rights and property restitution. For fear of upsetting the nationalist parties which are concentrated in war-torn areas, the primary destination for returnees, neither Mesić nor Račan seemed prepared to tackle the issue of returns head on.

The return of the nationalist HDZ party in December 2003 and the election of Ivo Sanader as Prime Minister raised a number of suspicions concerning inter-ethnic relations in Croatia. These fears were at least in part placated by the government's repeated statements on refugee returns and the expansion of the housing and social care schemes in early 2004. Since then the current government has been increasingly vocal about the need to provide a lasting solution to those who still seek to return.

Overall, however, and in spite of the current government's ambitions, the return project has been less than successful in Croatia.[28] The numbers of returnees has dwindled and only the most vulnerable are attempting to return. The local economy of Knin is now considerably worse off than other parts of the country and this fact has deterred many Serbs from attempting to return. The total Serbian population is just 3,164 down from more than three times that before the war. Even the European Commission noted that 'only the elderly return to Knin'.[29] Of more than 15,000 inhabitants (all ethnicities) in the city of Knin, only 3,103 were listed in the 2001 Census as having permanent income from work. More than twice that number, 7,219, were 'without income'. Only 1,463 persons received social welfare. In the neighbouring areas, the situation is even worse. For example, in 1991 Gospic had a population of 28,732 persons, of whom 64.3 per cent were Croatian, 31.3 per cent were Serbian, and 4.4 per cent were from other national groups. Since the war, the population has fallen and the town itself has a population of 12,980 of whom more than 90% are Croat. According to the 2001 Census, only 625 Serbs were registered in Gospic. Elsewhere as well, the percentage of Serbs has dwindled and as noted in the 2003 US State

Department Report, the majority of returnees are elderly Serbs whose only prospect is a state pension.[30] According to UNHCR, by 2003 approximately 240,000 Croatian Serbs remained in exile, mostly in Serbia and Montenegro.[31]

Bosnia and Hercegovina

By the end of the war in Bosnia, an estimated 2.2 million people had been displaced.[32] Of these more than 1 million were internally displaced, while the rest took refuge in neighbouring countries or in Western Europe. Approximately 700,000 enjoyed 'temporary protection' in Western Europe which began repatriating refugees in the two years following the Dayton Agreement.[33]

There were two main waves of return; the first occurred between 1996 and 1998 when refugees returned in both an organised manner and spontaneously to areas where they had been in the majority, primarily in the Croat-Muslim Federation; by 2001, there was a new wave of minority returns to areas in the Republika Srpska and elsewhere in the Federation. These migrations required considerable assistance from the international community that had established special institutions to support the General Agreement Framework for Peace (DPA) and address the challenges of integrating returning refugees. The most important of these institutions were the Office of the High Representative which created a Return and Reconstruction Task Force (RRTF) and the Commission for Displaced Persons and Refugees, later renamed the Commission for Real Property Claims of Displaced Persons and Refugees (CRPC).

The CRPC began to issue decisions in 1997 but there were several factors that undermined its legitimacy from the start. First, it did not offer applicants the right to appeal against negative decisions and, more important, it was created without enforcement mechanisms of its own. Since it did not deal with occupancy and evictions, or allocate temporary accommodation to those attempting to return to occupied property, it could do little to redress the situation. Consequently, local institutions did not feel compelled to uphold its decisions and it could do little more than serve as a repository of claims.[34] During its mandate the CRPC received 240,333 claims for 319,200 properties[35] and decision-making was notably slow.

In response to the slow pace of decisions, the OHR through its Human Rights department established the Return and Reconstruction Task Force (RRTF) which was co-chaired by UNHCR. The aim of the RRTF was to coordinate the international return efforts, above all monitoring. In addition, the High Representative imposed amendments to the property laws and created a new organising law – the Law on the Implementation of the Decisions to the Commission for Real Property Claims of Displaced Persons and Refugees (CRPC) – to ensure that holders of certificates could turn to national authorities for their enforcement.[36] In April 1998 a legal framework was established to enable property repossession to take place. This was followed by the adoption of laws in the Federation and Republika Srpska in late 1998.[37] These laws were amended by the OHR which helped to set up the Property Law Implementation Plan (PLIP).

The day-to-day operations of the PLIP were managed by a central committee, composed of representatives of UNHCR, OSCE, OHR, UN Mission in Bosnia and Herzegovina (UNMIBH) and the CRPC. In 2001 and 2003, the High Representative imposed two additional amendments to speed up the restitution process and limit the waste of alternative accommodation. This included reducing the deadline for the repossession of property, introducing fines for multiple occupants, and permitting the exchange of properties across the former Yugoslavia.

The implementation of the return project in Bosnia was complicated by the refugee flow and patterns of occupation by refugees from Bosnia and Croatia after Operations Storm and Flash. The initial source of frustration which prevented the restitution of properties lay with the emergency wartime legislation that had given licence to individuals and families to occupy the homes of displaced persons, often on the back of ethnic purges. Charles Philpott, former adviser to the OSCE Mission in Bosnia notes the corrupt manner in which property had been allocated during the conflicts in Bosnia.

Often the former inhabitants had been forcibly evicted, and the beneficiaries of such allocations were not necessarily displaced but young families, the politically well-connected or 'protected' classes, such as veterans or the families of fallen soldiers.[38]

Just as in Croatia, the allocation of war time properties was upheld by local courts and local authorities that granted licences for permanent occupancy to newcomers, at the expense of the original owners. By contrast, legal occupants who did not or could not return saw their rights curtailed by the application of Article 47 of the old Socialist Law on Housing Relations (Official Gazette of the Socialist Republic of Bosnia and Herzegovina, No. 14/84). The Law on Abandoned Apartments (Official Gazette of the Socialist Republic of Bosnia and Herzegovina, No. 6/92 (amended 8/92, 16/92, 13/94, 36/94, 9/95, 33/95) gave displaced occupants seven days to return and reclaim their property while refugees were given slighter longer – fifteen days. For this reason, some claim that decisions introduced in the post-war period consolidated the wartime allocations of property and thus failed to correct the ethnic cleansing that had taken place.[39] The wartime property laws were not repealed until 1998 with the introduction of 'laws on cessation' which established procedures for filing applications with the administrative authorities for the restitution of property. As of 30 April 2004, 92 per cent of 216,377 claims had been dealt with and closed.

The return project in Bosnia was further complicated by the country's domestic divisions – above all the role of ethno-nationalist factions in the Republika Srpska and parts of Hercegovina – and external decisions to repatriate refugees. There were several immediate challenges that compromised the process of accommodating returning refugees, even those whose readmission had been facilitated by international agencies on the ground. First of all, the physical security of returning refugees and displaced persons remained a major problem, especially in Republika Srpska, for several years after the DPA was signed. While returnees were subject to verbal harassment and damage to their property in the Federation, in the Republika Srpska, they were subject to 'the use of explosives, shooting, physical attacks, significant property damage, violent demonstrations, and sometimes even killings'.[40] Reports issued by human rights monitoring bodies, including the OSCE, substantiate this claim. It was only as a result of consistent intervention by the Office of the High Representative that intransigent groups in the Republika Srpksa and Hercegovina were brought into line and the violence lessened.

In addition, Bosnia was and still is heavily mined. The inability to demine large tracts of land prevented returnees from using valuable arable land and also endangered their security. For more than ten years the OSCE has recorded hundreds of incidents where civilians, including a large proportion of returnees, have been injured or killed in landmine incidents.

Related to the issue of physical security is the climate of fear that was created in the Republika Srpska where ICTY-indicted war criminals were given sanctuary and where more than a dozen remain at large to this day. The general unwillingness of the Republika Srpska administration to create a secure environment was exposed in June 2004 when the High Representative dismissed sixty Bosnian Serb officials for helping fugitive war criminals, including Radovan Karadžić, evade capture. Until 2003, the numbers of minorities who returned to settle in the Republika Srpksa paled in comparison to the number of returns in the Federation.

Second, the economic situation in Bosnia has proved to be a major deterrent to return. Ten years after the conflict, Bosnia remains a lower-middle-income country. In 1999, at a time when more than 200,000 refugees had been repatriated to Bosnia, GDP per capita was assessed at $970. A present it stands at $1,530 (Indicators Database, April 2005).[41] Official unemployment statistics are consistently estimated to be between 40–50 per cent of the population.[42] The war also destroyed much of the country's remaining industrial base, and industrial output accounts for less than 20 per cent of Bosnia's economy, which has been inflated by donor contributions and activity by the international community. For example, in 2001, it was estimated that 20 per cent of Sarajevo's revenue came from the international community and few commentators considered Bosnia's economic output to be sustainable in the long term.

By 2005, the governments of Croatia, Bosnia and Serbia and Montenegro met in Sarajevo to try to close the 'refugee chapter in the region'.[43] The '3×3 initiative' set a deadline of end 2006 to address most refugee issues either by voluntary return or local integration. The rationale for closing the refugee chapter was in part dictated by the improvement in returns dating from 2001 onwards but the main driving force was the rapid acceleration in European integration based on the Road Map for Bosnia and Stabilisation and Association Agreements signed between the European Council and its neighbours.

Serbia and Montenegro

Since 2001, Serbia and Montenegro have taken a number of steps to bring the country into line with West European standards regarding human rights, including problems associated with refugees and displaced persons. However, the legacy of previous legal instruments introduced during the socialist period, and later during Milošević's regime, created a poor legal basis for the protection of refugees. This legacy continues to have a bearing on the development of new policies towards refugees and displaced persons within the borders of Serbia and Montenegro (outside Kosovo). In particular, the design of the nationality policies associated with the former Socialist Federal Republic of Yugoslavia has influenced the creation of a dualistic approach to refugees and displaced persons, based on ethnic and national origin.

In the former Socialist Federal Republic of Yugoslavia (SFRY), citizenship was formally determined by the central government, while republics issued passports in which only place of birth and of permanent residence were recorded. Citizens of the federal state were recognised as belonging to *narodi*, a term used to denote constituent nations such as

Serbia, Croatia, Slovenia and *narodnosti* understood as other nationalities and ethnic groups that did not lay claim to a territorial unit within
the Federal state. Thus the nationalities policy in the former Yugoslavia
was determined on the basis of geography and ethnic origin.

Although the former Socialist Federal Republic of Yugoslavia was a
signatory to the 1951 United Nations Convention on Refugees and the
subsequent 1967 Protocol on Refugee Status, it instituted several local
and national laws which were incompatible with these international
instruments. After the breakout of war in the former Yugoslavia, and
faced with a massive influx of people who were residents of the other ex-
SFRY Republics, the government of the Republic of Serbia on 1 April
1992 adopted a Law on Refugees. This law has several serious shortcomings, including the use of the non-Convention definitions of the term
'refugee'. Instead, a refugee was defined on the basis of national origin.

The Constitutional Court Decision of 25 July 2002, on compliance of
the Law on Refugees with the FRY Constitution and the 1951 Convention, established that some of the provisions of the Republic of
Serbia Law on Refugees are not in compliance with the Constitution
and 1951 Refugee Convention. In particular, one may note provisions
regulating the issue of compulsory military service and work for refugees, and Article 18 providing that refugees lose that status if they refuse
to return to their place of origin when circumstances allow.

In the former SFRY while there was a law to regulate cases of asylum
applications, subsequent governments relied upon the 1980 Act on the
Movement and Stay of Foreigners which was enforced in the case of
asylum applicants. This Act set out conditions under which refugee
status could be obtained, described the competent body for establishing
refugee status as well as other decision-making bodies, and outlined the
provisions available to refugees in terms of accommodation, financial
assistance, health care, education and employment. However, several
regulations included in this act were not compatible with the Convention and Protocol, including the definition of a refugee. Under Article 50
of the Act on Movement and Stay of Foreigners a refugee is defined as:

A foreigner who has abandoned the country of residence, or the country whose
citizen he is, or who was a permanent resident of that country but without
citizenship in order to avoid persecution on grounds of his or her progressive
political views and leaning or national, religious, or racial descent may be
recognized by the status of refugee in the SFRY.[44]

In 1992, the Republic of Serbia introduced a further Law on Refugees
which covered refugees of Serb descent as a primary category. Non-
Serbs were considered as other potential beneficiaries of the law. In both

cases the law stipulated that beneficiaries must have residence permits in the territory of the SFRY. Non-residents were to be covered by the 1980 Act on the Movement and Stay of Foreigners. Thus, a dualistic approach towards refugees was created.

The reliance on two legal instruments – the 1980 Act on the Movement and Stay of Foreigners and the 1992 Act by the Serbian Republic – to define refugee status in Serbia reflected a bias that was expressed in inconsistent policies towards refugees throughout the 1990s. During the Milošević years, ethnic Serbs who sought refuge in Serbia were privileged over other categories of refugee. They were also used by the Belgrade authorities and nationalistic parties as a collective reminder of Serbian grievances in the Krajina, Eastern Slavonia, and ultimately Kosovo. According to the Belgrade Helsinki Committee, such victimisation prevented refugees from taking firm decisions regarding return or integration in Serbia and thus prolonged the refugee crisis.[45]

By 2000, the new Serbian government led by the former prime minister, Zoran Djindjić, attempted to resolve the ambiguous status of refugees by accelerating citizenship granting procedures to Serbs from Croatia and Bosnia. A government survey conducted after the publication of the 2001 Census paved the way for a new *National Strategy* which defined the government's commitment and outlined policy actions for return and integration. By 2002, the Federal Republic of Yugoslavia had begun to review its laws on asylum and refugees and instituted a new '*National Strategy for Resolving the Problems of Refugees and Internally Displaced Persons*' of 30 May 2002.

The *National Strategy* is based on two solutions to the refugee problem which reflect the dualistic tendency outlined above and include: facilitating the return of refugees and IDPs to their homes in Croatia, Bosnia and Kosovo; and, providing refugees with the option of integration through citizenship of Serbia and Montenegro. The return of IDPs to Kosovo is premised on the implementation of efficient mechanisms of property restitution and security guarantees.

As for integration, the Strategy stresses the need to provide conditions for local integration, 'meaning durable resolution of the essential existential problems of refugees and internally displaced persons as well as their families'. According to the Strategy, the basic aim of local integration is to help refugees achieve self-sufficiency and social equality.

The legal basis for the two options of repatriation and integration is found in Serbia's and Montenegro's commitments regarding refugee protection, return and repatriation. Alongside the agreements, national governments, the UN and its specialised agencies have introduced specific laws that have a direct bearing on refugees and their possibilities

for return. The most important of these include property and employment issues; as well as assistance programmes creating conditions
allowing refugees to make an informal choice, including in the form of
go-and-see visits, legal advice, application processing, support for the
journey itself and job placement schemes.

A government Task Force was created to oversee implementation of
the National Strategy and to operate as an inter-ministerial agency
including representatives of the Ministry of Social Welfare, Ministry for
Foreign Economic Relations, the Commissioner for Refugees, the
Ministry of Urban Planning and Construction, Ministry of Finance and
Economy, Ministry of Interior, Ministry of Labour and Employment
and Serbian Ministry of Foreign Affairs Coordinating Centre.

One of the central elements of the National Strategy is the provision
of affordable housing and social housing. A number of incentives were
proposed, including waiving taxes in part, municipal grants and construction loans. The Fund for Affordable and Social Housing was tasked
with implementing the social and subsidised housing construction policy
which was to be funded by donations and soft loans from the international community, refugees' own assets, and budget funds. The key
elements of the housing plan include: the construction of affordable
housing (i.e., apartments in multi-family houses in urban and other
residential areas); self-help construction of individual and other houses;
the purchase of old houses and garden plots in depopulated areas; aid to
start construction of beneficiary-owned housing units; and, providing
housing including garden plots by contracting agreements on life-long
sustenance. In addition, the National Strategy identifies a number of
programmes regarding medical and social-welfare institutions, including: the construction of social apartments in less urbanised areas;
transforming collective centers into elderly homes; expanding existing
accommodation capabilities of specialised social welfare institutions for
the most vulnerable and disabled; expanding existing accommodation
capacities of specialised medical institutions for the most vulnerable
medical cases.

Although the Strategy claims to focus on vulnerable communities, it
does not involve them in the process, and instead sets out some top-
down criteria to address the refugee problem. It specifies that refugees
should be resettled in depopulated areas by means of a dispersal policy.
It also attempts to define which families are able-bodied and which
categories of the population are most vulnerable: the disabled, the
elderly (above 55) and one/two parent families without sufficient income
to purchase apartments under loan schemes or to rent them under
market conditions.

Further evidence of the Strategy's top-down approach to the refugee problem is found in the declaration that 'refugees should be offered a possibility of local integration in the areas most similar to those where they lived before the exodus, respecting their original environment. Rural population should be directed to villages, and urban population to cities.'

A second element of the National Strategy is the gradual closing down of collective centres where hygiene and sanitary conditions are generally poor. Since only 18 per cent of refugees had their own housing in 2002, the provision of alternative accommodation was seen as a critical intervention for the government. Data collected in 2002 indicated that the majority of refugees lived in rented apartments (44 per cent), while others lived with relatives and friends (30 per cent). In 2003 the process of closing the centres was initiated, and by November 8,500 had been moved out of 135 closed centres. By 2005, there were 15,105 people living in camps, down from 35,000 just two years before.[46]

The most critical element of the Strategy in terms of ensuring a sustainable solution concerns creating economic conditions that will support employment in the region. With this aim in mind, the Strategy describes its intention to develop 'rapid employment' and identifies 150,000 potential beneficiaries. According to the basic employment programs, the primary objectives include: improvement of the social status of the most vulnerable refugee households; development of the economic environment for self-employment; strengthening local self-government; expansion of small family businesses and providing assistance through the Centres for Small Business Encouragement and Promotion.[47] To date, however, the prospect of employment is a far-off hope for many refugees and unemployment figures in Serbia are at least comparable to those in other parts of the former Yugoslavia.

Kosovo

The case of Kosovo is considerably different from those discussed above. In the first instance, the high-intensity conflict in Kosovo lasted only a matter of months and therefore those who fled the onslaught of Milošević's forces did not settle for long periods of time in neighbouring countries. Second, the process of stabilisation has been dictated by the United Nations Administration Mission in Kosovo (UNMIK) which has been responsible for ensuring that security mechanisms and democratic structures are put in place. Third, the case of Kosovo is most remarkable for the number of refugees and displaced persons who returned spontaneously following the NATO action of March 1999 and the growing number of minorities whose possibility for return has been challenged by inter-ethnic contest in subsequent six years.

During a period of just three months, Serb paramilitaries, special forces and regular forces caused the flight of 900,000 Kosovars. Most of these were ethnic Albanians who fled to Macedonia, Albania and, to a lesser extent Serbia and Montenegro, or remained inside Kosovo. A military technical agreement which marked the end of military action was signed on 9 June 1999. The Federal Republic agreed to the deployment in Kosovo of international and security presences under UN auspices and following the introduction of UN Security Council Resolution 1244, the United Nations Administration Mission in Kosovo was established.

The fate of the hundreds of thousands of displaced Kosovars forced UNMIK to focus its attention on creating mechanisms to facilitate their return. One major barrier to the return of displaced persons was the shortage of suitable housing and the problem of double occupancy. According to international surveys approximately 103,000 housing units had been destroyed or were uninhabitable.[48] In response to this challenge, UNMIK set up an *ad hoc* body, the Housing and Property Directorate (HPD) with a quasi-judicial independent branch, the Housing and Property Claims Commission (HPCC), on 15 November 1999. The rules governing the operations of the HPCC were laid down in UNMIK Regulation No. 2000/60 of 31 October 2000 which set out the following general principles for the repossession of housing:

(1) Any property right which was validly acquired according to the law applicable at the time of its acquisition remains valid, unless the regulations provide otherwise.

(2) Any person who lost residential property after 1989 as a result of discrimination has a right to restitution of property.

(3) Any transaction after 1989 which was illegal under a discriminatory law, but would otherwise have been legal, is valid.

(4) Any refugee or displaced person who has lost possession of residential property has a right to dispose of it, in accordance with the law.[49]

The HPD and the HPCC were given exclusive jurisdiction following the introduction of specific Regulation 1999/23. The HPCC has since been entrusted to review claims on behalf of those who lost property as a result of discrimination after the cancellation of Kosovo's autonomous status by Milošević on 23 March 1989. The HPCC was also trusted to regularise transactions of property concluded since 23 March 1989 which had been held up during the period of direct rule from Belgrade. Finally, the HPCC was authorised to review claims on behalf of refugees and displaced persons who lost property as a result of the 1999 conflict. While the HPCC adjudicated over property claims, the HPD was responsible for registering claims in the first instance and providing a mediation service.

It is important to mention that one feature that distinguished the policy of housing repossession in Kosovo from the other states considered in this study is the notion of compensation. Refugees and displaced persons who lost property as a result of the conflict in Kosovo are not entitled to compensation but are simply permitted to return.

Most Kosovo Albanians returned to their homes. By the end of 2003, approximately 807,000 refugees had returned. In contrast to the fast pace of returns of ethnic Albanians, the return of minorities (Serb, Roma, Bosniak, Ashkaelia and Egyptian) occurred only gradually and by May 2004, only 10,561 members of minority groups had returned to their pre-conflict homes.

In spite of the UNMIK presence, several factors have complicated the process of housing repossession and refugee returns. Many Albanian returnees occupied the homes of displaced Serbs and this has caused considerable administrative problems for the international community. Above all, however, the poor state of inter-ethnic relations has hampered the return of minority communities.

Since 1999, the Serb, Roma and other communities have been targeted with revenge attacks. The situation came to a head again in March 2004 when mass demonstrations led to inter-ethnic violence and civil unrest.

The March 2004 unrest resulted in the deaths of 19 civilians, 8 of whom were Serb. In addition, 950 people were injured and there was widespread destruction of property. Approximately 730 homes were damaged or destroyed as well as 36 churches, monasteries and religious sites. By 23 March more than 41,000 Serb, Roma, Ashkaelia, Egyptian and Albanian minority community members had been displaced[50] and return movement fell by 50 per cent based on 2003 figures.[51]

Although Kosovo Serbs have been the primary targets, other groups have been victimised.[52] For example, in Vushtrri/Vucitrn, the Ashkaelia neighbourhood was systematically attacked, and houses burned and looted. Some Bosniaks and Gorani, while not directly targeted, opted for self-evacuation. According to UNHCR, 'members of minority communities were regular targets of inter-ethnic harassment and violence from verbal assault, stone-throwing and systematic theft to physical assault, grenade attacks and killings'.[53]

Following the unrest in 2004, UNHCR advised Western governments against the forced return of Serb, Roma, Ashkaelia, Egyptian and Kosovo Albanian minorities claiming that 'such returns could contribute to further destabilise the situation in Kosovo' and that the risk was 'even higher where individuals may be forcibly returned to minority communities outside their place of origin'.[54] It also argued against the possibility of relocating refugees and displaced persons in other parts of Serbia or Montenegro.

As for Kosovo's Albanian population, international monitors noted that those living in northern municipalities continued to exist in a fragile environment which continued to deter the return of displaced persons. In particular, UNCHR noted certain categories of Albanians who had problems regarding return: those in mixed marriages and those who are perceived to have been associated with the Serbian regime.

While Western governments had started the process of removing ethnic Albanians and returning them to Kosovo on the grounds that the country was largely safe for their return, UNHCR issued guidelines which reminded the international community that traumatised individuals, and particularly those who had been subjected to serious persecution as well as victims of torture, survivors of sexual violence, or witnesses to crimes against humanity would not wish to return and should receive protection abroad.[55]

By 2005, the security situation had improved. Fewer serious crimes were reported and the UNMIK could boast that no ethnic violence had taken place since the killing of a 16-year-old Serb on 6 June 2004 in Gracanica in a drive-by shooting. There were other suggestions of stabilisation. For example, the elections on 23 October 2004 were conducted in a peaceful manner and the visit of Serbian President Boris Tadic on 13 February 2005 went smoothly. UNHCR also noted some progress in prosecuting those responsible for the March violence.[56]

In spite of the improvement in physical security, there are additional reasons why the refugees and displaced persons may be discouraged from returning. As for the ethnic Albanian majority, it is important to note that relations between remainees and returnees are not always harmonious.[57] Regarding the minority population, persistent discrimination in all areas of public administration has ensured that ethnic minorities face obstacles in accessing essential services in areas of health, education and justice. Finally, it should be borne in mind that just as in other post-conflict regions of the former Yugoslavia, unemployment is registered at over 50 per cent, a statistic which discourages individuals from returning voluntarily to Kosovo.

Sustainable returns?

The first part of this chapter introduced the concepts of justice, development and burden relief as possible explanations for return. While each of these may apply in individual cases, overall one cannot conclude that the pursuit of justice and the ambition of fostering economic development are driving the return process in the former Yugoslavia. As the above account demonstrates, there are several discrepancies between the declared objectives of the international community and respective governments and the outcome of the return programme. Such discrepancies appear both in the design of return programmes and in the practical implementation, suggesting that the process of return as a means of post-conflict stabilisation may not be sustainable in the end.

In terms of justice, one might argue that a well-developed notion of justice should include the participation of, and consultation with, victim groups who are best placed to define what justice means to them. This has certainly not happened in the former Yugoslavia where the pursuit of justice has been dictated by international and local institutions, above all the International Criminal Tribunal for the former Yugoslavia (ICTY) and national courts. Further, as evidenced by the persistence of violent crimes in Croatia and Bosnia until just a few years ago and most dramatically by the March 2004 unrest in Kosovo, the satisfaction of material needs, including housing, does not necessarily address broader issues of political security. A secure environment as advocated by Engelbrecht entails the creation of safe living conditions and the arrest of war criminals. It is arguable that in Croatia, where the judiciary has resisted the ideal of ethnic impartiality, and in Serbia and Bosnia's Republika Srpska where high profile indictees have been sheltered, that the concept of security is not yet sufficiently institutionalised to encourage refugees to return in the name of justice. Most returnees do not identify repossession with justice and their returns are motivated by other factors, many of which are beyond their control.

In terms of development, there is even less reason to suggest that return is linked to economic growth. Evidence of return as a means to economic development should be borne out by statistical data which demonstrates the positive benefits of the return of skills and labour for both the individual and society as a whole. As recorded above in the discussions of return in Croatia, Serbia, Bosnia and Kosovo, there is little to support the claim that return may advance economic growth. Rather, there is considerable evidence that the accommodation of returning refugees and IDPs has placed a great burden on receiving states which has not been recovered by the increase in the domestic market. Most regions where returnees are settling are characterised by high unemployment and few economic opportunities.

One irrefutable feature of return is the increasing trend in repatriation from West European countries. In the first two years after Dayton, hundreds of thousands of Croatian and Bosnian citizens were sent back from Germany, and to a lesser extent Austria. By 2001, this trend was also noticeable in the United Kingdom which began repatriating large numbers of Kosovars who failed to qualify for asylum. Once their temporary leave to remain expired, they too were removed and sent back. In the case of the former Yugoslavia, the burden-relieving argument, which is often justified in terms of appeasing domestic interests that are hostile to refugees and often Muslim communities, reflects a broader picture where Western governments have determined not only the manner but also the timing and rationale for return on their terms.

Conclusion

The programme of refugee returns has met with limited success in the former Yugoslavia. While a substantial number have returned, millions have sought asylum abroad and have opted for integration in their host states. In terms of policy implementation, there has been considerable improvement in the development of legal and administrative frameworks to process returns. However, the creation of institutions such as the CPRC in Bosnia and the HPD in Kosovo are dependent on the establishment of the rule of law and democratic practices for their continued success. The suggestion that these countries have now an established political culture which is conducive to the reintegration of returnees and displaced persons is still open to question. Over the past ten years the state public administration bodies, including the housing associations and other institutions of government, have at various times been subject to political corruption and retarded the prospect of return and reintegration.

Many refugees have been able to reclaim their homes through the various commissions and other quasi-judicial institutions created by the international community. However, it should be noted that it was international actors who instigated the processes of return and housing repossession by relying on both carrots and sticks to advance the pace of returns. Until the change of governments in Croatia, Bosnia and Serbia in 2000 and 2001, the pace of repossession was slow and conditioned by external factors, including the forced returns of thousands of former refugees from Western Europe. Since 2001, reform has taken place as a result of international intervention in the two largest refugee-producing states, Bosnia and Kosovo. Minority returns in Bosnia and Kosovo have occurred largely as a result of direct measures introduced by international authorities in the form of the high representative (OHR) and UNMIK. As for Croatia, Serbia and Montenegro, progress on return matters has tended to follow as a result of incentives, including conditional aid packages and the signing of Stabilisation and Association Agreements and in the case of Croatia, the opening of EU accession talks with the European Council. And yet, there is still evidence of discriminatory practices against minority groups and individuals seeking to return.

Returning to one's home does not signal the end of the process of post-conflict stabilisation. As demonstrated by the unrest in Kosovo in March 2004, persistent ethnic and political tensions between communities may create new refugee situations and rekindle the return-flight cycle. Thus the goal of political stabilisation cannot end with the return of refugees. Rather, there is a need to ensure that mechanisms are in place to provide continuing mediation between ethno-national groups and ensure that those who seek to return are better integrated in their home state.

It may be too early to conclude if the returns of the past decade are indeed sustainable. At present, there are many factors which suggest that such returns are not. Inter-ethnic tension and limited economic opportunities in all of the successor states of the former Yugoslavia are contributing to the non-return of many skilled persons who might otherwise have wished to return home. Since the security situation has improved in all the regions discussed in this chapter, including Kosovo, it is fair to conclude the economy is now the major drawback to return. Until the governments of the former Yugoslavia successfully embed the ideals of reconciliation and multi-ethnic existence across their societies, the return process will continue to be driven by external factors, above all the agendas of host states. This continued reliance on Western powers will only weaken the prospect of long-term sustainable returns.

Notes

1 The actual figure for internally displaced persons from Bosnia and Herzegovina, Croatia, Serbia and Montenegro, including Kosovo, and Macedonia was estimated at 564,934. See *UNHCR 2004 Global Refugee Trends*, http://www.unchr.ch/statistics.

2 See 'Bosnia and Herzegovina welcomes over 1 million returnees', UNHCR press release, 21 September 2004, http://www.unhcr.ch/cgi-bin/texis/vtx/news/opendoc.htm?tbl=NEWS&id=414fffba4&page=news

3 See, for example, Khalid Koser's study 'Return, readmission and reintegration: changing agendas, policy frameworks and operations programmes', in Bimal Ghosh, *Return Migration: Journal of Hope or Despair*, Geneva: International Organisation for Migration, 2000.

4 Between 1996 and 1999, the German government undertook a major programme of repatriating hundreds of thousands of refugees to the former Yugoslavia. Their resettlement in countries such as Bosnia has been described by international agencies as a return.

5 Elsewhere it has been argued that the pressure to demonstrate the success of return programmes is particularly strong following military intervention, and that the growing incidence of voluntary repatriation, the increasing number of restrictions on admission and the trend of removing unsuccessful asylum-seekers from Western countries has effectively narrowed the distinction between voluntary and forcible returns. See Brad K. Blitz, Rosemary Sales and Lisa Marzano, 'Non-voluntary return? The politics of return to Afghanistan', *Political Studies*, 53, 1 (2005), 182–200.

6 See Richard Black and Saskia Gent, *Defining, Measuring and Influencing Sustainable Return: The Case of the Balkans*, Development Research Centre on Migration, Globalisation and Poverty, Working Paper T7, December 2004, 2. http://www.migrationdrc.org/publications/working_papers/WP-T7.pdf

7 Walpurga Englbrecht, 'Bosnia and Herzegovina, Croatia and Kosovo: voluntary return in safety and dignity?' *Refugee Survey Quarterly*, 23, 3 (2004), 100–48.

8 See Black and Gent, *Defining, Measuring and Influencing*; Blitz, Sales and Marzano, 'Non-voluntary return'.

9 For a more developed account, see Monica Duffy Toft, '*Repatriation of Refugees: a Failing Policy*', John F. Kennedy School of Government, Harvard University, unpublished paper 2000.

10 See Black and Gent, 'Defining, Measuring and Influencing'; Brad K. Blitz, 'Refugee returns and minority rights in Croatia 1991–2004', *Oxford Journal of Refugee Studies*, 18, 3 (2005), 362–86; Blitz, Sales and Marzano, 'Non-voluntary return?'; and David Turton and Peter Marsden, 'Taking refugees for a ride? The politics of refugee return to Afghanistan', Afghanistan Research and Evaluation Unit, 2002. http://www.areu.org.af/publications/Refugees%20For%20a%20Ride%20English.pdf.

11 In the IOM's words, the return of qualified nationals programme 'aims to boost rehabilitation efforts in post-conflict Afghanistan through the progressive transfer of know-how of Afghan expatriate professionals to their home country. RQA will facilitate the short and long-term employment, return and reintegration of an estimated 1,500 professionals by the year 2004.'

12 See the evaluation documents by the IOM and the report submitted to the IOM by the African Centre for Technology Studies.

13 The desire of sending governments to promote returns may also come into conflict with the needs of the host government for reconstruction. See Turton and Marsden, 'Taking refugees for a ride', and Barry Stein, 'Refugee repatriation, return and refoulement during conflict', Paper presented to United States Agency for International Development, Promoting Democracy,

Human Rights, and Reintegration in Post-conflict Societies 30–31 October 1997, Washington, DC.

14 See Blitz, Sales and Marzano, 'Non-voluntary return?'.

15 Oliver Bakewell, 'Returning refugees or migrating villagers? Voluntary repatriation programmes in Africa reconsidered', *New Issues in Refugee Research*, Working Paper, No. 15, December 1999, p. 3. http://www.unhcr.ch/refworld/pubs/pubon.htm.

16 See Amnesty International Press Release of 28 April 2003, 'UK/Afghanistan: Forced return of Afghan asylum seekers unacceptable' which stated that 'returns for "symbolic" purposes are dangerous because they are motivated by public perception rather than a cool-headed and objective assessment of the reality on the ground'.

17 Now the Ministry of Public Works, Reconstruction, and Construction Office for Expelled Persons, Refugees and Returnees.

18 See Katarina Subasic, 'Croatia: new math', *World Press Review* 49, 8 (2002). http://www.worldpress.org/Europe/641.cfm.

19 The right to return is guaranteed by Article 12, paragraph 4 of the International Covenant on Civil and Political Rights to which Croatia is a signatory.

20 Organisation for Security and Cooperation in Europe, *Internally Displaced Persons, Refugees and Return*. OSCE Mission to Croatia: Zagreb, Croatia, 31 May 2001. http://www.osce.org/croatia/return/foreword

21 See Croatian Helsinki Committee Forced Evictions in the Republic of Croatia, Human Rights series, Zagreb, Croatia: Croatian Helsinki Committee, 1994, http://www.open.hr/com/hho/ english/izdanj1.htm and 'Information on Fires in Residential and Agricultural Facilities (Village Graveyards and Other) Recorded between 1 January and 15 April', Department for Severe Human Rights Violations, Zagreb Croatia: Croatian Helsinki Committee, 1998.

22 US Committee for Refugees, *Country Reports: Croatia* 1999, p. 2, http://www.refugees.org/world/countryrpt/europe/1999/croatia.htm

23 For a full account of these laws and other relating to return, see *Narodne Novine* (Official Gazette of the Republic of Croatia), NN 73/95, 27 September, Zagreb, Croatia, *http://www..nn.hr/sluzbeni-list/index.asp; Narodne Novine*, NN 7/96, 26 January, Zagreb, Croatia, http://www..nn.hr/ sluzbeni-list/index.asp; *Narodne Novine* NN 100/97, 26 September, Zagreb, Croatia, http://www..nn.hr/sluzbeni-list/index.asp; *Narodne Novine* NN 92/98. Zagreb, Croatia, 7 July, http://www..nn.hr/sluzbeni-list/index.asp

24 See OSCE, *Internally Displaced Persons*.

25 The Norwegian Refugee Council argued that 'the Return Programme perpetuates the effects of conflict-era law and policy and adds yet another layer of legal privilege and disadvantage on the basis of national origin and citizenship'. See Norwegian Refugee Council, *Briefing Paper*, 7 June 2001, http://www.db.idpproject.org/Sites/IdpProjectDb/idpSurvey.nsf/wViewSingle Env/E4AAEF766FFB579CC1256A7A00505393/$file/NRC+State-Statement+ 7+June+2001.pdf

26 Agence France Presse, 'Croatia renews calls for Serb refugees to return', 16 June 2003, http://www.reliefweb.int/w/rwb.nsf/o/aa8c8dd2dd 3f283a49256d4800229e18?

27 RFE/RL NEWSLINE (2002) 'Bosnian Croats face eviction from Knin', 6 September, http://listserv.acsu.buffalo.edu/cgi-bin/wa?A2=;ind0209a&L= albanews&F=&S=&P=2271

28 Blitz, Sales and Marzano, 'Non-voluntary return'.

29 European Commission, 'Commission Staff Working Paper: Croatia–Stabilization and Association Report 2003', COM (2003) 139 Final, Document Number SEC (2003) 341, 26 March, http://europa.eu.int/comm/external_ relations/see/sap/rep2/com03_139_en.pdf European Commission Stabilisation Report, p. 11.

30 See US State Department, 'Country Reports on Human Rights Practices', released by Bureau of Democracy, Human Rights and Labour, 31 March 2003, http://www.state.gov/g/drl/rls/hrrpt/2002/18359.htm

31 UNHCR Estimate of Refugees and Displaced Persons Still Seeking Solutions in South-Eastern Europe, 18 December 2002;

32 UNHCR, 'Update on conditions for return to Bosnia and Herzegovina', January 2005, http://www.unhcr.ba/publications/B&HRET0105.pdf

33 From 1996 to 2000, IOM BiH assisted 178,994 Bosnian refugees to return home from Germany, providing them with travel assistance and a small repatriation grant to facilitate their reintegration.

34 Charles Philpott, 'Though the dog is dead, the pig must be killed: finishing with property restitution to Bosnia-Hercegovina's IDPs and refugees', *Journal of Refugee Studies*, 18 (2005), 1–24.

35 CRPC 2004, p. 3.

36 In March 2001, another Dayton institution, the Human Rights Chamber, ruled that the non-enforcement of the decisions of the CPRC constituted a violation under the European Convention for the Protection of Human Rights and Fundamental Freedoms and awarded the CPRC decision-holders non-pecuniary damages.

37 These laws were passed by both entities and included: the Law on the cessation of the Application of the Law on Abandoned Apartments; Law on the Cessation of the Application of the Law on Temporary Abandoned Real Property Owned by Citizens; Law on the Taking Over of the Law on Housing Relations (Official Gazette – Federation 11/98); Law on the Cessation of the Application of the Law on the Use of Abandoned Property (and instructions), RS Official Gazette 38/1998 11 December 1998; Official Gazette 1/99 of 21 January 1999.

38 Philpott, 'Though the dog is dead, the pig must be killed', p. 2.

39 Ibid.

40 Englbrecht, 'Bosnia and Herzegovina, Croatia and Kosovo', p. 104.

41 See World Bank, 'Bosnia and Herzegovina Data Profile', 2005, http:// devdata.worldbank.org/external/CPProfile.asp?SelectedCountry=BIH&C CODE=BIH&CNAME=Bosnia+and+Herzeusand+HerzegovinaPTYPE =CP

42 See European Commission, *The Western Balkans in Transition, Enlargement Papers No. 23, European Economy of December 2004*, Brussels: European

Commission. http://europa.eu.int/comm/economy_finance/publications/ en-largement_papers/elp23_en.htm

43 See UNHCR, 'Balkan governments seek to close refugee chapter in region', 31 January 2005, http://www.unhcr.ch/cgi-bin/texis/vtx/news/opendoc.htm? tbl=NEWS&id=41fe4b4b4&page=news

44 See Helsinki Committee for Human Rights in Serbia (2002), p. 262.

45 Ibid.

46 See UNHCR, *Global Refugee Trends*, 2004.

47 The Strategy identifies five types of employment scheme: including grants in kind; interest-free loans and micro-credits; self-employment programmes which include loans to set up small businesses; employment in existing and 'successful' companies; training to prepare refugees for employment, which includes providing scholarships for high school and university students as well as retraining programmes for workers.

48 See Hans Das, 'Restoring property rights in the aftermath of war', *International and Comparative Law Quarterly*, 53 (April 2004), 429–44.

49 Ibid., p. 435.

50 UNHCR, 'Position on the continued international protection needs of individuals from Kosovo', August 2004, p. 3.

51 See report of Secretary General on United Nations Interim Administration Mission in Kosovo S/2005/88 (15 February 2005), para. 12.

52 According to UNHCR 82 per cent of the displaced were Serbs.

53 UNHCR 2004.

54 Ibid., p. 8.

55 Ibid., p. 6.

56 See UNHCR Position on the Continued International Protection Needs of Individuals from Kosovo, March 2005.

57 See Black and Gent, *Defining, Measuring and Influencing Sustainable Return.*

Bibliography

Abramowitz, Morton, 'The complexities of American policymaking on Turkey', *Insight Turkey*, 2, 4 (2000), 3–35.

Abramowitz, Morton (ed.), *Turkey's transformation and American policy*, New York: Century Foundation Press, 2001.

Adanir, Fikret, 'The Macedonians in the Ottoman Empire, 1878–1912', in Andreas Koppeler (ed.), *The formation of national elites*, New York: New York University Press, 1992, 161–90.

'The socio-political environment of Balkan nationalism: the case of Ottoman Macedonia, 1856–1912', in Heinz-Gerhard Haupt, Michael G. Müller and Stuart Woolf (eds.), *National identities in Europe in the XIXth and XXth Centuries*, The Hague: Kluwer Law International, 1998, 221–54.

Agence France Presse, 'Croatia renews calls for Serb refugees to return', 16 June (2003), http://www.reliefweb.int/w/rwb.nsf/0/aa8c8dd2dd3f283a49256d4800229e18?

Agnew, John, and Corbridge, Stuart, *Mastering space: Hegemony, territory and international political economy*, London/ New York: Routledge, 1995.

Almond, Mark, *Europe's backyard war: the war in the Balkans*, London: Heinemann, 1994.

Altmann, Franz-Lothar, 'Regional economic problems and prospects', in Judy Batt (ed.), *The Western Balkans: Moving on*, Institute for Security Studies, Chaillot Paper No. 70, October 2004, 69–74.

Amnesty International, 'UK/Afghanistan: forced return of Afghan asylum seekers unacceptable', Press Release, 28 April (2003).

Auden, W. H., *The dyer's hand*, New York: Random House, 1967.

Bach, Jonathan, 'One step forward, three steps back? Germany, the European Community, and the recognition of Croatia and Slovenia', paper presented at the German Studies Association Conference, Washington, DC, 1993.

Baker, James Addison, and DeFrank, Thomas M., *The politics of diplomacy: Revolution, war, and peace, 1989–1992*, New York: Putnam, 1995.

Bakewell, Oliver, 'Returning refugees or migrating villagers? Voluntary repatriation programmes in Africa reconsidered', *New Issues in Refugee Research*, Working Paper, No. 15, December (1999), http://www.unhcr.ch/refworld/pubs/pubon.htm

Bal, Idris (ed.), *Turkish foreign policy in post Cold War era*, Boca Raton: Universal Publishers/BrownWalker, 2004.

Ball, Howard, *Prosecuting war crimes and genocide: The twentieth century experience*, Lawrence: University Press of Kansas, 1999.

Banac, Ivo, *The national question in Yugoslavia*, Ithaca, NY: Cornell University Press, 1984.

Barker, Elisabeth, *Macedonia: Its place in Balkan power politics*, London, 1950, reprint, Westport: Greenwood Press, 1980.

Bass, Gary Jonathan, *Stay the hand of vengeance: The politics of war crimes tribunals*, Princeton: Princeton University Press, 2000.

Bastian, Jens, 'Knowing your way in the Balkans: Greek foreign direct investment in southern Europe', *Journal of Southeast European and Black Sea Studies*, 4, 3 (2004), 463–4.

Beeley, Brian, 'People and cities: migration and urbanization' in Beeley (ed.), *Turkish transformation: New century new challenges*, Huntingdon, UK: The Eothen Press, 2002, 36–58.

Beeley, Brian (ed.), *Turkish transformation: New century new challenges*, Huntingdon, UK: The Eothen Press, 2002.

Beigbeder, Yves, *Judging war criminals: The politics of international justice*, New York: St. Martin's Press, 1999.

Bell, John, 'Bulgaria's search for security,' in Bell (ed.), *Bulgaria in transition*. Boulder, CO: Westview Press, 1998, 314–15.

'The 'Ilindentsi': Does, Bulgaria have a macedonian minority?' in Bell (ed.), *Bulgaria in transition* Boulder, CO: Westview Press, 1998, 189–206.

Biberaj, Elez, *Albania in transition: The rocky road to democracy*, Boulder, CO: Westview, 1999.

Bildt, Carl, *Peace journey*, London: Weidenfeld & Nicholson, 1998.

Black, Richard, and Gent, Saskia, *Defining, measuring and influencing sustainable return: The case of the Balkans*. Development Research Centre on Migration, Globalisation and Poverty, Working Paper T7, December 2004, http://www.migrationdrc.org/publications/working_papers/WP-T7.pdf

Blitz, Brad K., 'Refugee returns in Croatia: Contradiction and reform', *Politics*, 23, 3 (2003), 181–91.

'Refugee returns, civic differentiation, and minority rights in Croatia 1991–2004', *Journal of Refugee Studies*, 18, 3 (2005), 362–86.

Blitz, Brad K., Sales, Rosemary and Marzano, Lisa, 'Non-voluntary return? The politics of return to Afghanistan', *Political Studies*, 53, 1 (2005), 182–200.

Boas, Gideon, and Schabas, William A. (eds.), *International criminal law developments in the case law of the ICTY*, Leiden: Martinus Nijhoff, 2003.

Bogoev, Ksente, 'The Macedonian revolutionary organization (V.M.R.O.) in the past hundred years', *Macedonian Review*, 23 (1993), 2–3, 118–28.

Bolaffi, Angelo, 'Foreign reactions to xenophobia', *Der Spiegel*, 14 December 1992, no. 51, 28f, reprinted in Jarausch and Gransow (eds.), *Uniting Germany: Documents and debates 1944–93*, Oxford: Berghahn Books, 1994, 263–5.

Bonner, Raymond, 'Tactics were barrier to top Serb's indictment', *New York Times*, 29 March 1999, 9.

Boot, Max, *The savage wars of peace: Small wars and the rise of American power*, New York: Basic Books, 2002.

Bourantonis, Dimitris, and Tsakonas, Panayotis, 'The Southeastern Europe Multinational Peace Force: Problems of and prospects for a regional security agency', *Politics*, 23, 2 (2003), 75–81.

Bourdieu, Pierre, *The field of cultural production*, Cambridge: Polity, 1993.

Boyer, Peter J., 'General Clark's Battles', *The New Yorker*, 17 November 2003.

Bugajski, Janusz, *Ethnic politics in eastern Europe*, Armonk, NY: M. E. Sharpe, 1995.

Bulgarian Ministry of Foreign Affairs, 'Declaration on the development of equal in rights and mutually beneficial relations with the Russian Federation', Bulgaria, http://.www.mfa.bg/policy/Russia_e.htm

Cameron, Fraser, *The foreign and security policy of the European Union: past, present and future*, Sheffield: Sheffield Academic Press, 1999.

Cameron, Fraser, and Quille, Gerard, *The ESDP-State of Play*, EPC Working Paper Number 11, European Policy Centre, (September 2004).

Çarkoglu, Ali, and Rubin, Barry (eds.), *Turkey and the European Union: domestic politics, economic integration and international dynamics*, London/Portland: Frank Cass, 2003.

Carvel, John, 'Young Brits still bashing the Boche', *The Guardian*, 10 June 1996, 2.

Chalaby, Jean-Karim, 'Nationalism as a discursive strategy', *The ASEN Bulletin*, no. 1, 4, 6 (1993–4), 19–25.

Cigar, Norman, *Genocide in Bosnia: The policy of ethnic cleansing*, College Station, TX: Texas A&M University Press, 1995.

Clark, Wesley, *Waging war*, New York: Random House, 2001.

Clement, Sophie, *Conflict prevention in the Balkans*, Chaillot Paper 30, October 1997.

Clyatt, Jr., Oscar W., *Bulgaria's quest for security after the Cold War*, Washington, DC: The Institute for National Strategic Studies, 1993.

Cohen, Leonard J., *Broken bonds: Yugoslavia's disintegration and Balkan politics in transition*, Boulder, CO: Westview, 1995.

Cohen, Nick, 'And you thought the war was over', *Independent on Sunday*, 5 May 1996, 16.

Cohen, Philip, *Serbia's secret war*, College Station: Texas A&M University Press, 1996.

Collins, Randal, 'German-bashing and the theory of democratic modernization', *Zeitschrift für Soziologie*, 24, (1995), 3–21.

Conversi, Daniele, 'Central secession: Towards a new analytical concept? The case of former Yugoslavia', *Journal of Ethnic and Migration Studies*, 26, 2 (2000), 333–56.

'Domino effect or internal developments? The influences of international events and political ideologies on Catalan and Basque nationalism', *West European Politics*, 16, 1 (1993), 245–70.

'Moral relativism and equidistance: British attitudes to the war in former Yugoslavia', in T. Cushman and S. Mestrovic (eds.), *This time we knew: Western responses to genocide in Bosnia*, New York: New York University Press, 1996, 255–62.

German-bashing and the breakup of Yugoslavia, Seattle: University of Washington/ Henry M. Jackson School of International Studies, 1998.

Crawford, Beverly, 'Explaining defection from international cooperation: Germany's unilateral recognition of Croatia', *World Politics*, 48, 4 (1996), 482–521.

Crnobrnja, Mihailo, *The Yugoslav Drama*, London: Taurus, 1994.

Croatian Helsinki Committee, 'Information on Fires in Residential and Agricultural Facilities Recorded between 1 January and 15 April', Department for Severe Human Rights Violations., Zagreb Croatia: Croatian Helsinki Committee, 1998.

  Forced Evictions in the Republic of Croatia, Human Rights series, Zagreb, Croatia: Croatian Helsinki Committee, 1994, http://www.open.hr/com/hho/english/izdanj1.htm

Crossette, Barbara, 'UN details its failure to stop '95 Bosnia massacre', *New York Times*, 16 November 1999, col. 8, 12.

Cushman, Thomas, and Mestrovic, Stjepan, *This time we knew: Western responses to genocide in Bosnia*, New York: New York University Press, 1996.

Daianu, Daniel, 'Reconstruction in southeastern Europe', *The Southeast European Yearbook 1998–99*, Athens: ELIAMEP, 1999.

Danforth, Loring M., *The Macedonian conflict: Ethnic nationalism in a transnational world*, Princeton: Princeton University Press, 1995.

Das, Hans, 'Restoring property rights in the aftermath of war', *International and Comparative Law Quarterly*, 53 (2004), 429–44.

Daskalov, Roumen, *The making of a nation in the Balkans: Historiography of the Bulgarian revival*, Budapest: Central European University Press, 2004.

Demokratsiia, 'Vnushnanta politika e tolkova po-dobra, kolkoto e po-razuman', *Demokratsiia*, 2 September 1992.

Deutsche Presse Agentur, 'Possible recognition of Croatia, Slovenia urged', *Deutsche Presse Agentur* (DPA), 12 July 1991, translated in *Foreign Broadcast Service* (FBIS), *Daily Report* (WEU, Western Europe), 13 July 1991, 15.

Dimitras, Panayote Elias, *Greece: Albanian immigrants for hire or expulsion*, War Report, Number 46, October (1996), Greek Helsinki Monitor.

Djilas, Milovan, *Tito: The story from inside*, New York: Harcourt, Brace, 1980.

  Wartime, New York: Harcourt, Brace, 1977.

Drezov, Kyril, 'Macedonian identity: An overview of the major claims', in James Pettifer (ed.), *The new Macedonian question*, Mcmillan Press, 1999, 47–59.

East Europe, 'Ganev assesses results of London conference', Foreign Broadcast Information Service, *Daily Report, East Europe*, 10 September (1992).

Economist Intelligence Unit, *The Country Report: Romania, Bulgaria, Albania*, no. 1 (1991), 5; and no. 4 (1994).

Eliade, Mircea, *The myth of the eternal return: Cosmos and history*, Princeton: Princeton University Press, 1974.

ELIAMEP, *Kosovo: Avoiding another Balkan War*, Athens, 1998.

Englbrecht, Walpurga, 'Bosnia and Hercegovina, Croatia and Kosova: voluntary return in safety and dignity?' *Refugee Study Quarterly*, 23, 3 (2004), 100–48.

Engelbrekt, Kjell, 'A vulnerable Bulgaria fears a wider war', *RFE/RL Research Report*, no. 12 (1993), 7–12.

European Commission, 'Commission staff working paper: Croatia–Stabilization and association report 2003', COM (2003) 139 Final, Document Number SEC (2003) 341. 26 March. http://europa.eu.int/comm/external_relations/see/sap/rep2/com03_139_en.pdf

The *Western Balkans in transition: Enlargement papers No. 23, European economy of December 2004*, Brussels: European Commission, 2004, http://europa.eu.int/comm/economy_finance/publications/enlargement_paperselp23/en.htm

European Stability Initiative 2004, *The Lausanne Principle: Multiethnicity, territory and the future of Kosovo's Serbs*, European Stability Initiative, Berlin/Pristina, 7 June 2004, http://www.esiweb.org/pdf/esi_document_id_53.pdf

EU–Western Balkans Summit, *Declaration*, Thessaloniki, 21 June 2003, http://www.eu 2003.gr/en/articles/ 2003 /6/23/3135/index.asp

Evening News, 'Ve haf vays of making you hate ze Germans', *Evening News*, 12 June 1996, 23.

Filipova, Liliana, 'Sus siuzheta za kvotite Dogan se muchi da tushira krizata v sobstvenata si partiia', *Demokratsiia*. http://www.eunet.bg/bgnews/show_story.html?issue=149208535&media=1523776&class=1946720&story=149209911

Friedman, Victor A., 'Macedonian language and nationalism during the nineteenth and early twentieth centuries', *Balkanistica*, 2 (1975), 83–98.

'The sociolinguistics of literary Macedonian', *International Journal of the Sociology of Language*, 52 (1985), 31–57.

Gall, Carlota, 'NATO soldiers fire on Kosovo Albanians', *New York Times*, 8 March (2001).

Gallagher, Tom, *Outcast Europe: The Balkans 1789–1999: From the Ottomans to Milošević*, London: Routledge, 2001.

Geary, James, 'Politics and massacres: Did France tacitly trade a Bosnian 'Safe Haven' to the Serbs for the return of peacekeeper hostages?', *TIME*, 147, 26, 24 June 1996.

Gellner, Ernest, *Nations and nationalism*, Oxford: Blackwell, 1983.

Genscher, Hans-Dietrich, *Rebuilding a house divided: A memoir by the architect of Germany's reunification*, New York: Broadway Books, 1997. (Translation of *Erinnerungen* (Memoirs), Berlin: Siedler, 1995, 1st edn).

Giatzidis, Emile, *An introduction to postcommunist Bulgaria: Political, economic and social transformation*, Manchester: Manchester University Press, 2002.

Gilbert, M., 'The roots of appeasement', in Kleine-Ahlbrandt and W. Laird (eds.), *Appeasement of the dictators: Crisis diplomacy?* New York: Holt, Rinehart & Winston, 1970.

Glenny, Misha, 'Germany fans the flames of war', *New Statesman and Society*, 27 December 1991, 145ff.

The fall of Yugoslavia: The third Balkan War, New York: Penguin Books, 1994.

The Balkans: Nationalism, war and the great powers 1804–1999, London and New York: Granta Books, 2000.

Gow, James, *Legitimacy and the military: Yugoslav crisis*, New York: St. Martin's Press, 1992.

Great Britain, Parliament, *House of Commons. Official Report. Parliamentary Debates* (Hansard). London: HMSO (daily), vol. 260, no. 112, 31 May 1995, cols. 999–1102.

House of Lords. Official Report. Parliamentary Debates (Hansard). London: HMSO, 564, 96, 31 May 1995, cols. 1117–1172.

Gutman, Roy, *A witness to genocide: The 1993 Pulitzer Prize-winning dispatches on the 'ethnic cleansing' in Bosnia*, New York: Macmillan, 1993.

'UN's deadly deal', *New York Newsday*, 29 May 1996, A7, A24–A25, A31.

Hagan, John, *Justice in the Balkans: Prosecuting war crimes in the Hague Tribunal*, Chicago: University of Chicago Press, 2003.

Hall, Brian, 'Rebecca West's war', *The New Yorker*, 15 April 1996, 74–83.

Hazan, Pierre, *La justice face à la guerre: De Nuremberg à la Haye*, Paris: Stock, 2000.

Hedges, Chris, 'As UN organizes, rebels are taking charge of Kosovo', *The New York Times*, July 29 1999.

Hikmet Alp, Ali, 'Balkan region in Turkey's security environment', in Ali L. Karaosmanolu and Seyfi Taşhan (eds.), *The europeanization of Turkey's security policy: Prospects and pitfalls*, Ankara: Foreign Policy Institute, 2004, 190–91.

Hill, Christopher, 'The capability expectations gap: Conceptualizing Europe's international role', *Journal of Common Market Studies*, 31, 3 (1993), 305–28.

Hislope, Robert, 'Between a bad peace and a good war: Insights and lessons from the almost-war in Macedonia', *Ethnic and Racial Studies*, 26, 1 (2003), 129–51.

Hoare, Marko Attila, *How Bosnia armed*, London: SAQI Books/Bosnia Institute, 2004.

Hobsbawm, Eric, and Range, Terence (eds.), *The invention of tradition*, Cambridge: Cambridge University Press, 1983.

Hodge, Carole, 'Slimy Limeys', *New Republic*, 9 January 1996, 21–2.

Holbrooke, Richard, *To end a war*, New York: Random House, 1998.

Honig, Jan Willem, and Both, Norbert, *Srebrenica: record of a war crime*, UN Srebrenica Report, London: Penguin, 1997.

Horowitz, Donald, *Ethnic groups in conflict*, Berkeley: University of California Press, 1985.

Human Rights Watch/Helsinki Watch, *Destroying ethnic identity: Selective persecution of Macedonians in Bulgaria*, New York: Human Rights Watch, 1991.

Greece. Free speech on trial: Government Stifles Dissent on Macedonia, New York: Human Rights Watch, 1991.

Denying ethnic identity: The Macedonians of Greece, New York: Human Rights Watch, 1994.

Human Rights in the Former Yugoslav Republic of Macedonia, New York: Human Rights Watch, 1994.

Human Rights Watch, *Human rights in the former Yugoslav Republic of Macedonia*, New York: Human Rights Watch, 1994.

The fall of Srebrenica and the failure of UN peacekeeping, New York: Human Rights Watch, 1995.

Croatia: Human rights in eastern Slavonia during and after the transition of authority, New York: Human Rights Watch, 1997, http://www.hrw.org/reports/1997/croatia/Croatia-04.htm

Broken promises: Impediments to refugee return to Croatia, 2003, http://www.hrw.org/reports/2003/croatia0903/croatia0903.pdf

Croatia fails Serb refugees: Ethnic discrimination slows refugee return, New York: Human Rights Watch, 2003, http://www.hrw.org/press/2003/09/croatia090203.htm

Huntington, Samuel, 'The clash of civilizations?', *Foreign Affairs*, 72, 3 (1993), 21–49.

Hyde, Andrew G., 'Seizing the initiative: The importance of regional cooperation in SEE and the prominent role of the Southeast EU Cooperation Process', *Journal of SEE and Black Sea Studies*, 4, 1 (2004), 18–19.

Ignatieff, Michael, 'The virtual commander: How NATO invented a new kind of war', *The New Yorker*, 2 August 1999.

Virtual war: Kosovo and beyond, New York: Henry Holt, 2000.

International Criminal Tribunal for the Former Yugoslavia, *The prosecutor of the Tribunal against Vojislav Seselj*, Indictment (Case No. IT), Initial Indictment, 14 February 2003, www.un.org/icty/indictment/english/ses-ii030115e.htm.

Internal Displacement Monitoring Centre, 'Croatia: reforms come too late for most remaining ethnic Serb IDPs', 18 April 2006. http://www.internal-displacement.org/8025708F004BE3B1/(httpInfoFiles)/5A32E9E12C172-B9AC125714F00538ED1/$file/Croatia)_overview_April2006.pdf

International Herald Tribune, 'For Balkan stability', *International Herald Tribune*, 4 August 1999.

Ivankovic, Nenad, *Bonn: Druga hrvatska fronta*. Zagreb Mladost, 1993.

Izetbegovic, Alija, *Islamska deklaracija*, BOSNA: Sarajevo, 1990.

Jacobsen, C. J., 'Washington's Balkan strategy. Aberration or herald?' *South Slav Journal*, 17, 1/2 (1996), 67–70.

Jagger, Bianca, 'The betrayal of Srebrenica', *The European*, 15 September – 1 October 1997, 14–19.

Jarausch, Konrad H., *The rush to German unity*, Oxford: Oxford University Press, 1994.

Jarausch, Konrad H., and Gransow, Volker, 'The new Germany: Myths and realities', in Jarausch and Gransow (eds.), *Uniting Germany: Documents and debates, 1944–1993*, Providence/ Oxford: Berghahn Books, 1994.

Jović, Borisav, *Poslednji Ddani SFRJ*, Belgrade: Politika, 1995.

Jurgen-Axt, Heinz, 'Did Genscher disunite Yugoslavia? Myths and facts about the foreign policy of united Germany', in Gunay Goksu Özdogan and Kemali Saybasili (eds.), *Balkans: A mirror of the new international order*, Instanbul: Eren Publishers, 1995, 221–42.

Drezov, Kyril, 'Bulgaria', in John B. Allcock, Marko Milivojevic, and John Horton (eds.), *Conflict in Yugoslavia: An encyclopedia*, Santa Barbara: ABC-CLIO, 1998.

Kadijević, Veljko, *Moje Vvidjenje Rraspada*, Belgrade: Politika, 1993.

Karahasan, Dževad, *Il centro del mondo: Sarajevo, esilio di una cittá*, Milan: Il Saggiatore, 1995.

Karakasidou, Anastasia, 'Politicizing culture: Negating ethnic identity in Greek Macedonia', *Journal of Modern Greek Studies*, 11 (1993), 1–28.

Karaosmanolu, Ali, 'Turkey's objectives in the Caspian region', in Gennady Chufrin (ed.), *The security of the Caspian Sea region*, Oxford: Oxford University Press, 2001.

Kasper, Martin (ed.), *Language and culture of the Lusatian Sorbs throughout their history*, Berlin: Akademie-Verlag, 1987.

Katardzhiev, Ivan, AI. M. O. R. O., in two parts, *Macedonian Review*, vol. 20, nos. 1–2 (1990), 31–49; and no. 3, 139–61.

Kelsey, Tim, and Leppard, David, 'The thief, the Serbian link and the financing of Britain's ruling party', *The Independent*, no. 1, 2, 990, 20 May 1996, 1, 13.

'Tories probe Serb links to funding', *The Guardian*, 20 May 1996, 1–2, 8.

'Serbs gave Tories £100,000', *The Sunday Times*, no. 8/960, 19 May 1996, 1, 24.

Kerr, Rachel, *The International Criminal Tribunal for the Former Yugoslavia: An exercise in law, politics, and diplomacy*, Oxford: Oxford University Press, 2004.

Kertzer, David I., *Ritual politics and power*, New Haven: Yale University Press, 1988.

Kinzer, Stephen, 'Demonstrations for tolerance', *New York Times*, 13 January 1993, reprinted in K. H. Jarausch and V. Gransow (eds.), *Uniting Germany: Documents and debates, 1944–1993*, Providence/ Oxford: Berghahn Books, 1994, 267–9.

Kisselinchev, Chavdar, 'A world divided and polarized', *Sofia Western News*, no. 44, September 1999.

Klau, T., 'Angst vor dem bösen "Boche" geht in Frankreich wieder um', *Bonner Rundschau*, 28 March 1990, reprinted in K. H. Jarausch and V. Gransow (eds.), *Uniting Germany: Documents and debates, 1944–1993*, Providence/ Oxford: Berghahn Books, 1994, 131–2.

Knaus, Gerald, and Martin, Felix, 'Lessons from Bosnia and Herzegovina: Travails of the European Raj', *Journal of Democracy*, 14, 3 (2003).

Knežević, Djurdja, 'The enemy side of national ideologies: Croatia at the end of the 19th century and in the first half of the 20th century', in László Kontler (ed.), *Pride and prejudice: National stereotypes in 19th and 20th - century Europe East to West*, Budapest: Central European History Department, Working Paper, series 2 (Budapest: CEU, 1995), 105–18.

Kofos, E., and Veremis, T., 'Kosovo: Efforts to solve the impasse', *The International Spectator*, 33, 2 (1998) (Rome), 131–46.

Koser, Khalid, 'Return, readmission and reintegration: Changing agendas, policy frameworks and operations programmes', in Bimal Ghosh, *Return Migration: Journal of hope or despair*, Geneva: International Organisation for Migration, 2000.

Krishtanovskaia, Olga, and White, Stephen, 'From nomenklatura to new elite', in Vladimir Shlapentokh, Christopher Vanderpool and Boris Doktorov (eds.), *The new elite in post-communist Europe*, College Station, TX: Texas A&M University Press, 1999.

Kurspahic, Kemal, *Prime time crime: Balkan media in war and peace*, Washington, DC: US Institute of Peace Press, 2003.

Lampe, John R., 'Working toward the EU: Bulgaria's progress and Serbia's struggles', EES NEWS, May–June 2005, 9–11.

Larrabee, F. Stephen, and Lesser, Ian O., *Turkish foreign policy in an age of uncertainty*, Santa Monica: RAND, 2003.

Layne, Christopher, and Schwarz, Benjamin, 'For the record', *The National Interest*, Fall (1999), 13, cols. 1 and 4.

Lebor, Adam, *Milošević: A biography*, New Haven: Yale University Press, 2004.

Lefebvre, Stephane, 'Bulgaria's foreign relations in the post-communist era: a general overview and assessment', *East European Quarterly*, 28, 4 (1995).

Lehne, Stefan, 'Has the "hour of Europe" come at last? The EU's strategy for the Balkans', in Judy Batt (ed.), *The Western Balkans: Moving on*, Institute for Security Studies, Chaillot Paper No. 70, October (2004), 111–24.

Lenkova, Mariana, 'Positive and negative stereotypes in the media of seven Balkan countries', Greek Helsinki Monitor, 1997, http://www.greekhelsinki.gr/english/media/GHM-Media%20Monitoring-Bulgaria.htm

'Hate speech' in the Balkans, Vienna: International Helsinki Federation for Human Rights, 1998.

Libal, Michael, *Limits of persuasion: Germany and the Yugoslav crisis, 1991–1992*, Westport: Praeger, 1997.

Lunt, Horace G., 'Some sociolinguistic aspects of Macedonian and Bulgarian', in A. Stolz, I. R. Titunik, and Lubmoir Dolezel (eds.), *Language and literary theory*, Ann Arbor, MI: Michigan Slavic Publications, 1984, 83–132.

Lytle, Paula, 'Electoral transitions in Yugoslavia', in Y. Shain and J. Linz (eds.), *Between states: Interim governments in democratic transitions*, Cambridge Studies in Comparative Politics, Cambridge: Cambridge University Press, 1995, 237–54.

Magas, Branka, *The destruction of Yugoslavia: Tracing the break-up 1980–92*, New York: Verso, 1993.

Magas, Branka, and Zanic, Ivo, *The war in Croatia and Bosnia-Herzegovina 1991–95*, London: Frank Cass, 2001.

Malcolm, Noel, *Kosovo: A short history*, London: Macmillan, 2002.

Mark Thompson, *Paper House: The ending of Yugoslavia*, New York: Pantheon Books, 1994.

Marsh, David, *Germany and Europe: The crisis of unity*, London: Mandarin, 1994.

McCarthy, Patrick, Maday, Tom, Rohde, David, and Susic, Lejla, *After the fall: Srebrenica survivors in St. Louis*, Missouri Historical Society Press, 2001.

Mestrovic, Stjepan G., *The Balkanization of the West: The confluence of postmodernism and postcommunism*, London/New York: Routledge, 1994.

Michas, Takis, *Unholy alliance: Greece and Milošević's Serbia*, College Station: Texas A&M University Press, 2002.

Milošević, Slobodan, *Godine rasjzleta*, Belgrade, 1989.

Minority Rights Group International, *Minorities in Croatia*, London: Minority Rights Group International, September 2003.

Misirkov, Krste P., *On Macedonian matters*, trans. by Alan McConnell, Skopje: Macedonian Review Editions, 1974.

Mitev, Petur-Emil, 'Popular attitudes toward politics', in John Bell (ed.), *Bulgaria in transition*, Boulder, CO: Westview Press, 1998.

Naimark, Norman, and Case, Holly (eds.), *Yugoslavia and its historians: Understanding the Balkan wars of the 1990s*, Stanford: Stanford University Press, 2003.

Narodne Novine (Official Gazette of the Republic of Croatia), NN 73/95, Zagreb, Croatia, 27 September (1995), http://www..nn.hr/sluzbeni-list/index.asp

NN 100/97, Zagreb, Croatia, 26 September (1997), http://www..nn.hr/
sluzbeni-list/index.asp

NN 92/98, Zagreb, Croatia, 7 July (1998), http://www..nn.hr/sluzbeni-list/
index.asp

NN 7/96, Zagreb, Croatia, 26 January (1996), http://www.nn.hr/sluzbeni-list/
index.asp

Neuburger, Mary, *The Orient within: Muslim minorities and the negotiation of
nationhood in modern Bulgaria*, Ithaca and London: Cornell University Press,
2004.

Newhouse, John, 'The diplomatic round: Dodging the problem', *New Yorker*,
24 August 1992.

Norwegian Refugee Council, *Briefing paper*, 7 June 2001, http://www.db.
idpproject.org/Sites/IdpProjectDb/idpSurvey.nsf/wViewSingleEnv/E4AAEF
766FFB579CC1256A7A00505393/$file/NRC+Statement+7+June+2001.pdf

Organisation for Security and Cooperation in Europe, *Internally Displaced
Persons, Refugees and Return*, OSCE Mission to Croatia: Zagreb, Croatia,
31 May (2001), http://www.osce.org/croatia/return/foreword

    *OSCE Status Report No. 12, Assessment of Issues Covered by the OSCE Mission to
    the Republic of Croatia's Mandate since 12 November 2000*, 3 July 2003, http://
    www.osce.org/documents/mc/2003/07/450_en.pdf

Organisation for Security and Cooperation Mission in Kosovo, *Human Rights
Challenges following the March Riots*, May 2004, http://www.osce.org/
documents/mik/2004/05/2939_en.pdf

Owen, David, *Balkan odyssey*, New York: Harcourt Brace, 1996.

Palmer, Jr., Stephen E. and King, Robert R., *Yugoslav communism and the
Macedonian question*, Hamden: CO: Archon Books, 1971.

Pavlowitch, Stevan, *The improbable survivor: Yugoslavia and its problems,
1918–1988*, London: Hurst, 1988.

Perl, Lila, *Yugoslavia, Romania, Bulgaria: New era in the Balkans*, New York: EP
Dutton, 2000.

Perry, Duncan M., *The politics of terror: The Macedonian revolutionary movement,
1893–1903*, Durham, NC: Duke University Press, 1988.

    'The Macedonian question revitalized', RFE/RL, *Report on Eastern Europe*, I,
    34 (1990), 5–9.

    'The republic of Macedonia: Finding its way', in Karen Dawisha and Bruce
    Parrot (eds.), *Politics, power and the struggle for democracy in South-East
    Europe*, Cambridge: Cambridge University Press, 1997, 226–81.

Philpott, Charles, 'Though the dog is dead, the pig must be killed: Finishing
with property restitution to Bosnia-Herzegovina's IDPs and refugees',
Journal of Refugee Studies, 18 (2005), 1–24.

Physicians for Human Rights, *War crimes in Kosovo: A population-based
assessment of human rights violations of Kosovar Albanians by Serb forces*,
15 June (1999), www.phrusa.org/past_news/kexec.html

Pomfret, John, and Hockstader, Lee, 'In Bosnia, a war crimes impasse: NATO
differences with U.N. Tribunal mean few are arrested', *Washington Post*, 9
December 1997, A1.

Poropat, Liviana, *Alpe-Adria e iniziativa centro-Europea: Cooperazione nell'Alpe-Adria e nell'area danubiana*, Naples: Edizioni Scientifiche Italiane, 1993.

Poulton, Hugh, *Balkans: Minorities and states in conflict*, London: Minority Rights Group Publications, 1993.

Who are the Macedonians?, Bloomington: Indiana University Press, 1995.

Powell, Colin, and Persico, Joseph E., *My American journey*, New York: Ballantine Books, 1996.

Power, Samantha, *A problem from hell: America and the age of genocide*, New York: Basic Books, 2002.

Pribicevic, Ognjen, 'Serbia after Milošević', *Journal of Southeast European and Black Sea Studies*, 4, 1 (2004), 107–18.

Pribichevich, Stoyan, *Macedonia: Its people and history*, University Park: Pennsylvania University Press, 1982.

Priest, Dana, 'Kosovo land threat may have won war', *The Washington Post*, 19 September 1999, A1.

Proceedings of the Symposium on 'Recent Developments in the Practice of State Recognition', *European Journal of International Law*, 4, 1 (1993).

Rakate, P. K., 'The shelling of Knin by the Croatian Army in August 1995: A police operation or a non-international armed conflict?', *International Review of the Red Cross*, no. 840, 31 December 2000, 1037–52.

Ramet, Sabrina Petra, 'The radical Right in Germany', *In Depth*, 4, 1 (1994), 43–68.

'The Macedonian enigma', in Ramet and Ljubiša S. Adamovich (eds.), *Beyond Yugoslavia: Politics, economics and culture in a shattered community*, Boulder, CO: Westview Press, 1995.

RFE/RL NEWSLINE, 'Bosnian Croats face eviction from Knin', 6 September (2002), http://listserv.acsu.buffalo.edu/cgi-bin/wa?A2=ind0209a&L=albanews&F=&S=&P=2271 RFE/RL Newsline, vol. 3, no. 192, part I, 1 October (1999).

Robbins, Keith, *Appeasement*, Oxford/ New York: Blackwell, 1988.

Robbins, Philip, *Suits and uniforms: Turkish foreign policy since the Cold War*, London: Hurst and Company, 2003.

Robertson, Geoffrey, *Crimes against humanity: The struggle for global justice*, New York: The New Press, 1999.

Rohde, David, *Endgame, the betrayal and fall of Srebrenica: Europe's worst massacre since World War II*, Boulder, CO: Westview Press, 1998.

Rossos, Andrew, *Russia and the Balkans: Inter-Balkan rivalries and Russian foreign policy 1908–1914*, Toronto: University of Toronto Press, 1981.

'The Macedonians of Aegean Macedonia: A British officer's report, 1944', *Slavonic and East European Review*, 69, 2 (1991), 282–309.

'The British Foreign Office and Macedonian national identity, 1918–1941', *Slavic Review*, 53, 2 (1994), 369–94.

'Macedonianism and Macedonian nationalism on the left', in Ivo Banac and Katherine Verdery (eds.), *National character and national ideology in interwar Eastern Europe*, New Haven: Yale Center for International and Area Studies, 1995.

'Incompatible allies: Greek communism and Macedonian nationalism in the Civil War in Greece, 1943–1949', *Journal of Modern History*, 69, 1 (1997), 42–76.

Rubin, Barry, and Kirisci, Kemal (eds.), *Turkey in world politics: An emerging multiregional power*, London: Lynne Rienner, 2001.

Sahara, Tetsuya, 'The Islamic world and the Bosnian crisis', *Current History*, 93, 586 (1994), 386–9.

Scharf, Michael, *Balkan justice*, Durham: Carolina Academic Press, 1998.

Schierup, Carl-Ulrik (ed.), *Scramble for the Balkans: Nationalism, globalism and the political economy of reconstruction*, New York: St. Martin's Press, 2000.

Schöpflin, George, 'Nationhood, communism and state legitimation', *Nations and Nationalism*, 1, 1 (1995), 81–91.

The new politics of Europe: Nations, identity, power, London: Hurst, 2000.

Sekelj, Laslo, *Yugoslavia: The process of disintegration*, New York: Columbia University Press, 1993.

Sell, Louis, *Slobodan Milošević and the destruction of Yugoslavia*, Durham, NC: Duke University Press, 2003.

Seton-Watson, Robert William, *Absolutism in Croatia*, London: Constable & Co, 1912.

Shain, Yossi, and Linz, Juan, *Between states: Interim governments in democratic transitions*, Cambridge Studies in Comparative Politics, Cambridge: Cambridge University Press, 1995.

Shashko, Philip, 'The past in Bulgaria's future', *Problems of Communism*, 39, September–October (1990), 75–83.

Shea, John, *Macedonia and Greece: The struggle to define a new Balkan nation*, Jefferson, NC: McFarland, 1997.

Shoup, Paul, *Communism in the Yugoslav national question*, New York: Columbia University Press, 1968.

Silber, Laura, and Little, Allan, *Yugoslavia: The destruction of Yugoslavia: Death of a nation*, London: Penguin Books/BBC Books, 1997.

Simic, Andrei, *The peasant urbanites: A study of rural–urban mobility in Serbia*, New York: Seminar Press, 1973.

Simms, Brendan, 'Bosnia: The lessons of history?', in T. Cushman and S. Mestrovic (eds.), *This time we knew: Western responses to genocide in Bosnia*, New York: New York University Press, 1996.

'The unknown accomplices in the Holocaust', *The Times Higher Education Supplement*, 4 October 1996, 25.

Sinnot, Richard, '*European public opinion and security policy*', Chaillot Paper No. 28, July (1997).

Sletzinger, Martin, 'The consequences of the war in Kosovo', *Kosovo and NATO. Impending challenges*, The Woodrow Wilson International Center for Scholars, East European Studies, Washington, DC, 1999, 3–5.

Sontag, Susan, 'Why are we in Kosovo?' *New York Times Magazine*, 2 May 1999, 52, col. 1.

Spillmann, Kurt R., and Krause, Joachim (eds.), *Kosovo: Lessons learned for international cooperative security*, Studies in Contemporary History and Security Policy, vol. 5, Bern: Peter Lang, 2000.

Spinelli, Barbara, 'Gli ipocriti mea culpa dell' Ovest. La fine della Bosnia', *La Stampa*, 30 June 1993.

Stanchev, Krasen, 'Sega sa nuzhni usloviia za investitsii', Demokratsiia, 24 November (1999), http://www.eunet.bg/bgnews/show_story.html?issue=158232609&media=1523776&class=2414656&story=158235712.

Stein, Barry, 'Refugee repatriation, return and refoulement during conflict', Paper presented to United States Agency for International Development, Promoting Democracy, Human Rights, and Reintegration in Post-conflict Societies, Washington, DC, 30–31 October (1997).

Stover, Eric and Peress, Giles, *The graves: Srebrenica and Vukovar*, Zurich: Scalo Publishers, 1998.

Straubhaar, Thomas, *International mobility of the highly skilled: Brain gain, brain drain or brain exchange*, HWWA Discussion Paper 88, Hamburgisches Welt-Wirtschafts-Archiv (HWWA), Hamburg Institute of International Economics, 2000, http://www.hwwa.de/Publikationen/Discussion_Paper/2000/88.pdf

Students Against Genocide, et al., Appellants v. Department of State, et al., Appeal from the United States District Court for the District of Columbia (No. 96cv00667), Decided 7 August 2001, http://www.ll.georgetown.edu/federal/judicial/dc/opinions/99opinions/99-5316a.html

Subasic, Katarina, 'Croatia: New math', *World Press Review*, 49, 8 (2002), http://www.worldpress.org/Europe/641.cfm

Sudetic, Chuck, *Blood and vengeance: One family's story of the war in Bosnia*, New York: W.W. Norton & Company, 1996.

Tanner, Marcus, *Croatia: A nation forged in war*, New Haven: Yale University Press, 1997.

Thomas, Robert, *Serbia under Milošević: Politics in the 1990s: How Milošević won and exercised power*, London: Hurst & Company, 1999.

Tokgöz, Mina, 'The economy: Achievements and prospects', in B. Beeley (ed.), *Turkish transformation: New century new challenges*, Huntingdon, UK: The Eothen Press, 2002, 141–64.

Treverton, Gregory F., 'The new Europe', *Foreign Affairs*, 71, 1 (1992), 94–112.

Troebst, Stefan, 'Yugoslav Macedonia, 1944–1953: Building the party, the state and the nation', *Berliner Jahrbuch für osteuropäische Geschichte*, 1 2 (1994), 103–39.

Troxel, Luan, 'Bulgaria and the Balkans', in Constantine P. Danopoulos, and Kostas Messas (eds.), *Crises in the Balkans: views from the participants*. Boulder, CO: Westview Press, 1997, pp. 195–210.

Tsentur, Nauchen, 'Za Bulgarska Natsionalna Strategiia', *Bulgariia prez dvadeset I purviia vek*, Bulgarska natsionalna doktrina, Sofia, 1997.

UNHCR, 'Position on the continued international protection needs of individuals from Kosovo', March and August (2004).

'Balkan governments seek to close refugee chapter in region', 31 January (2005), http://www.unhcr.ch/cgi-bin/texis/vtx/news/opendoc.htm?tbl=NEWS&id=41fe4b4b4&page=news

'Bosnia and Herzegovina welcomes over 1 million returnees', UNHCR press release, 21 September 2004, http://www.unhcr.ch/cgi-bin/texis/vtx/news/opendoc.htm?tbl=NEWS&id=414fffba4&page=news

'Update on conditions for return to Bosnia and Herzegovina', January 2005, http://www.unhcr.ba/publications/B&HRET0105.pdf

UNHCR 2004 Global Refugee Trends, http://www.unchr.ch/statistics

UNHCR Briefing Note: Kosovo, 25 June 1999, http://www.reliefweb. int/w/rwb.nsf/0/3ea3e43e357094ba8525679b00488f6e?OpenDocument

United Nations General Assembly, *The fall of Srebrenica: Report of the Secretary-General pursuant to General Assembly resolution 53/35*, United Nations General Assembly Document A/54/549, 15 November 1999.

US Committee for Refugees, *Country Reports: Croatia 1999*, http://www. refugees.org/world/countryrpt/europe/1999/croatia.htm

US State Department, 'Country reports on human rights practices', Released by the Bureau of Democracy, Human Rights and Labour, 31 March 2003, http://www.state.gov/g/drl/rls/hrrpt/2002/18359.htm

Uslu, Nasuh, *The Turkish–American relationship between 1947 and 2003: The history of a distinctive alliance*, Hauppaug, NY: Nova Science Publishers, 2003.

Turkish foreign policy in the post-cold war period, Hauppaug, NY: Nova Science Publishers, 2003.

Veremis, Thanos, 'The ever-changing contours of the Kosovo issue', in Dimitrios Triantaphyllou (ed.), *What status for Kosovo?*, Institute for Security Studies, Chaillot Paper No. 50, October (2001), 85–7.

Vlassidis, Vlassis, 'We and others: The Greek image in the mass media and the educational system of FYROM', *Athens-Skopje*, Athens: Papazissis, 2003, 297–366.

West, Rebecca, *Black lamb and grey falcon*, London: Macmillan, 1942.

West, Richard, 'Yugoslavia really is one nation', *The Sunday Telegraph*, 30 June 1991.

Wheeler-Bennett, John, 'The road to appeasement', in William Laird Kleine-Ahlbrandt (eds.), *Appeasement of the dictators: Crisis diplomacy?* New York: Holt, Rinehart & Winston, 1970.

Williams, Paul, and Scharf, Michael, *Peace with justice? War crimes and accountability in the former Yugoslavia*, Langham, MD: Rowman and Littlefield, 2002.

Wintour, Patrick, 'Major goes to war with Europe', *The Guardian*, 22 May 1996, 4, 8, 9.

Woodward, Susan L., *Balkan tragedy: Chaos and dissolution after the cold war*, Washington, DC: Brookings Institution, 1995.

World Bank, 'Bosnia and Herzegovina data profile', World Bank, 2005, http:// devdata.worldbank.org/external/CPProfile.asp?Selected Country =BIH& CCODE=BIH&CNAME=Bosnia+and+Herzegovina&PTYPE=CP

Zhelev, Zheliu, *V goliamata politika*, Sofia: Knigoizdatelska kushta Trud, 1998.

Zheliazkova, Antonina, 'Bulgaria's Muslim minorities,' in J. Bell (ed.), *Bulgaria in transition*, Boulder, CO: Westview Press, 1998, 165–87.

Zheliazkova, Antonina (ed.), *Relations of compatibility and incompatibility between Christians and Muslims in Bulgaria*, Sofia: International Center for Minority Studies and Intercultural Relations Foundation, 1995.

Zimmermann, Warren, 'Origins of a catastrophe: Memoirs of the last American ambassador to Yugoslavia', *Foreign Affairs*, 74, 1 (1995), 2–20.

Origins of a catastrophe, New York: New York Times Books, 1996.

Zuvela, Maja, 'Bosnian Serbs reveal 31 new Srebrenica mass graves', *Reuters Report*, 4 June (2004), http://www.alertnet.org/thenews/newsdesk/L04568018.htm

Index